Writing on Skin in the Age of Chaucer

Buchreihe der ANGLIA/ ANGLIA Book Series

Edited by
Lucia Kornexl, Ursula Lenker, Martin Middeke, Gabriele Rippl, Hubert Zapf

Advisory Board
Laurel Brinton, Philip Durkin, Olga Fischer, Susan Irvine,
Andrew James Johnston, Christopher A. Jones, Terttu Nevalainen,
Derek Attridge, Elisabeth Bronfen, Ursula K. Heise, Verena Lobsien,
Laura Marcus, J. Hillis Miller, Martin Puchner

Volume 60

Writing on Skin
in the Age of Chaucer

Edited by
Nicole Nyffenegger and Katrin Rupp

DE GRUYTER

For an overview of all books published in this series, please see
http://www.degruyter.com/view/serial/36292

ISBN 978-3-11-070961-2
e-ISBN (PDF) 978-3-11-057813-3
e-ISBN (EPUB) 978-3-11-057587-3
ISSN 0340-5435

Library of Congress Control Number: 2018941014

Bibliographic information published by the Deutsche Nationalbibliothek
The Deutsche Nationalbibliothek lists this publication in the Deutsche Nationalbibliografie;
detailed bibliographic data are available on the Internet at http://dnb.dnb.de.

© 2020 Walter de Gruyter GmbH, Berlin/Boston
This volume is text- and page-identical with the hardback published in 2018.
Printing: CPI books GmbH, Leck

www.degruyter.com

Table of Contents

Acknowledgements —— VII

Nicole Nyffenegger and Katrin Rupp
Introduction:
    Writing on Skin in the Age of Chaucer —— 1

Part I: Reading Diseased Skin

Sealy Gilles
Doctrinal Dermatologies —— 19

Michael Leahy
The "Scabbe of Synne:"
    Reading Leprous Skin in Late Medieval Culture —— 55

Sharon E. Rhodes
Legible Leprosy:
    Skin Disease in the *Testament of Cresseid*, Chaucer's Summoner, and *Amis and Amiloun* —— 77

Part II: Textual Skins

Catherine S. Cox
Chaucer's Ethical Palimpsest:
    Dermal Reflexivity in the General Prologue —— 97

Erin E. Sweany
The Cook's "Mormal:"
    Reading Disease, Doubt, and Deviance on the Body of Chaucer's Cook —— 119

Nicole Nyffenegger
Blushing, Paling, Turning Green:
    Hue and Its Metapoetic Function in *Troilus and Criseyde* —— 145

Part III: Writing Dermal Identities

Pax Gutierrez-Neal
Like a Second Skin:
Appropriation and (Mis)interpretation of Identities in *Sir Gawain and the Green Knight* and *William of Palerne* —— **169**

Roberta Magnani
Queer Skin in the "Wife of Bath's Prologue" and Its Manuscript Glosses —— **195**

M.W. Bychowski
Reconstructing the Pardoner:
Transgender Skin Operations in Fragment VI —— **221**

Elizabeth Robertson
Afterword: Skin Matters —— **251**

Contributors —— **265**

Index —— **269**

Acknowledgements

We are very grateful to a number of people and institutions without whose generous support this volume would not have been possible. Special thanks go to the contributors of this volume, whose inspiring paper proposals for and stimulating presentations at the New Chaucer Society Nineteenth International Congress in Reykjavík in 2014 provided the starting point for this volume: Sealy Gilles, Michael Leahy, Sharon E. Rhodes, Catherine S. Cox, Erin E. Sweany, Pax Gutierrez-Neal, Roberta Magnani, M.W. Bychowski. Elizabeth Robertson's generous engagement with our project in the afterword is highly appreciated by all of us. We thank our colleagues and friends at our home institutions for their ongoing support: Annette Kern-Stähler, Virginia Richter, Ursula Kluwick, Zoë Lehman Imfeld, Kathrin Scheuchzer, Martin Hilpert, François Spangenberg, and our students, who keep inspiring us. We thank Lara Portmann for her invaluable copy-editing work, as well as Pauline Bachofner and David Jost for their work on the manuscript at different stages. Thanks are also owed to the Department of English of the University of Bern and the Institute of English Studies of the University of Neuchâtel for their financial support, as well as to the UniBern Forschungsstiftung that funded a research stay at the Wellcome Collection in London at a very early stage of this project. We thank the editors of the Anglia Series at De Gruyter, and especially Ursula Lenker and Lucia Kornexl, for including our volume in the series, as well as Ulrike Krauss and Katja Lehming at De Gruyter for their work on the book. We are also grateful to Roberto Fighetti from the Veneranda Fabbrica del Duomo di Milano for his prompt support in obtaining the permission to reproduce the picture of St. Bartholomew included in the introduction of this volume. Nicole's special thanks, as always, go to Rolf, Lucien, Jules, and Michelle Nyffenegger for their patience and generosity. Katrin's special thanks go to her parents, Erika Rupp, and Gerhard Blättler for their loving support.

Bern and Neuchâtel, June 2018
Nicole Nyffenegger and Katrin Rupp

Nicole Nyffenegger and Katrin Rupp
Introduction:
Writing on Skin in the Age of Chaucer

> Adam scriveyn, if ever it thee bifalle
> Boece or Troylus for to wryten newe,
> Under thy long lokkes thou most have the scalle,
> But after my makyng thow wryte more trewe;
> So ofte adaye I mot thy werk renewe,
> It to correcte and eke to rubbe and scrape,
> And al is thorugh thy negligence and rape.
> — (Chaucer's "Wordes unto Adam, His Owne Scriveyn")[1]

In his "Wordes unto Adam, His Owne Scriveyn" Geoffrey Chaucer famously explores the relationship between human skin and parchment. He wishes his scribe Adam to get scabs on his head as a punishment for his careless copying when he writes *newe* Chaucer's works rather than being true to his original *makyng* of them. This carelessness, in turn, leads to Chaucer having to *renewe* Adam's work. The rubbing and scraping necessary to correct the product of Adam's negligence on the parchment resonate suggestively with the rubbing and scraping that would be necessary for poor Adam's relief if Chaucer's malediction became reality. The continuous palimpsestic renewal and rewriting of each other's works in which scribe and poet are engaged here extends to Adam's human skin, which is thus presented as an inscribable surface. With Chaucer's appropriation of the material side of literary production from his scribe (the rubbing and scraping of the parchment, the rewriting of the poems on it), one wonders whether to picture Chaucer himself bringing quill to parchment for these particular words or to imagine that, in a malicious gesture of dominance, he had his scribe write his own scabs into their literary existence.[2]

---

[1] 'Adam scribe, if ever it should happen / that you write Boece or Troilus anew, / then under your long locks you shall have the scabs, / unless you write more truly after my making; / so often must I renew your work daily, / to correct it and also to rub and scrape, / and all is through your negligence and haste.' Our own translation into modern English. The Middle English Chaucer quotations are from Benson (1987).

[2] Mize (2001: 359) hints at both options and discusses the parchment-skin relation here as a *contrapasso*, "the peculiar appropriateness or symmetry of a fault's sequel to the fault itself." For the wider context of scribes' roles in literary production, see, e.g., Wakelin (2014); Fisher (2012). Leahy discusses the different meanings of scabs (*MED scabbe* n.) in this volume, see also Cox in this volume.

The written and overwritten text, the writing surface, and the skin as the surface of the writer thus enter into a complex relationship in Chaucer's short poem. They do so even more because this particular Chaucer, this Adam, and this palimpsestic skirmish may well be a product of Chaucer's (or another, unknown author's)[3] imaginative writing rather than a representation of a real situation. This goes beyond Carolyn Dinshaw's (1989: 4) seminal reading of the poem as presenting a "figurative identification [...] between the human body and the manuscript page, the text" exactly because it is not the body of Adam we are looking at but his skin. Instead of the one-to-one figurative identification of body and page that Dinshaw's quote is usually understood to advocate, we encounter a layering of human and animal skins: Chaucer's itch to correct his scribe's faults and the resultant abuse of the parchment are figuratively transferred unto Adam's skin while both the correcting efforts and the conjured disease exist only by virtue of having been etched into and preserved on processed animal skin.[4]

This layered text-parchment-skin relation is further complicated by the fact that material and metaphorical uses of skin coexist and arguably intermingle in this poem. This creates an effect of oscillation that medieval readers, used as they were to encountering writing on processed animal skin, may have found easier to disentangle than we do today. Our choice of the phrase "writing on skin" for the title of this volume reflects this layering. The phrase means both, that human skin is conceived of as inscribable both in the material and in the figurative sense, and that human skin is a topic to write about. Often, the two actually concur: The fact that the marks of leprosy were read as signs of sin inscribed on human skin is only evident to us because medieval authors writing on religion and medicine considered skin a topic worth writing about, as our two opening contributions show. The temporal focus on "the age of Chaucer" that completes our title allows for a dense synchronic approach to the textuality of human skin in Chaucer's works (most prominently the *Canterbury Tales*), in

---

[3] Mooney (2006) identifies Chaucer's main scribe and the Adam of the short poem as Adam Pinkhurst. Various scholars are critical about the poem's attribution to Chaucer (Lerer 1990, 1993; Boffey and Edwards 1998; Edwards 2012) or about taking Chaucer's harsh criticism of Adam at face value (e.g., Gillespie 2008; Wakelin 2014). With several critics (e.g., Dinshaw 1989; Gillespie 2008), we disagree with Mooney (2006: 102) that her identification of Adam "puts to rest arguments as to the primarily figural interpretation of Adam's name in this poem." Cox (this volume) discusses Chaucer's short poem and its implications for Chaucer's other works in more depth.

[4] This layering may in fact be implied by Dinshaw's addition of "the text" to the "manuscript page," if it is read as suggesting a difference between the two rather than a specification of the latter. For a reading of this quote as advocating a one-to-one figurative relation, see, e.g., Fee's (1994: 55) otherwise very convincing "Productive Destruction."

works influenced by him (such as Robert Henryson's *Testament of Cresseid*), or in works that were influential at his time (such as Guy de Chauliac's *Cyrurgie*). This narrow time frame and our focus on English literature allow us to discuss pertinent aspects of the human skin's textuality in depth.

What, then, do we understand by the textuality of human skin? In the Middle Ages especially, conceptualisations of skin as inscribable and readable are based on the human skin's relatedness to parchment as it is apparent in Chaucer's short poem. Establishing this relatedness requires a focus on the surface of human skin, which, as Karl Steel (2013: 183) points out, leads to "a materialist attentiveness to the *stuff* of skin" (emphasis in original). In her study of the connections between body and language, Karmen MacKendrick (2004: 24) likewise proposes "to think, not in the depths, but at the edges, on the skin, at the surface of the page on which we write" and consequently theorises skin as something that can be touched, folded, and cut. Thus, while the long established theoretical paradigm of the inscribed body (and the nonexistence of a body prior to inscription) as influentially discussed by Michel Foucault (1977), Judith Butler (1990), and Elizabeth Grosz (1990) forms an important basis for the theorising of inscribed skin,[5] the parchment-skin relation offers theoretical angles that are related to but separate from those of the inscribed body. The skin's materiality, established by its being a surface as well as two-dimensional (especially in MacKendrick's notion of folding), invests it with the potential to work as a powerful metaphor alongside the parchment, the material stuff that most medieval literature is written on. The skin's materiality even enables it to work as a metaphor for much farther-reaching concepts such as time, as Isabel Davis (2013: 99) claims: "Skin and time were thought to share the same mechanical properties: both could stretch, fold, and tear."

In this volume, our attention is on the relations between text, parchment, and skin. In what follows, we present four different aspects of these relations as they have been discussed in recent scholarship and we outline the interventions the contributors of this volume aim to make in the field. These four aspects are, first, the (mostly figurative) resonances between parchment-making and transformations of human skin, second, parchment as a space of contact between animal and human spheres, third, human skin and parchment as sites where identities are negotiated, and fourth, the place of medieval skin studies within cultural studies and its relationship to the major concerns of cultural

---

[5] For developments of these theories towards tattoo and body modification theory see also, e.g., DeMello (2000), Pitts (2003), Caplan (2000), and Nyffenegger (2013).

studies: the difficult demarcation of skin from body, the instability of any inscription, and the skin's precarious state as an entity of its own.

The first aspect of the text-parchment-skin relation is the fact that the skin of a living animal can be turned into parchment and thus resonates with the potential, though mostly figurative, transformations of the skin of a living human. Sarah Kay (2006: 45 f.) points to the "Charter of Christ" poems and the *Ovide moralisé* among other related texts, in which the tortures inflicted on Christ's body are likened to the processes of parchment production in order for his skin to finally be presented as "the original legal charter confirming man's redemption" (2006: 45) or as a richly decorated manuscript respectively. However, human skin is not only represented as parchment, it is also echoed by the parchment on which any thematic treatment of skin is inscribed in the Middle Ages. Kay terms this resonance a 'mute doubling.' Folios bearing marks of their production, she claims, "constitute a mute doubling of the kinds of suffering undergone by the protagonists of many of the texts that are written on them" and "may have been seen as a graphic realization of the text's content" by their readers (2006: 36). We propose in this volume to think of the complex interrelations between different material and figurative representations of human and animal skin not as a doubling but as a 'layering' instead. Adrienne Williams Boyarin discusses a 'layering of textual images' in the Katherine group *Saint Margaret* that is akin to the one we discussed above for Chaucer's poem. The nourishment provided to Margaret by the narrator/writer Teochimus during her imprisonment, Boyarin (2009: 97) claims, is an investment in the quality of the *boc-felle*, the parchment that her life will eventually be written on. The marks left on Margaret's skin during torture disappear shortly before her death and are then transferred onto a different skin, a manuscript page by Teochimus (Nyffenegger 2013: 279 f.).[6]

A similar transfer from one skin to another, and consequently a layering of skins appears in **Sharon E. Rhodes'** discussion of *Amis and Amiloun* in the context of Chaucer's "Summoner's Tale" and Henryson's *Testament of Cresseid*. Rhodes re-examines readings of the Summoner's and Cresseide's leprosy as brought about by their lechery. In *Amis and Amiloun*, the idea that leprosy is contracted as a result of personal wrongdoings is taken a step further. Amiloun, Rhodes shows, is disfigured with leprosy in acceptance of a retribution that actually concerns his friend Amis. While the two friends initially look alike, Amiloun's infected skin now marks them as two distinct persons. When Amiloun (unlike Cresseid and the Summoner) is miraculously cured of his disease, his

---

[6] See also Lewis (2000).

skin becomes once again identical with that of Amis. Consequently, it is rendered illegible, both as a signifier for sin and as a signifier for a sinful individual as distinct from another.

Roberta Magnani tackles the layering of text, parchment, and skin in her contribution on the "Wife of Bath's Prologue." She contends that the *prente of seinte Venus seel*[7] presents Alisoun's gender identity as inscribed on her skin by patriarchal discourse. This cutaneous inscription resonates with the anti-feminist writings on parchment that Alisoun's fifth husband enjoys reading. Both are presented as violent, aimed at containing and controlling Alisoun's agency, and underlined by the glosses in the Ellesmere manuscript that Magnani discusses as strategies of surveillance. Against this male, anti-feminist epistemology, Magnani proposes a queer hermeneutics that recognises the fact that "skin signifies queerly, that is, in multiple and divergent ways." Marked skin is not a stable signifier, and Venus' seal on Alisoun's skin consequently becomes a site where gender identity is played out and complicated beyond hetero-normative binaries. Similar to this textual mark on skin, the manuscript page that Alisoun tears from the anti-feminist codex Janekyn is reading becomes a space where gender dichotomies can be rethought as queer. Magnani further discusses one Ellesmere manuscript gloss on foreskin, which, like Alisoun's skin, opens up a space for feminine and queer hermeneutics because "the cut of circumcision bleeds meaning across categories."

In her discussion of Chaucer's short poem addressed to Adam Scriveyn and of the pilgrims' portraits in the General Prologue to the *Canterbury Tales*, **Catherine S. Cox** explores the layering of skins further. Starting from her reflections on a wide range of palimpsests from the Anglo-Saxon Exeter Riddle #24 to Jeannette Winterson's (1992) novel *Written on the Body*, she claims that human skin itself figures as a palimpsest inscribed from the inside by the character's moral choices. She examines this connection between morality and skin marked by disease in "Adam Scriveyn" as well as in the General Prologue portraits of the Summoner, the Cook, and the Wife of Bath. Extending Sharon E. Rhodes' reading of the Summoner's skin as specifically leprous, Cox argues that "something untoward in the Summoner's abuse of office and ethics has occurred" which is made manifest on his skin. Similarly, the pus oozing from the Cook's *mormal* is suggestive of some inward corruption. However, in both cases, "an exact diagnosis remains purposefully elusive" and Cox argues that instead, the characters are "a means for the narrator Chaucer to intensify his sequential correlations of skin and ethics." And while the Wife of Bath's red complexion is traditionally

---

7 'imprint of Venus' seal'

seen as a sign of her lustful desires, she primarily *talks* about such desires, thus producing a palimpsest that forecloses any clear-cut interpretation. While skin is thus conceptualised as inscribable from the inside, its readability remains problematic.

The second aspect of the text-parchment-skin relation is that the parchment of a medieval manuscript is a space where human and animal spheres touch: it is a man-made product stemming from the body of a living animal, a product processed and marked by humans that may occasionally "touch back" as Lara Farina (2013), Bruce Holsinger (2009, 2010) and Sarah Kay (2004, 2006, 2011), among others, argue. Consequently, categorisations along the species divide may become unstable and need to be renegotiated. This has become a pertinent discussion especially in medievalist human-animal studies. In an experimental piece, Holsinger (2010) creatively explores such negotiations by reverting the positions of man and animal. He has his alter ego and "a certain Dr. Lollius" discover and reveal to the scholarly community that all Chaucerian manuscripts are in fact written on the skins of slaughtered humans. Animals as a recurrent motif in medieval literature of all genres and in art, Holsinger's alter ego concludes, can be attributed to the fact that "for a millennium our human forebears lived with their flesh just inches from the parchmenter's blade – and all the imaginative work of becoming-animal was merely a fantasy of survival" (2010: 136). Kay (2011: 16 f.), in a later companion piece to her article discussed above, admits to having eclipsed animals from her previous discussions and comes to the conclusion that in addition to her earlier question of how "readers felt about parchment acting as a double of their own skin," further questions that need to be asked concern the fact that parchment is animal skin: "to what extent do texts written on parchment give readers the sense of having an animal skin?"

Pax Gutierrez-Neal explores this question in the hunting scenes of the two fourteenth-century romances *Sir Gawain and the Green Knight* and *William of Palerne*. There, the terms used for the skinning of the animals to obtain their hides and the terms used for the arming of the knight overlap, producing "mirrored transfigurations of shape." Human and non-human identities become blurred, the boundaries between them are left open. Further, Gutierrez-Neal reads Gawain's scar, obtained from the Green Knight's third axe-blow, as a central signifier of his post-traumatic new identity and parallels it with William's "skinning" from his various identities. Both newly acquired signifiers are however misconstrued and misread by the protagonists' respective societies and thus again point to the precarious readability of skin.

The third aspect of the text-parchment-skin relation is that identity more generally (in addition to the boundaries between animal and human) is negotiated on both human skin and parchment, as Gutierrez-Neal points out. Didier

Anzieu's (1995) concept of the 'Skin-Ego' has been especially influential in medieval skin studies.[8] It is based on his vision of the skin as being, at the same time, a container, an interface (demarcating the outer world and protecting what is inside from penetration) and a tool for communication with others. In addition, skin is also the receptible surface on which the signs of relations with the outside world are inscribed (1995: 39–40). According to Anzieu then, skin has two sides but three dimensions: It has an inside in its role as container, an outside that serves for communication, both by the self and by the outside world that leaves its traces on it, and it has a middle dimension that separates the inside from the outside.

Marco d'Agrate's Renaissance statue of the skinned apostle St. Bartholomew (1562) in the Cathedral of Milan can serve as an impressive visualisation of this concept. The saint stands erect, holding in his left hand a Bible and in his right hand a tail of his flayed skin, which is loosely thrown around his neck and shoulders like a cloak. Despite the missing skin, St. Bartholomew's body remains wholly functional, with its subtle mechanisms enhanced by a detailed attention to the anatomical play of muscles and sinews that the saint's posture requires and that the removal of his skin has exposed to full view. The martyr's agony was deep enough to have left traces of furrows on the flesh of his cheeks and forehead. These traces on the flesh may well be a witness to the Aristotelian notion that it is not the skin that feels but the flesh beneath it.[9] Consequently, skin and body here appear as closely related but distinct entities. Skin envelops the body like a garment; it protects and holds together the flesh, bones, and inner organs. But skin not only dresses the body, it also acquires a markedly textile quality of its own in its cloak-like presentation on the statue. Skin here becomes a text inscribed with meaning by both the body from the inside and the world from the outside, something which is further underlined by the etymological analogy of *text* and *textile*, which both derive from Latin *texere*, 'to weave.'[10]

The skin's double-sidedness apparent both in Anzieu's concept of the 'Skin-Ego' and in the statue of St. Bartholomew relates to the question of the agent behind an inscription on skin. Such inscriptions happen from the inside or from the outside and they can be self-chosen marks or marks made by an 'other,' be it God, an illness, or an oppressing cis-normative force such as is discussed

---
8 E.g., Kay (2004, 2006), Benthien (2002), as well as Mills, Steel, and Small in Walter's (2013) *Reading Skin*.
9 "The skin, when cut, is in itself devoid of sensation; and this is especially the case with the skin on the head, owing to there being no flesh between it and the skull" (Aristotle, *Historia Animalium*, III: 11).
10 Kay (2006) discusses skin in the iconography of St. Bartholomew at length.

Figure 1: St. Bartholomew in the Cathedral of Milan. Reproduced with permission of the Veneranda Fabbrica del Duomo di Milano.

in **M.W. Bychowski's** article. In her critical trans approach, she examines how the skin of Virginia in the "Physician's Tale" and the skin of the Pardoner respectively invite us to rethink notions of gender and sexuality in favour of trans identities. Virgins and castrates (such as, potentially, the Pardoner) share a physical likeness owing to their skin's smooth pre- or post-sexual condition respectively. Both Virginia's and the Pardoner's skins are broken by a knife, thus testifying to the fact that "wholeness [of skin] is not itself a naturally fixed state but requires constant rhetorical operations of sharp-machines." Both Virginia (albeit only temporarily) and the Pardoner offer resistance to the workings of the knife on skin, and thus invite us to reconsider the violent construction of gendered identities.

While the incisions discussed by Bychowski are clearly inscriptions by an outside 'other,' the question of agency is complicated by inscriptions on skin made by an illness such as, most prominently, leprosy. Some medieval interpretations of diseased skin see the sinful subjects bringing the disease upon themselves, while others find the sick to be *quasi Christi*, chosen to suffer. The agent of writing may be moral, physiological, or divine, originating either from the inside or from without, but the occasion of the inscription in all cases is the human being inside the skin. **Sealy Gilles** traces medieval approaches to leprosy back to the Bible, arguing that the Old Testament readings of diseased skin range from the clinical, in Leviticus, to evidence of chastisement, and, conversely, a test of faith, as in Job. The New Testament, more consistently, mandates compassion in imitation of Jesus' healing of ten lepers. Gilles shows how church fathers such as Pope Gregory and Isidore of Seville resort to these biblical models to offer divergent perspectives on the disease and how medieval poets take up these (sometimes competing) theological ideas. In Béroul's late twelfth-century *Tristran et Iseut*, the leprous bandit Ivain is seen as marked by lust, while Tristran's choice of the guise of a leper questions such a reading of the leprous skin. In *Ami et Amile*, the hero is afflicted with leprosy due to a bigamous vow made to save his dear friend, so here disease is an occasion for self-sacrifice and redemption. In his *Testament of Cresseid*, Robert Henryson offers a more consistently negative concept of leprosy. In the fifteenth century, when the number of people afflicted with leprosy dwindles, the leper becomes an imaginary figure that serves as a site of projection of a variety of fears. In the case of Cresseid, her disease, caused by her blasphemy, embodies the danger of sexual deviance and contagion, even as Henryson deviates from well-known medical protocols for assessing cutaneous infections. As Gilles argues, "Henryson ensures that Cresseid's affliction is at once etiologically ambiguous and clinically unequivocal."

Michael Leahy also analyses Henryson's *Testament of Cresseid*. He does so, however, with a focus on medieval medical discourses of leprosy and thus complements the theological approaches discussed by Gilles. Taking the description of leprosy in the Middle English translation of Guy de Chauliac's *Chirurgia magna* as an example, Leahy demonstrates how this writer-surgeon conceives of the disease in moral and metaphorical ways. Leahy argues that Cresseid's leprosy is not uniquely a result of her sexual excess, but that the moral significance of the disease is fluid throughout the poem. The visible signs on the skin of the morally corrupt soul serve as an index to viewers to beware of sins and keep away from the treacherous spots that symbolise them. Conversely, narratives of the affective tradition, such as Margery Kempe's *Book*, suggest that these marks should be touched as a means of gaining access to the divine. The salvific embracing of lepers advocated in affective narratives goes back to the attitude towards leprosy in the New Testament that Gilles outlines in her article. Both medical and religious readings of marked skin thus aim at reaching beyond the cutaneous surface of the body. As Virginia Langum (2013: 146) points out, "the human interior – whether physiological or moral – is not as easily perceived and interpreted as the external body" and it therefore takes the expertise of a medical and religious person to "read through the skin."

The fourth and final aspect to be discussed here is the place of medieval skin studies within the field of cultural studies and its relationship to the major concerns of cultural studies. The relatively new field of medieval skin studies has emerged and is further developing in the context of feminist, queer, and human-animal studies' preoccupations with the constructedness and fluidity of various categorisations. Three of its principal concerns have been, first, the difficult demarcation of skin from body and flesh that we have tentatively answered above by suggesting to focus on the skin's two-dimensionality, two-sidedness, and materiality. Second, the instability of any writing on skin as it is exemplified in the continual palimpsestic renewal in Chaucer's address to Adam, and third, the skin's precarious state as an entity in its own right (rather than the surface of the body or flesh) leading to its "relative invisibility" in medieval texts (Connor 2004: 11). In what follows, we discuss the second and third of these concerns in more detail.

As for the instability of any writing on skin, it is central to think not only of the writer and the possibility of continual palimpsestic reinscription but also of the agent of reading. In addition to asking "who or what writes onto skin," we must ask the questions of "who reads" and "in which context." Our opening articles by Leahy and Gilles problematise the different perspectives on the same topic by medical and religious "readers" of diseased skin. Ulrike Landfester (2012) points out how the interpretation of marks on skin depends on the context within which they are read. Punitive or ownership tattoos on the skins of Roman slaves, for example, were invested with great symbolic potential in the new context of Christ's passion (2012: 119–121). While we do not specifically engage with tattoos here, the possible appropriation of dermal inscriptions and of readings of such inscriptions that deviate from their "original intent" are relevant to several of our articles.

Erin E. Sweany in particular picks up on the unreliable legibility of the Cook's skin as discussed also by Cox and reads the Cook's *mormal* against the likewise open nature of the unfinished tale. She proposes that leprosy be added to the catalogue of possible causes of the *mormal* and the Cook's other suspicious bodily symptoms. However, she also urges us not to reduce the diagnosis of the Cook's health problems to leprosy, but instead to recognise the fact that the diversity of symptoms caused by leprosy (outlined in this book's introductory chapters) underscores the indeterminate nature of the Cook's physical and spiritual disorder. Understanding the Cook's leprosy as "an embodied uncertainty," she suggests that the *mormal* is a site that demands interpretation by the reader. It is exactly this indeterminacy that may be at the core of the Cook's marked skin. Sweany suggests that our own perception of modern medicine and our myths about its medieval predecessor may have made us miss Chaucer's clues "that the pilgrims are misreading the cook's body" as a pointer to the difficulty of reading bodies in general.

Another preoccupation of medieval skin studies has been to make skin visible in the first place against Steven Connor's (2004: 11) positing its "relative invisibility" in the Middle Ages. Connor (2004: 9–49) explains this relative invisibility as a result of the inherited Aristotelian conceptions of skin as neither a separate entity nor a sensory organ.[11] Quite on the contrary, Katie Walter (2013: 3) finds, "skin is far from invisible" and "is made to speak in wide-ranging ways to its aesthetic, philosophical, ethical, and political preoccupations." In fact, both Connor and Walter are right: Skin is indeed nearly invisible in many medieval texts. When we look for the Middle English terms for skin (*hid*, *fel*, and *skin*) in Chaucer's works, the findings suggest that Connor's claim of the skin's relative invisibility is tenable. There are no occurrences of *hid* or *fel* in the whole of the *Canterbury Tales*. The few instances of *skin* refer to animal skin or are idiomatic, with the slack skin of January's neck as the only exception ("Merchant's Tale," l. 1364). However, as Walter points out, this does not mean that skin is not present or that it does not play an important role in medieval lit-

---

11 Jablonski (2006: 2) points out that still today "few people [...] think of our skin as an organ of the human body."

erature. In medieval culture and literature, skin did matter. Many of the articles in Walter's volume touch on the readability of skin, but the book's overall approach is broader than ours, offering an insight into the human skin's multifarious meanings from the construction of the cultural other to political ideologies or the experience of the divine expressed through skin.

In this present volume, we focus on the skin's textuality in more depth. The example of the *Canterbury Tales* shows that, while explicit references to human skin as such are difficult to find, there are many references to human skin that is in some way marked. The term *MED heu* n. (modern 'hue') for example appears regularly, denoting in its restricted sense the colour of the face that is caused by outside or inside influences (e. g., the Shipman's sun-tanned skin or the Wife of Bath's reddened skin revealing her humoural disposition) or the colour of the face that is caused by overwhelming feelings (e. g., Palamon's and Arcite's changing hue in fear of each other in the "Knight's Tale"). **Nicole Nyffenegger** engages with hue in *Troilus and Criseyde* and argues that the layering of text, parchment, and skin is particularly intricate where hue is concerned. Hue not only makes skin visible in medieval texts that do not contain explicit skin references; as an inscription on skin it also invites conceptualisations of the human face as a *mise en abyme* of the parchment page. Since hue is inherently connected to change (the acts of blushing, paling, turning green all emphasise the moment when the colour changes), it invests the human skin with a palimpsestic fluidity that makes it a suitable surface for the inscription of feelings. Nyffenegger argues that hue in *Troilus and Criseyde,* apart from betraying a character's feelings at distinct moments in the narrative, fulfils several overarching functions: First, the distribution of hue references underlines the structure of the narrative in a way that resembles manuscript rubrication. Second, hue reinforces the intricate connections between visual dynamics, emotions, and agency in the work. Third, the narrator uses hue as a figure for the specific generic conventions of romance and thus gives it a metapoetic function. Through hue, Nyffenegger argues, Chaucer reflects on his poetic options when writing about love.

Skin, while always present and important, is not always easily visible in the texts. However, it comes into sharper focus when it is marked (by choice, by God, by an illness), when it gains visibility not as skin but as inscribed skin. Consequently, we focus on representations of marked, inscribed, and potentially readable skin in different texts and contexts in the age of Chaucer. The three different angles we take in the discussion are, first, that of the precarious readability of diseased skin ("Reading Diseased Skin"), second, that of skin as inscribable and written on ("Textual Skins"), and third, that of skin as the locus of negotiations of identity along the boundaries of gender and species constructions ("Writing Dermal Identities"). Naturally, the three angles inform one another.

Diseased skin especially is not only a topic in literary texts, it also forms the basis for some of our discussions of skin as textual and of the marked skin's role in identity construction. We shed light on these questions from different perspectives: When the works discussed overlap, different foci are set and when similar questions are asked, they are so in relation to different texts. Thus, we hope to present a dense and in-depth exploration of the different aspects of the human skin's textuality in this volume, showing that writing on skin, both in the sense of material and figural inscriptions and in the sense of texts written about skin was a pertinent topic in the age of Chaucer.

Works Cited

Primary Sources

Benson, Larry D. (ed.). 1987. *Geoffrey Chaucer: The Riverside Chaucer*. 3rd ed. Boston: Houghton Mifflin.

Wentworth Thompson, D'Arcy (trans.). *Aristotle: Historia Animalium*. Book III. *Internet Classics Archive*. <classics.mit.edu/Aristotle/history_anim.3.iii.html> [accessed 26 April 2017].

Winterson, Jeanette. 1992. *Written on the Body*. London: Jonathan Cape.

Secondary Sources

Anzieu, Didier. 1995. *Le Moi-Peau*. Psychismes. Nouvelle édition revue et augmentée. Paris: Dunod.

Benthien, Claudia. 2002. *Skin: On the Cultural Border Between Self and the World*. Trans. Thomas Dunlap. New York: Columbia University Press.

Boffey, Julia and A. S. G. Edwards. 1998. "'Chaucer's Chronicle,' John Shirley, and the Canon of Chaucer's Shorter Poems." *Studies in the Age of Chaucer* 20: 201–218.

Butler, Judith. 1990. *Gender Trouble: Feminism and the Subversion of Identity*. Thinking Gender. New York: Routledge.

Caplan, Jane (ed.). 2000. *Written on the Body: The Tattoo in European and American History*. Princeton: Princeton University Press.

Connor, Steven. 2004. *The Book of Skin*. London: Reaktion Books.

Davis, Isabel. 2013. "Cutaneous Time in the Late Medieval Literary Imagination." In: Katie L. Walter (ed.). *Reading Skin in Medieval Literature and Culture*. The New Middle Ages. New York: Palgrave Macmillan. 99–118.

DeMello, Margo. 2000. *Bodies of Inscription: A Cultural History of the Modern Tattoo Community*. Durham: Duke University Press.

Dinshaw, Carolyn. 1989. *Chaucer's Sexual Poetics*. Madison: University of Wisconsin Press.

Edwards, A. S. G. 2012. "Chaucer and 'Adam Scriveyn'." *Medium Aevum* 81.1: 135–138.

Farina, Lara. 2013. "Wondrous Skins and Tactile Affection: The Blemmyae's Touch." In: Katie L. Walter (ed.). *Reading Skin in Medieval Literature and Culture*. The New Middle Ages. New York: Palgrave Macmillan. 11–28.

Fee, Christopher R. 1994. "Productive Destruction: Torture, Text, and the Body in the Old English *Andreas*." *Essays in Medieval Studies* 11: 51–62.

Fisher, Matthew. 2012. *Scribal Authorship and the Writing of History in Medieval England*. Columbus: Ohio State University Press.

Foucault, Michel. 1977. *Discipline and Punish: The Birth of the Prison*. New York: Pantheon Books.

Gillespie, Alexandra. 2008. "Reading Chaucer's Words to Adam." *The Chaucer Review* 42.3: 269–283.

Grosz, Elizabeth. 1990. "Inscriptions and Body-Maps: Representations and the Corporeal." In: Anne Cranny-Francis and Terry Threadgold (eds.). *Feminine, Masculine and Representation*. Sidney: Allen and Unwin. 62–74.

Holsinger, Bruce. 2009. "Of Pigs and Parchment: Medieval Studies and the Coming of the Animal." *PMLA* 124.2: 616–623.

Holsinger, Bruce. 2010. "Parchment Ethics: A Statement of More than Modest Concern." *New Medieval Literatures* 12: 131–136.

Jablonski, Nina G. 2006. *Skin: A Natural History*. Berkeley: University of California Press.

Kay, Sarah. 2004. "Flayed Skin as *objet a*." In: Jane E. Burns (ed.). *Medieval Fabrications*. The New Middle Ages. New York: Palgrave Macmillan. 193–205.

Kay, Sarah. 2006. "Original Skin: Flaying, Reading and Thinking in the Legend of Saint Bartholomew and Other Works." *Journal of Medieval and Early Modern Studies* 36.1: 35–73.

Kay, Sarah. 2011. "Legible Skins: Animals and the Ethics of Medieval Reading." *postmedieval: A Journal of Medieval Cultural Studies* 2.1: 13–32.

Landfester, Ulrike. 2012. *Stichworte: Tätowierung und europäische Schriftkultur*. Berlin: Matthes & Seitz.

Langum, Virginia. 2013. "Discerning Skin: Complexion, Surgery, and Language in Medieval Confession." In: Katie L. Walter (ed.). *Reading Skin in Medieval Literature and Culture*. The New Middle Ages. New York: Palgrave Macmillan. 141–160.

Lerer, Seth. 1990. "Textual Criticism and Literary Theory: Chaucer and His Readers." *Exemplaria* 2.1: 329–345.

Lerer, Seth. 1993. *Chaucer and His Readers: Imagining the Author in Late-Medieval England*. Princeton: Princeton University Press.

Lewis, Katherine J. 2000. "'Lete Me Suffre.' Reading the Torture of St Margaret of Antioch in Late Medieval England." In: Jocelyn Wogan-Browne, Rosalynn Voaden, Arlyn Diamond, Ann Hutchison, Carol M. Meale and Lesley Johnson (eds.). *Medieval Women: Text and Contexts in Late Medieval Britain. Essays for Felicity Riddy*. Turnhout: Brepols, 69–82.

MacKendrick, Karmen. 2004. *Word Made Skin: Figuring Language at the Surface of Flesh*. New York: Fordham University Press.

Mills, Robert. 2013. "Havelok's Bare Life and the Significance of Skin." In: Katie L. Walter (ed.). *Reading Skin in Medieval Literature and Culture*. The New Middle Ages. New York: Palgrave Macmillan. 57–80.

Mize, Britt. 2001. "Adam, and Chaucer's Words Unto Him." *The Chaucer Review* 35.4: 351–377.

Mooney, Linne R. 2006. "Chaucer's Scribe." *Speculum* 81.1: 97–138.
Nyffenegger, Nicole. 2013. "Saint Margaret's Tattoos: Empowering Marks on White Skin." *Exemplaria* 25.4: 267–283.
Pitts, Victoria. 2003. *In the Flesh: The Cultural Politics of Body Modification*. New York: Palgrave Macmillan.
Small, Susan. 2013. "The Medieval Werewolf Model of Reading Skin." In: Katie L. Walter (ed.). *Reading Skin in Medieval Literature and Culture*. The New Middle Ages. New York: Palgrave Macmillan. 81–97.
Steel, Karl. 2013. "Touching Back: Responding to Reading Skin." In: Katie L. Walter (ed.). *Reading Skin in Medieval Literature and Culture*. The New Middle Ages. New York: Palgrave Macmillan. 183–195.
Wakelin, Daniel. 2014. *Scribal Correction and Literary Craft: English Manuscripts 1375–1510*. Cambridge: Cambridge University Press.
Walter, Katie L. (ed.). 2013. *Reading Skin in Medieval Literature and Culture*. The New Middle Ages. New York: Palgrave Macmillan.
Williams Boyarin, Adrienne. 2009. "Sealed Flesh, Book-Skin: How to Read the Female Body in the Early Middle English *Seinte Margarete*." In: Kathryn Kerby-Fulton (ed.). *Women and the Divine in Literature before 1700: Essays in Memory of Margot Louis*. Victoria: ELS Editions. 87–106.

Part I: **Reading Diseased Skin**

Sealy Gilles
Doctrinal Dermatologies

Abstract: Leprosy, or Hansen's disease, and related skin afflictions have long been linked to doctrinal deviancy and sexual transgression, as in Robert Henryson's *Testament of Cresseid*. However, the perverse 'leper' is only one end of the spectrum occupied by *lepra* in the European Middle Ages. This article charts medieval leprosy's erratic course from a clinically attested affliction that nevertheless bore a range of significations to an unequivocal expression of corruption. As outbreaks of Hansen's disease bedeviled European communities from the tenth to thirteenth century, the struggle to interpret the disease and respond to the suffering it causes reflected the protean nature of skin afflictions. Physicians, ecclesiasts, poets, and civil authorities drew on a wide range of sources as they worked to care for the sick and protect their communities. For some, leprosy offered salvation and marked the sufferer as *quasi Christi*. For others, it provided a figure for heresy and punishment for the blasphemer. In the late Middle Ages and early modern era, as the disease disappears, readings of leprous skin narrow and darken. In the post-pandemic climate of the late Middle Ages, the careful parsing of disease that had governed attempts to identify the sick and mandate their care gives way to fears of contamination and vagrancy. Sufferers from epidermal disease are increasingly relegated to one unmediated identity, the 'leper,' sexually promiscuous and doctrinally suspect.

> And if þe world haue hem in hate, neuerþelatter God haue hem not in hate. Ȝe, but he loued Lazer, þe leprouse man, more þan oþer men.
>
> — (Guy de Chauliac, *The Cyrurgie*, 381 ll. 15–17)[1]

In the second half of the fifteenth century, when the Scottish poet Robert Henryson rewrites the end of Geoffrey Chaucer's *Troilus and Criseyde*, he afflicts the heroine with Hansen's disease, or leprosy, a fate never contemplated in his source. In a radical addendum to Chaucer's ambivalent portrait of a "lady fre" (*Troilus and Criseyde*, 5.144),[2] Henryson's compressed text specifies blasphemy

---

[1] 'And even if the world loathes them, nevertheless God hates them not. Yea, but he loved Lazarus, the leprous man, than other men.' Quotations from *The Cyrurgie of Guy de Chauliac* are from Ogden (1971), cited by page and line number in the main text. Translations are my own.
[2] Chaucer's ambivalence is underlined here by Criseyde's circumstances and by the identity of the speaker, Diomede, who is leading her into the Greek camp. Quotations from *Troilus and Criseyde* are from Benson (1987). They are cited by book and line number in the main text.

as an immediate cause for the disease but also suggests a proximate cause, promiscuity. The double etiology is not without precedent; the ties between leprosy, doctrinal deviancy, and sexual transgression have a long pedigree. Nevertheless, the perverse 'leper' is only one end of the spectrum occupied by Hansen's disease and related skin disorders in the Middle Ages; medieval leprous identities were far more complex and nuanced than Henryson's portrait of a corrupt lady leads us to believe. In this article, I attempt to chart medieval leprosy's erratic career from a clinically attested affliction that nevertheless bore a range of significations to an unequivocal expression of corruption. I find that in the eleventh and twelfth centuries the diseased skin's motility as text, combined with the quotidian presence of *leprosi*, mitigated against conflating patient and pathogen into a single degraded prototype. Late in the Middle Ages, as leprosy outbreaks subside in most of Western Europe, representations of the sick diverge from the carefully articulated profiles and protocols of medical professionals. Leprosy is increasingly read as evidence of depravity and the 'leper,' especially in her literary incarnations, becomes corrupt and dangerously contagious.

Physicians, theologians, and civil authorities from the sixth century to the first half of the fourteenth century drew on Biblical sources, on medical science, and on their own observations to develop taxonomies and protocols that governed responses to the leprous and that guided communities struggling with the competing claims of public safety and private care. Poets cast a wider net still as they worried about the impact of the disease on intimate relationships and puzzled out its place in moral and eschatological economies. Throughout the twelfth and thirteenth centuries, the struggle to interpret this multifaceted disease and to respond to the suffering it inflicted reflected the protean nature of leprosy itself. In the late Middle Ages and early modern era, however, representations of the leprous narrow and darken as the sick are increasingly relegated to one unmediated identity – the sexually promiscuous and doctrinally suspect deviant.

The often paradoxical array of responses to leprosy derives in part from the rich indeterminacy of skin. Skin, whether animal or human, seems declarative but is inherently unstable. Most articulate in its corrupted state, a marked skin promises revelation even as it obscures; at best, our outermost organ bears fitful and unstable witness to our internal workings. Looking outward, we also find that the skin we count on to protect us from incursion is instead the intersection between self and world. Increasingly, skin has become understood as, in Claudia Benthien's terms, "a place of encounter," both a canvas and an "organ of communication and contact" (Benthien 2002: 2, 6–7). For many medieval physicians and ecclesiasts, diseased skin also made visible the state of the soul, although, as with any text, glosses could differ widely. Moreover, medieval interest in skin went well beyond the individual organ. The post-modern engagement with bodily surfaces, as reflected in this volume, returns us to medieval encounters with parchment, with the penetrated body of Christ, with the hairy hide of the werewolf, and, of course, with the leprous.

Given the instability of the term *lepra* and the long history of *leper* as a pejorative, it behooves us to be self-conscious in our nomenclature. After G. H. Armauer Hansen's discovery of *mycobacterium leprae* in 1873, the preferred term for leprosy has been 'Hansen's disease,' which has the advantage of diagnostic accuracy and clinical dispassion. It follows that the term *leper* is now properly eschewed as derogatory, whether it refers to victims of Hansen's disease or to individuals shunned as if they were infected with a contagious and disfiguring illness. Furthermore, as Albert Bourgeois points out, other than the Latin term *leprosus*, medieval texts commonly used *ladre,* or *lazar,* a derivative of *Lazarus*, *mesel* or "wretched," or simply *infirmus* (Bourgeois 1972: 21). Nevertheless, *leprosy* and *leprous* remain useful as historically situated terms for conditions that included but were not limited to Hansen's disease. In addition, I use *leper* to characterize someone who is wholly defined by epidermal disease in ways that extend well beyond their medical condition.[3] Like substantives such as *cripple* or *lunatic, leper* becomes a 'pathonym' – my neologism for a label that replaces the complexities of individual identity with an imagined totality completely determined by disease or disability. I argue here that even this hijacked identity was not necessarily, or even primarily, demeaning in medieval disease discourse. Henryson's Cresseid is only at the extreme end of a spectrum that includes the ascetic and the lustful, the saint and the heretic.

At first, medieval responses to leprosy mirrored the affliction itself in their diversity. The sick might be seen as pitiable, as corrupt, or as sanctified. Literary representations of those afflicted range from Ivain, the sexual predator in Béroul's *Tristran and Iseut*, to the self-sacrificing hero of *Ami et Amile;* ecclesiastical sources are similarly diverse, housing both saints and heretics. Nevertheless, beginning in the late fourteenth century, as the disease retreated from European communities, its complexities were subsumed into the 'leper,' a pathonymic repository of moral, doctrinal, and sexual deviancies. This essay argues that the retreat of Hansen's disease, especially in England, allowed for the emergence of a chimeric pariah whose skin, voice, and hair testify to the corruptive power of the disease but not to its redemptive or salvific qualities. That pariah

---

[3] As Rawcliffe (2006) points out, medieval *leprosus, lepra*, and their cognates referred to a variety of skin disorders. See her discussion of nomenclature issues (2006: 11–12).

emerges as a vehicle for a plague-troubled society fearful of social unrest and beset by a new venereal pox.

Lepra in the Vulgate Bible – Diagnosis, Chastisement, and Blessing

Reading skin is always a tricky business, but when we turn to epidermal disease integumental legibility is further compromised by shifting symptoms and episodes of remission and relapse. This fluidity confounds diagnosis – particularly in regard to accounts from the distant past. The Vulgate Bible's *lepra*, for example, may refer to scabies, viral infections such as measles and smallpox, eczema, or any one of a host of other afflictions (Lieber 2000: 99–107); in addition, cutaneous boundaries dissolve as Old Testament *lepra* extends to molds and fungal infestations contaminating homes and garments. Elsewhere in the Old Testament, the clinical, detached guidelines in Leviticus give way to links between *lepra* and transgression. The Gospels, on the other hand, yield renderings of the sick as worthy of mercy, as occasions for miracle working. This wealth of scriptural precedent, together with charitable imperatives in the eleventh and twelfth centuries, authorized a wide, sometimes contradictory, range of doctrinal responses to the leprous.

Biblical sources on skin disorders suggest that the demonization and marginalization of the sick is neither natural nor inevitable. Leviticus attests to the care that must be taken in diagnosis and insists that priests, who are charged with examining the sick, leave open the possibility of reentry into the community. The oft-cited chapters Leviticus 13 and 14, for all of their specificity, refrain from casting blame on the diseased and lay out elaborate protocols for diagnosis and reentry into the community once the threat of contagion is past.[4] The focus throughout is on skin, but the range of disorders is wide. *Lepra*, the Vulgate's translation of the Hebrew *zara'ath*, refers to a number of dermatological diseases, including scabies, psoriasis, measles, and simply rash. In recognition of the complexity of these conditions and the heavy price the patient pays for quarantine, priests are charged with making a thorough assessment over an extended time period:

> If, however, the shiny place is white in the skin and no deeper in the flesh and the hair in it is its former color the priest shall seclude [the patient] for seven days and on the seventh day examine him and if the disease has not spread further in the skin beyond its former

---

4 See Demaitre (2007: 234–235).

extent, seclude him seven more days, and on the seventh day he shall be examined. If the leprous spot is hard to see and it has not grown on the skin, he is clean, it is only scabies, and the man shall wash himself and his clothes and he shall be clean. (Leviticus 13.4–6)[5]

Further diagnostic guidelines cover boils, swellings, white patches, burn-like spots, itching, and loss of hair. In recognition of the dangers of infection and the price of expulsion, the scripture prescribes that the sufferer determined to have a persistent skin condition appear as a mourner and remove himself from the camp:

> Whoever therefore is spotted shall be [judged] leprous and set apart in accordance with the judgment of the priest. He shall wear torn clothes, bare his head, cover his mouth, and proclaim himself infected and unclean. As long as he is leprous and unclean he shall live outside the camp. (Leviticus 13.44)[6]

Human skin is not the only vulnerable integument in this text. A garment, "whether wool or linen [...] or [...] skin or anything that is made of skin" (Leviticus 13.47–48),[7] may be leprous as well, and, like the afflicted person, shall be judged clean or unclean based on careful examination at the beginning and end of a seven-day quarantine. Houses in Canaan are also at risk. If a house is seen to be leprous, it must be examined by a priest "[a]nd should he see in the walls of the house pale or reddish pitted deformities and they are below the surface" (Leviticus 14.37)[8] the house must be closed up for seven days, after which time the priest must look again. If the disease has spread within the house, it must be scraped and cleaned and replastered. A house that cannot be cleansed must be destroyed:

---

[5] "sin autem lucens candor fuerit in cute nec humilior carne reliqua et pili coloris pristini recludet eum sacerdos septem diebus et considerabit die septimo et siquidem lepra ultra non creverit nec transierit in cute priores terminos rursum includet eum septem diebus aliis et die septimo contemplabitur si obscurior fuerit lepra et non creverit in cute mundabit eum quia scabies est lavabitque homo vestimenta sua et mundus erit." Scriptural passages are taken from the Latin Vulgate (Weber 1969). Translations are my own unless otherwise stated.
[6] "Quicumque ergo maculatus fuerit lepra et separatus ad arbitrium sacerdotis habebit vestimenta dissuta caput nudum os veste contectum contaminatum ac sordidum se clamabit omni tempore quo leprosus est et immundus solus habitabit extra castra." For a detailed discussion of skin disease in the Old Testament see Lieber (2000). Lieber is working directly with the Hebrew Bible while I base my discussion on the Vulgate.
[7] "vestis lanea sive linea [...] aut certe pellis vel quicquid ex pelle confectum est."
[8] "et cum viderit in parietibus illius quasi valliculas pallore sive rubore deformes et humiliores superficie reliqua."

> If [after cleansing and replastering] the *lepra* returns and the priest, having entered, sees a sprinkling of leprous blemishes on the walls, the *lepra* is persisting and the house is unclean. They must immediately cast its stones and timbers and dust [plaster] outside the walls into an unclean place. (Leviticus 14.44–45)[9]

In these chapters, *lepra* is suspected of a motility that enables it to cross from stone to flesh, from flesh to fabric: "He who enters the house when it is closed up will be unclean until the evening and he who sleeps in the house or eats in it shall wash his garments" (Leviticus 14.46–47).[10]

Lepra compromises boundaries between skin, walls, and garments; its fungible nature compels us to "reconsider[] human specificity," in the words of Sarah Kay (2011: 14).[11] Creaturely skins dried, scraped, and sewn, plaster mixed and smoothed over stone, human skin pulsing with blood: in Leviticus, all integuments come under the law for *lepra*:

> This is the law for all *lepra* – both for *lepra* that strikes clothing and the scarring of houses, and of the breaking out into blisters, shiny spots and in various kinds of changing colors – in order to know when it is clean and when unclean. (Leviticus 14.54–57)[12]

Diseased integument in persons or things must be detected, isolated, and monitored lest the community suffer more widespread infection – either corporeal or material. Nevertheless, recuperation is also possible for the diseased, should the symptoms abate. Leviticus 14.4–32 prescribes elaborate rituals in order that the leprous – human or domicile – may be cleansed according to the "ritus leprosi" ('rite of the leprous') and reintegrated into the community (Leviticus 14.2). The ceremony calls for the recently healed patient to bathe and shave his head, eyebrows, and beard. His reentry into the camp is effected through the sacrifice of lambs and doves; he is anointed with their blood (Leviticus 14.1–32).[13] Similarly,

---

9 "ingressus sacerdos viderit reversam lepram et parietes aspersos maculis lepra est perseverans et immunda domus quam statim destruent et lapides eius ac ligna atque universum pulverem proicient extra oppidum in loco inmundo."
10 "qui intraverit domum quando clausa est inmundus erit usque ad vesperum et qui dormierit in ea et comederit quippiam lavabit vestimenta sua."
11 Kay is speaking of the skin-to-skin contact between medieval readers and parchment, the non-human animal remains foundational to medieval literacy, a contact zone that will recur here in the discussion of twelfth-century anti-heresy figurations.
12 "ista est lex omnis leprae et percussurae leprae vestium et domorum cicatricis et erumpentium papularum lucentis maculae et in varias species coloribus inmutatis ut possit sciri quo tempore mundum quid vel inmundum sit."
13 The Vulgate's prescriptions begin "hic est ritus leprosi quando mundandus est" ('Here is the rite for the leprous when he is being cleansed,' Leviticus 14.2).

a house that is no longer leprous must be cleansed with the blood of a bird, while, for both human and house, a second bird is freed "to fly freely into the field as [the priest] prays for the house that it may be justly cleansed" (14.53).[14]

Lepra in Leviticus is an external affliction that attaches itself to animate bodies and inanimate objects. It is not the expression of an internal condition – an intrinsic corruption – nor is it inflicted as retribution for particular transgressions, as will happen elsewhere in the Old Testament. Isolation of the sick protects the community from infection, and seems not to be intended as punishment (Lieber 2000: 133). The cleansing rituals in Leviticus 14 do call for a penitential sacrifice, "sacrificium pro peccato" (14.19), to make atonement for any offense, perhaps inadvertent, that has contributed to the suffering of the leprous. There is little in either chapter 13 or 14, however, to indicate that the sick bring the condition upon themselves any more than clothes or houses are likely to earn their affliction. Moreover, even though the leprous may be contagious, they do not necessarily pollute.

The distinction between contagion and pollution becomes clearer when we compare Leviticus 13 and 14 on *lepra* to the strictures on men and women who experience genito-urinary discharges: pus, semen, or menstrual blood. These effluents require vigilance and repeated cleansing, in order that the sons of Israel "not die in their uncleanness when they defile [the Lord's] tabernacle that is in their midst" (Leviticus 15.31).[15] In addition, the menstrual woman and the man who experiences "an issue of seed" defile any clothes, beds, saddles, vessels that they touch (Leviticus 15.26–27). For the seven days of her quarantine, the woman is forbidden human contact lest she contaminate others, who then must be shunned as well. Here there are no diagnostic protocols and no strictures detailing the priest's responsibility to those experiencing the discharge; they are seen as impure, rather than diseased, and are therefore not susceptible to treatment. Although the cleansing rituals bear some resemblance to those for a patient cured of *lepra*, for the menstrual woman there is no cure for her recurring defilement.

Elsewhere in the Hebrew Bible cutaneous infection is reserved for humans, and anxieties regarding leprous fabrics and walls disappear. At the same time, the disease becomes an instrument of divine chastisement; often those smitten with *lepra* are suffering because they have shown themselves to be arrogant, blasphemous, or simply insubordinate. When Miriam, sister of Moses, complains of her brother's marriage to a Cushite, God's anger "was raised against [Miriam

---

14 "avolare in agrum libere orabit pro domo et iure mundabitur."
15 "non moriantur in sordibus suis cum polluerint tabernaculum meum quod est inter eos."

and Aaron] so that when the cloud that had been over the tabernacle receded [...] behold Miriam appeared white with *lepra* as if with snow" (Numbers 12.9–10).[16] Even here, however, the case is far from hopeless and the culprit deserves compassion. Aaron's plea on Miriam's behalf envisions further corporeal disintegration, a characteristic of Hansen's disease: "Let her not be like the dead, and leprous like the aborted, expelled from his mother's womb, of whom, look, the flesh is already half devoured" (Numbers 12.12).[17] Moses pleads for Miriam as well and after seven days isolation she returns to the camp, no longer anathema.[18]

For others, there is no return. Uzziah had ruled Jerusalem well for fifty-two years, but "grew proud, to his destruction" (2 Chronicles 26.16).[19] In the Chronicles account, he enters the temple to burn incense, properly the role of the priests only. The consecrated priests, the sons of Aaron, warn him, but he is without contrition:

> and when he threatened the priests there was suddenly leprosy on his forehead [...] Azariah, the high priest, and all the other priests, looked and he was leprous in his forehead and they expelled him quickly, and he himself hurried to leave, because the Lord had stricken him. Thus Uzziah, the king, was leprous to the day of his death, and because he was fully leprous lived in a house apart, for he was excluded from the house of the Lord. (2 Chronicles 26.19–21)[20]

Uzziah will become an exemplum of the arrogant blasphemer, anathema to the faithful.

Whereas in Uzziah's case disease inscribes divine castigation on the skin of the transgressor, in the Book of Job the body becomes a contested site in an epic struggle between God and Satan for the soul of the just. Satan dares God: "take your hand and touch [Job's] bone and his flesh, and then you shall see [if] he will

---

[16] "iratusque contra eos abiit nubes quoque recessit quae erat super tabernaculum et ecce Maria apparuit candens lepra quasi nix."

[17] "ne fiat haec quasi mortua et ut abortivum quod proicitur de vulva matris suae ecce iam medium carnis eius devoratum est lepra."

[18] Lieber (2000: 107–111) discusses this episode in detail and suggests that Miriam suffers from psoriasis.

[19] "elevatum est cor eius in interitum suum." In the Vulgate, the Chronicles are the Libri Paralimpomenon.

[20] "minabatur sacerdotibus statimque orta est lepra in fronte eius [...] Azarias pontifex et omnes reliqui sacerdotes viderunt lepram in fronte eius et festinato expulerunt eum sed et ipse perterritus adceleravit egredi eo quod sensisset ilico plagam Domini fuit igitur Ozias rex leprosus usque ad diem mortis suae et habitavit in domo separata plenus lepra ob quam et eiectus fuerat de domo Domini."

praise you to your face" (Job 2.5).²¹ Job is given over to Satan who strikes Job "with horrible sores from the sole of his foot to the crown of his head" (Job 2.7).²² In despair Job curses the day of his birth and longs for death "in the anguish of [his] spirit" but stops short of cursing God (Job 7.11). For this he will be rewarded, made whole. Job's innocence and his steadfast refusal to deny his God put him outside the retributive model that gave us Uzziah; Job prepares the Christian reader for the leprous sick, healed by Jesus, and for Lazarus, whose suffering earns him divine favor.

In the New Testament, Gospel accounts mitigate, even forbid, harsh treatment of the leprous, and those injunctions thread their way through later patristic and sermon literature. Matthew describes Jesus healing a leprous man, and, citing Isaiah, says Christ "took on our infirmities and endured our diseases" (Matthew 8.17).²³ The evangelists, and later medieval commentators, return again and again to the prophet's account, which delineates the messiah's kinship with the diseased: "Truely he has borne our infirmities and endured our sorrows and we have thought of him as a leper, and as one stricken by God and brought down" (Isaiah 53.4).²⁴ Isaiah's language will resonate throughout the Middle Ages.²⁵

Lazarus, who gave the medieval *leprosus* the name 'lazar,' may not have been afflicted with Hansen's disease at all. A beggar, Lazarus, like Job, is beset with sores, "ulceribus plenus" (Luke 16.20), but he becomes leprous only in post-Gospel tradition. Needy and sick, he lies before a rich man's gate in perennial reproach: "There was a rich man and he dressed in purple and in linen and he ate at a splendid banquet every day and there was a beggar named Lazarus who lay at the rich man's gate full of sores, desiring to be fed with the crumbs that fell from the rich man's table" (Luke 16.19 – 21).²⁶ The parable gains much of its power from Lazarus' post-mortem elevation to rest in the bosom of Abraham and selfish Dives' descent into hell (Luke 16.22).

---

21 "mitte manum tuam et tange os eius et carnem et tunc videbis quod in facie benedicat tibi."
22 "percussit Iob ulcere pessimo a planta pedis usque ad verticem eius." *Lepra* is not used in the Vulgate for Job's disease. Nevertheless, his afflictions will earn him a role as a precursor of the medieval leper.
23 "ipse infirmitates nostras accepit et aegrotationes portavit."
24 "vere languores nostros ipse tulit et dolores nostros ipse portavit, et nos putavimus eum quasi leprosum et percussam a Deo et humilitatum."
25 See Orlemanski (2012), "How to Kiss a Leper," for a cogent discussion of Isaiah 53 and the "embodied sublime." See also Pichon (1984: 354 – 355).
26 "Homo quidam erat dives et induebatur purpura et bysso et epulabatur cotidie splendide et erat quidam mendicus nomine Lazarus qui iacebat ad ianuam eius ulceribus plenus cupiens saturari de micis quae cadebant de mansa divitis."

Even as the beggar ascends directly to the bosom of Abraham upon his death, so the leprous in the Middle Ages were often assured of immediate salvation by virtue of their affliction, a promise increasingly worked out in the doctrines of purgatory that emerge in the twelfth century.[27] Moreover, the sufferer is blessed with salvific power beyond his or her own sphere. Dives, the rich man who is cast into Hades and begs for a drop of cool water from Lazarus' fingertip, has his own descendants in the wealthy donors whose anxiety concerning the afterlife prompts the building of leprosaria and the underwriting of masses ensuring their salvation.

Lepra in Patristic Sources – Glossing Skin

Just as *lepra* elicited a range of responses in the scriptures, epidermal afflictions provided the sixth-century Christian theologians Isidore of Seville and Gregory the Great with a rich trove of analogy and metaphor. The threat of contagion and the skin's alluring kinship to parchment offered intuitive links to heresy's dangers,[28] but Isaiah 53 and the examples of Job and Lazarus insisted on suffering as the gateway to salvation. Patristic readings of leprous skin informed later eleventh- and twelfth-century attempts to address a multivalent disease that struck kings and commoners alike.

Isidore of Seville (c. 560–536 C.E.), in keeping with the generic demands of his encyclopedic project, eschews the ambiguities of the Old Testament accounts for elaborate taxonomies of heterodoxy. In Isidore's commentary on Leviticus, the cutaneous markers that once served to distinguish those who must be kept separate from those who could safely remain within the camp become metaphoric shorthand for the heresies besetting the true church.[29] In "De Lepris," Isidore first establishes the link between *lepra* and 'falsa doctrina' and then launches into a catalogue of heresies and the analogous symptoms belonging to leprosy:

> False doctrine is leprosy. Consequently it is not unreasonable that heretics be understood to be leprous, who, not having the oneness of true faith, avow various teachings in error, and

---

27 See Le Goff (1984: 209–234).
28 Touati (2000) argues that theories on the threat of contagion and poisoned air emerge late in the Middle Ages.
29 Forrest (2005: 155) points out in *The Detection of Heresy* that the analogy between dissent and contagious disease was used in the anti-heresy polemic to explain the spread of heresy from person to person "at a seemingly exponential rate."

mix truth with falsehood: just as leprosy pollutes human bodies with variegated spots both true and false. (Isidore of Seville, *Quaestiones in vetus testamentum*, XI.1–2)[30]

The various heresies are then characterized based on the location of leprous symptoms; the body becomes a doctrinal microcosm in which *lepra* of the head is the most pestilential because "[h]e who bears leprosy on his head has sinned against the divinity of the Father, or against the godhead, which is Christ" (XI.4).[31] This is the leprosy of the Jews, the Manicheans, the Arians, and their ilk. The eight sections that follow identify specific heresies as leprosies of the beard, of baldness, of skin, of the livid scar, of the flesh, and of various colors.[32]

Isidore's near contemporary, Pope Gregory I (c. 540–604 C.E.), also uses leprous skin to embody the deformations and dangers of heresy. In Part I, Book Five of his *Magna Moralia*, an exposition on the Book of Job, the sixth-century pope notes that heretics employ mixtures of good and evil to seduce and deceive the unwary. He uses the lesions symptomatic of Hansen's disease to figure the partial truths and shiny deceptions of heresy:

> In leprosy, certainly, a part of the skin is made bright and part retains its healthy color. Lepers in this way are a figure for heretics because, just as they mix the straight with the deformed [*prava*], they sprinkle the color of health with blemishes. (Gregory the Great, *Magna Moralia*, Liber V, cap. XI, 237)[33]

Prava here is often translated as 'evil,' or 'wrong,'[34] but the context of Gregory's passage suggests we retain the primary meaning of *pravus:* 'crooked, irregular, deformed,' with connotations of perversity and depravity. Nevertheless, the analogy also offers hope. Blending Chronicles with the Gospel of Luke, Gregory tells us that, just as Jesus miraculously healed the ten 'lepers' as recounted in Luke,

---

[30] "Lepra doctrina est falsa. Proinde leprosi non absurde intelliguntur hæretici, qui, unitatem veræ fidei non habentes, varias doctrinas profitentur erroris, veraque falsis admiscent: sicut et lepra veris falsisque locis humana corpora variando commaculat." Quotations of Isidore of Seville are taken from Migne (1850). Also see *Isidore of Seville: The Etymologies*, book IV, ch. VIII (Barney, Beach, and Berghof 2006: 112–113).
[31] "In capite lepram portat, qui in divinitatem Patris, vel in ipso capite, quod Christus est, peccat."
[32] See Caput XI, sections 3–13. For a discussion of Isidore's analogies see J. Stearns (2011: 44).
[33] "In lepra quippe et pars cutis in fulgorem ducitur et pars in colore sano retinetur. Leprosi itaque hæreticos exprimunt, quia dum rectis praua permiscent, colorem sanum maculis aspergunt." Gregory also likens Job's friends to heretics who disguise a poisoned drink with a taste of honey on the rim of the cup. Quotations from the *Magna Moralia* are from Adriaen (1979).
[34] Bliss in Marriott and Bliss (1844: 262), for example, translates *perversis* as 'wrong' and *prava* as 'evil.'

sometimes the teachings of the church are able to reform the heretic and return him to divine favor. As with some of the friends of Job, the leprous in Gregory's argument are salvageable:

> Hence, in order to be healed, they cry out, "Jesus, Master." For indeed in these words they signify they have erred, here they who are about to be saved humbly call him master; as soon as they come to recognize the master once again, so soon are they brought to a state of health. (*Magna Moralia*, Liber V, cap. XI, 237)[35]

In keeping with the Vulgate's rich trove of figures, leprosy provides Gregory with the language of both infectious error and spiritual healing.

When Gregory turns from exegesis to homiletic narrative, diseased skin no longer threatens; instead, it demands compassion. In his homily on the monk Martyrius, Gregory expands upon Matthew's account of the miraculous healing of a leprous man and invokes Isaiah's portrayal of the messiah as at once stricken and redemptive. Martyrius, on his way to visit a monastery, rescues a leprous man, "whose limbs were made foul with clustered sores of elephantiasis" (Gregory the Great, *Homiliarum in evangelia*, col. 1301).[36] He carries the 'leper' to the gates of the monastery, where the sick man is revealed to be Christ and ascends into heaven. In his conclusion, Gregory invokes Isaiah 53 to join the abject and the sublime together:

> Who indeed in human flesh is more sublime than Christ who is exalted above angels? And who in human flesh is more abject that the leprous, who is deformed with swelling wounds and filled with fetid exhalations? But behold in the form of a leper he appears; and he who is revered above all is not ashamed to be seen as despised below all men. (*Homiliarum in evangelia*, Homilia XXXIX, col. 1301)[37]

---

35 "Unde et bene ut saluentur, clamant: *Iesu praeceptor*. Quia enim in eius uerbis se errase significant, hunc saluandi humiliter praeceptorum uocant; cumque ad cognitionem praeceptoris redeunt mox ad formam salutis recurrunt."

36 "quem densis vulneribus elephantinus morbus per membra fœdaverat." Quotations from *Homiliarum in evangelia* are from Migne (1857).

37 "Quid enim in humana carne sublimius carne Christi, quae est super angelos exaltata? Et quid in humana carne abjectius carne leprosi, quæ tumescentibus vulneribus scinditur, et exhalantibus fetoribus impletur? Sed ecce in specie leprosi apparuit; et is qui est reverendus super omnia, videri despectus infra omnia dedignatus non est." See discussion by Rawcliffe (2006: 63).

The pope's rhetorical construct forges an intimate link between the leprous beggar's abasement and his saviour's apotheosis.[38]

Touched by God – Twelfth-Century Responses to Suffering

The emergence of Hansen's disease as endemic in eleventh-century Europe lent new immediacy to the patristic exegesis of skin. As in Isidore's commentary, the condition's extensive symptomatology proved fertile ground for taxonomies of sin, but the quotidian presence of the sick insisted that attention also be paid to suffering. *Lepra* was not unknown in early medieval Europe, but, as the numbers of visibly diseased sufferers increased, responses to the disease became both more concrete and more complex. The leprous were no longer an abstraction confined to sermons and patristic glosses; the presence of the afflicted mitigated against wholesale categorization of the sick. We see a particularly potent mix of doctrine and pastoral care in the work of Jacques de Vitry, an authority on preaching who served as Bishop of Acre from 1216 to 1225. In a model sermon, Jacques draws on both Leviticus and the gospels, using an elaborate catalogue indebted to Isidore. However, instead of figuring heresies, his schema links the visible symptoms of leprosy with the invisible maladies of the soul: *lepra efflorens*, or scaly skin, testifies to vanity, lividity to jealousy, *nigra*, or blackened skin, to a guilty conscience, and so forth.[39] Jacques does not end with these humoural analogies, but uses them to argue that when Christ cures the ten 'lepers' who cry out to him (Luke 17.11–19) he is treating the ten effects of sin on the soul, which parallel ten effects of leprosy on the body. Nicole Bériou finds that Jacques brings an attentive and warning gaze, "un regard attentif et averti," to bear on the world of the *leprosi* and that, for Jacques, the suffering bodies of the leprous become open books of flesh fashioned by God as earthly testaments, both legible and susceptible to cure (Bériou and Touati 1991: 69).

---

[38] The trope of Christ's skin as a surface to be read emerges in the fourteenth-century Middle English "Long Charter of Christ." Speaking from the cross, Christ describes his skin as parchment, stretched and washed with blood, marked with wounds and spit. For texts see Spalding (2006), especially 26 ll. 75–90.

[39] The complete list is as follows, with Bériou's links to relevant vices (in my translation): lepra efflorens [vainglory], pallida [faint-heartedness], liuida [envy], uolatilis [changeability], nigra [guilty conscience], alba [conceit], rubea [cupidity and carnal desire], lepra cutis [lustfulness], lepra uestis [vain finery], lepra domus [needlessly luxurious accommodations], lepra capillorum [unseemly tonsure and hair], lepra cicatricis [sins repeated] (*Sermo II* in Bériou and Touati 1991: 123 ll. 159–170).

In Jacques' model sermons, Uzziah and Lazarus converge as the malady is construed a tool to both discipline the recalcitrant flesh and achieve a transformation, a turn towards God. Jacques explains to his auditors that God tests them, just as a buyer tests a new pot. If he strikes the vessel and hears a clear tone, he takes it as his own. If the vessel responds discordantly, he repudiates it. In this way, God strikes the leprous, then chooses those who willingly and with gratitude welcome their affliction.[40] Distinguishing between *lepra anime* and *lepra corporis*, Jacques assures those who suffer bodily disease that "[i]ndeed leprosy of the body is purgatory in this life and if you patiently endure it as your martyrdom you will have no other purgatory" (*Sermo II*, 123 ll. 152–154).[41] The notion that the leprous sufferer is chosen for this arduous path, is destined for a higher purpose, is also reflected in Jacques' placement of the leprosarium residents in his *ad status* manuals for preachers, collections assembled after he became Bishop of Acre. Within the hierarchy of sermon audiences he locates *leprosi* immediately below the religious orders and above paupers, pilgrims, crusaders, and merchants (Bériou and Touati 1991: 39–40 n. 15).[42]

Jacques de Vitry's elevation of those stricken with leprosy conforms to other evidence from medieval France. Near the end of the twelfth century and the beginning of the thirteenth, documents admitting the sick into lazar houses characterize the disease in providential terms that declare the sufferer to be chosen, divinely afflicted. Again Isaiah 53.4 is invoked; twelfth-century records, in attesting to the status of the diseased, bear witness to the divine imprint as the sufferer is "stricken by God and brought low" (*percussam a Deo et humilitatum*).[43] In 1183, Raginaldus from Danumvilla is "made leprous by the will of God" (*voluntate Dei leprosus factus*), and, in 1188, Nivelon, son of Geoffroi de Grand-pont, is "adorned with leprosy by the will of God" (*Dei voluntate lepra sigillatus*) (Merlet and Jusselin 1909: 49, 54 as quoted in Bériou and Touati 1991: 14–15). An affliction that was once at a rhetorical remove in the simile "we thought of him him *as*

---

40 "Sicut autem qui ollas nouas emere uolunt manu percutiunt et si clare sonant illas accipiunt, si rauce sonant et quassum sonum reddunt respuunt et non emunt, ita Deus infirmitate uos percussit. Si libenter et cum gratiarum actione suscipitis, Dominus acceptat et recipit." (Jaques de Vitry, *Sermo I*, 115 ll. 351–356). Quotations from *Sermo I* and *Sermo II* are from Bériou and Touati (1991).

41 "Lepra enim corporis est uobis purgatorium in hac uita quam si patienter sustineatis pro martyrio uobis reputabitur et aliud purgatorium non habebitis."

42 See also Hugh of St. Victor's account of the healing of the ten lepers: *Allegoriae in Novum Testamentum, Opera omnia*, PL 175, Liber IV, cap. XXV, col. 823 (Migne 1854). See Rawcliffe (2006: 111–112) for a discussion of Hugh's reasoning.

43 Jacques de Vitry assures patients in his first model sermon that "God has stricken you with this affliction" (*ita Deus infirmitate vox percussit*) (See Bériou and Touati 1991: 115 ll. 354–355).

a leper" (*nos putavimus eum quasi leprosum,* Isaiah 53.4) has become an unmediated blow that nevertheless offers the possibility of heavenly reward.

The promise of purgatorial remission finds direct expression in the voices of two poets stricken with leprosy: Jean Bodel (c. 1165–c. 1210) and Baude Fastoul, who writes in the third quarter of the thirteenth century. Both Bodel and Fastoul address their affliction in their late work; both articulate the hope that their tribulations in this world will exempt them from suffering in the next. Bodel, writing in 1202, has relinquished his hope for earthly succor, even from God:

> Nor do I expect God to intervene
> To staunch this suffering in me
> On the contrary, may he inflict my body with that very pain
> By which my soul may be free from debt. (93 ll. 213–216)[44]

Baude Fastoul's plea is more vivid, more corporeal. Here, epidermal affliction is the mark of grace upon the body, a sign of divine, if stringent, solicitude, as in the Book of Job. Baude Fastoul tells us that

> God, who has made to light upon me
> A sickness through which I must be marked,
> Says that before him I will be blessed. (107 ll. 10–12)[45]

Here, the sickness ("mal") that inscribes the skin of the sick man comes directly from the hand of God, not as chastisement but as the stigmata marking those chosen to suffer in order that they may be saved. Just as the human scribe has recorded affliction upon the skin of a flayed sheep, so the divine Author has ornamented (*sigillatus*) and marked (*il m'estuet musir*) the skin of the *lazar*. However, we are also reminded that, unlike parchment, leprous skin refuses separation from the suffering body it encloses. The scribal analogy validates these human skins as legible, but their lesions and nodules insist on the text's origin in subdermal disease. The three-dimensionality of leprous skin militates against the reading of the epidermal apart from the corporeal. These are neither flayed corpses nor disembodied hides, but bodies recording their own testaments – to suffering and to the hope of transcendence through divine favor.[46]

---

[44] "Ne ja Diex ne s'en entremete / Que il ceste dolor m'estanche, / Ains doinst au cors tel penitanche / Par quoi l'ame soit fors de dete." Quotations are taken from Ruelle (1965).
[45] "Dix, ki a fait sur moi luisir / Un mal dont il m'estuet musir, / Dist que devant lui souef flaire." Quotations are taken from Ruelle (1965).
[46] For a discussion of the active responses of patients to their sponsors and questioners, see Stemmle (2015).

Contagion – Twelfth-Century Deviants

For Fastoul, leprous skin bears God's mark and warranty. But the capacious nature of leprosy makes other readings, and authorships, possible, even inevitable. The purgatorial sufferers of the twelfth century co-exist with a much less benign figure indebted to the sixth-century taxonomies of Isidore of Seville cited earlier. In Isidore's classification, the 'leper,' a diseased grotesque, represents threat rather than divinely inspired suffering. In this figure, the blasphemy of Uzziah joins the fear of physical contagion to fuel anti-heresy diatribe.

Leprosy, with its terrifying symptoms, proves a potent source of figures for doctrinal corruption. Raymond of Toulouse, in 1177, cites putrid leprous sores, or *tabes*, as the visible signs of heresy.[47] Eckbert of Schönau uses the analogy to make the threat of doctrinal contagion visceral. He says of the Cathars' message: "the sermon creeps into the heart like a cancer, and like leprosy it spreads swiftly, far and wide, infecting the precious limbs of Christ" (*Sermones contra catharos*, Sermo I col. 13).[48] William the Monk in his diatribe against Henry of Lausanne recalls Leviticus 14 in its imbrications of body and leprous garment. Here, we also hear an early version of Cynthia's "bill" against Cresseid in Henryson's *Testament of Cresseid*. William (as quoted in Moore 1975: 57) writes:

> You too are a leper, scarred by heresy, excluded from communion by the judgement of the priest, according to the law, bare-headed, with ragged clothing, your body covered by an infected and filthy garment; it befits you to shout unceasingly that you are a leper, a heretic and unclean, and must live alone, outside the camp, that is to say outside the church.[49]

In these passages, cutaneous infection, at times seen as contagious and always dreaded for its horrifically distorting effect on the body, proves an ideal vehicle for the construction of heresy as both rampant and grotesque. Heresy, in its turn, enables the anathematization of the sick – as 'leper,' a kissing cousin to the Jew, intimate with enemies of the faith.[50]

---

47 "haec put[r]ida hæresis tabes prævaluit." See Raymond V's address to the General Chapter of the Cistercians in Stubbs (1875: 270). Also addressed in Moore (1976: 3).
48 "nam sermo corum serpit ut cancer, et quasi lepra volatilis longe lateque discurrit, pretiosa membra Christi contaminans." Quotations are taken from Migne (1855).
49 An edition of the debate can be found in Manselli (1953).
50 Discussions of the heretic as diseased can be found in the Moore (1975) and Fudge (2013: 61ff).

Leprous Heroes – The Ambiguities of Twelfth-Century Narrative

As attacks on dissidents intensified in the twelfth century, leprosy played a crucial role in the triangulation of doctrinal transgression, sexual deviance, and bodily corruption, a dynamic well understood and exploited by Robert Henryson three centuries later. However, just as we find divergent readings of the disease in theological sources, so romance and *chanson de geste* testify to a range of interpretive possibilities. The popular story of Ami and Amile, for example, is indebted both to anti-heresy polemics and to pastoral recuperation of the 'leper.' In this narrative, which survives in Latin, French, Anglo-Norman, and Middle English versions from the eleventh to late fourteenth centuries,[51] a protagonist is caught between the irreconcilable demands of *trouth* and friendship. The tale celebrates the friendship of Ami and Amile, unrelated by blood but born on the same day and identical in appearance. In the Old French version, the two are given identical gold cups by the Pope upon their christening. They serve nobly at the court of Charlemagne. Amile, however, is seduced by the emperor's daughter, Belissant, and must prove his innocence in judicial combat, a trial he is sure to lose. Ami, who can truthfully swear he has never slept with the princess, jousts in Amile's place and defeats Amile's accuser. To avoid exposing his friend he swears a false oath of betrothal to Belissant and an angel tells him that: "Affliction and torment of the flesh will be your lot; you will be a loathsome leper; your eyes will dim and teeth drop out. And from neither kith nor kin will you have any help" (*Ami et Amile, st. 90*, ll. 1816–1819).[52] As foretold, he is beset with leprosy and his wife abandons him: "His nose had become sunken and sore, and his tongue had grown thick [...] Lubias] refused any longer to look at him or touch him or offer him her body" (st. 103 ll. 2059–2065).[53] Lubias attempts to divorce her sick husband, expels him from their home, and refuses him sustenance. Finally, Ami takes to the road as a "ladre forain," or itinerant *lazar*, with two faith-

---

51 See Le Saux (1993: 1–17).
52 "Moult grans martyres de ta char t'en atent: / Tu seras ladres et meziaus ausiment, / Ne te parront oil ne bouch ne dent, / Ja n'i avraz aïde d'ami ne de parent." Quotations for *Ami et Amile* are taken from Dembowski (1969). I am using Rosenberg and Danon's (1996: 82) translation.
53 "Moult li abaisse et angoisse li nés / Et li retranche durement li parlers, / [...] [Lubias] nel deingna veoir ne esgarder / Ne de son cors servir ne honorer." Translation by Rosenberg and Danon (1997: 89).

ful serfs for companions.⁵⁴ The poem is unequivocal in its condemnation of the wife. Conversely, Ami retains the allegiance of his people, and his son, although too young to help, is passionate in his defense. Garin and Haymmes, the two serfs who accompany Ami in exile, remain devoted to him even as the disease takes its toll.

Maimed and desperate, Ami begs outside a palace at Riviers, not knowing that it is the home of Amile and Belissant. Amile, unlike Dives, responds to news of a leprous beggar by offering him food and wine. Ami's golden cup, the only vestige left of his former life, triggers a reunion. In the poem's *dénouement*, Ami is restored to health, made whole, by Amile's willingness to sacrifice his own children to heal his friend by bathing him in their blood. Those who have abandoned Ami suffer retribution in the end; those who succored him are redeemed. Even the children are restored to life! Here, a bigamous vow brings on disease, but there is no contamination of others, and the corruption is contained, and finally resolved, within one salvageable, even transcendent, body.⁵⁵

Even in his most desperate moments, Ami, the friend who swears a false oath, bears no resemblance to the sexually perverse 'leper' that emerges in the medical literature and some anti-heresy diatribes.⁵⁶ In stark contrast, the figure of Ivain in Béroul's late twelfth-century *Tristran* draws upon this nightmarish predator, whose disease results in increased sexual appetite and who is eager to rape and infect the innocent. In Béroul, the cuckolded husband, King Marc, finally convinced of Tristran and Yseut's guilt, plans to execute his queen by fire. The stake is readied and the fire laid, but Ivain, leader of a gang of bandit *leprosi*, offers Marc a sadistic alternative:

> Look: I have here one hundred [leprous] comrades.
> Give us Yseut, to be possessed in common.
> No woman has suffered a worse fate.
> Sire, in us there is such a great lust!
> There is no woman under heaven

---

54 See Bourgeois (1972: 64–67) for an account of those diagnosed as leprous but without the status or resources to secure a place in a leprosarium. His evidence is largely from fifteenth and sixteenth-century Pas-de-Calais.
55 The Middle English version is *Amys and Amylion* (Le Saux 1993). In English, the leprous friend is Amylion. See Rhodes' more detailed discussion of the Middle English version in this volume. The spelling of the names varies.
56 Characterization of sufferers from *elephantia* as lustful is found as early as Aretaeus of Cappadocia. See Demaitre (2007: 208–209) for specific sources. See also Rhodes (this volume) for links between lust and leprosy.

> Who could endure intercourse with us for one day.
> (Béroul, *Tristan*, ll. 1192–1197)[57]

Gang rape, humiliation, and a life of physical disintegration and pain – these are the wages of infidelity for a beautiful woman and they will reappear as such in Henryson's *Testament of Cresseid*. In Béroul, leprosy promises to avenge the lost marital honor Marc can no longer salvage and it serves a similar purpose for Troilus in Henryson's *Testament*. Disease destroys the body that betrays.[58]

In Béroul's romance, however, neither leprous bandit nor king has the last word. Tristran rescues Iseut and the lovers have their idyll in the forest until the expiration of the love potion, combined with the hardships of wilderness survival, drives them to renounce their love and return to court. When we see leprosy return, it is in a far more ambiguous guise. Yseut is put to the test, at her own suggestion, in a trial by oath hosted by King Arthur and his court. At Mal Pas, the boggy ford between Marc's land and Arthur's tents, Tristran, following his beloved's directions, awaits in the guise of a leprous beggar. When Arthur arrives he calls out:

> Sire, King Arthur, I am a sick man,
> Hunchedback, leprous, deformed and feeble.
> [...]
> I have come in search of alms.
> [...]
> King Arthur, do you see how I scratch myself?
> I am freezing, although some may be hot.
> Before God, give me your leggings. (ll. 3715–3730)[59]

---

[57] "Veez: j'ai ci compaignons cent: / Yseut nos done, s'ert conmune. / Paior fin dame n'ot mais une. / Sire, en nos a si grant ardor! / Soz ciel n'a dame qui un jor / Peüst soufrir nostre convers." Quotations for Béroul's *Tristan* are taken from Lacy (1998); they are cited by line number in the main text. With the exception of Arthur, I have followed the spelling of names in the Lacy edition.

[58] Touati traces the increasing dominance of the Ivain and his type to a late thirteenth-century shift in *mentalité* following Lateran IV. He argues that the diametrically opposed images of the lazar chosen by God and the depraved 'leper' had always coexisted but that the thirteenth-century movement to regularize religious communities contributed to a marginalization of the leprous (Bériou and Touati 1991: 31–32).

[59] "Sire Artus, rois, je sui malades, / Bociez, meseaus, desfaiz et fades. / [...] / Ça sui venuz l'aumosne querre. / [...] / Roiz Artus, voiz com je me grate? / J'ai les granz froiz, qui quait les chauz. / Por Deu me donne ces sorchauz."

In addition to engaging in insults, some fisticuffs, and off-color badinage, the 'leper' plays a practical joke, misdirecting his enemies into the mire, and addresses a veiled insult to King Marc. When Yseut arrives, however, the masquerade becomes a matter of survival. In a startling move, she orders the 'leper' to carry her across the ford. Reproving his show of hesitation, Yseut invokes the belief that a promiscuous woman could be a carrier of leprosy without becoming ill herself. She scolds the 'leper:'

> "Pay attention," she said, "put yourself in place.
> Do you believe that your sickness will take hold of me?
> Have no doubt, it will not." (ll. 3923–3925)[60]

The queen rides astride his broad back, as the assembled courts watch:

> They all watched, both king and nobles.
> Her thighs pressed against his staff.
> He raised one foot, then the other;
> Often he pretended to fall;
> He made a great show of his pain.
> Yseut the beautiful rode him astride,
> One leg here and the other there.
> (ll. 3934–3940)[61]

As Neda Chernack Zovic (1996: 90) points out, the queen's horseback ride is a parody of the sexual act, shamelessly flaunted before the assembled courts. Nevertheless, Yseut's unorthodox ride across the mire on the back of a beggar will save her life:

> Lords, she said, for the mercy of God!
> I see here holy relics.
> Now listen to what I swear here,
> So that it satisfies the king;
> [...]
> That no man has entered between my thighs
> Except for the leper who made himself a packhorse,

---

[60] "'Cuite.' faite ele, 'un poi t'arenge. / Quides tu que ton mal me prenge? / N'en aies doute, non fera.'" For a discussion of women's immunity to leprosy and their role as carriers of disease, see Jacquart and Thomasset (1988: 188–190).

[61] "Tuit les gardent, et roi et conte. / Ses cuises tient sor son puiot. / L'un pié sorlieve et l'autre clot, / Sovent fait senblant de choier, / Grant chiere fai de soi doloir. / Yseut la bele chevaucha, / Janbe deça, janbe dela." See discussion of this passage in Lacy (1998: 215).

[and] who carried me over the ford,
And my husband, King Marc. (ll. 4197–4200, 4205–4208)[62]

Practical joker and romance hero, Tristran as trickster destabilizes the leprous identity; he does so in conspiracy with his lover, who implicates herself even as she outwits her male adversaries. Béroul exploits anxieties about contagion and promiscuity to mock the two cuckolded kings. His heroine, having escaped the clutches of the 'leper' Ivain, embraces the protean Tristran, thereby surviving to love again. Henryson's Cresseid will not be so lucky.

Parsing Disease – Physicians, Surgeons, and Juries

Sacrificial friend, sexual predator, charlatan beggar, blasphemer, *quasi Christi*: leprous skin articulated a bewildering array of identities. However, an even greater range of symptoms and classifications lurked behind these often fantastic personae. Medieval physicians struggled to anatomize the leprous body and set treatment protocols for a disease they understood to be incurable once it had taken hold. Even as they acknowledged the dangers they believed *lepra* presented to their communities, authorities such as Bernard de Gordon (1270–1330) and Guy de Chauliac (1300–1368) asserted the medical professional's responsibility to ground his reading of a patient's condition in scrupulous examination. To this purpose they developed batteries of symptoms and carefully delineated protocols. Guy de Chauliac formalized Bernard's signs into lists easily followed by practitioners. 'Equivocal' signs were not exclusive to leprosy and included many of the dermatological symptoms characteristic of *lepra* more broadly defined: dark and spotted skin, loss of hair, ulcerations, anesthesia. 'Unequivocal' signs, such as tuberous eyebrows, swollen nostrils and lips, distorted voice, fetor, and fixed gaze (inability to blink), pointed conclusively to the disease:

> Rowndenesse of þe eyȝen and of þe eres, spredynge of þe browes, and writhinge or crokynge of þe nose þirles, [...] fowlenesse of þe lippes, an hose voyce as þoghe he spak with his nose þirles, stynkynge of brethe and of al þe persone, stable lokynge and horrible in þe maner of a beste þat highte satoun. (Guy de Chauliac, *The Cyrurgie*, 380 ll. 3–9)[63]

---

[62] "'Seignors,' fait el, 'por Deu merci! / Saintes reliques voi ici. / Or escoutez que je ci jure, / De quoi le roi ci aseüre: / [...] / Qu'entre mes cuises n'entra home / Fors le ladre qui fist soi some, / Qui me porta outre les guez, / Et li rois Marc mes esposez.'"
[63] 'rounding of the eyes and ears, swelling of the eyebrows, and twisting or deviation of the nostrils [...] coarseness of lips, a hoarse voice as though he spoke through his nostrils, fetor

Demaitre points out that the diagnostic catalogues changed little over the centuries, except to expand as symptoms were added, elaborated, and reorganized. Demaitre (2007: 207) adds that "attempts to improve the diagnosis consisted in compiling more symptoms, describing them with greater precision, differentiating and organizing them methodically, and evaluating their reliability." Uroscopy and hematoscopy could indicate a predilection towards leprosy and the examination of the blood, in particular, might confirm a diagnosis, but external signs dominated diagnostic protocols.[64] Far from offering only superficial indicators, skin provided a three-dimensional map to the contours of disease. Examiners were encouraged to employ sight, touch, and smell as they tested for discoloration, lumps, open sores, insensitivity to pinpricks, and odor.

Even as medical authorities advised care and compassion, the guidelines and catalogues of symptoms emerging from schools of medicine such as the University of Montpellier were often couched in language that placed them at several removes from the bodies they describe. In contrast, records from the screening panels that used those guidelines to evaluate the sick can be heartbreakingly specific. Very few records survive from England and we have scant documentation from any locale before the late fourteenth century, when Hansen's disease was in decline in Western Europe.[65] Nevertheless, a trove of financial accounts and judgments from the Pas-de-Calais region, assembled by Albert Bourgeois, affords a window into the often laborious process of evaluating those suspected of leprosy. Late medieval expense reports and verdicts from *iudicia leprosorum* in Saint-Omer, Arras, Béthune, and Aire testify to a reluctance to isolate the sick without a clear diagnosis. Although priests played a significant role before the mid-thirteenth century, the late medieval juries documented by Dr. Bourgeois were first composed primarily of residents, *ladres,* from the leprosarium that would receive the patient, although others, such as town officials, the master or chaplain of the leprosarium, or *ladres* from neighboring towns, might assist in determinations. Beginning in the early fifteenth century, juries were increasingly composed of medical professionals, physicians or barber-surgeons, in addition to leprosarium residents (Bourgeois 1972: 27–29). Regardless of their training, these panels followed the advice of Guy de Chauliac and others in their reluctance to act quickly in removing a patient from his or her home. Those

---

of breath and of the body, a fixed stare as of the beast they call an ape.' See Demaitre (2007: 216–219) for a discussion of Guy's diagnostics.

[64] See Bourgeois (1972: 30) for the relative importance of external clinical signs and examination of blood and urine. See also Demaitre (2007: 235–237).

[65] On the irony of a disease only documented as it disappears, see Baudot and Candille (1972: 12–13.)

whose diagnosis was uncertain were often told to return in six months, after following a health regimen designed to alleviate symptoms.[66] Even unequivocal signs were sometimes not enough to condemn the examinee, as we see in the example of Leurens Waultier of Aire.

On October 5, 1532, Leurens was examined, *mis a l'espreuve*, for leprosy. The panel included physicians, surgeons and *lazars*. They agreed that Leurens had "morphea of the head" (Bourgeois 1972: 186 n. 43.b) and suspicious nodules on his nostrils but differed as to the diagnosis and disposition. The medical professionals declared those symptoms "insufficient evidence to judge the body of Leurens completely leprous" (Bourgeois 1972: 186 n. 43.b),[67] whereas the leprosarium residents concluded that "Leurens is leprous and must be separated from interactions with the healthy" (Bourgeois 1972: 186 n. 43.b).[68] Leurens was allowed to go, but two and a half years later the disagreement was settled in favor of the residents when Leurens was reexamined and diagnosed as suffering from *lèpre brune*. He was then separated from the healthy (Bourgeois 1972: 30–31, 185–186 n. 43.b).[69] In this and other cases, judges recognized that reading epidermal disease required expertise and time; their work was colored by the daunting responsibility not to sequester precipitously even as they fulfilled their obligation to the public.

As the Sick Disappear – Leprosy in the Late Medieval Imagination

The texts cited above – Biblical passages, scriptural glosses, anti-heretical diatribes, autobiographical poems, model sermons, romance narratives, medical treatises – participate in, and rely upon, the creation of categories and distinctions. Sorting, listing, glossing, and temporal ordering are all called into service as communities and authorities work to identify the sick accurately, define hospital communities, care for those diagnosed with the disease, and interpret epidermal disorders in a doctrinal context. From Leviticus to Guy de Chauliac, the

---

66 For an example of deliberations involving an interim regimen and a waiting period, see Bourgeois (1972: 314 n. 108).
67 "ne sont souffissans indices pour jugier le corps dudit Leurens totallement lépreux"
68 "Leurens est lépreux et par ce doibt estre séparé hors de la conversacion du poeuple sain"
69 "aprez laquelle visitate et espreuve iceulx maîtres phizicien, chirurgiens et ladres ont unaniement et d'un commun accord dit, déclaré et jugié ledit Leurens estre entachié de la maladie de lèpre [...] au moyen de quoy icellui Leurens doibt estre séparé et déboulté hors de la conversacion du poeuple sain" (Bourgeois 1972: 186, n. 43).

symptoms of *lepra* are carefully parsed in order to map the progression of disease and justify medical, ecclesiastical, and legal responses. When communities across Western Europe were struggling with outbreaks of Hansen's disease, elaborate articulations of the 'leper' as a moral and social construct had to take into account the presence of *leprosy*, the physiological condition. In other words, the imagined 'leper' was continually juxtaposed to the quotidian presence of the leprous.

Beginning in the late thirteenth century, Western Europe saw the incidence of Hansen's disease decrease. The disease persisted in a number of northern locales and subsided at varying rates elsewhere in Europe,[70] but evidence from late medieval insular communities indicates that it had almost disappeared in England by the fourteenth century. Some fifty years before Robert Henryson wrote his *Testament of Cresseid*, England's leprosaria were either almost empty or primarily home to the non-leprous: the indigent, the elderly, the disabled (Carlin 1989: 23–24). Max Satchell (1998: 13) estimates that one third of English leprosaria "disappear from the documentary record" in the fourteenth and fifteenth centuries. Peter Richards notes that by the fourteenth century only 200 leprosaria hospitals remained in Britain and that many of those housed few Hansen's patients or none. There were fewer than 2000 hospitalized lazars out of a population of perhaps three million (Richards 1977: 11). St. Julian's hospital near St. Albans was typical: By 1344 only two or three *leprosi* were in residence.[71]

As we have seen, the screening panels and medical authorities of the late Middle Ages continued to rely on a mixture of observation and tradition to parse the disease. In catalogues of symptoms, palliative regimens, and *iudicia leprosorum*, "premodern medicine [...] treated leprosy as a 'malady of the whole body'" (Demaitre 2007: 279). However, when we turn to representations of the leprous in late medieval literary, penitential, and judicial discourse, we find divergence from the sober assessments of medical practitioners. In these texts, the 'leper' emerges as the distorted avatar of the leprous.

In his account of the "cultural deployment of leprosy" in the late Middle Ages, Michael Leahy (this volume) argues that diseased skin remained a principal signifier that "continued to exert ethical and metaphorical power." For example, in the sermons of Hugo Legat, a fourteenth-century Benedictine monk, lep-

---

[70] See Richards (1977: ch. 2 *passim*) for a detailed look at Hansen's disease in the island parishes of Finland and elsewhere in seventeenth-century Scandinavia.
[71] Even these numbers may be too high. Orme and Webster find that Sherburn (Durham), one of the biggest leprosaria in England, had only 65 inmates in 1316. Most were much smaller with fewer than a dozen residents, many of whom were not afflicted with Hansen's disease (1995: 36).

rosy is both metaphor for sin and the price for succumbing to gluttony. In effect, as we saw in Jacques de Vitry, leprosy "materialis[es] [...] the effects of sin on the soul" (Leahy, this volume). In Jacques, however, those material effects are carefully parsed and catalogued. In Legat's sermons, and elsewhere in late medieval sources, Leahy (this volume) finds that the "hazy and imprecise nature of the disease" makes it available as a figure for a wide range of deviancies. Those figurations, in turn, authorize the disciplining of the imagined 'leper.'

Late medieval juridical texts cast those suspected of leprosy as dangerous deviants, intent on the physical and moral corruption of their fellows. Edward III issued an edict in 1346 excluding *leprosi* from London because, he proclaimed, they deliberately sought to contaminate others, through their speech, their breath, and through "carnal intercourse with women in stews and other secret places" (Riley 1868: 230–231).[72] Authorities in Berwick-upon-Tweed threatened to strip the clothes from and expel any 'leper' found within town walls.[73] Other regulations forbade churchgoing by *leprosi* (1427) and threatened those who harbored the afflicted with banishment (1466) (Mathews 2002: 60).

Although Hansen's disease had a longer life in the north, in Robert Henryson's time it is likely that the lazar houses of Scotland, including one in Dunfermline, Henryson's home town, were increasingly populated by the non-leprous or were closing. Nevertheless, in 1428, Scotland's King James I mandated

> That no leper folk, neither men nor women, shall from henceforth enter any borough of the realm other than three times in the week: that is to say each Monday, each Wednesday and each Friday, from ten o'clock until two in the afternoon. And when fairs and markets fall on these days, they should postpone their visits and come on the [following] morning to get their living.[74]

---

[72] Rawcliffe (2006: 275) calls this edict "unprecedented – and unique" in England and points out that Edward was attempting to clear trouble-makers from the streets of London before leaving on a military expedition.

[73] In the fourteenth century, authorities in Bristol declared that no lepers or prostitutes were permitted within town precincts (Bickley 1900: I, 33). In 1374–1375, a Norwich borough court expelled Thomas Tytel, webster and leper (Hudson 1892: 58–60). At Berwick-upon-Tweed, *leprosi* found in violation of a town ordinance forfeited all their garments and those suspected of infection were cast out (Rawcliffe 2006: 275–276; Thomson and Innes 1814–1865: I, 2, cap. XVIII).

[74] "That na lipper folk, nouther man nor woman, enter na cum in a burgh of the realme bot thrise in the oulk, that is to say, ilk Monounday, Wednesday and Friday, fra ten houris to two eftrnoon and quhair fairis and mercattis fallis in they dayes, that thay leift thair entrie in the burrowis and gang on the morn to get thair leving" (Thomson and Innes, 1814–1875: II, 16, cap. 8). Rawcliffe's translation (2006: 289–290). See Bourgeois (1972: 66) for similar restrictions on begging as well as hostility towards leprous beggars in Pas-de-Calais in the fifteenth century.

The king's pronouncement is notable, not for an erasure of the "leper folk" – four hours a day, three days a week hardly amounts to total exclusion – but rather for its attempt to manage a putative leprous presence. On market days, James insists that lazars wait until the following morning to earn their living, leaving the crowded (and more lucrative) fairs to healthy vendors. Rawcliffe (2006: 7–8, 93, 253, 289) sees the edict, and others like it, as part of the late fourteenth-century response to a very different disease, an expression of a "siege mentality" in a post-pandemic climate of repeated local bubonic plague outbreaks.[75] Rawcliffe also notes concerns about a perceived threat from vagabonds and the need to control a more mobile and less tractable generation of young people freed from ties to the land, anxieties that became entangled with the fear of contagion.

These late medieval responses to leprosy suggest a changing and increasingly hostile environment for those suspected of the disease. As long as sufferers from Hansen's disease remained present in medieval towns, the communities that harbored them seemed able to tolerate a wide range of competing identities for the leprous. However, with the subsidence of the disease, which for England begins in the late thirteenth century, the quotidian patient was replaced by an imagined 'leper' who was increasingly feared and despised. This spectral 'leper' is evident in royal edicts, church documents, and in the literary figure of the leprous lady, rife with venereal disease.[76]

Henryson's Cresseid – Fifteenth-Century Exemplum

In his *Testament of Cresseid*, Robert Henryson gives us just such a corrupt 'leper,' a 'patient zero,'[77] well positioned to pass her condition and her guilt to her literary progeny, who are female, sexually suspect, and dangerously contagious. The clarity and discipline in Henryson's account of Cresseid's disease gives the poem a clinical tone much admired by modern editors and critics.[78] The central epi-

---

[75] See also Rawcliffe's account of public anxieties in *Urban Bodies* (2013: 4–8, *passim*).
[76] The reimagining of the 'leper' in the absence of leprosy bears a strong resemblance to the creation of the virtual or spectral Jew after the expulsions of 1290 (England), 1306 (France), and 1492 (Spain), a dynamic ably delineated in separate studies by Tomasch (2002) and Kruger (2006).
[77] 'Patient zero' was the term Shilts (1987: 147, 156, *passim*) used to designate Gaétan Dugas, a French-Canadian airline attendant, as the origin of the AIDS epidemic in North America. The label has long since lost scientific credibility but retains its stigmatizing power.
[78] See M. Stearns (1944); Parr (1945); Fox (1968: 25–28); Hume (1969).

sode mimics the Biblical account of Uzziah's infection in its clear delineation of cause and effect and in the rapidity of divine retribution. Cresseid commits blasphemy, is called to account, immediately becomes visibly leprous, and is cast out from temple and community. However, as Michael Leahy points out in this volume, the poem never makes up its mind as to the cause of Cresseid's affliction. In the preamble to his protagonist's blasphemous outburst, Henryson invokes a complex and murky etiology. Blasphemy acts as the functional cause of Cresseid's leprosy, but the poem grounds the disease in the sexually promiscuous body. Cresseid's desertion of Troilus marks her as unfaithful, as an oath breaker, and, as the poem begins, she is described as no better than a camp follower (Henryson, *Testament of Cresseid*, ll. 74–77).[79] The triangulation of blasphemy, sexual deviance, and disease renders Cresseid, a romance heroine praying to pagan gods, heir to twelfth-century Cathars accused of infecting the communal body of Christendom.[80]

After Cresseid complains of mistreatment by Venus, Saturn pronounces judgment upon her. That speech act enacts the penalty instantly as disease overruns the guilty body. Saturn's remorseless cataloguing of Cresseid's infection conflates cause and origin in a sequence of brief but damning apothegms that somatize moral and doctrinal degeneracy, fusing the medical and the juridical. Thus Saturn and Cynthia pronounce a sentence of "pane," "torment sair," "seiknes incurabill," and, most telling of all, a guarantee that she will be "to all louers [...] abhominabill" (ll. 306–308).[81] As Leahy (this volume) points out, the anacoluthon insists on the intimate link between Cresseid's prior identity as the model lover, "the flour and A per se / Of Troy and Grece" (ll. 78–79)[82] and her current status as "abiect odious" ('contemptible outcast,' l. 133). Having sketched out the general outlines of his judgment, Saturn proceeds to the price it exacts. Without naming the disease, he articulates the leprous condition, both internal and external, humoural and communal, as, above all, a condition of radical dissolution and exclusion. Beauty, vitality, fair features he will "exclude fra the for euermair" (l. 315),[83] just as the blasphemer will be excluded from the society that valued her for these attributes. Her moist heat is transmuted into the cold dry-

---

[79] Quotations from *Testament of Cresseid* are taken from Fox (1968) and cited by line number in the main text.
[80] See Rhodes (this volume) for a discussion of the multiple causes of Cresseid's affliction.
[81] Quotations from *Testament of Cresseid* will be translated in the footnotes. The gods decree that Cresseid be oppressed with 'suffering,' 'tormented with disease,' and 'incurable illness.' They also condemn her to be an abomination to lovers everywhere.
[82] "the flower and perfection of Troy and Greece"
[83] 'banish from you for evermore'

ness of melancholy, her wantonness into "greit diseis" or great distress (l. 320). He leaves it to Cynthia, with her leaden, borrowed light, to name the condition: "This sall thow go begging fra hous to hous / With cop and clapper lyke ane lazarous" (ll. 342–343).[84]

Etiological protocols are not the only casualties here. In the instantaneous onset of disease Henryson abrogates the painstaking analysis of emerging symptoms laid out by medieval authorities such as Guy de Chauliac (379–381), and the poem's temporal disjunctions make a mockery of the carefully considered narrative pathologies found in much medical discourse throughout the Middle Ages.[85] Although at first glance, the onset of disease is clinically detailed, the *Testament* is in fact driven by the conflation and disjunction belonging to the imploding language of anathema. The time warp begins with a series of preemptive exclusions long before Cresseid exhibits any symptoms of leprosy.[86] Before the poem opens, she is, of course, removed from Troy as part of the exchange repatriating Antenor and restoring her to her father. Then, well before Saturn lays his "frostie wand" ('icy wand,' l. 311) upon her head, she is repudiated and cast out by Diomede, who, having had his fill of her, abandons her to the general camp:

> [He] send to hir ane lybell of repudie
> And hir excludit fra his companie.
> Than desolait scho walkit up and doun,
> And sum men sayis, into the court, commoun. (ll. 74–77)[87]

Shamed by Diomede's abandonment of her, Cresseid, in yet another retreat, takes refuge in her father's house but "[i]nto the kirk wald not hir self present" (l. 117),[88] and instead withdraws further into "ane secreit orature, / Quhair scho micht weip hir wofull destyny" (ll. 120–121),[89] a destiny not yet revealed to her. Ignorant of her fate, Cresseid nevertheless bewails it. Her querulous outburst to Cupid and his mother defines her as already leprous:

---

[84] 'Thus you shall go begging from house to house / with cup and clapper like a leprous one.'
[85] For example, see Demaitre's (2007: 210–215) account of Bernard of Gordon's diagnostic guidelines.
[86] See Riddy (1997: 232–233) for successive exclusions.
[87] '[Diomede] sent her a declaration of divorce / and banned her from his company. / Then, abandoned, she wandered up and down, / and, some men say, as a common woman, into the court.' "Commoun" here refers to Cresseid, or to her position in the court, possibly as a woman men use in common. See Fox (1968: 92, note for line 77).
[88] 'she would not appear in church'
[89] 'a secluded chapel, where she might lament her sorrowful destiny'

> Now am I maid ane vnworthie outwaill,
> And all in cair translatit is my joy.
> Quha sall me gyde? Quha sall me now conuoy,
> Sen I fra Diomeid and nobill Troylus
> Am clene excludit, as abiect odious? (ll. 129–133)[90]

In the Kafkaesque world of Saturn's court, that heartrendingly prescient protest and the complaint that follows it elicit the juridical process by which leprosy is imposed. As articulated by the lunar Cynthia, the verdict recapitulates symptoms of leprosy:

> Fra heit of bodie [here] I the depryue,
> And to thy seiknes sall be na recure
> Bot in dolour thy dayis to indure.
> Thy cristall ene mingit with blude I mak,
> Thy voice sa cleir vnplesand, hoir, and hace,
> Thy lustie lyre ouirspred with spottis blak,
> And lumpis haw appeirand in thy face (ll. 334–340)[91]

Henryson has been lauded for his realism, and the poem's commitment to taxonomies is certainly reflected in the precise listing of Cresseid's symptoms.[92] The cataclysmic and instantaneous nature of her illness, however, testifies to a very different representational strategy. Whereas medieval physicians and juries often mandated six-month waiting periods in order to assess the progress of disease, the progression of leprosy's symptoms is here collapsed into an instant metamorphosis – a reification of Cresseid's prior self-identification as "abiect odious."[93] As in the diatribes against Cathars and other heretics, the distinction between pathogen and victim is erased in an etiological sleight-of-hand.

---

90 'I am now made a despised outcast / and my joy is entirely changed to sorrow. / Who shall guide me? Who shall now protect me / Since I from Diomede and noble Troilus / am entirely banished, as a hateful outcast?'
91 'I here deprive you of the body's vital heat, / And there shall be no remedy for your sickness / Except to suffer your days in sorrow. / I mix with blood your crystal clear eyes. / Your voice, so clear, [I make] unpleasing, rough, and hoarse, / Your lovely complexion covered in black spots, / and leaden lumps appearing on your face.' Leahy (this volume) points out that these symptoms, especially the "spottis blak," have their precursors in Chaucer's poem.
92 See, for example, Parr (1945), M. Stearns (1944), and, more recently, Wynne-Davies (1993).
93 Compare the two-year gestation period and progressive deterioration of the leper in the Middle English *Amys and Amylion* (Le Saux 1993: 75, st. 124–126).

Once Cresseid becomes leprous, Henryson distorts the well-attested chronology of leprosy by accelerating the heroine's corporeal deterioration. Cresseid herself takes inventory:

> My cleir voice and courtlie carrolling,
> Quhair I was wont with ladyis for to sing,
> Is rawk as ruik, full hiddeous, hoir and hace:
> [...]
> Now is deformit the figour of my face. (ll. 443–448)[94]

Her "Complaint" uses that inventory, the declaration of a corrupt self, to haunt the "ladyis fair of Troy and Grece" with the spectre of things to come:

> Nocht is ȝour fairnes bot ane faiding flour,
> Nocht is ȝour famous laud and hie honour
> Bot wind inflat in vther mennis eris,
> ȝour roising reid to rotting sall retour. (ll. 461–464)[95]

Here the "roising reid" of a lady's cheek is destined, not simply to rot, but to return to rotting, as if the flowering of her beauty were simply a phantom moment of wholeness between decay and dissolution.

The poem's most audacious, and most puzzling, manipulation of leprosy's progression comes when Troilus, resurrected out of Chaucer's fifth book and fresh from victories on the battlefield, having "strikken doun / Knichtis of Grece in number mervellous" (ll. 486–487),[96] processes triumphantly into Troy past the clamorous colony of lepers. Cresseid casts her eyes up to her former lover and yet fails to recognize him when he stoops over her in pity. Troilus, ignorant of her identity, sees a vestige of his beloved in the horribly distorted face and is moved to tumble jewels into her lap, but she is, in effect, stricken with a selective and preemptive blindness and must later ask "Quhat lord is ȝone?" (l. 533).[97]

Cresseid's brief testament follows closely on the heels of this encounter. In it, she invokes, even more explicitly than in her lament, the preemptive language of a transi-tomb's banderole: "Heir I beteiche my corps and carioun / With wor-

---

[94] 'My clear voice and courtly caroling, / When I was accustomed to sing with ladies / Is raucous as a rook's, full hideous, rough, and hoarse / [...] / now deformed are the lineaments of my face.'
[95] 'Now is your beauty but a fading flower, / Now is your glory and high honor / But the breath of wind in other men's ears, / Your rosy face shall to rot return.'
[96] 'cut down / Knights from Greece in astonishing numbers'
[97] 'What lord is that?'

mis and with taidis to be rent" (ll. 577–578).[98] Consistent with medieval protocols for the interment of the leprous, Cresseid's body is buried without delay, "withouttin tarying" (l. 593), and all that remains is epitaph. Troilus, in addressing the audience that Cresseid herself consistently invoked, dispassionately reduces her to her final condition: "Lo, fair ladyis, Cresseid of Troy [the] toun, / Sumtyme countit the flour of womanheid, / Under this stane, lait lipper, lyis deid" (ll. 607–609).[99] The narrator is quick to follow suit, asking the women in his audience to "Beir in your mynd this sor[e] conclusion" (l. 614), as if the entire poem were nothing but codicil.[100]

In its preemptive instantiation of disease, the *Testament of Cresseid* abrogates the scrupulous protocols of Guy de Chauliac and Bernard de Gordon. Henryson turns instead to the collapsed etiology of the anti-heresy diatribes. As the lazar house of Dunfermline is emptied of its patients, Robert Henryson's Cresseid succumbs to a sickness no longer governed by empirical protocols of observation, diagnosis, and palliative treatment. By multiplying the causes of disease and by collapsing the progression of its symptoms Henryson ensures that Cresseid's affliction is at once etiologically ambiguous and clinically unequivocal. Her disease is not so much a sickening as it is the inadvertent performance of a corrupt self – disloyal, troth-breaking, promiscuous, and blasphemous. That corruption, moreover, declares itself in bloodshot eyes, a hoarse voice, and, above all, the blemished, rotting skin of the 'leper.' If, as Judith Butler (2006: 132) argues, the body is the "site for pollution and endangerment," Cresseid's quarantine and death testify to the triumphant containment and excision of the polluted and polluting other. Infected as she is with what is believed to be a devastatingly contagious disease, she gives herself little opportunity to pose a danger to others. Troilus' "ressoun," or assertion, engraved on her tomb, circumscribes her even as it memorializes her; the flower of womanhood is now simply "lait lipper" (l. 609). The temporal collapse is so complete that, as Felicity Riddy (1997: 233) says: "In the end the narrative itself [...] exclude[s] her." Cresseid's fate is emblematic of a healthy, triumphant system, and that triumph is inscribed upon the surface of her defeated body. Riddy (1997: 244) argues that "the *Testament of Cresseid* shows [...] the struggle to constitute a stable masculine identity; its constant risk of dissolution; its relation to repression, law,

---

[98] 'Here I bestow my corpse and carrion / With worms and with toads to be torn.'
[99] 'Behold, fair ladies, Cresseid of the town of Troy, / Once counted the flower of womanhood, / Under this stone, late a leper, lies dead.'
[100] 'Bear in mind this painful conclusion.' Of course, in the tradition of Chaucer editions, the *Testament of Cresseid* is but a codicil. It begins its life in England as the sixth book of Chaucer's poem in the edition compiled by William Thynne in 1532.

and punishment; and above all its need to exclude the feminine." The woman's mutilated skin can be read as testifying to the success of this project – to the simultaneous containment and excision of the deviant woman.

Lepra forces itself through and onto skin; the body writes itself from the inside out, and that eruption compels a response. Benthien's (2002: 11–12) characterization of skin as a site for engagement implies opportunities for exchange and negotiation. The diseased skin of the leprous patient was a particularly fraught site for such encounters. Many medieval observers, like the priests of Leviticus, argued that the difficulty of glossing often ephemeral cutaneous signs and the high price of a mistaken reading mandated patience. Bernard of Gordon and Guy de Chauliac warned against the danger of hasty diagnosis and worked out elaborate protocols to preclude errors. They remind us that once the dreaded designation was made patients faced pain, debility, and separation. For them, as for Jacques de Vitry, leprous skin also bore witness to the sufferings of Christ. The affliction promised remission from purgatory, and offered the healthy redemption through good works. The pathonymic readings of leprous skin found in Isidore, in Raymond of Toulouse, and in Robert Henryson, on the other hand, abandon process and foreclose exchange. In the absence of the *lazar*, *lepra*, read only from the outside in, becomes a vehicle for anathema.

Works Cited

Primary Sources

Adriaen, Marcus (ed.). 1979. *Gregory the Great: S. Gregorii Magni moralia in Iob*. CCSL 143. Libri I–X. Turnhout: Brepols.

Barney, Stephen A., W. J. Lewis, J. A. Beach and Oliver Berghof (eds. and trans.). 2006. *Isidore of Seville: The Etymologies of Isidore of Seville*. Cambridge: Cambridge University Press.

Benson, Larry D. (ed.). 1987. *Geoffrey Chaucer: The Riverside Chaucer*. 3rd ed. Boston: Houghton Mifflin.

Bériou, Nicole and François-Olivier Touati (eds.). 1991. "Jacques de Vitry: Sermo I and II." In: Nicole Bériou and François-Olivier Touati. *Voluntate dei leprosus: Les lépreux entre conversion et exclusion aux XIIe et XIIIe siècles*. Spoleto: Centro italiano di studi sull'alto medioevo. 101–128.

Bickley, Francis B. (ed.). 1900. *The Little Red Book of Bristol*. 2 vols. Bristol and London: W. C. Hemmons.

Dembowski, Peter F. (ed.). 1969. *Ami et Amile, chanson de geste*. Paris: Librairie Honoré Champion.

Fox, Denton (ed.). 1968. *Robert Henryson: Testament of Cresseid*. London: Nelson.

Hudson, William (ed.). 1892. *Leet Jurisdiction in the City of Norwich During the XIIIth and XIVth Centuries: With a Short Notice of Its Later History and Decline from Rolls in the Possession of the Corporation*. Edited for the Selden Society. London: Bernard Quaritch.

<https://archive.org/stream/leetjurisdiction00norwrich/leetjurisdiction00norwrich_djvu.txt> [accessed 20 December 2016].

Lacy, Norris J. (ed. and trans.). 1998. "Béroul's *Tristran*." In: Norris J. Lacy (ed. and trans.) *Early French Tristran Poems*. Volume 1. Cambridge: D. S. Brewer. 12–216.

Le Saux, Françoise (ed.). 1993. *Amys and Amylion*. Exeter: University of Exeter Press.

Marriott, Charles (ed.) and James Bliss (trans.). 1844. *S. Gregory the Great, the First Pope of that Name: Morals on the Book of Job*. Oxford: John Henry Parker.

Merlet, René and Maurice Jusselin (eds.). 1909. *Cartulaire de la léproserie du Grand-Beaulieu et du prieuré de Notre-Dame de la Bourdinière*. Chartres: E. Garnier. <https://catalog.hathitrust.org/Record/009032949> [accessed 20 November 2016].

Migne, Jacques-Paul (ed.). 1850. *Isidore of Seville: Quaestiones in vetus testamentum: In leviticum*. "De lepris." PL 83. Cap. XI.

Migne, Jacques-Paul (ed.). 1854. *Hugh of St. Victor: Allegoriae in novum testamentum: Opera omnia*. PL 175. Liber IV.

Migne, Jacques-Paul (ed). 1855. *Eckbert of Schönau: Sermones contra catharos*. PL 195. Sermo I.

Migne, Jacques-Paul (ed.). 1857. *Gregory the Great: Homiliarum in evangelia*. PL 76. Liber II, Homil. XI.

Ogden, Margaret S. (ed.). 1971. *Guy de Chauliac: The Cyrurgie of Guy de Chauliac*. EETS OS 265. Oxford and London: Oxford University Press.

Riley, H. T. (ed.). 1868. *Calendar of Close Rolls, 1346–49: Memorials of London and London Life in the Thirteenth, Fourteenth and Fifteenth Centuries*. London: Longmans & Greens.

Rosenberg, Samuel N. and Samuel Danon (trans.). 1996. *Ami and Amile: A Medieval Tale of Friendship*. Ann Arbor: University of Michigan Press.

Ruelle, Pierre (ed.). 1965. *Les Congés d'Arras (Jean Bodel, Baude Fastoul, Adam de la Halle)*. Paris: Presses Universitaires de France.

Spalding, Mary C. (ed.). 2006. *The Middle English Charters of Christ*. Ann Arbor: University of Michigan Library. <http://name.umdl.umich.edu/AFW1075.0001.001> [accessed 6 December 2016].

Stubbs, William (ed.). 1875. *Raymond of Toulouse: Chronica. The Historical Works of Gervase of Canterbury*. London: Longmans.

Thomson, Thomas and Cosmo Innes (eds.). 1814–1875. *Acts of the Parliament of Scotland*. <http://www.rps.ac.uk/trans/1428/3/9> [accessed 20 December 2016].

Weber, Robert (ed.). 1969. *Biblia Sacra iuxta vulgatam versionem*. Stuttgart: Württembergische Bibelanstalt.

Secondary Sources

Baudot, Marcel and Marcel Candille. 1972. "Préface." In: Albert Bourgeois (ed.). *Lépreux et maladreries du Pas-de-Calais (X^e–XVIIIe siècles)*. Volume XIV². Arras: Mémoires de la commission départementale des monuments historiques du Pas-de-Calais. 9–13.

Benthien, Claudia. 2002. *Skin: On the Cultural Border Between Self and the World*. Trans. Thomas Dunlap. New York: Columbia University Press.

Bériou, Nicole and François-Olivier Touati. 1991. *Voluntate dei leprosus: Les lépreux entre conversion et exclusion aux XIIe et XIIIe siècles*. Spoleto: Centro italiano di studi sull'Alto Medioevo.

Bourgeois, Albert. 1972. *Lépreux et maladreries du Pas-de-Calais (X^e–XVIIIe siècles)*. Volume XIV². Arras: Mémoires de la commission départementale des monuments historiques du Pas-de-Calais.

Burton Russell, Jeffrey. 1965. *Dissent and Reform in the Early Middle Ages*. Berkeley: University of California Press.

Butler, Judith. 2006. *Gender Trouble: Feminism and the Subversion of Identity*. Thinking Gender. New York and London: Routledge.

Carlin, Martha. 1989. "Medieval English Hospitals." In: Lindsay Granshaw and Roy Porter (eds.). *The Hospital in History*. New York and London: Routledge. 21–40.

Demaitre, Luke. 2007. *Leprosy in Premodern Medicine: A Malady of the Whole Body*. Baltimore: Johns Hopkins University Press.

Forrest, Ian. 2005. *The Detection of Heresy in Late Medieval England*. Oxford: Clarendon.

Fox, Denton. 1968. "Introduction." In: Denton Fox (ed.). *Robert Henryson: Testament of Cresseid*. London: Nelson. 1–58.

Fudge, Thomas A. 2013. *The Trial of Jan Hus: Medieval Heresy and Criminal Procedure*. Oxford: Oxford University Press.

Hume, Kathryn. 1969. "Leprosy or Syphilis in Henryson's *Testament of Cresseid*?" *English Language Notes* 6.4: 242–245.

Jacquart, Danielle and Claude A. Thomasset. 1988. *Sexuality and Medicine in the Middle Ages*. Princeton: Princeton University Press.

Kay, Sarah. 2011. "Legible Skins: Animals and the Ethics of Medieval Reading." *postmedieval: A Journal of Medieval Cultural Studies* 2.1: 13–32.

Kruger, Steven F. 2006. *The Spectral Jew: Conversion and Embodiment in Medieval Europe*. Minneapolis: University of Minnesota Press.

Le Goff, Jacques. 1984. *The Birth of Purgatory*. Trans. Arthur Goldhammer. Chicago: University of Chicago Press.

Lieber, Elinor. 2000. "Old Testament 'Leprosy,' Contagion, and Sin." In: Lawrence Conrad and Dominik Wujastyk (eds.). *Contagion: Perspectives from Pre-Modern Societies*. Burlington: Ashgate. 99–136.

Magilton, John, Frances Lee and Anthea Bayleston (eds). 2008. *Lepers Outside the Gates: Excavations at the Cemetery of the Hospital of St. James and St. Mary Magdalene, Chichester*. Chichester Excavations 10. York: Council for British Archaeology.

Manselli, Raoul. 1953. "Il monaco Enrico e la sua eresia." *Bullettino dell'Istituto storico italiano per il Medio evo, Archivio Muratoriano* 65: 1–63.

Mathews, Jana. 2002. "Land, Lepers, and the Law in *The Testament of Cresseid*." In: Emily Steiner and Candace Barrington (eds.). *The Letter of the Law: Legal Practice and Literary Production in Medieval England*. Ithaca, NY: Cornell University Press. 40–66.

Moore, Robert I. 1975. *The Birth of Popular Heresy*. Toronto: University of Toronto Press.

Moore, Robert I. 1976. "Heresy as Disease." In: W. Lourdaux and D. Verhelst (eds.). *The Concept of Heresy in the Middle Ages (11th-13th C.): Proceedings of the International Conference, Louvain, May 13–16, 1973*. Leuven: Leuven University Press. 1–11.

Orlemanski, Julie. 2012. "How to Kiss a Leper." *postmedieval: A Journal of Medieval Cultural Studies* 3: 142–157.

Orme, Nicholas and Margaret Webster. 1995. *The English Hospital, 1070–1570*. New Haven and London: Yale University Press.

Parr, Johnstone. 1945. "Cresseid's Leprosy Again." *Modern Language Notes* 60: 487–491.

Pichon, Geneviève. 1984. "Essai sur la lèpre du haut Moyen Age." *Le Moyen Age* 90.3: 331–356.

Rawcliffe, Carole. 2006. *Leprosy in Medieval England*. Woodbridge: Boydell Press.

Rawcliffe, Carole. 2013. *Urban Bodies: Communal Health in Late Medieval English Towns and Cities*. Woodbridge: Boydell Press.

Richards, Peter. 1977. *The Medieval Leper and His Northern Heirs*. Cambridge: D. S. Brewer.

Riddy, Felicity. 1997. "'Abject Odious:' Feminine and Masculine in Henryson's *Testament of Cresseid*." In: Helen Cooper and Sally Mapstone (eds.). *The Long Fifteenth Century: Essays for Douglas Gray*. Oxford: Oxford University Press. 229–272.

Satchell, Max. 1998. "The Emergence of Leper Houses in Medieval England, 1100–1250." Unpubl. PhD dissertation, Oxford University.

Shilts, Randy. 1987. *And the Band Played on: Politics, People, and the AIDS Epidemic*. New York: St. Martins Press.

Stearns, Justin K. 2011. *Infectious Ideas: Contagion in Islamic and Christian Premodern Thought in the Western Mediterranean*. Baltimore: Johns Hopkins University Press.

Stearns, Marshall W. 1944. "Robert Henryson and the Leper Cresseid." *Modern Language Notes* 59.4: 265–269.

Stemmle, Jennifer. 2015. "From Cure to Care: Indignation, Assistance and Leprosy in the High Middle Ages." In: Anne M. Scott (ed.). *Experiences of Charity: 1250–1650*. Burlington: Ashgate. 43–61.

Tomasch, Sylvia. 2002. "Post-Colonial Chaucer and the Virtual Jew." In: Sheila Delaney (ed.). *Chaucer and the Jews: Sources, Contexts, Meanings*. New York and London: Routledge. 69–85.

Touati, François-Olivier. 1998. *Maladie et société au Moyen Âge, la lèpre, les lépreux et les léproseries dans la province ecclésiastique de Sens jusqu'au milieu du XIVe siècle*. Brussels: De Boeck.

Touati, François-Olivier. 2000. "Contagion and Leprosy: Myths, Ideas and Evolution in Medieval Minds and Societies." In: Lawrence I. Conrad and Dominik Wujastyk (eds.). *Contagion: Perspectives from Pre-Modern Societies*. Burlington: Ashgate. 179–202.

Wynne-Davies, Marion. 1993. "Spottis Blak: Disease and the Female Body in *The Testament of Cresseid*." *Poetica: An International Journal of Linguistic Literary Studies* 38: 32–52.

Zovic, Neda Chernack. 1996. *Les espaces de la transgression dans le* Tristran *de Béroul*. New York: Peter Lang.

Michael Leahy
The "Scabbe of Synne:"
Reading Leprous Skin in Late Medieval Culture

Abstract: This chapter examines how leprosy was represented across different genres of writing in late medieval England. It focuses on how medical knowledge, particularly complexional theory, offered a means of reading diseased skin that proved amenable not only to medical descriptions of leprosy but to literary and religious depictions too. It challenges critical perspectives that make absolute distinctions between medical and nonmedical approaches to the disease in the Middle Ages. It argues that attempts to find a register to convey what medical authors saw as the unique and destructive qualities of leprosy led them to use complex imagery and rhetoric to describe it, not dissimilar to nonmedical representations of the disease. This chapter analyses some examples of these various engagements with leprosy including a Middle English translation of the surgical writings of Guy de Chauliac; Robert Henryson's *Testament of Cresseid*; Middle English sermons by Hugo Legat; and the *Book of Margery Kempe*. In doing so, it points to the diverse meanings which constellated around diseased skin in the late medieval period.

One of the effects of the increased circulation of medical knowledge in the later Middle Ages was the absorption of a technical vocabulary in religious and literary texts which enabled authors to connect internal moral states with the external body.[1] Whilst the idea of deciphering a person's thoughts and emotions through observing the body had been an important feature of classical medicine, it was consolidated within the more integrated system of scholastic medicine in twelfth-century Western Europe.[2] This knowledge, which seeped into the English vernacular during the age of Chaucer, foregrounded *complexio*, a theory outlining how the balance of the primary qualities and humours in the body affected

---

[1] On the dissemination of medical knowledge in late medieval England see Voigts (1984, 1995); Taavitsainen and Pahta (2004); Getz (1988); Green (2000).
[2] Physiognomy, the field of knowledge concerned with interpreting character through facial features, extended back to classical medicine; see Swain (2007). See Cox's contribution in this volume for a discussion of Chaucer's use of portraiture to reveal inner characteristics in the General Prologue to the *Canterbury Tales*. See also Friedman (1981); Braswell-Means (1991).

health, behaviour, and character.[3] Whilst, in medical theory, *complexio* had a wide range of applicability, describing the multiple and mutable causes and effects of humoural balance, it was appropriated by literary and religious authors in more specific ways. In particular, it offered a technical matrix which enabled one to represent both a person's permanent character – melancholic, phlegmatic, etc. – and their more volatile shifts of temperament by reference to their bodily appearance, especially their skin (Groebner 2004: 365–366).

The capacity of complexional theory to account for "physical, physiological, and even psychological changes" (Groebner 2004: 366) accounts for why it found applicability in the wider late medieval culture beyond the sphere of medical learning. It accounts for much of the crossover between medical, moral, and literary responses to leprosy described in this chapter and, in particular, the importance which authors placed on reading and decoding diseased skin. In the following pages, I explore how leprosy was considered by late medieval writers to be a superlative disease characterised by its multiple and extravagant bodily effects and associated with egregious behaviour. Both medical and nonmedical authors responded to it by combining expressions of awe at its effects with a desire to understand it through constructing taxonomies, many of which were indebted to complexional theory. But I argue that the numerous and pronounced symptoms associated with the disease overstretched the medical terminology used to describe it and encouraged authors to resort to dense metaphors and rhetoric to try to encapsulate it. The application of complexional theory to account for leprosy, far from offering a neat correspondence between the condition and its causes, led to a proliferation of meanings around the condition. Thus I argue that leprosy, as imagined by late medieval authors, was a disease characterised by multiple and unstable meanings.

This chapter contributes to the concern with reading skin in this wider volume by proffering some examples drawn from the myriad references to leprosy in literary, moral, and mystical writings. Following Sealy Gilles' analysis of the religious basis of understanding diseased skin in the foregoing chapter, this chapter emphasises the importance of medical perspectives of leprosy. Beginning with the fourteenth-century French surgeon Guy de Chauliac and his extensive discussion of leprosy in his *Chirurgia magna*, I show how, even in its most practical utterances, the condition had moral resonances. I go on to discuss how references to the disease and its sufferers in Robert Henryson's *Testament of*

---

[3] The idea of balance between and amongst the primary qualities – hot, cold, wet, dry – and the four constituent humours of the body – blood, phlegm, choler and black bile – formed the cornerstone of medieval scholastic theory (or complexional theory) derived from classical medicine; see Kaye (2014); O'Boyle (1998); García-Ballester (2002); Jacquart (1998); Groebner (2004).

Cresseid; a collection of sermons; and the *Book of Margery Kempe* drew upon or paralleled its representation in medical writings.

This analysis is subtended by a perspective of the importance of language and imagery in exploring cultural attitudes to disease. Thus, whilst practical accounts of disease in medical writings might differ from the more explicitly moral orientation of religious or literary texts, the shared lexicon between these genres of writing reveal stronger correspondences than has often been allowed by critics. Given this intertwining of medical and cultural views of leprosy, I contend that it is problematic when analysing its representations in late medieval writings to tease apart 'leprosy,' the cultural legacy, from 'Hansen's disease,' the biomedical term for the condition. By reading medical texts alongside literary and religious ones, I hope to show that our understanding of medieval definitions of leprosy is intractable from the language with which they were articulated and the cultural associations they accrued.

Categorising Disgust: Medical Views of Leprosy

Although leprosy was understood in terms of its potential effect on all bodily organs, its ability to rupture and degrade skin was often foregrounded. This was due not only to its most obvious manifestations being on the skin's surface but also because of the cultural importance of skin in affirming bodily integrity. Medieval medical authors emphasised the role of skin in maintaining balance between the body and the external environment. The canonical works of two surgeon-authors – Lanfranc of Milan (d. 1315) and Guy de Chauliac (c. 1300–1368) – both translated into Middle English, describe skin as composed of little threads of veins, arteries, and nerves. Lanfranc states that skin is the "governoure of alle þe body" (*Science of Cirurgie*, 29)[4] and mentions its role in providing the body or human subject with knowledge of the qualities, temperature, and texture of objects in the world. Skin is thus configured as simultaneously the boundary separating the body from the world and that which mediates between both.[5] It is the presence of the nerves – referred to by Lanfranc and others as the *synwes* ('sin-

---

4 'governor of all the body.' Quotations are from Fleischhacker (1984); page numbers from this edition follow quotations in the main text. All modern translations from Middle English are the author's.
5 My reading of the cultural resonance of skin in medieval writings is indebted to the philosophical explorations in Connor's (2004) *The Book of Skin*, although, as the editors point out in the introduction to this volume, Connor pays little attention to the significance of skin in medieval culture.

ews') – in the skin that enables the body to be "sensible" of external things.[6] Whilst this idea of the skin comprising of nerves diverges from the Aristotelian view, prevalent in much late medieval medical theory, which suggests that the nerves extend from the brain only as far as the flesh beneath the skin, at other points Lanfranc seems to follow this distinction between skin and sinews: "ȝif þe skyn were as sensible as a ȝenewe, a man myȝte noȝt dwellen in colde eyre, ne in hote eyre" (29).[7] The ambiguity seems to arise from the two functions he ascribes to skin: It both allows one to feel external objects and qualities; but it is also a shell which protects the internal body from excessive sensation, which might harm it. As much as the skin was seen as a boundary protecting and hiding the internal organs, it was the role of the medical practitioner to know the operations of the internal body. A comprehensive understanding of *complexio* was crucial to the practitioner's effective treatment of illness. A patient's complexion could be discerned by a combination of factors including displays of temperament, uroscopy, and astrology; of primary importance in this endeavour though was the appearance of the patient's skin. The skin was understood as a screen on which was projected a confluence of disease symptoms, humoural qualities, and personality traits. It was thought to render legible the state of the patient's invisible, internal body and soul, although as I show below the information it yielded could often be ambiguous.

In the case of leprosy, concerns and anxieties relating to a loss of bodily integrity were foregrounded in medical taxonomies outlining its symptoms.[8] Guy de Chauliac calls leprosy the "raþest" (*The Cyrurgie*, 377),[9] or most principal, of diseases and notes that it compromises the shape or form of the body. When discussing its symptoms he prioritises its dermatological effects detailing how it manifests itself as "foule coloure, morphe, scabbe, and stinkynge filþes" (379)[10] and he goes on to mention foul lips, writhing nostrils, stinking breath, and hoarseness. The variety of symptoms that accumulate around the condition present problems of definition particularly as only a few are required to be present in order to effect a diagnosis. Furthermore, the focus on ulcerated or festering skin with adjectives underlining disgust – "foule," "stinkynge," "horrible" – signals profound unease towards a condition characterised by the disintegration of the body particularly where the skin breaks to reveal its fleshly underside. Such

---

6 See Walter (2013: 122).
7 'if the skin was as sensible as a sinew, a man might not dwell in cold air, or in hot air'
8 For views of leprosy by medieval medical scholars see Grigsby (2004: 51–58); Boeckl (2011).
9 Quotations for *The Cyrurgie of Guy de Chauliac* are from Ogden (1971). The page numbers from this edition follow quotations in the main text.
10 'discoloration, scurf, scabs, and stinking discharges'

apprehensions may have informed worries about contagion that circulated around leprosy.

These fears were accented by the legacy of the term leprosy and its conflation with skin ailments. Various Middle English terms were used to refer to the disease: *lepre* and *mesel* regularly appear in writings as does *lazer*, which denotes the leprous subject as well as a leper hospital.[11] The confused scriptural legacy surrounding the medieval use of the Latin word *lepra*, discussed in this volume by Sealy Gilles and Sharon E. Rhodes, helped to render it particularly amenable to a variety of metaphorical and moral uses.[12] This moral potency of leprosy can also be seen in the term's obstinacy in late medieval culture despite the apparent demise of the medical condition in the fourteenth and fifteenth centuries in Europe.[13] However, leprosy remained a mainstay of medical writings and continued to exert ethical and metaphorical power through its persistent invocation in late medieval English culture. This implies the ideological and symbolic resilience of a condition that eluded any single definition or interpretation.

Medical historian Luke Demaitre (2009: vii) argues that the focus by scholastic medical authors on the ternary system of "signs, causes, and cures" and their application of such a model to leprosy set physicians apart from those literary and religious writers who framed it in terms of "metaphor and moralisations." However, although descriptions of leprosy in medical texts tend to follow a rigid taxonomic framework, its superlative features are conveyed through recourse to rhetorical excess. Guy de Chauliac's overview of the disease is expressed in such terms:

> It is an evel compleccioun, colde and drye, even and dyuerse, in partie and in all [...] it is rottynge of þe schappe [...] it is called lepra, þe leper, a lepore nasi (i. of þe coppe and of þe

---

11 These terms are largely interchangeable: Whilst medical authors tend to use *leper* (*elefancie* to refer to the most severe cases and, sometimes, *mesel* to refer to non-leprous skin conditions), authors of religious texts, romances, and chronicles use all three. *Lazer* is an abbreviation of a composite Lazarus-figure comprising the leprous beggar in Christ's parable "Dives and Lazarus" in Luke 16.13–91 and the Lazarus whom Christ raised from the dead in John 11.1–44; see Richards (1977: 8).

12 For more discussion of the development of medieval ideas of leprosy see Weissenrieder (2003: 133–138); Rawcliffe (2006: 72–74); Richards (1977: 9).

13 Historians believe that it receded from much of the continent over the fourteenth and fifteenth centuries and cite the evidence of diminishing numbers of *leprosaria*, or leper hospitals, during this period. Boeckl (2011: 5) cites circumstantial evidence provided by Meyers and Binford (1976: 205–225) that the crusades contributed to a dramatic rise in leprosy cases in Europe, but this theory remains inconclusive. See also Demaitre (2009: vii–ix); Rawcliffe (2006: 107–110). For discussion of theories explaining the decrease of leprosy in the later Middle Ages see Gottfried (1983: 14–15).

nose) for þe tokens þerof apperyn þerynne raþest and moste verraily. Or it is saide of þe worde lupus, a wolfe, for it devoureþ alle þe membres as a cancrouse wolfe [...]. And þerfore it is cleped of Avicen a commune cancre to all þe body. (377–378)[14]

There is a curious mix of order and decomposition here as Guy's careful and extensive definition and categorisation of the disease rubs against his description of the bodily disintegration it engenders. The use of the adjective *evel* is instructive: It is a common appellation in Middle English medical writings and signified a diseased or deformed condition but carried connotations of malevolence or iniquity too.[15] He goes on to outline the disease as distinctive through the way it can attack both individual bodily organs and all of them and through its disfiguring effects on the form, or "schappe" of the body. The sense of proliferation and escalation of leprosy is paralleled by the variety of names for the disease. His etymology for *lepra* has two bases: First, the proximity of the Latin word for hare, *lepus*, with *lepra* prompts a connection between the hare's nose, *lepore nasi*, and the disfigured nose of the sufferer where, he claims, leprosy can appear soonest. Second, he makes a metaphorical association between the wolf, *lupus*, and the effects of leprosy: "for it devoureþ alle þe membres as a cancrouse wolfe."[16] The evenness of the wolf metaphor – the comparison of the disease's ferocity and disintegrating effects with the wolf's quality of devouring its prey – collapses into a description of the wolf *itself* as "cancrouse." This metaphorical conflation emerges from the demands placed on language to convey a sense of leprosy's destructive qualities. Likewise when Chauliac, quoting the Arabic medical author Avicenna (980–1037), refers to leprosy as a "commune cancre," he develops the cancerous-wolf metaphor by classifying leprosy itself as a cancer. A cancer was normally defined in medieval medicine as a spreading ulcer or swelling; but, in Chauliac's usage in this passage, it seems to operate as another sign of leprosy. Leprosy, then, seems resistant to the attempts to define and describe it because of its exclusivity but also in the way that its protean features encourage conflation with other conditions. Its rhetorical representation in

---

14 'It is a diseased complexion, cold and dry, consistent and diverse, in single body parts and in all [...] it is a rotting of the body form [...] it is called alternatively *lepra*, leprosy or *lepore nasi* (i.e. referring to the tip of the nose and the nose) for the signs of the condition appear in that part most quickly and most visibly. Or it is related to the word *lupus*, a wolf, for it devours all the members like a cancerous wolf [...]. And therefore Avicenna calls it a cancer common to all the body'

15 For the religious connotations of descriptors of disease in medical texts see Ziegler (1998: 48–49).

16 'for it devours all members as a cancerous wolf'

Chauliac's text shows how it both mitigates the bodily integrity of the sufferer and subsumes other diseases.

This passage reveals how, even in a text that is oriented towards descriptive and taxonomic modes, leprosy could be prone to highly figurative renderings. Demaitre (2009: 80–81) does acknowledge that popular associations between leprosy and evil may have been bolstered by those same associations advanced by authors like Guy de Chauliac. Yet, he argues, these were instances where medical language is infiltrated by other discursive strands, where "notions of impurity and judgement tainted some discussions of causes and consequences" (Demaitre 2009: 91). However, there is no untainted medical language that exists outside of its articulations in such writings, and any attempt to extrapolate value-neutral language from these definitions and descriptions of leprosy is to risk re-aligning Chauliac's text according to the demands of an objective, scientific discourse, reflecting the expectations we bring to modern medical writings. The above analysis of the description of leprosy provides an example of how late medieval medical writings are wholly oriented towards configuring leprosy in ideological ways. It signals how, when religious authors turned to scholastic medicine and complexional theory for a register through which they could develop moral or metaphorical ideas of leprosy, they would have encountered one richly resonant and amenable to such an application.

Leprosy and Lovesickness

The connection between medical and moral perspectives of leprosy is a prominent feature of Robert Henryson's (c. 1460–1500) *Testament of Cresseid*, particularly in its description of the affliction of its protagonist with leprosy. Henryson begins his poem by invoking Chaucer's *Troilus and Criseyde* – for which the *Testament* provides a sequel of sorts – and asks "Quha wait gif all that Chauceir wrait was trew?" (*Testament of Cresseid*, l. 65).[17] The questioning of Chaucer's veracity appears to revolve around the issue of his representation of Criseyde's infidelity in abandoning Troilus for the Greek warrior Diomede, and the exemption from punishment she is subsequently afforded. Henryson attempts to offer a cor-

---

[17] 'Who knows if all that Chaucer wrote was true?' Quotations from the *Testament of Cresseid* are from Fox (1981: 111–131); they are referenced by line number in the main text.

rective version featuring Cresseid's abandonment by Diomede, followed by her subsequent, and unspecified, dishonourable behaviour amongst the Greeks.[18]

This connection between moral behaviour and disease is substantiated by Henryson's recourse to medical learning in describing the onset of Cresseid's leprosy. After she has blamed the gods for Diomede's abandonment and for her subsequent destitution, they convene to discuss her punishment. This results in Saturn and Cynthia, goddess of the moon, afflicting her with leprosy through a series of performative utterances.[19] The presence of both deities reflects the medical belief that the astrological confluence of the moon and Saturn could engender leprosy (Rawcliffe 2006: 101). The placing of the gods' punishment within a medical framework is maintained when Saturn pronounces that he will remove Cresseid's beauty and "change [her] mirth into melancholy" (l. 316); an excess of the humoural fluid, black bile, or melancholy, was thought by medical writers like Chauliac to be a principal cause of leprosy.[20] As the gods continue with their pronouncement, they outline the principal symptoms of the condition, as well as the social ostracism it was sometimes understood to engender:

> Thy cristall ene mingit with blude I mak,
> Thy voice sa cleir vnplesand hoir and hace,
> Thy lustie lyre ouirspred with spottis blak,
> And lumpis haw appeirand in thy face:
> Quhair thow cummis, ilk man sall fle the place.
> This sall thow go begging fra hous to hous
> With cop and clapper lyke ane lazarous. (ll. 337–343)[21]

---

[18] Pearsall (2000: 173) argues that Henryson's version is a response to Chaucer's leaving Criseyde's "moral position unresolved" whilst Edmondson (2008) claims that Henryson's text should be best understood as a judgement on and negation of Chaucer's text rather than one of lineage and inheritance.

[19] The term 'performative utterance' refers to Austin's speech-act theory and his identification of 'illocutionary acts' where language, particularly ceremonial language, is used to achieve or enact something, instead of merely representing a thing; see Austin (1975: 94–108). The use of performative language in the gods' judgement in the *Testament* gives a sense of the ineluctable and sudden onset of leprosy. As Gilles shows in the foregoing chapter, Henryson's depiction of the sudden physical transformations of leprosy is in contrast to its progressive character in medical and legal writings.

[20] Critics have commented on the close alignment between Henryson's description of leprosy in this poem and contemporary medical descriptions of the condition; see Stearns (1944); Rowland (1964).

[21] "'Your crystal eyes mingled with blood I make, / Your voice so clear unpleasant rough and hoarse / Your lovely complexion overspread with black spots, / And white lumps appearing in your face: / Where you come, each man shall flee the place. / Thus shall you go begging from house to house / With cup and clapper like any leper'"

The passage emphasises the dramatic disintegration of Cresseid's beauty: Her clear voice is to become hoarse and croaky; her "lustie lyre," or beautiful skin, will be covered with black spots. Whilst these transformations appear to her, and those who see her, as sudden, the reader, through being accorded access to the gods' dispensation of punishment upon her, understands the hidden machinations through which her offenses have been transformed into physical blemishes and deformities.

Even though Henryson evokes the medical understanding of the causes and symptoms of leprosy to describe the transformation of moral behaviour into physical disease, this passage is ambiguous as to the particular acts that are being punished. The poem's opening stanzas insist upon Cresseid's sexually licentious behaviour, and many of its critics accept that as the reason why she is struck with leprosy.[22] Yet the gods' vengeful convention suggests that it is her blasphemy that is being punished. The matter is confused even further when, later in the poem, the narrator claims that she suffers both for betraying Troilus' love (ll. 613–616) and as a result of the turning of the wheel of fortune (ll. 461–469). Throughout the poem, then, the moral significance of leprosy is constantly shifting and ambiguous, a quality that corresponds with its disintegrating capacity. Indeed, similar to the diagnostic issues thrown up by the multiple signs of leprosy in Chauliac's account, it points to the difficulty of deciphering a person's character or moral state through reading their skin.[23]

The indistinct coordinates which frame Chauliac's description of the disease underlining its permeability in relation to other conditions is reflected in the etiological integration between Henryson's *Testament* and its fourteenth-century antecedent, Chaucer's *Troilus and Criseyde*. The alignment of the uncertain significances of leprosy with the indeterminacy with which lovesickness is represented in *Troilus and Criseyde* shows that Henryson's poem does not differentiate itself from Chaucer's text as much as its opening lines, as well as its modern critics, affirm.[24] The two works share a concern with the way that the body manifests internal, subjective states and simultaneously triggers an obfuscating semantics of disease. In Chaucer's text, we are told of Troilus' falling in love with Criseyde in physical terms: his heart swells, he endures a loss of appetite and insomnia, and these effects soon become apparent on his external body:

---

[22] See Pearsall (2000: 175–176); Rowland (1964); Patterson (1973: 697–698); Brody (1974: 175).
[23] On the indeterminacy of deciphering skin, see Sweany's chapter in this volume.
[24] The depiction of Troilus' love as illness, whilst a feature in Giovanni Boccaccio's (1313–1375) *Il filostrato*, Chaucer's principal source for *Troilus and Criseyde*, is developed more completely in Chaucer's poem. For a study of the differences between both texts see Windeatt (1983).

> And fro this forth tho refte hym love his slep,
> And made his mete his foo, and ek his sorwe
> Gan multiplie, that, whoso tok kep,
> It shewed in his hewe both eve and morwe.
> (Chaucer, *Troilus and Criseyde*, I, ll. 484–487)[25]

As his sorrows proliferate, they become susceptible to bodily imperatives: his "hewe" reveals his lovelorn state to anyone who notices.[26] His condition undermines his knightly stature, as he engages in warfare to protect his besieged Troy from the encroaching Greek army, leading to his equivocation that "he hadde a fevere and ferde amys" (I, l. 491).[27]

The word "hewe" refers to appearance, including form and shape, as well as skin colour. It therefore suggests a significant alteration to Troilus' physical appearance (*MED heu* n.). It crops up again later in the poem when Troilus, who has retired to a private chamber feigning illness in order to set up a surreptitious first meeting with Criseyde, is about to declare his love to her:

> In changed vois, right for his verray drede,
> Which vois ek quook, and therto his manere
> Goodly abaist, and now his hewes rede,
> Now pale. (III, ll. 92–95)[28]

The irony of a feigned illness bearing the symptoms – quaking voice and an alternating skin complexion – of an actual one is key to the representation of lovesickness, or *amor heroes*, throughout the poem where it persistently shuttles between an ailment and a courtly pose.

This depiction of lovesickness in terms of bodily symptoms in *Troilus and Criseyde* is based upon its presence as a melancholic condition in medieval medical writings. Medical scholars such as Constantine the African (1017–1087) and Gerard of Berry (d. c. 1200) identified lovesickness as a malady that led to humoural excess producing effects such as sleeplessness, aversion to eating, faulty

---

[25] 'And from this time onwards love robbed him of his sleep, / And made his food his foe, and also his sorrows / Began to multiply, so that, whoever took heed, / It showed in his complexion both night and day.' Quotations from *Troilus and Criseyde*, referenced by book and line number in the main text, are from Benson (1987).
[26] See also Nyffenegger (this volume).
[27] 'he had a fever and fared badly'
[28] 'In altered voice, due to his absolute dread, / Which voice also shook, and also his manner / Graciously abashed, and now his complexion red, / Now pale'

judgement, and, in extreme cases, death.²⁹ Such views are articulated in Chaucer's *Troilus and Criseyde* but are counterpoised with a conception of lovesickness as a cynical pose assumed by the knight when pursuing his lady. This tension is exemplified in the above scene where Troilus' attempt to *act* sick transforms into the real thing on meeting Criseyde. In the courtly world of Chaucer's Troy, lovesickness, as distinct from fever, carries suggestions of weakness, moral instability, and culpability.³⁰

There are clear parallels between the descriptions of bodily manifestations of internal sorrow or states in *Troilus and Criseyde* and the symptoms of leprosy in Henryson's poem. Julie Orlemanski (2013), in charting the links between both poems, proposes that the *Testament* enacts its own form of justice by proffering leprosy as a truer sign of Cresseid's falseness and corruption. She argues that whilst its moral lesson may be subverted throughout the poem, the *Testament* ultimately enacts "its own move to a different regime of narrative poetics" (Orlemanski 2013: 169). Although I agree that the generic distinction between both poems relates to their different perspectives towards the character and actions of Criseyde/Cresseid, I suggest that the relationship between lovesickness and leprosy in both poems should be understood more in terms of continuity. Thus, just as Cresseid's internal moral state is manifested on her skin in the *Testament*, her remote, otherworldly beauty in *Troilus* is inseparable from her character – "So aungelik was hir natif beaute, / That lik a thing inmortal semed she / As doth an hevenyssh perfit creature" (I, ll. 102–104).³¹ The manifestation of Criseyde's character is again foregrounded when Troilus asks her to elope with him before she is forced to leave Troy and join her father at the Greek encampment, as part of an exchange between both armies. Her refusal is framed in terms of her moral integrity:

> And also thynketh on myn honeste,
> That floureth yet, how foule I sholde it shende,

---

29 The understanding of an extreme form of erotic love as pathological derived from the classical world; see Beecher and Ciavolella (1990). For the development of medical ideas of erotic melancholy in the West see Wack (1990: 31–50, 179–193); Beecher and Ciavolella (1990: 70–71).
30 More specifically, there is an implication that Troilus' nobility within Trojan society may be undermined if it became known that he has fallen in love with Criseyde, a widow whose father, Calchas, has deserted Troy to side with the Greek army.
31 'So angelic was her natural beauty / that she seemed like an immortal thing / as does a heavenly perfect creature'

> And with what filthe it spotted sholde be,
> If in this forme I sholde with yow wende. (IV, ll. 1576–1579)³²

Criseyde is represented in terms of an alluring flower throughout the poem; but at this point the leitmotif is invoked to refer to an alliance between her physical beauty and her honesty or moral integrity "'that floureth yet'." The layered imagery thus plays on the idea of smeared beauty, implicating Criseyde's virtue and her physical appearance with the spots of filth that she affirms would be the outcome of an elopement. This, then, provides the moral template from which Henryson draws upon in his focus on Cresseid's spots and disfigurement resulting from the punitive onset of her leprosy. Physical change and an unseemly complexion also characterises Criseyde's last private meeting with Troilus in Chaucer's poem:

> With broken vois, al hoors forshright, Criseyde
> To Troilus thise ilke wordes seyde:
> "O Jove, I deye, and mercy I beseche!
> Help, Troilus!" And therwithal hire face
> Upon his brest she leyde and loste speche [...]
> And thus she lith with hewes pale and grene,
> That whilom fressh and fairest was to sene. (IV, ll. 1147–1155)³³

The final couplet, contrasting Criseyde's former floral-like beauty with her pale and colourless complexion, underlines her sudden and radical transformation.

In the *Testament*, then, Cresseid's fate is to suffer a condition that (at least in part) correlates with the melancholic suffering she is understood to have instigated in the previous narrative. The fear that Criseyde expresses in Chaucer's text of being morally compromised is actualised in Henryson's version through the presence of spots on her diseased body, as well as her hoarseness and physical weakness. Lovesickness in Chaucer's text could carry over into leprosy in Henryson's poem because both are represented as having the potential to manifest hidden emotions and immoral behaviour on the skin. Both Chaucer and Henryson participate in a late medieval poetics where medical language, particularly that describing sicknesses prone to moral or metaphorical deployment, like leprosy and

---

32 "'And also consider my honesty, / That flowers yet, how miserably I should harm it, / And with what filth it should be spotted, / If in this manner I should go with you'"

33 'With broken voice, all hoarse from shrieking, Criseyde / To Troilus these same words she said: / "O Jove, I die, and mercy I beseech! / Help, Troilus!" And with that her face / Upon his breast she laid and lost her speech [...] / And thus she lay there with a pale and green complexion, / Who once was fresh and fairest to see'

lovesickness, is mobilised to trace the problematic relationship between behaviour or desire and the purportedly legible body.

Sin on Skin: Moral Leprosy

The evocation of leprosy as an index to a variety of physical and moral states is also evident in its more overtly didactic articulations. An early fifteenth-century anti-Lollard sermon, written in the vernacular by Hugo Legat (fl. c. 1399–1427), a monk and Benedictine prior at St. Albans, Hertfordshire, exemplifies the diversity of moral conditions that could be associated with the disease. In one of his sermons, Legat develops the trope of leprosy as a figure for a host of sins. He begins by referring to Christ's healing ministry and focuses on the account in Luke 17.12–14 of his healing of ten lepers. Legat goes on to link exegetically the lepers in this account to "al maner o volk þat liggen her e þis world e þe siknes & te sorw of dedli synne" (29).[34] The employment of leprosy as a means to imagine sin is enabled by the legibility of diseased skin: "ʒif þe be e þe scabbe, e þe lepur o dedli synne, þe art mor vowler & mor horrible e þe sith o God þanne euer was any mesel þat euer was maad her be-fore" (29).[35]

Legat's reference to "scabbe" is instructive: the term was used in Middle English to refer to any one of a variety of skin diseases and signified, more generally, blotchy or ulcerated skin. It was often mentioned as a prominent characteristic of leprosy – as it is in Guy de Chauliac's treatise – and the conflation between both in Legat's text is another example of the overlapping of leprosy with other ailments (MED scabbe n.). The fact that the "scabbe" is used interchangeably with leprosy in Legat's metaphor for sin shows how the employment of leprosy is based primarily on its visibility on the skin. The visual force of the metaphor depends, first, on its evocation of the disgust the reader or hearer is expected to experience on beholding leprous skin and, second, on this disgust being a shadow of the revulsion God feels on beholding the sinner's soul. Leprosy thus offers a productive means of materialising Christian views of the effects of sin on the soul.

The disgust that leprosy engenders is yoked to the idea of skin as offering a medical hermeneutics of the body. Legat develops the metaphor to visualise the

---

[34] 'all manner of folk that lie here in this world in the sickness and the sorrow of deadly sin.' Quotations are taken from Grisdale (1939). Page numbers from this edition follow quotations in the main text.
[35] 'if you are in the scab, in the leprosy, of deadly sin, you are more foul and more horrible in the sight of God than ever was any leper that ever was made here before'

skin as a screen on which sins are revealed as leprous sores. He composes a prayer, which he advises his hearer to recite: "'Lord God, take hede' þe schalt seye, 'to me sowle & be-hold how vowl it is be-spottid with þe leprus in-to þe scabbe of synne & deliuere it from al þe vilþe & vnclennes þat is trine'" (29).³⁶ The emphasis in medical writings of the marks and "spots" of leprosy as outward signs of effects taking place within the body is paralleled in Legat's text by the idea of the soul having a skin, or some kind of surface, where spots, or the "scabbe," are visible to the privileged sight of God indicating the penitent's internal condition of "vilþe & vnclennes." Just as the physician can read diseased skin and diagnose a condition such as leprosy, God can see the "scabbe of synne," know its internal condition and, through forgiveness, enable the sinner's deliverance.

Legat goes on to outline a framework where the principal effects of leprosy are associated with particular sins. In one, he links leprosy's ability to bring about physical deformities with the effects of gluttony on the body; both, he says, can efface beauty. He cites an exemplum from the *Policraticus* of John of Salisbury (1120–1180) that tells the story of Dionysius, King of Sicily, "as fair of face, as bewtewus o bodi & as lusti vor to loke vpon as any man" (30),³⁷ who falls sick as a result of leading a gluttonous lifestyle. In relating this, Legat moves from the metaphorical use of disease as an image of sin to the idea that it can itself be the *effect* of such conditions:

> But afterwarde, whan a ʒaf hym to lustis & lykyngis of his flesche, to delices o mete & drynk & to misrule [...], a-non rith a lost al þe flowres of his fair-hede, al þe helþe of his body & in-to gret siknes & strong disese & a-mong al oþer a lost þe sithte o boþe his eʒen [...] and ter-vro vor Cristes sake, be-war o þis vis & tis synne & specialiche e þis tyme o lente. (30)³⁸

The sicknesses that Dionysius suffers from are constituted here as the effects of his lifestyle yet they are intrinsically linked to the hearer's moral behaviour as

---

36 "'Lord God, take notice' you shall say, 'to my soul and behold how foully it is be-spotted with the leprosy within the scab of sin and deliver it from all filth and uncleanness that is therein'"
37 'as fair of face, as beauteous of body and as handsome for to look upon as any man'
38 'But afterward, when he gave himself over to the desires and appetites of his flesh, to the pleasures of food and drink and to bad governance [...], immediately he lost all the flowers of his beauty, all the health of his body and fell into great sickness and grave disease and, along with all of this, he lost the sight of both eyes [...] and therefore for Christ's sake, beware of this vice and this sin and especially in this time of Lent'

evidenced in the author's appeal to observe abstinence in Lent.³⁹ They also encompass social disease in the form of Dionysius' misrule of his kingdom. Legat goes on to mention the specific illnesses that can result from gluttony including gout and dropsy before describing it again in terms of spiritual leprosy: "Vor þer is no lepur e þe world þat semyþ so vowl & so orrible in owr sichte as doþ a glotun e þe siþte of God" (30).⁴⁰ Therefore, incorporated within the guiding metaphor of leprosy, we find a proliferation of other physical and spiritual illnesses linking gluttony and political ineptitude.⁴¹

Legat locates in leprosy similar generative qualities as Henryson does: Leprous skin is indexed to sin and moral failure; the disgust it engenders can be employed to promote edification. Whereas physical beauty is contrasted with the disfigurements of leprosy, it is implicated in its onset through its arousal of sexual desire – as evident in the figures of Cresseid and Dionysius. Whilst the link between sexual excess as both a cause and a symptom of leprosy is one that was made by late medieval moralists and medical writers, its importance has sometimes been exaggerated by scholars. Sexual behaviour and disease was just one of the many associations that cleaved to leprosy. The fluidity with which leprosy is presented by Legat, both in terms of its physical manifestations and the variety of its moral indices, provides a corrective to views that place an exclusive correspondence between leprosy and sexual behaviour in medieval culture. It reveals how it was understood to operate in much more subtle and multifarious ways.⁴²

Intimacy and Estrangement: Devotion and Leprosy

The fluctuating nature of leprosy, as evinced in the metaphorical treatments described above, resonates with a late medieval pietistic tradition of advancing leprosy as a means of devotional access. Yet, whereas in Legat's and Henryson's configurations leprosy provides a means of mapping the soul onto the diseased body, the affective tradition locates edifying opportunities and divine access

---

39 The exemplum can be connected, in this sense, with the popular late medieval genre of health regimens. These texts advised their readers to maintain good health through issuing advice on diet, sleep and exercise as well as morally sound behaviour; see Wallis (2010: 548).
40 'For there is no leper in the world that appears so foul and so horrible in our sight as does a glutton in the sight of God'
41 See also Gilles' discussion of the links between leprosy and heresy in this volume.
42 Pearsall (2000: 176), for instance, argues that the tracing of moral qualities in physical degradation in Henryson's *Testament* is underlined by the association between leprosy and sexual disease in the later Middle Ages.

through the associations triggered by encounters with the leprous body – although both moral and affective modes can often be mutually present in a narrative. The bases of such material can be traced to accounts of Christ's healing of lepers in the New Testament and from his commandment to treat the sick and poor as if they were Christ.[43] Whilst Legat's leprosy imagery insists upon the soteriological need to overcome or maintain distance from the sin-infested soul, affective narratives articulate a desire for a contemplative or tactile relationship with lepers in order to either imitate Christ or treat lepers as if they themselves were surrogates of Christ.

Yet again the distinctions that are often set up between medical and religious medieval engagements with leprosy are belied by Guy de Chauliac's inclusion of conventional religious responses, particularly from the affective tradition, in advising his surgeon-reader on how to treat those suspected of having leprosy. Chauliac's awareness of the – at least partial – sequestration that attends the most severe cases of leprosy due to its presumed contagious nature leads him to stress the care that is to be undertaken in diagnosing such cases.[44] He includes advice about how one should reassure patients:

> Firste, in clepynge Goddes help, he [the surgeon] schall conforte ham and saie þat this passioun or sekenesse is saluacioun of þe soule [...] and if þe world haue hem in hate, neuerþelatter God haue hem not in hate. ȝe, but he loued Lazer, þe leprouse man, more þan oþer men. (381)[45]

Such consolation provides relief to his later dramatic account of the steps to be taken in the event of a diagnosis of the severest forms of the condition:

> If he haue forsothe many even-voycede tokens and fewe vnvoycede tokens, he is comunely cleped fordone or destroyed. And soche ben bitterly to be warned þat þai halde gode gouernance [...] and þat þai drawe hem to þe north parties of here mansions (i. dwellyng places) and þat þai come noght mykel among þe peple, for þay ben entred into leper. If þai haue forsoþe many even-voycede tokens and many vnuoycede tokens, þai schal be wiþdrawen fro þe peple with good counseillynge words and ledde into þe mesondeux. (383)[46]

---

[43] These passages are respectively Luke 17.12–14 and Matthew 25.36–40.

[44] In her historical analysis of medical attitudes towards leprosy in medieval England and France, Brenner (2015) argues that religious beliefs influenced the compassion shown to leprosy sufferers by medical practitioners.

[45] 'First, in calling God's help, he shall comfort them and say that this passion or sickness is salvation for the soul [...] and if the world holds them in hate, nevertheless, God holds them not in hate. Yea, for he loved Lazarus, the leprous man, more than other men'

[46] 'If he has indeed many ambiguous signs and a few unambiguous signs, he is commonly regarded as ruined or destroyed. And such people should be sharply warned to govern themselves

The advice assumes a ritualistic tone in the specific instructions about how the patient in the less severe instance should be warned in stringent terms about how to conduct and orient himself following the diagnosis. The degree of agency afforded to the patient in this instance is removed in the case of the patient with the most severe condition, a change signalled by a shift to the passive register as Chauliac describes how the patient should be removed from the community and placed in a hospital.

Chauliac's instructions on the treatment of leprosy, hovering between asserting the need for some degree of sequestration and stressing the importance of consoling patients who have been diagnosed with the condition, blends two types of discourse which were often enunciated in late medieval responses to leprosy. On the one hand, he repeats the instructions found in various medical texts, *leprosaria* customaries, and official writs stressing the importance of keeping those with leprosy at a distance from the wider community; on the other, he repeats the comparisons of lepers with Christ and the need to provide comfort to them typical of devotional and hagiographical literature.

The idea that leprosy can be a means of expressing Christological devotion is found in the fifteenth-century spiritual autobiography of Norfolk devotee Margery Kempe. Kempe charts her spiritual growth in part through a narrative of her engagement with the lepers she encounters on the streets of her hometown of Lynn. As a young business-woman, occupied with the material world, we are told that Kempe viewed lepers as "lothful" ('loathsome') and "abhomynabyl" ('abominable,' *Book of Margery Kempe*, 176).[47] Yet following her commitment to a devotional life, they remind her instead of Christ's sufferings:[48]

> Sche myth not duryn to beheldyn a laȝer er anoþer seke man, specialy ȝyf he had any wowndys aperyng on hym. So sche cryid & so sche wept as ȝyf sche had sen owr Lord Ihesu Crist wyth hys wowndys bledyng [...] for thorw þe behldyng of þe seke man hir mende was al takyn into owr Lord Ihesu Crist. (176)[49]

---

well [...] and to remove themselves to the north sides of their mansions (i.e. homes) and that they come not much among the people, for they have been entered into leprosy. If they have indeed many ambiguous signs as well as many unambiguous signs, they shall be withdrawn from the people with good advice and led into the hospital'

47 Quotations are taken from Meech and Allen (1940) and referenced by page number in the main text.

48 For a discussion of the late medieval tradition of imagining Christ in the Passion as being like a leper and the importance of leprosy in affective piety in general see Sealy Gilles' foregoing chapter.

49 'She might not endure to behold a leper or another sick man, especially if he had any wounds appearing on him, without crying and weeping as if she had seen our Lord Jesus Christ

The passage makes clear the lepers' role as a channel through which Kempe's mind can become suffused with contemplation of Christ.⁵⁰ The employment of the verb *beheldyn* is important in this sense because it links sight with touch and suggests that the tableau of the lepers exert a psychosomatic effect on her prompting her to become "al takyn into" Jesus. If such a description resounds with fears of physical contact and transmission that sometimes accumulated around the subject of leprosy, it enacts a reversal through proffering Kempe as an exemplary figure who can transform leprous touching from a threatening gesture into a devotional event. Indeed, there is a degree of correspondence between this saintly touching and the touch of the medical practitioner in Guy de Chauliac's text; both seem to have the ability to come into physical contact with lepers without risking contagion themselves.

Whilst Kempe's text is in marked contrast in tone and content to Chauliac's practical treatise, they both draw from similar conventional discourses attached to leprosy, particularly in terms of the dynamic between consoling and distancing lepers. This is articulated in Kempe's confessor's injunction that she should not act on her desire to kiss the – presumably male – lepers in Lynn's streets. He does however allow her to go to "a place wher seke women dwellyd" (177)⁵¹ where she encounters lepers in the relatively controlled space of a hospital. She meets and embraces two female lepers and, similar to Chauliac's instructions, exhorts them to accept their illness with patience and meekness. One of the women, a virgin, responds:⁵² "þan þe oon woman had so many temptacyons þat sche wist not how sche myth best be gouernyd [...] and sche was labowryd wyth many fowle & horibyl thowtys, many mo þan sche cowde tellyn" (177).⁵³ Jonathan Hsy (2010: 192) proposes that "as much as this passage intimates lechery, its evasive prose style also evokes the discursive specter of sodomy, 'that utterly confused category' that gathers together any number of non-heteronorma-

---

with his wounds bleeding [...] for through beholding the sick man, her mind was consumed with our Lord Jesus Christ.'

50 In this Kempe emulates the self-abasing charity of saints towards those with leprosy and the sick in general described in hagiographies. It forms part of what McMurray Gibson (1989: 47) describes as the *Book*'s "calculated hagiographic" enterprise. For more discussion of the hagiographical purposes in the *Book* see Staley (1994); Lewis (2004). For discussion of works of charity and mercy in the *Book* see Cullum (2004: 178–179).

51 'a place where sick women dwelled'

52 On the possible significances of the leper's virginity in the context of the wider text see Voaden (1997: 183).

53 'then one of the women had so many temptations that she knew not how she might best be governed [...] and she was laboured with many foul and horrible thoughts, many more than she could tell'

tive acts and desires."[54] The passage insists upon the multiple and unbounded quality of the woman's thoughts: her "*many* fowle & horibyl thowtys" are amplified to "*many mo* þan sche cowde tellyn" (emphases added). The *Book* implies that the proliferation of such thoughts and/or their appalling nature means that they are rendered uncommunicable. The association of "fowle and horibyl thowtys" with leprosy recalls the overlap between the physical disease and the condition of the soul in Hugo Legat's sermons and Henryson's *Testament*. At the same time, they echo Chauliac's repeated use of "horrible" and "fowle" in describing the bodily effects of leprosy. The hazy and imprecise nature of the disease in late medieval culture allows it to stand as a figure, not for one set of sexual sins, but for a wide variety of illicit behaviours and emotions. In the leper's confession to Kempe, the admission of her foul and ungoverned emotions would signal, for the reader, a multiplicity of vague and monstrous desires saddled to the formless and egregious features attending articulations of leprosy.

The leper's speech to Kempe in the *Book* overlays a confessional discourse, emerging out of the condition of leprosy and its moral resonances, upon a one based on edification through a Christological empathy with leprous bodies. It reflects the various ways that the condition is deployed in Middle English writings and how authors invoke and deploy a productive disgust towards the skin of lepers to provoke desires for haptic engagement with it as well as for its effacement. The overwhelming nature of leprosy, attacking all members of the body and undermining dermatological integrity, demands recourse to metaphor and analogy and, with its biblical inheritance, asserts itself as a spiritual as well as a physical malaise. But, as we have seen, its many symptoms allow it to be configured in various ways: it is linked to blasphemy, gluttony, erotic excess, political misrule, and the exemplary sufferings of Christ. Its protean qualities allow it to assume moral and devotional potency across medical writings, romance literature, didactic prose, and devotional works; its projection of the internal body and soul upon the sufferer's skin enables articulations of disgust, fear, devotion, and desire.

---

54 The reference to sodomy as an "utterly confused category" comes from Michel Foucault (1978: 101). On the notion of deviant sexuality in the description of Margery's care for lepers see Vandeventer Pearman (2010: 142).

Works Cited

Primary Sources

Benson, Larry D. (ed.). 1987. *Geoffrey Chaucer: The Riverside Chaucer.* 3rd ed. Boston: Houghton Mifflin.

Fleischhacker, Robert V. (ed.). 1894. *Lanfrank: Science of Cirurgie.* EETS OS 102. London: Kegan Paul, Trench, Trübner & Company.

Fox, Denton (ed.). 1981. *Robert Henryson: The Poems of Robert Henryson.* Oxford: Clarendon Press.

Grisdale, D. M. (ed.). 1939. *Hugo Legat: Three Middle English Sermons from the Worcester Chapter Manuscript F.10.* Kendal: University of Leeds.

Meech, Sanford B. and Hope E. Allen (eds.). 1940. *Margery Kempe: The Book of Margery Kempe.* EETS OS 212. London: Oxford University Press.

Ogden, Margaret S. (ed.). 1971. *Guy de Chauliac: The Cyrurgie of Guy de Chauliac.* EETS OS 265. Oxford and London: Oxford University Press.

Secondary Sources

Austin, John L. 1975. *How to Do Things with Words.* 2nd ed. Oxford: Clarendon Press.

Beecher, Donald A. and Massimo Ciavolella. 1990. "Love Melancholy as a Medical Idea in the Ancient World." In: Donald A. Beecher and Massimo Ciavolella (eds.). *A Treatise on Lovesickness.* Syracuse: Syracuse University Press. 39–58.

Binford, C. H. and W. M. Meyers. 1976. "Leprosy." In: Chapman H. Binford and Daniel H. Connor (eds.). *Pathology of Tropical and Extraordinary Diseases.* Volume 1. Washington: Armed Forces Institute of Pathology. 205–225.

Boeckl, Christine M. 2011. *Images of Leprosy: Disease, Religion, and Politics in European Art.* Kirksville: Truman State University Press.

Braswell-Means, Laurel. 1991. "A New Look at an Old Patient: Chaucer's Summoner and Medieval Physiognomia." *The Chaucer Review* 25: 266–275.

Brenner, Elma. 2015. "Between Palliative Care and Curing the Soul: Medical and Religious Responses to Leprosy in France and England, c.1100–c.1500." In: Naoë Kukita Yoshikawa (ed.). *Medicine, Religion and Gender in Medieval Culture.* Cambridge: D. S. Brewer. 221–235.

Brody, Saul N. 1974. *The Disease of the Soul: Leprosy in Medieval Literature.* Ithaca, NY: Cornell University Press.

Connor, Steven. 2004. *The Book of Skin.* London: Reaktion Books.

Cullum, P. H. 2004."'Yf lak of charyte be not owerhynderawnce:' Margery Kempe, Lynn and the Practice of the Spiritual and Bodily Works of Mercy." In: John H. Arnold and Katherine J. Lewis (eds.). *A Companion to the Book of Margery Kempe.* Cambridge: D. S. Brewer. 177–194.

Demaitre, Luke. 2009. *Leprosy in Premodern Medicine: A Malady of the Whole Body.* Baltimore and London: Johns Hopkins University Press.

Edmondson, George. 2008. "Henryson's Doubt: Neighbors and Negation in *The Testament of Cresseid*." *Exemplaria* 20.2: 165–196.
Foucault, Michel. 1978. *The History of Sexuality: An Introduction*. Trans. Robert Hurley. Volume 1. New York: Vintage.
Friedman, John B. 1981. "Another Look at Chaucer and the Physiognomists." *Studies in Philology* 78.2: 138–152.
García-Ballester, Luis. 2002. "On the Origin of the 'Six Non-Natural Things' in Galen." In: Jon Arrizabalaga, Montserrat Cabré, Lluis Cifuentes and Fernando Salmon (eds.). *Galen and Galenism: Theory and Medical Practice from Antiquity to the European Renaissance*. Aldershot: Ashgate. 105–115.
Getz, Faye M. 1988. *Medicine in the English Middle Ages*. Princeton: Princeton University Press.
Gottfried, Robert S. 1983. *The Black Death: Natural and Human Disaster in Medieval Europe*. New York: Free Press.
Green, Monica H. 2000. *Women's Healthcare in the Medieval West: Texts and Contexts*. Aldershot: Ashgate.
Grigsby, Bryon L. 2004. *Pestilence in Medieval and Early Modern English Literature*. New York and London: Routledge.
Groebner, Valentin. 2004. "*Complexio*/Complexion: Categorizing Individual Natures, 1250–1600." In: Lorraine Daston and Fernando Vidal (eds.). *The Moral Authority of Nature*. Chicago and London: University of Chicago Press. 361–383.
Hsy, Jonathan. 2010. "'Be more strange and bold:' Kissing Lepers and Female Same-Sex Desire in *The Book of Margery Kempe*." *Early Modern Women: An Interdisciplinary Journal* 5: 189–195.
Jacquart, Danielle. 1998. "Medical Scholasticism." In: Mirko D. Grmek (ed.) and Antony Shugaar (trans). *Western Medical Thought from Antiquity to the Middle Ages*. Cambridge (MA) and London: Harvard University Press. 197–240.
Kaye, Joel. 2014. *A History of Balance, 1250–1375: The Emergence of a New Model of Equilibrium and Its Impact on Thought*. Cambridge and New York: Cambridge University Press.
Lewis, Katherine J. 2004. "Margery Kempe and Saint Making in Later Medieval England." In: John H. Arnold and Katherine Jane Lewis (eds.). *A Companion to the Book of Margery Kempe*. Cambridge: D. S. Brewer. 195–216.
McMurray Gibson, Gail. 1989. *The Theatre of Devotion: East Anglian Drama and Society in the Late Middle Ages*. Chicago and London: University of Chicago Press.
MED = *Middle English Dictionary*. 1952–2001. Ed. Hans Kurath, Sherman M. Kuhn, John Reidy and Robert E. Lewis. Ann Arbor: University of Michigan Press. <http://quod.lib.umich.edu/m/med/>.
O'Boyle, Cornelius. 1998. *The Art of Medicine: Medical Teaching at the University of Paris, 1250–1400*. Leiden: Brill.
Orlemanski, Julie. 2013. "Desire and Defacement in *The Testament of Cresseid*." In: Katie L. Walter (ed.). *Reading Skin in Medieval Literature and Culture*. The New Middle Ages. New York: Palgrave Macmillan. 161–181.
Patterson, Lee W. 1973. "Christian and Pagan in *The Testament of Cresseid*." *Philological Quarterly* 52: 696–714.

Pearsall, Derek. 2000. "'Quha wait gif all that Chauceir wrait was trew?' Henryson's *Testament of Cresseid*." In: Susan Powell and Jeremy J. Smith (eds.). *New Perspectives on Middle English Texts: A Festschrift for R. A. Waldron*. Cambridge: D. S. Brewer. 169–182.

Rawcliffe, Carole. 2006. *Leprosy in Medieval England*. Woodbridge: Boydell Press.

Richards, Peter. 1977. *The Medieval Leper and His Northern Heirs*. Cambridge: D. S. Brewer.

Rowland, Beryl. 1964. "The 'seiknes incurabill' in Henryson's *Testament of Cresseid*." *English Language Notes* 1: 175–177.

Staley, Lynn. 1994. *Margery Kempe's Dissenting Fictions*. Philadelphia: Pennsylvania State University Press.

Stearns, Marshall W. 1944. "Henryson and the Leper Cresseid." *Modern Language Notes* 59.4: 265–269.

Swain, Simon. 2007. "Polemon's Physiognomy." In: Simon Swain (ed). *Seeing the Face, Seeing the Soul: Polemon's Physiognomy from Classical Antiquity to Medieval Islam*. Oxford and New York: Oxford University Press. 125–201.

Taavitsainen, Irma and Päivi Pahta. 2004. "Vernacularisation and Medical Writing in its Sociohistorical Context." In: Irma Taavitsainen and Päivi Pahta (eds.). *Medical and Scientific Writing in Late Medieval English*. Cambridge and New York: Cambridge University Press. 1–18.

Vandeventer Pearman, Tory. 2010. *Women and Disability in Medieval Literature*. The New Middle Ages. New York: Palgrave Macmillan.

Voaden, Rossalynn. 1997. "Beholding Men's Members: The Sexualizing of Transgression in *The Book of Margery Kempe*." In: Peter Biller and Alastair J. Minnis (eds.). *Medieval Theology and the Natural Body*. York: York Medieval Press. 175–190.

Voigts, Linda Ehrsam. 1984. "Scientific and Medical Books." In: Jeremy Griffiths and Derek Pearsall (eds.). *Book Production and Publishing in Britain, 1375–1475*. Cambridge: Cambridge University Press. 345–402.

Voigts, Linda Ehrsam. 1995. "Multitudes of Middle English Medical Manuscripts, or the Englishing of Science and Medicine." In: Margaret R. Schleissner (ed.). *Manuscript Sources of Medieval Medicine*. New York: Garland. 183–196.

Wack, Mary. 1990. *Lovesickness in the Middle Ages: The Viaticum and Its Commentaries*. Philadelphia: University of Pennsylvania Press.

Wallis, Faith (ed.). 2010. *Medieval Medicine: A Reader*. Toronto: University of Toronto Press.

Walter, Katie L. 2013. "The Form of the Formless: Medieval Taxonomies of Skin, Flesh, and the Human." In: Katie L. Walter (ed.). *Reading Skin in Medieval Literature and Culture*. The New Middle Ages. New York: Palgrave Macmillan. 119–140.

Weissenrieder, Annette. 2003. *Images of Illness in the Gospel of Luke: Insights from Ancient Medical Texts*. Tübingen: J. C. B. Mohr.

Windeatt, Barry. 1983. "Chaucer and the *Filostrato*." In: Piero Boitani (ed.). *Chaucer and the Italian Trecento*. Cambridge and New York: Cambridge University Press. 89–114.

Ziegler, Joseph. 1998. *Medicine and Religion, c.1300: The Case of Arnau de Vilanova*. Oxford and New York: Oxford University Press.

Sharon E. Rhodes
Legible Leprosy:

Skin Disease in the *Testament of Cresseid*, Chaucer's Summoner, and *Amis and Amiloun*

Abstract: Three Middle English poetic texts – the Testament of Cresseid, the characterisation of the Summoner in Chaucer's *Canterbury Tales*, and *Amis and Amiloun* – illustrate the social function performed by skin disease, 'leprosy,' in medieval literature. Skin marred by disease marks questionable characters such as Cresseid, Amiloun, and the Summoner as the perpetrators of grave sins. Consequently, we can read their skin, and presumably contemporary readers did, as evidence of and special emphasis on the sinful state of the physically marred characters' souls. Such texts demand that we read the skin of leprous characters as an indication of their misdeeds. Moreover, they suggest that anyone that follows the bad example of such characters risks having their own face inscribed with sin.

In 1850, Nathaniel Hawthorne marked his anti-heroine with a scarlet letter "A," theoretically preventing her from being seen as anything beyond the sin for which the letter stood. Yet however prominent the colour or size of this patch, Hester Prynne's letter cannot have been as conspicuous, or as difficult to conceal, as the "bylis blak" ('black boils,' l. 399)[1] with which Robert Henryson disfigured the face of Cresseid as punishment for her disloyalty to Troilus and blasphemy against love in the *Testament of Cresseid*, his late fifteenth-century addendum to Chaucer's *Troilus and Criseyde*.[2] While Hawthorne's *Scarlet Letter* details the psychological pain of being branded a harlot, Cresseid's marks both brand her and cause her physical pain. Moreover, Hester's letter does not cut her off from society to the same extent as Cresseid's newly sullied visage: After Cynthia spread "spottis blak" ('black spots,' l. 260) over Cresseid's formerly beautiful face, Cresseid moves from her father's house to the leper colony at the edge of

---

1 Quotations for the *Testament of Cresseid* are taken from Fox (1968) and referenced by line number in the main text. Unless otherwise noted, all translations of Middle English and Latin are my own.
2 Just such an objection was raised by Hester Prynne's fellow townswomen who complained that the magistrates "should have put the brand of a hot iron on [her] forehead" because "she may cover [the letter] with a brooch." (Hawthorne 1851: 64).

https://doi.org/10.1515/9783110578133-005

the Greek encampment wherein the inhabitants' identities are limited to the label of 'leper.' Much as Cresseid becomes identified by her disease, the first attribute Chaucer mentions in his introduction of the lecherous Summoner in the General Prologue to his *Canterbury Tales*, other than his disreputable occupation, is his "fyr reed [...] saucefleem" ('fire-red [...] pimpled,' ll. 624–625)[3] face that none of the medical treatments available at the time were able to alleviate. Finally, in the Middle English verse romance of *Amis and Amiloun*, the two eponymous characters cannot be distinguished until leprosy renders Amiloun unrecognisable. While Hester accepts her letter "A," it is a penalty imparted by mortal men that she could easily remove or obscure. Cresseid, the Summoner, and Amiloun are punished directly by God and cannot escape the marks of God's dissatisfaction. Although a modern medical professional would diagnose each of these skin conditions differently, according to medieval medicine, each of these characters can be said to suffer from a form of leprosy. Such "leprosy," of course, is not the result of infection with a specific bacterium, but a broad category of skin diseases rooted in sin. While these skin conditions may not reveal the exact nature of the sinners' misdeeds, the unmistakability of the presence of skin disease legibly marks them as people to avoid – indeed, Chaucer tells us that "children were aferd" ('children were afraid,' l. 628) of the Summoner's face – and makes each character a cautionary tale: a negative and viscerally grotesque exemplum. In sum, each story suggests that however private or subtle a sin may be, the sins of Cresseid, Amiloun, and the Summoner erupt through their skins and allow anyone to read the states of their souls.

'Lepros' in the Middle Ages – Biblical Roots and Aetiology

According to medieval thought all disease was rooted in sin, but Carol Rawcliffe (1999: 14) argues that lepers particularly "fell victim to the belief that their fate must, of necessity, have come as chastisement from God." Indeed, there is ample biblical precedent for such an attitude toward leprosy. Among the many examples of the Old Testament are Miriam, King Ozias and Gehazi, a servant of the prophet Elisha, all of whom are stricken with leprosy for their sins against God and his servants.[4] Additionally, Naaman, a Syrian, is miraculously *cured* of leprosy by one of God's prophets, perhaps as a reward for turning to

---

[3] Quotations for Chaucer's *Canterbury Tales* are taken from Benson (1987) and referenced by line number in the main text.
[4] See also Gilles' discussion of leprosy in the Bible in this volume.

the true God for help. This is far from an exhaustive list of the occurrences of leprosy in the Bible, but the cases of these characters are particularly interesting when compared to Middle English literature as they make "the connection between leprosy and a moral violation [...] explicit" (Brody 1974: 114). More importantly, in the two cases in which leprosy is cured – Miriam and Naaman – the cure comes from God rather than the treatment of a physician or an application of medicine.

When looking at the history of leprosy it is important to note that the symptoms described in these Old Testament stories – such as Miriam's "candens lepri quasi nix" (Numbers 12.10)[5] – are incongruous with both the medieval and the modern understanding of the disease denoted as "leprosy."[6] Luke Demaitre (1985: 327) writes that we must distinguish "[m]edieval leprosy [...] from the skin ailment called *lepra* in biblical and classical antiquity." It was not until the late nineteenth-century that Armauer Hansen – the eponym of 'Hansen's disease,' a modern term for leprosy – attributed his namesake to chronic infection with *mycobacterium leprae*; a type of precision in pathology that was, of course, impossible before the advent of the microscope.[7] Stanley Rubin (1974: 150) explains that "[t]he word *lepra* meaning scaly was, as far as the Greeks were concerned, used not in relation to leprosy [...] but to refer to the many scaling skin diseases such as eczema and psoriasis."[8] What became known in the Middle Ages as *leprosy* was, to the Greeks, *elephantiasis*. However, this technical distinction between different disease aetiologies does not at all alter the symbolic value of the word *leprosy* in literature, whether medieval or biblical. Semiotically, *leprosy* is not a singular biomedical disease in the *Testament of Cresseid*, Chaucer's *Canterbury Tales*, and *Amis and Amiloun* or, for that matter, in the cases of Miriam, Ozia, Gehazi, and Namaan. Rather, it is a superficial manifestation of inner guilt. Whatever the exact cause of a skin condition – that is, whether modern medicine would diagnose these particular conditions as infection with a specific bacterium or virus, allergic reaction, or fungal overgrowth – the moral implications and deterrent value in medieval and biblical accounts of leprosy do not rest on a scientific understanding of its pathogenesis. Leprosy in medieval and biblical literature is significant because it is only skin deep. While Hansen's disease is a systemic infection with serious implications for the lungs and nervous sys-

---

5 'bright white [...] leprosy like snow'
6 See also 4 Kings 5.27.
7 See also Gilles' discussion of Hansen's disease (this volume).
8 For a thorough and concise explanation of the history of the term *leprosy* and the distinction made between the disease now classified as leprosy or Hansen's disease and previous uses of the term see Eichman (1999).

tem as well as the skin, the leprosy of the Bible and Cresseid, Amis, and the Summoner is an outward affliction. Its public presentation, consequent legibility, and lack of cure – except, as we will see, through divine means – allow leprosy to act as a trope that can be read by those within and outside a given text.

In Numbers, God smites Miriam with leprosy after Miriam and Aaron criticise Moses for marrying an Ethiopian woman: "locuta[] est Maria et Aaron contra Mosen propter uxorem eius aethiopissam" (Numbers 12.1).[9] In response to this dissension, God speaks directly to the three siblings: "ore enim ad os loquor ei et palam non per enigmata et figuras Dominum videt quare igitur non timuistis detrahere servo meo Mosi" (Numbers 12.8).[10] To fully impart the lesson that one should avoid speaking ill of God's servants, a form of blasphemy, "Maria apparuit candens lepra quasi nix" (Numbers 12.10)[11] after God left the tabernacle. Aaron begs Moses to not let Miriam become "quasi mortua" ('like a dead person,' Numbers 12.12) and, in turn, Moses prays that she be healed. After seven days' exile from the camp, the leprosy disappears and Miriam rejoins the society of the living. It is significant that Miriam is not cured by a human medical treatment but by Moses' prayer and her own penance – here seven days' exile. Moreover, it is interesting that Aaron explicitly makes a connection between leprosy and death; while a leper may not die – and, in the case of infection with *mycobacterium leprae*, is unlikely to die – for many years after the initial infection, the segregation required by societal views of the disease makes lepers practically dead. In other words, in being cut off from other living people, lepers die metaphorically. Later, in 2 Chronicles, King Ozias is struck with leprosy when he attempts to burn incense in the temple, even after the priests warned him "non est tui officii Ozia ut adoleas incensum Domino sed sacerdotum hoc est filiorum Aaron qui consecrati sunt ad huiuscemodi ministerium" (2 Chronicles 26.18).[12] When Ozias disregarded the priests, "statimque orta est lepra in fronte eius" (2 Chronicles. 26.19–21)[13] and the priests cast him out. Unlike Miriam, "fuit [...] Ozias rex leprosus usque ad diem mortis suae et habitavit in domo separata plenus lepra" (2 Chronicles 26.19–21).[14] Given his lifelong affliction with

---

[9] 'Miriam and Aaron spoke against Moses because of his Ethiopian wife'
[10] 'For mouth to mouth I speak to him and plainly, not through puzzles or figures does he see the lord. Why therefore do you not fear to disparage my servant Moses?'
[11] 'Miriam appeared bright white with leprosy, like snow'
[12] 'it is not your office to burn incense to the Lord but [that of] the priests, that is, the sons of Aaron who were set apart for this sort of service'
[13] 'immediately a leprosy sprang up in his forehead'
[14] 'King Ozias was a leper until the day of his death and he dwelled in a separate house full of leprosy'

leprosy and his subsequent ostracisation, we can conclude that Ozias' presumption of serving as a priest in the temple is a far graver sin than Miriam's objections to Moses' wife. Lastly, in 4 Kings, the Syrian general, Naaman is not punished with leprosy for a specific sin against the Hebrew God, but is rewarded with health when he seeks a cure from Elisha, God's prophet (4 Kings 5.8).[15] However, Gehazi, Elisha's servant, becomes "leprous like snow" (*leprosus quasi nix*) and brings the curse of leprosy on his descendants when he greedily took for himself the gifts Naaman had entrusted him to deliver to Elisha (4 Kings 5.27).

Saul Nathaniel Brody (1974: 108) points out that the connection between morality and leprosy predates the Bible. However, Brody adds that "even if it is not the source of the leper's reputation for sinfulness, no other document can claim to have helped so much in propagating that reputation." Certainly this is true of the popular conception of leprosy in the later Middle Ages by which time, fed by these and other biblical stories, leprosy had become a touchstone for the sin/disease link. In fact, Rawcliffe (1999: 14) writes that "medieval theologians took a harsh view of leprosy [...] sometimes portraying the disease as a symbol of deep-seated moral decay or as a real, physical manifestation of wickedness on the part of the sufferer or his parents;" a view supported by the case of Gehazi and his descendants. As an extension of this vein of thought "the heretic was frequently described in medical terms as a spiritual leper, infected by a poisonous contagion from which his soul was unlikely to recover, expelled from the community of the faithful and driven by uncontrollable sexual urges to contaminate others" (Rawcliffe 1999: 14). For instance, in *Handlyng Synne* – an exhaustive poem of more than 12,000 lines on the multitudinous forms of wrongdoing – Robert Mannyng utilises just such a schema: "He þat ys yn dedly synne, / Gostly, he ys a mesel wyþ ynne" (ll. 11475–11476).[16] Conversely, this view of the physical leper allowed "poets and storytellers [to] further elaborate[] the theme of leprosy as a punishment for crime or depravity" (Rawcliffe 1999: 15). In fiction, as opposed to moralising poems like Mannyng's, those "yn dedly synne" can be marked externally as the spiritual lepers they are. Consequently, Henryson's Cresseid, Chaucer's Summoner and Amiloun all *appear* as lepers. These charac-

---

15 After Naaman is "restituta est caro eius sicut caro pueri parvuli et mundatus est" ('flesh was restored, like the flesh of a little child and was clean') he said, "vere scio quod non sit Deus in universa terra nisi tantum in Israhel obsecro itaque ut accipias benedictionem a servo tuo" ('truly I know that there is no God in all the world except in Israel,' 4 Kings 5.14–15).
16 'He that is in deadly sin is, spiritually, a leper within.' Quotations are taken from Furnivall (1973). For more on heretics and leprosy see Gilles (this volume).

ters' skins publicly broadcast their private wickedness, allowing – even forcing – the audience to visualise the effects of sin which would otherwise be unreadable.

Cresseid's Skin, Cresseid's Sin

The character of Cresseid, ignominious already at the end of Chaucer's *Troilus and Criseyde*, becomes a physical and moral disgrace in Henryson's *Testament of Cresseid*. When Henryson takes up Chaucer's story in his addendum, he claims to have "fand the fatall destenie / of fair Cresseid, that endit wretchitlie" (ll. 61–63).[17] According to Henryson, not only does Diomede abandon Cresseid once he "had all his appetyte / And mair fulfillit of this fair ladie" (ll. 71–72),[18] she is also punished for her infidelity to Troilus and her blasphemous complaint to Cupid and Venus to whom she prays after Diomede abandons her. Her prayer, far from deferential, is vehemently accusatory:

> O fals Cupide, is nane to wyte bot thow
> And thy mother, of lufe the blind Goddes.
> Ye causit me alwayis understand and trow
> The seid of lufe was sawin in my face. (ll. 134–136)[19]

This prayer alone certainly surpasses the blasphemous qualities of Miriam's complaint concerning Moses' wife; after all, Miriam only spoke against God's servant, not God. After much deliberation among the planetary gods, Cynthia declares that she will destroy Cresseid's beauty with the following hallmarks of leprosy:

> Thy cristal ene muglit with blude I mak;
> Thy voice sa clair unplesand, hoir, and hace;
> Thy lustie lyre ouirspred with spottis blak. (ll. 337–338)[20]

The effect on Cresseid's eyes and voice are in keeping with a medieval medical diagnosis of leprosy: Guy de Chauliac, a fourteenth-century French physician,

---

[17] 'discovered the fatal destiny of fair Cresseid, who ended wretchedly.' Quotations for the *Testament of Cresseid* are taken from Fox (1968) and referenced by line number in the main text.
[18] 'had all of his appetite and more filled by this fair lady'
[19] 'Oh, false Cupid, is anyone to blame except you and your mother, the blind goddess of love. You made me always to understand and trust that the seed of love was sewn into my face.'
[20] 'Your crystal eye I will muddy with blood; your clear and pleasant voice, rough and hoarse; your fair complexion covered with black spots.'

notes in his *Cyrurgie* that in addition to the telltale sores, a leper might have "an hose voyce as þoghe he spak with his nose þirles" and "graynes [...] vnder þe eyȝe liddes" (380).²¹ These symptoms also helped to obliterate Cresseid's former identity as a noblewoman. Yet Cresseid's skin, although not her only attribute to be destroyed by the gods' sentence, is given two lines where her eyes and voice are each given only one. Cynthia concludes her curse by announcing that Cresseid is henceforth destined to live "lyke ane lazarous" (that is, 'like a leper,' l. 343) meaning that she will not only be found unattractive but that "[q]uhair [Cresseid] cummis, ilk man sall fle the place" (ll. 341–343).²² In other words, she is to live in exile from the society of the living just as Miriam did for seven days and as King Ozias did for the remainder of his life.

Some scholars, such as Edwin D. Craun (1985), argue that Cresseid's leprosy is brought on only through her blasphemous prayer. Julie Orlemanski (2013: 166) reasons that "Cresseid's blasphemy forms an isolated episode – upon which all the subsequent events nonetheless depend." However, her primary blasphemy against Cupid and Venus is not her complaint itself, but her betrayal of love, that is, her betrayal of Troilus. The disrespectful prayer with which Henryson's story begins is only the last straw in a series of blasphemies against Cresseid's "awin god[s]" (l. 275). As Cupid states in Cresseid's trial

> quha will blaspheme the name
> Of his awin god, outher in word or deid,
> To all goddis he dois baith lak and schame,
> And sculd have bitter panis to his meid (ll. 274–277).²³

Cresseid has blasphemed her own gods in word *and* deed. In addition to her irreverent prayer, Cresseid abused the gods' gift – her beauty – through her actions.²⁴ The first act of blasphemy is her infidelity to Troilus. The second is her promiscuity in "the court, comoun ('the court shared by all,' l. 77) after Diomede has abandoned her. As in the biblical precedents, there is no human cure for leprosy in the *Testament of Cresseid*. Moreover, in this medieval story, the characters

---

21 'a hoarse voice as though he spoke through his nostrils' and 'grains under the eyelids.' Quotes for *The Cyrurgie of Guy de Chauliac* are from Ogden (1971). The page number of this edition is given in the main text.
22 'where Cresseid comes, each man shall flee that place'
23 'whoever would blaspheme the name of his own god, either in word or deed, does both dishonour and shame to all gods, and should have bitter pains as his reward'
24 In line 137, Cresseid laments that the gods "causit me alwayis understand and trow / The seid of lufe was sawin in my face" ('made me understand and believe the the seed of love had been sewn in my face,' ll. 136–137).

know that there is no cure and so when Cresseid's father "luikit on hir uglye lipper face"[25] he despaired "[f]or he knew weill that their was na succour / To hir seiknes, and that dowblit his pane" (ll. 376–377).[26] This is no mere illness but divine punishment. Brody (1974: 129) argues that "leprosy was commonly assumed to be a venereal disease" and Andrew Higl (2010: 176) suggests that Cresseid contracted leprosy through her promiscuous behaviour after Diomede abandoned her. In their respective chapters of this volume, Michael Leahy and Sealy Gilles deconstruct medieval leprosy and its role in the *Testament of Cresseid* through their own lenses. Leahy argues that Cresseid's leprosy is directly linked to Troilus' lovesickness as portrayed in Chaucer's *Troilus and Criseyde*. Leahy notes too that Criseyde's beauty before she leaves the city is closely linked to her honesty. Gilles views Cresseid's leprosy as primarily punitive but grounded in Cresseid's promiscuous body. Ultimately, Gilles draws our attention to the potential social effect of a disease as readily apparent as leprosy. Indeed, the gods' trial of Cresseid suggests that in the *Testament of Cresseid*, leprosy does not result from sexual acts but as punishment for Cresseid's blasphemous behaviour – her betrayal of Troilus – and her blasphemous prayer. Although in this particular instance, leprosy is not meted out by the Judeo-Christian God, it is, nevertheless, akin to the divine punishment of Miriam's blasphemy.

Knowing that others – including all potential lovers – will flee her presence and not wanting to be seen in her new guise, Cresseid elects exile in the "hospital at the tounis end" (l. 382).[27] And again, Henryson describes her skin in morbidly depressing detail:

> Sum knew hir weill, and sum had na knawledge
> Of hir becaus scho was sa deformait,
> With bylis blak ouirspred in her visage
> And hir fair colour faidit and alterait. (ll. 393–296)[28]

Henryson's focus on Cresseid's skin shows it to be so thoroughly marred by its wounds that she is not entirely recognizable even to those who once knew her. Leprosy, the curse of the gods, has so altered Cresseid that she is no longer

---

[25] 'looked at her ugly leper face'
[26] 'because he knew well that there was no cure for her sickness, and that doubled his pain.' See also Chaucer's Summoner, discussed below, who, it is implied, tried many different salves and ointments without success.
[27] 'hospital at the edge of town'
[28] 'Some knew her well, and some had no knowledge of her because she was so deformed, with black boils spread over her face and her fair colour faded and altered.'

herself. The person that was Cresseid, once afflicted by leprosy, reads, first and foremost, as a leper. Cresseid herself does eventually lament the loss of her "cleir voice and courtlie carrolling" (l. 443),[29] but she, and the audience, know that the ability to sing would not save her from the disgrace of having a face covered in "bylis blak" ('black boils,' l. 395). Accordingly, the lament of her lost voice and "port" is a mere prelude to another description of her most conspicuous symptoms:

> Of lustines I was hald maist conding.
> Now is deformit the figour of my face;
> To luik on it, na leid now lyking hes. (ll. 447–449)[30]

Cresseid's disfigurement renders her a stranger to many, but by far the most cutting example of a formerly familiar person that fails to identify the leprous Cresseid is Troilus himself who – "[w]ith greit tryumphe and laude victorious" (l. 488)[31] – rides past a group of begging lepers – Cresseid among them. Being the virtuous hero of the story, Troilus has pity on the lepers and approaches them. When he sees the leprous Cresseid, Troilus is reminded – to his mind inexplicably – of "fair Cresseid, sumtyme his awin darling" (l. 504).[32] This nostalgia for his former lover, untarnished by her inconstancy, moves him to throw "[a]ne purs of gold" (l. 521)[33] into her skirt. Although Cresseid, her eyes "minglit with blude" ('clouded with blood,' l. 337), does not recognise Troilus, another leper does. When the latter informs her of the identity of her generous benefactor, she is devastated anew and "cryit scho thus: / O fals Cresseid and trew knicht Troylus" (ll. 545–546).[34] She then elaborates on the moral and behavioural differences between Troilus and herself: Troilus was faithful, but she was "fickill and frivolous" ('fickle and frivolous,' l. 552). Further, while Troilus "keipt gude continence" ('kept well his continence,' l. 554), Cresseid "[w]as inclynit to lustis lecherous" (l. 559).[35]

The lessons implicit in the *Testament* are patent, but Henryson still has his anti-heroine state it unequivocally in a direct address to women: "in your mind

---

[29] 'clear voice and courtly caroling'
[30] 'Of loveliness I was held most worthy. Now the figure of my face is deformed; no one has pleasure in looking on it now.'
[31] 'with great triumph and victorious praise'
[32] 'fair Cresseid, once his own darling'
[33] 'a purse of gold'
[34] 'she cried thus: Oh, false Cresseid and true knight Troilus'
[35] 'was inclined toward lusty lecherousness'

ane mirrour mak of me / As I am now" (ll. 457–458).³⁶ Her full warning is an extensive and generic reminder that "[n]ocht is your fairnes bot ane faiding flour" (l. 549),³⁷ and that, consequently, one's beauty is not to be counted upon. The addition of "[a]s I am now" reminds us that Cresseid's flower faded much faster than necessary because "[s]a elevait [she] was in wantones" (l. 549).³⁸ Thus, the subtext of her warning to women is that the flower of female beauty can be lost to immorality as well as to time. After her lament and warning, Cresseid "maid hir testament" ('made her testament,' l. 576) and died immediately thereafter. Henryson closes his story with the rumour that Troilus had a marble tomb made for his wayward lover on which he had inscribed in beautiful golden letters another warning to women:

> "Lo, fair ladyis, Cresseid, of Troyis toun,
> Sumtyme countit the flour of womanheid,
> Under this stan, lait lipper, lyis deid" (ll. 603–609)³⁹

The most beautiful remnant of Cresseid's life is a golden inscription on a tomb summarising her unfortunate – and hideous – end. Normally, the lepers' readable sin would die with them, but Troilus, in memorialising Cresseid, immortalises her legible leprosy by literally writing out her condition at death so that Cresseid's leprosy – and what it signifies – outlives her.

Saving Face in *Amis and Amiloun*

In *Amis and Amiloun*, a romance about two sworn friends who, initially, look identical, Amiloun contracts leprosy after disregarding a warning from God, much as Ozias ignored the warning of God's priests.⁴⁰ Amis is accused, correctly, of having fornicated with Belisaunt, the daughter of the duke he was serving; he agrees to a duel to prove his innocence, but, as he is not innocent, he is bound to die in the duel.⁴¹ So, his uncanny lookalike Amiloun swears on his own innocence, wins the duel and thereby persuades the bystanders and the duke that

---

36 'make a mirror of me as I am now in your mind'
37 'your beauty is nothing but a fading flower'
38 'she was so embroiled in wantonness'
39 'Lo, fair lady, Cresseid, from the city of Troy, once thought the flower of woman hood, lies dead under this stone, as a leper.'
40 Although the story of *Amis and Amiloun* is recorded in many different medieval languages, I am confining my own discussion exclusively to the Middle English version.
41 See also Brody (1974: 160).

Amis and Belisaunt had not had intimate relations. However, this stratagem does not seem to please God, whose angel, before the duel, warns Amiloun that:

> Yif thou this bataile underfong,
> Thou schalt have an eventour strong
> Within this yeres thre;
> And or this thre yere be al gon,
> Fouler mesel nas never non
> In the world, than thou schal be! (ll. 1255–1260)[42]

While Amiloun succeeds in duping his fellow mortals by taking on his friend's challenge, he does not deceive God. Moreover, Amiloun does not merely take on his friend's fight but his lecherous sin and its punishment, leprosy. Views on the logic of Amiloun's leprosy vary widely. On the one hand, Kathryn Hume (1973: 27–29) argues that Amiloun contracts leprosy simply because of his "unjust fight." That is, had Amis fought his own duel he would have lost because he was guilty of the crime of which he was accused. However, although the crime had occurred Amiloun can swear that *he* did not commit it. Although presumably such deceit would not please God, leprosy, as punishment for this alone, seems cruel and unusual. Ojars Kratins (1966: 351), on the other hand, views Amiloun's leprosy not as punishment at all, but as "a visitation of divine grace with the goal of verifying, before the tale is over, that both friends in the severest of trials 'trew weren in al þing' as the poem states at the outset." Kratin's assessment is not far off the mark, but ignores the possibility that a test of friendship might – and here, I argue, does – include the acceptance of punishment that, by rights, belongs to someone else. I propose that, had Amis fought his own fight, he would have died as the concept of trial-by-ordeal dictates. However, in taking on his friend's fight, Amiloun takes on the sin of lust that led to the ordeal and is punished accordingly.

Just as Cresseid exiles herself and the Summoner frightens children, Amiloun's condition results in ostracisation: As the angel warned Amiloun, his wife and family shun him when he develops leprosy. Amiloun's loss of his high place in society, however, is gradual. This slow removal from society reflects the slow development of Amiloun's symptoms in contrast to Cresseid's disease which appears as soon as her trial by the gods has concluded. First, Amiloun's

---

[42] Quotations for *Amis and Amiloun* are taken from Leach (1960) and referenced by line number in the main text. 'If you undertake this battle, you will have a powerful adventure within three years; and before these three years have passed, there will no leper more foul in this world than you.'

wife makes him "[t]o eten at the tables ende" (l. 1582),⁴³ as opposed to eating at the high table, his due as lord. Then she declares that "[h]e is so foule a thing, / It is gret spite to al mi kende" (ll. 1593–1594)⁴⁴ and forces him to move into a "litel loge" ('small lodge,' l. 1613) near the gate. Finally, she drives him off the estate altogether saying that even if Amiloun "for hunger and cold / Dyed ther he lay" (ll. 1664–1665)⁴⁵ she would not give him anything more to eat or drink.

Because Amiloun is the hero of a medieval romance, the only people who will accept him in his leprous state – beyond his loyal servant Amoraunt – are those whose sin he has taken on himself: Amis and Belisaunt. As Troilus does not recognise the leprous Cresseid, Amiloun's dearest friend, Amis, does not initially recognise the leprous Amiloun. In fact, Amis assumes that Amiloun has been killed and the leper has stolen the gold cup that matches his own because "[i]n al this world were coupes nomo / So liche in al thing / save min and mi brothers" (ll. 2054–2056).⁴⁶ Amiloun, a leper first and foremost, does not make any claims to his name when his friend does not recognise him. This failure of recognition serves as a dramatic device, but it also reinforces the idea that lepers are defined by their disease rather than any previous identity. Instead, after Amis has "sleynt [Amiloun] in the lake" (l. 2073)⁴⁷ and otherwise threatened his life, Amiloun's faithful servant, Amoraunt, tells Amis:

> thou art unhende
> And of thi werkes unkende,
> To sle that gentil knight.
> Wel sore may him rewe that stounde
> That ever for the toke he wounde
> To save thi liif in fight. (ll. 2107–2112)⁴⁸

Here, by not simply identifying the leper as Amiloun, Amoraunt makes the most direct statement concerning the root of Amiloun's condition: Amiloun's leprosy is the "wounde" that he took to save Amis' life. Once Amis and Belisaunt learn the leper's former identity, and that they are the cause of his diseased state, they welcome him into their home.

---

43 'to eat at the end of the table'
44 'he is such a foul thing that it is a great torment to all of my kin'
45 'died where he lay of hunger and cold'
46 'in all this world there were no cups so alike in all regards, except mine and my brother's'
47 'thrown Amiloun into the lake'
48 'you are discourteous and ignoble in your actions, to slay that gentle knight. He will rue that time sorely that he ever took wounds to save your life in a fight.'

Perhaps because the sexual sin is not his own, Amiloun – unlike Cresseid or the Summoner – is offered a full cure. In keeping with biblical tradition, this cure comes from God and at quite a price: in order to make "[h]is brother [...] as fair a knight / As ever he was biforn" (ll. 2213–2214),[49] Amis must kill his own children and anoint Amiloun with their blood. Although Amis is "[w]el loth [...] his childer to slo" (l. 2218)[50] he is "wele lother his brother forgo" (l. 2219)[51] and so he kills his children to save his friend from his disfiguring condition. In the end, both Amis and Amiloun are linked to Christ: Amiloun because he takes on and suffers for the sin of another and Amis because, like God the father, he is willing to sacrifice his children to save Amiloun. As in the stories of Miriam and Naaman, it is only "[t]hrough grace of Goddes sonde" (l. 2409)[52] – not mortal medicine – that leprosy in medieval literature may be cured. Fortunately for Amis, the romance of *Amis and Amiloun* does not conclude with Amiloun's cure and two dead children but with a happy miracle: After the children have been slain and Amiloun's leprosy is cured by their blood, Amis finds his children "[w]ithout wemme and wound / Hool and sound" (ll. 2419–2420).[53] Through the cure of Amis' own sacrifice, Amiloun's sin disappears and his skin becomes once more identical to Amis' and, significantly, illegible.

Chaucer's Pimpled Pervert

Finally, Chaucer's Summoner, like Cresseid, appears to be guilty of sexual sin, but his disease is not the sentence of a council of planetary gods and, so far as we know, does not appear suddenly. Nor, as in the case of *Amis and Amiloun*, is the Summoner's imminent contraction of leprosy announced by an angel. In the *Canterbury Tales*, the Summoner is already a leper when we meet him. After Chaucer briefly describes his Summoner's face – "a fyr-reed cherubynnes face" (*Canterbury Tales*, l. 624)[54] – he reports that the Summoner was as "lecherous as a sparwe" (l. 626)[55] before elaborating on his physical condition which, in addition to pimples, includes "scalled browes" ('scabbed brows,' l.

---

49 'his brother as fair a knight as ever he was before'
50 'very loath to kill his children'
51 'far more loath to forsake his brother'
52 'through the grace of God's messenger'
53 'without blemish or wound, whole and sound'
54 'a fire-red cherubim's face.' Quotations are taken from Benson (1987), the line number is given in the main text.
55 'lecherous as a sparrow'

627), a "piled berd" ('patchy beard,' l. 627) and "whelkes white" ('white pustules,' l. 632). Pimples, a patchy beard and pustules could all be minor imperfections, but Chaucer adds that "children were aferd" ('children were afraid,' l. 628) of the Summoner's face, undermining any notion that his symptoms are mild. It's likely that the disturbing nature of his appearance was not limited to the very young; we can reasonably presume that older onlookers were simply more polite in their reactions. Although Chaucer does not explicitly designate his Summoner a leper as Henryson does Cresseid, his portrait too aligns with contemporary descriptions of leprosy. It's important to note, however, that modern physicians would not describe the Summoner as a sufferer of Hansen's Disease (leprosy). Indeed, Thomas J. Garbáty (1963) argues that the Summoner actually had secondary syphilis. However, the material issue here is not a specific disease's aetiology according to modern medicine, but the moral function of *medieval* leprosy.[56] Chaucer describes two symptoms that reflect Guy de Chauliac's "tokenes" of leprosy: "fallynge of the heres" and "rudy droppe (i. sausflewme)" (*The Cyrurgie*, 380).[57] Perhaps most significantly, however, Chaucer lists a number of medical treatments that did nothing to mitigate the Summoner's pimples, scalp infection, facial hair loss and pustules:

"Ther nas quyk-silver, lytarge, ne brymstoon,
Boras ceruce, ne oille of tartre noon,
Ne oynement that wolde clense and byte." (ll. 629 – 631)[58]

Walter C. Curry (1922: 403) and many scholars since have cited this detailed list of treatments in their diagnoses of the Summoner's condition – whether as leprosy, some other skin disease or syphilis – but in the context of the story these remedies are most notable for their failure to improve, let alone cure, the Summoner's ailments.

The significance of the Summoner's condition does not lie in its exact symptoms or modern classification but the ultimate spiritual cause presented in the text: his sparrow-like lechery.[59] In addition to the quicksilver and other prepara-

---

56 For more on this modern medical diagnosis see Garbáty's (1963) "The Summoner's Occupational Disease," a superbly researched and very well argued article.
57 'hair loss' and 'rosacea like reddening [ulcers of the skin].' Quotations for *The Cyrurgie of Guy de Chauliac* are taken from Ogden (1971). Page numbers of that edition are given in the main text.
58 'There was no mercury, lead monoxide, or sulphur, borax, white lead or oil of tartar, or or ointment that would cleanse and burn.'
59 In John of Trevisa's translation of *Bartholomaeus Anglicus De Proprietatibus Rerum*, the sparrow is described as a "ful hoot bridde and lecherous, and here fleische ofte itake in mete excitiþ

tions that Guy de Chauliac suggests for the treatment of leprosy he asserts that lepers "schal eschewe fro leccherye and fro all þing þat may chaufe here nature" (385).⁶⁰ Abstinence, however, does not appear among the remedies that the Summoner has tried: not only could he "[f]ul prively a fynch [...] pull" (l. 652),⁶¹ but his relationship to the "yonge girles of the diocise" (l. 664)⁶² does not seem entirely above board.⁶³ Chaucer further reports that his new travelling companion "wold suffre for a quart of wyn / a good felawe to have his concubyn" (ll. 649– 650).⁶⁴ This trading of privileges for wine constitutes simony which Brody (1974: 128) finds "[a]mong the damnable sins which ecclesiastical writers connect[ed] with leprosy." Of course, the Summoner's occupation makes his behaviour still more offensive for its hypocrisy. As Thomas J. Garbáty (1963: 348) puts it, the *Canterbury Tales*' "religious figures [...], all of whom were guilty of some kind of clerical abuse, came in for severe comment" and

> the most vicious sketch of all is that of the Summoner, an officer of the Church whose duty it was to ferret out delinquents in morals, especially in matters of fornication and adultery, and to bring them before the ecclesiastical courts.

Garbáty concludes that the Summoner's skin condition is venereal, but the medieval understanding of sexually transmitted disease does not exactly correspond to the modern one. While some diseases were said to be passed *through* sex, others, leprosy among them, were sometimes said to develop *from the act itself* regardless of the disease-state of one's partner. Indeed, Chauliac suggests that sex can be dangerous for those predisposed toward leprosy not because of contagion but because the act itself might "chaufe [a leper's] nature" (385).⁶⁵ Along these lines, it is interesting to note that a seventh-century patriarch of Jerusalem attributed leprosy not to sexual intercourse or intercourse with lepers, but specifically to "intercourse with menstruating women" (Miller and Nesbitt 2014: 40). As with Cresseid, I assert that the root of the Summoner's skin condition is in his sins – or his female lovers' time of the month – and not in any contact he may have had with leprous women when indulging the sin of lust. Regardless of the cause or precise nature of the Summoner's disease, it is clear

---

seruyse to Venus" ('a very hot and lecherous bird, and the flesh thereof often inspires service to Venus,' *On the Property of Things*, 639). Quotation taken from Seymour (1975).
60 'should avoid lechery and all things that might inflame their nature.' See also Wood (1971).
61 'secretly pluck a finch'
62 'young girls of the diocese'
63 For an explanation of the idiom *to pull a finch* see Benson (1987: 823 n. 652).
64 'for a quart of wine he'd allow a good fellow to have his concubine'
65 'inflame a leper's nature'

that his lifestyle does little to ease his condition and perhaps this is what motivates him to undertake the pilgrimage to Canterbury, the "hooly blisful martir for to seke, / that hem hath holpen whan that they were seeke" (ll. 17–18).[66] After all, according to Rubin (1974: 162), lepers could procure "[h]oly water made from a drop of St. Thomas' blood" in Canterbury which was said to cure the leprosy of true penitents.

Unlike Cresseid and Amiloun, the Summoner does not retreat to a leper colony or otherwise appear to be ostracised from the healthy. However, as I mentioned briefly above, "children were aferd" of the Summoner's appearance suggesting that, if his condition continued to worsen, he was en route to becoming a true pariah. Adults may have been more hesitant to read the Summoner's face as leprous, and certainly his abusive use of his position might motivate would-be accusers to hold their tongues, but children, free from such apprehensions, can clearly read the Summoner's wickedness in his face.

Conclusions: Leprous Literacy

Just as the Puritan magistrates use a scarlet letter to publicly shame Hester Prynne, leprosy in medieval literature publicises the leper's sins for other characters at the story level as well as for the audience. In the *Testament of Cresseid*, the character of Chaucer's Summoner and in *Amis and Amiloun,* diseased and disfigured skin is a superficial and clearly visible brand of serious misdeeds. Were it not for the curse of leprosy – which destroyed her means of lechery – Cresseid might have had any number of affairs before her beauty faded in the natural course of time. Her blasphemy, however, brings retribution from the gods. The specific punishment of leprosy warns away lovers and thereby physically prevents Cresseid from further misusing romantic love while at the same time putting a horrific face on the consequences of, at least, female infidelity. The story of *Amis and Amiloun* illustrates not only the connection between sin and disease, but shows that whatever one may convince humanity of, God cannot be fooled. However, this story ends on a hopeful note: although sin is punished and manifests hideously in Amiloun's skin, Amis' sacrifice cures him. Finally, the figure of Chaucer's Summoner suggests the negative consequences of lechery somewhat more subtly: The Summoner does not soliloquise what brought him to his present diseased state; nor does he, within the existing text of the *Canterbury Tales*, repent of his lechery or the abuse of his position in

---

[66] 'to seek the holy blissful martyr that helped them when they were ill'

the ecclesiastical court system.[67] However, his child-frightening face cannot have served as an inducement to mimic him and surely would have driven away anyone with whom he might indulge in lechery no matter the favours he might be able offer them.

Rawcliffe (1999) and Rubin (1974), among others, report that by the later Middle Ages the incidence of leprosy had declined steeply. Yet the spectre of the disease and its theological significance lingered. While pure moralists and sermon writers depended on the metaphor of spiritual leprosy as Robert Mannyng did in *Handlyng Synne*, poets and romance writers utilised the disease to mark sinful characters and thus make their misdeeds known within and without the confines of the stories they inhabited. The *Testament of Cresseid*, Chaucer's Summoner and *Amis and Amiloun* deter sin by reminding the audience that lepers do not merely suffer from their disease but from their status as outcasts. In these stories, sin does not result only in posthumous penalties, but in immediate consequences which, effectively, bring hell to earth.

Works Cited

Primary Sources

Benson, Larry D. (ed.). 1987. *Geoffrey Chaucer: The Riverside Chaucer*. 3rd ed. Boston: Houghton Mifflin.

Fischer, Bonifatius, Jean Gribomont, H. F. D. Sparks, Walter Thiele and Robert Weber (eds.). 1994. *Biblia Sacra iuxta vulgatam versionem*. Stuttgart: Württembergische Bibelanstalt.

Fox, Denton (ed.). 1968. *Robert Henryson: Testament of Cresseid*. London: Nelson.

Furnivall, Frederick J. (ed.). 1973. *Robert of Brunne's* Handlyng Synne, *and Its French Original*. Millwood, NY: Kraus Reprint.

Hawthorne, Nathaniel. 1851. *The Scarlet Letter*. London: Knight and Son.

Leach, MacEdward (ed.). 1960. *Amis and Amiloun*, London: Oxford University Press.

Ogden, Margaret S. (ed.). 1971. *Guy de Chauliac: The Cyrurgie of Guy de Chauliac*. EETS OS 265. Oxford and London: Oxford University Press.

Seymour, M. C. (ed.). 1975. *John Trevisa: On the Properties of Things: John Trevisa's Translation of* Bartholomaeus Anglicus De Proprietatibus Rerum. Volume 1. Oxford: Clarendon Press.

---

[67] Although unrepentant within the received text, it is possible that the Summoner's pilgrimage to the shrine of the "hooly blisful martir" ('holy blessed martyr,' l. 17) in Canterbury heals him spiritually and physically.

Secondary Sources

Brody, Saul N. 1974. *The Disease of the Soul: Leprosy in Medieval Literature.* Ithaca, NY: Cornell University Press.

Craun, Edwin D. 1985. "Blaspheming Her 'Awin God:' Cresseid's 'Lamentatioun' in Henryson's 'Testament'." *Studies in Philology* 82.1: 25–41.

Curry, Walter C. 1922. "The Malady of Chaucer's Summoner." *Modern Philology* 19.4: 395–404.

Demaitre, Luke. 1985. "The description and diagnosis of leprosy by fourteenth-century physicians." *Bulletin of the History of Medicine* 59.3: 327–344.

Eichman, Phillip. 1999. "The History, Biology and Medical Aspects of Leprosy. *The American Biology Teacher* 61.7: 490–495.

Garbáty, Thomas J. 1963. "The Summoner's Occupational Disease." *Medical History* 7.4: 348–358.

Higl, Andrew. 2010. "Henryson's Textual and Narrative Prosthesis onto Chaucer's Corpus: Cresseid's Leprosy and Her *Schort Conclusion*." In: Joshua R. Eyler (ed.). *Disability in the Middle Ages: Reconsiderations and Reverberations.* Surrey: Ashgate. 167–181.

Hume, Kathryn. 1973. "'Amis and Amiloun' and the Aesthetics of Middle English Romance." *Studies in Philology* 70.1: 19–41.

Kratins, Ojars. 1966. "The Middle English Amis and Amiloun: Chivalric Romance or Secular Hagiography." *PMLA* 81.5: 347–354.

Miller, Timothy S. and John W. Nesbitt. 2014. *Walking Corpses: Leprosy in Byzantium and the Medieval West.* Ithaca, NY: Cornell University Press.

Orlemanski, Julie. 2013. "Desire and Defacement in *The Testament of Cresseid*." In: Katie L. Walter (ed.). *Reading Skin in Medieval Literature and Culture.* The New Middle Ages. New York: Palgrave Macmillan. 161–181.

Rawcliffe, Carole. 1999. *Medicine & Society in Later Medieval England.* London: Sandpiper Books.

Rubin, Stanley. 1974. *Medieval English Medicine.* London: David & Charles Newton Abbot.

Wood, Chauncey. 1971. "The Sources of Chaucer's 'Garleek, Onyons, and Eke Lekes'." *The Chaucer Review.* 5.3: 240–244.

Part II: **Textual Skins**

Catherine S. Cox
Chaucer's Ethical Palimpsest:
Dermal Reflexivity in the General Prologue

Abstract: This essay considers the role of skin in relation to social interaction and the construction of the ethical self within those relationships. In a short poem, Chaucer famously scolds his scrivener, Adam, likening the animal skin of the corrupted (that is, error riddled) text to the human skin of the hapless scribe upon whom the curse of skin disease, "scalle," is hypothetically placed as fitting retribution for the rubbing and scraping of the parchment of animal origin undergoing correction. The amusing and ironic anecdote provides a starting point for exploring the ways by which Chaucer's self-reflexive representations of skin germane to textuality correspond thematically to representations of skin as corporeal texts, signifying indeterminately the character and composition of their occupants. An illustrative portrait sequence is analyzed – the Summoner, the Cook, the Wife of Bath – suggesting that related to the tantalizing ultimate unknowability of the words in palimpsest, hidden and elusive and only partially recoverable at best, Chaucer sees a productive correlation between the material reality of a text's literary and social construction and the abstract, intangible potentialities thereby generated.

In his charmingly odd short poem, "Chaucer's Wordes Unto Adam, His Owne Scriveyn," cited and discussed by volume editors Katrin Rupp and Nicole Nyffenegger in their introductory chapter, above, Chaucer famously scolds his scribe, Adam, for necessitating the author's intervention in correcting errors that the scribe has made in producing manuscript copies of the author's works – a scolding that, it seems, the hapless scribe dutifully records. In the context of fourteenth-century literary production, the brief poem aptly conveys the relationship between the "maker," as Chaucer and other writers of verse referred to themselves as "makers" of creative works, and the scribes, whose taking of dictation and recording and recopying of the makers' words produced the material manuscripts of literary texts.[1] As Carolyn Dinshaw (1989: 1–12, 189 n. 4 and n. 6) and

---

[1] As Partridge (2012: 148 n. 72) observes, "There was some overlap in the terms used for copying and composition," which, while not necessarily "exploit[ed] for artistic ends," arguably occurs in Chaucer's *Retractions*, the "makere of this booke" notation, but also, quite likely, in the "Adam" text as well. The enterprise we now call "poetry" would have been referred to as "mak-

others (Mooney 2006; Horobin 2010; Mooney and Stubbs 2013) have observed, maker and scribe understood literary production as a cooperative, if hierarchical, social enterprise, the final review prior to release reserved for the maker's eye. Self-reflexively illustrating the dynamics of a handwritten, collaborative manuscript culture, Chaucer's poem regards the discovery of errors as unsurprising, implicitly routine, and gives as a rationale for the author's annoyance the effort invested in the established measures of scraping and reworking the palimpsest, to be routinely undertaken for the purpose of eliminating the errors and ensuring the release and dissemination of an accurate copy into the social world of literary purchase and reception.[2]

Thus we find dramatized here the author Chaucer's reaction to the discovery of errors in Adam's writing of Chaucer's words – the possibility of textual distortion having been realized and the means of correction delineated in anticipation of subsequent need. Chaucer, asserting authority, removes Adam's written words and replaces them with his own; once again, he suggests, he must "renewe" the physical surface.[3] Chaucer describes his handling of the palimpsest and expresses frustration at his having to erase the errors by scraping the parchment in order to create a fresh surface for new, and presumably more accurate, ink. Within this ironically dramatized metanarrative, Chaucer asserts his own authority and ensures that he, the author, has the final word, even if he must do the secretarial

---

ing" by those who "made" poetry in medieval England, distinct from the "poets" of classical antiquity. On these distinctions, see Olson (1979), Schmidt (1987: 144–146), Cox (1997: 1–4).

2 Volume editors Rupp and Nyffenegger observe in their introduction, above, "[O]ne wonders whether to picture Chaucer himself bringing quill to parchment for these particular words or to imagine that, in a malicious gesture of dominance, he had his scribe write his own scabs into their literary existence." My own reading here leans more towards the latter, or the appearance of such, rather, as conveyed by the poem's thematic rendering of the relationship between Chaucer and his perhaps merely imagined scribe. Gillespie (2008: 276) notes: "Shirley picks up on the claim Chaucer makes to ownership of his texts, 'my makyng,' and magnifies its importance, making it 'more truwe.' These words are 'Chauciers.' The point made by the genitive case can be made another way: these words are 'a Geffrey,' where the preposition 'a' signals *appartenance*. These words are spoken to Adam, but he is not merely Adam Pinkhurst, or even Adam the scrivener, he is 'his,' 'Chauciers.' Adam is more than just 'his' in fact; he is 'his owen.' And who could know so much about that which Chaucer so emphatically possesses? None other than the omniscient third-person narrator of all the stories of English literature that the reader has been privy to in Trinity R.3.20: John Shirley. As he constructs his own Chaucer from Chaucer's words, Shirley ensures that his readers can make their Chaucer from the same words, and, by that process, assign Shirley a fêted role in Chaucerian tradition."

3 On manuscript copying, book production, and palimpsest, see Hanna (2004), Johnston (2014: 90–127), Gillespie and Wakelin (2011), Kwakkel (2014), Reimer (2015).

work himself and "correcte"[4] the results of his employee's faulty discharge of duty. The doubled verbs of removal, "rubbe and scrape," underscore both the physical effort needed for the task and the exasperation on the part of Chaucer that his words have been distorted.

Foregrounding a parallel between the animal skin of the corrupted text and the human skin of the hapless scribe himself, Chaucer hypothetically curses Adam with the skin disease "scalle," a disfiguring inflammation accompanied by intense itching,[5] as fitting retribution for the disfigured parchment and the rubbing and scraping that accompanies its resolve. The texture, appearance, and wear upon the animal-skin parchment due to the process of his placing new text over the previous text in palimpsest find correlation in the living, but damaged, skin (likewise in texture, appearance, and wear) of the scribe. Given the litany of curses popular in dramatized late-medieval exchanges, it is no mere coincidence that Chaucer, as a crucial component of his scolding words, evokes the image of disfigured and inflamed skin. While words of ill wishes have no properties of instrumentality, and, obviously, no capacity to cause physical harm, the exasperation behind those words and the image they evoke tie into the thematic gist of the metanarrative's dermal trope: the behavior of the negligent scribe ("thy negligence and rape") is figuratively likened to the appearance of his faulty workmanship and extended hypothetically to his own physical appearance. As Rupp and Nyffenegger (this volume) observe:

> This layered text-parchment-skin relation is further complicated by the fact that material and metaphorical uses of skin coexist and arguably intermingle in this poem. This creates an effect of oscillation that medieval readers, used as they were to encountering writing on processed animal skin, may have found easier to disentangle than we do today.

This amusing and ironic anecdote, through which Chaucer's implicitly ethical metaphor of the palimpsest figures prominently, provides a starting point for exploring the ways by which Chaucer's self-reflexive representations of skin germane to textuality correspond thematically to representations of skin as corporeal texts, potentially signifying the character and composition of the humans

---

4 Quotations of Chaucer's works cite the Riverside edition (Benson 1987); locations provided in text. Translations are my own except where indicated.
5 The first attributed use of the word *scalle* is that of Chaucer in "Adam," according to the *OED* entry: "Etymology: probably < Old Norse *skalle* a (naturally) bald head (Swedish *skalle*) Obs. exc. Sc. and *north. dial.* A. A scaly or scabby disease of the skin, *esp.* of the scalp. dry scall: psoriasis. humid or moist scall : eczema. honeycomb scall, milk scall, milky scall, ringworm scall: see the qualifying words. α. c1374 CHAUCER *To Scriv.* 3 Vnder þy long lokkes þowe most haue þe scalle."

bearing it. Just as the hapless "Adam" provides an illustrative example of a human being (however fictive) whose skin is described as hypothetically bearing the marks, scars, and traces of its owner's erring, so too the fictive pilgrims of Chaucer's literary pilgrimage are described as bearing their own marks, scars, and traces, implicitly and explicitly associated with conventionally problematic moral lapses, both biblical and popular, owing to their metaphoric conjunctions of manuscript production and dissemination.

Cutaneous Habitations

To appreciate Chaucer's palimpsest trope, it is useful first to recall the place of the physical parchment manuscript in the historical trajectory of material textual production. As succinctly described in the descriptions accompanying the Getty Museum's (2003) "The Making of a Medieval Book" exhibit:

> Most medieval manuscripts were written on specially treated animal skins, called parchment or vellum (paper did not become common in Europe until around 1450). The pelts were first soaked in a lime solution to loosen the fur, which was then removed. While wet on a stretcher, the skin was scraped using a knife with a curved blade. As the skin dried, the parchment maker adjusted the tension so that the skin remained taut. This cycle of scraping and stretching was repeated over several days until the desired thinness had been achieved. Here, the skin of a stillborn goat, prized for its smoothness, is stretched on a modern frame to illustrate the parchment making process.

Interestingly, the Getty Museum specifies that a "stillborn" animal's skin is used in the exhibit, distancing the process of parchment preparation from the reality of the deaths of animals necessitated by parchment demand during the medieval era, during which, as Bruce Holsinger (2009: 619) notes, a single book could consume the skin of dozens, or in rare but documented cases, hundreds, of animals.[6]

---

[6] Kwakkel (2014) comments on the oversized volumes and the production materials required: "My favourite activity is to touch, smell, and listen to the crackling sound of cows and sheep that have been dead for a thousand years. That's right, I am talking about medieval parchment, the standard material for books made between the fifth and thirteenth centuries. Animal skin replaced papyrus (standard up to the fifth century) and would ultimately be challenged by paper, which competed for dominance during the later medieval period." See also Rudy (2015: 18–40).

The reality, of course, is that even the most meticulous production methods netted a final product revealing of its origins; as Sarah Kay (2006: 36) notes of one's handling of medieval manuscripts:

> Just occasionally you can make out on its velvety surface a trace of its genesis, most commonly a pattern of hair follicles, or a filigree of tiny veins: subliminal reminders that it cannot altogether escape the time-bound world of mortality. In less luxurious manuscripts, however, the parchment retains traces of the processes by means of which it was made. If it came from a damaged or parti-colored animal it may be scarred or blotchy. It may further be scraped, cut, split, holed, torn, stretched, strained, or dried to a hornlike consistency, all blemishes which are consequent on the flaying, scraping, stretching, and drying of hides.

That a manuscript page was once the living property of a living animal wasn't lost on medieval scribes and authors,[7] who not only overtly identify their materials, the skin parchment and quill nib that constituted the writing surface and instrument, but additionally anthropomorphize their parchment and acknowledge its biological history with an imagined sentience of its origin and transformation. And although Dolores Warwick Frese and Katherine O'Brien O'Keeffe (1997: xi) too easily dismiss the trope of living words and dead skin in the Middle Ages as having already become a cliché, they note that "the image of writing (literally and metaphorically) on living bodies continued to have power."[8]

While more given to accepting as matter-of-fact the reality of slaughter and the pervasive presence of flayed skin conjoined with textual transmission and readers' reception, medieval readers, writers, scribes, and others participatory in the process of bringing manuscripts into being nonetheless show on occasion insight into the reality of human-animal relationships and correspondences, hi-

---

7 Shoaf (2001: 95), in establishing Chaucer's use of metonymy, offers the following correlation: "[...] what I take to be one of the most vivid metonymies I can cite. I mean my skin. Pause with me for a moment to think about it. The largest organ in my body, my skin, is denominated by the verb that means to cut my skin off, to flay me, to strip me of it [...]. Any dictionary of the English language will tell you that the noun *skin* is immediately derived from the verb *to skin*. It is a metonymy of cause-effect, just like *cut* – the effect of the verb, the result of its action, is applied as name to what which underoges of suffers the action of the verb." On contemporary theoretical perspectives on human skin, see Jablonski (2006) and MacKendrick (2004).
8 Nyffenegger (2013: 280) observes, "Postmodern theories of body modification, and in particular of tattooing and piercing, can help medievalists to further explore the modified bodies of medieval martyrs. However, body modification theories often read skin as text or as the (not quite) blank page. For medievalists, skin as a writing matter is nothing out of the ordinary. The fact that animal skin was the primary writing matter may have opened different perspectives on inscribed human skin to medieval thinkers and writers."

erarchical yet unavoidable. As Jacques Derrida (2002: 380) notably observes in his landmark 1997 essay "The Animal That Therefore I Am:"

> What stakes are raised by these questions? One doesn't need to be an expert to foresee that they involve thinking about what is meant by living, speaking, dying, being and world as in being-in-the-world or being to-wards the world, or being-with, being-before, being-behind, being-after, being and following, being followed or being following, there where I *am*, in one way or another, but unimpeachably, *near* what they call the animal. It is too late to deny it, it will have been there before me who is (following) after it. *After* and *near* what they call the animal and *with* it – whether we want it or not and whatever we do about it.

Perhaps the best known illustration of parchment production and the hints of thematic correlation with the textual contents of the finished manuscript is the description found in the Exeter Riddle #24, part of the Old English collection of riddles included with other known writings of the Anglo-Saxon era in the ninth-century Exeter Book manuscript, the first part of which is quoted here:

> Mec feonda sum   feore besnyþede
> woruldstrenga binō   wætte siþþan
> dyfde on wætre   dyde eft þonan
> sette on sunnan   þær ic swiþe beleas
> herum þam þe ic hæfde   heard mec siþþan
> snað seaxses ecge   sindrum begrunden
> fingras feoldan.[9]

Though the author of this riddle is anonymous, the parchment itself metaphorically speaks with the voice of authenticity and authority, describing its transformation from living animal to dead skin (parchment) and finally a book, usually interpreted to be the Christian Bible. In this regard it is similar to the riddles of the eighth-century Tatwine and Eusebius that likewise trace production from living animal to the parchment surface upon which are written the contents of a holy book, a full Bible or a portion thereof. Here, Tatwine's "De Membranis:"

> Eiferus exuviis populator me spoliavit,
> Vitalis pariter flatus spiramina dempsit,
> In planum me iterum carnpum sed verterat auctor.

---

[9] 'An enemy came   and took away my life / and my strength also   in the word; then wetted me, / dipped me in water;   then took me thence; / placed me in the sun,   where I lost all my hair. / he knife's edge cut me—   its impurities ground away; / fingers folded me.' Quotation taken from Baum (1967). See also Williamson (1977: 178): "This Bible or book riddle is probably the earliest sustained piece of book-art poetry in English."

> Frugiferos cultor sulcos mox irrigat undis,
> Omnigenam nardi messem mea prata rependunt,
> Qua sanis victum et lzesis praestabo medelam.¹⁰

And, similarly, Eusebius' speaking manuscript page, emphasizing that the dead parts of the animal have the capacity, figuratively, to speak:

> Antea per nos vox resonabat verba nequaquam,
> Distincta sine numc voce edere verba solumus;
> Candida sed cum arva lustramur milibus atris;
> Viva nihil loquimur, responsum mortua famur.¹¹

The process of production – slaughter, washing, scraping, cutting, finishing – is voiced by the skin itself, recalling its living material reality as the cutaneous covering of a living animal and its undead afterlife as parchment, specifically having been used for the production of a holy book, collectively the Christian Bible. Kay (2006: 36) notes of such parchment production, "[t]hese causes of damage – scraping, cutting, splitting, tearing, holing, stretching, drying out – are all processes that, inflicted on a living human body rather than on a dead animal, would be forms of torture."

What is so telling about the voice of Riddle #24, therefore, is that while readers typically assert that the solution is "Bible," in fact the first-person voice cannot in any accurate way be identified as the Bible, or any book for that matter, speaking but rather the dead animal whose skin has been transformed into the parchment that constitutes the book's material form. The shift in perspective near the end, a twofold conflation of Bible and voice, material and content, not only occludes the voice's autobiographical anecdote of origin but also conflates the dead animal with the finished product, shifting the reader's attention away from the material parchment to the sacred texts occupying that surface. To be sure, literary conflations of flesh and blood with the Book and its Passion narratives of suffering and sacrifice are not uncommon; as Kay (2006: 36) observes:

---

10 'A fierce robber ripped off my hide, / Plundered the breath-pores of my skin. / I was shaped by an artist and author / Into a flat field. Furrowed and wet, / I yield strange fruit. My meadows bloom / Food for the healthy, health for the sick.' Quotation from Wright (1872: 526); translation from Williamson (1982: 178).

11 'Once silent, voiceless, wordless, dumb – / Now voiceless, silent, bearing words we come, / White fields crossed by myriad black tracks: / Alive we are dumb – dead, answer back.' *Enigma*, cited by Bitterli (2009: 183). Translation from Williamson (1982: 178).

> Folios bearing defects like these thus constitute a mute doubling of the kinds of suffering undergone by the protagonists of many of the texts that are written on them. When turning the pages of a pious text especially, medieval readers would be faced, in the substance of the parchment on which it was copied, with one or both of the aspects of the dichotomy with which the work was centrally concerned: the torments of mortal life and the blissful eternity to which it would lead.

In Exeter Riddle #24, the conflation is with an animal whose fate is both exploited and ignored. Bruce Holsinger (2009: 622), in his pioneering work with conjunctions of the ethical and the materials of writing, observes of this riddle's speaking parchment, "[t]he animal's *mec*, its 'me,' holds up an ethical mirror to the centuries of slaughter that gave us a millennium of medieval writing."[12] The overall trajectory, then, is the foregrounding of the material surface of the written page by way of the anthropomorphic voice of skin delineating its stages of life, death, and post-death, as parchment, overtly identifying skin as its medium even as the poem privileges the Word as its message. In Exeter Riddle #24, the perfection signified by the admiring words of the Bible's host, as it were, evades the obvious reality that in the course of manuscript production, mistakes could be made even if, once corrected, their presence is nearly invisible.

In the material culture of the fourteenth century, the concept of the palimpsest, a reworked and reused parchment, corresponds to both economic and ideological concerns. Economic, in that parchment could be scraped and re-used, conserving resources in order to avoid absorbing the cost of having a new suitable piece of animal skin prepared or purchased for the necessary document preparation; and ideological, in that an unmistakable symbolic value attaches to the act of replacing one text with another, prioritizing the validity of the new material over that which it displaces, as in the case of religious texts, for example, where, in early Christian centuries, non-Christian "pagan" texts provided the parchment for Christian-oriented commentaries and letters. The traces or residue of the earlier material could in some cases be discerned, and the visible and tactile evidence of someone's having rubbed and scraped it attested to the parchment's having been re-used, perhaps more than once. As evident in the Archimedes Palimpsest, for example, the digital images of which are available on the project's website, even without the aid of digital technologies, parts of a palimpsest can sometimes, with effort, be discerned, a process of recovery both la-

---

[12] Holsinger's insightful analysis helped solidify the 'animal studies' scholarship of the past five years, with a particular emphasis on the ethics of the non-human and what that means for medievalists.

borious and fortuitous.[13] And even when the original contents cannot be discerned, the history of the parchment's past is understood, that supplanting and replacing has occurred; as codicology and paleography scholar Eric Kwakkel (2014) observes, "[w]ell known are cases where scribes and readers erased text with a knife, either because the reading was wrong or because they disagreed with it." Given the challenges of authenticating authorship and establishing authoritative editions of popular texts, as Root, Windeatt, McGann, Ruggiers, and others have long noted (Benson 1987: 795–797),[14] the hidden history contained in a palimpsest's multivalent, residual layers tantalizes with the possibilities of documentation and material evidence of a text's historical journey from author to reader.

Although technologies of textual production have since rendered the handwritten palimpsest obsolete, as paper began to replace parchment and as textuality and literacy transitioned into the early modern era,[15] the concept of the layered, erased, residual prepared skin surface and its figurative sense of past and present, history and reception, codification and interpretation, remains an elucidating trope, with a self-reflexive figurative dimension when used thematically to call attention not only to the symbolic meaning within the parameters of the literary fiction but also to the process of that literature's composition, dissemination, and reception.[16] Contemporary novelist Jeanette Winterson, for example, in her 1992 novel *Written on the Body*, delves into this twofold characteristic of the palimpsest, its layering of text and the prioritized visibility of the text currently occupying the surface space. She observes via her narrator that "Writ-

---

[13] "Only occasionally can one just discern, at right angles to the prayer book text, the erased writings that the current project is attempting to recover" (*Archimedes Palimpsest*).

[14] See the introduction to the Explanatory Notes to the *Canterbury Tales* in the *Riverside* (Benson 1987: 795–797), which discusses manuscript tradition and textual editions.

[15] Manly and Rickert (1940: I.8, 24–25) found in compiling all available extant manuscripts of the *Canterbury Tales*, "[o]f the MSS, including fragments, fifty-one are on vellum, twenty-eight on paper, and four use both vellum and paper," and describe the evidence of correction: "The study of corrections by themselves is a many-sided problem. There is the passing over of mistakes through reluctance to spoil the appearance of a fine vellum MS; there is the meticulous correction from the exemplar of small errors by the careful scribe – erasing, striking out, interlining, writing in the margin; there is the correction by the thoughtful scribe according to his own ideas, of supposed or real errors in his exemplar (cf # Ha2); there are supposed improvements on Chaucer introduced by the editorially minded scribe; there is the correction (sometimes to error) by comparison with one or more other MSS."

[16] Though beyond the scope of the present essay, of related interest are figurative associations of manuscript illumination and corporeal markings. On manuscript illumination and its relationship to reading, writing, and reception, see, for instance, Gellrich (1985), Desmond and Sheingorn (2003), Mann (2014), Rudy (2015).

ten on the body is a secret code only visible in certain lights; the accumulations of a lifetime gather there. In places the palimpsest is so heavily worked that the letters feel like braille" (Winterson 1992: 89). Here, an instructive parallel is drawn between the skin of a lover's living body and the life thus far experienced by the person within it – it records moments and memories, the newer replacing the older like a palimpsest. The record, then, is fragmentary and partial, more imagined than documented. That Winterson's anonymous narrator observes the surface's having been "heavily worked" owing to the sequential rewritings, much as Chaucer's palimpsest is reworked in replacing Adam's former, inaccurate, words, is indicative of subsequent and sequential rewritings. Traces of damage on the skin's surface convey the fact of there being a history behind them; they are the evidence of a past that cannot be erased, even if their appearance is inconclusive and ambiguous regarding the particulars of their origins.

Unlike decorative, deliberate markings and piercings on the surface of the skin (tattoos, brands, earrings, etc) or temporary cosmetic coverings or enhancements similarly placed,[17] the marks of damage (scars, sores, inflammation, infection, rosacea, for example) signify a history of injury and/or illness rather than personal expression by choice. In this sense, damaged skin communicates not its owner's ideas, opinions, ideological affiliations, aesthetics, desire for self-expression, or attention-seeking, but rather its owner's material history, the chronological, linear timeline punctuated by events leaving traces, the extent of their significance not necessarily correlating with the prominence of the physical marks that incite curiosity, revulsion, or both. Although words of wishful thinking, like Chaucer's curse that Adam be stricken by the "scalle," have no instrumentality themselves, and, realistically, damaged skin may or may not have a story to tell that implicates its owner in immoral or unethical behavior,[18] within the world of material textuality and the craft of making, Chaucer implies, a possible symbolic correlation may be gleaned between a fictive person's ethical character and their skin's appearance, particularly where eruptions, scars, and inflammation signal some degree of its wearer's having a proclivity for behaviors and desires that are themselves transgressive within the ethical parameters of late medieval Christian ethics as represented in art and literature. This isn't to

---

[17] On tattoos and other markings described in medieval texts, see Nyffenegger (2013). For historical background and current perspectives, see Caplan (2000), DeMello (2000).

[18] See also Rhodes (this volume): "[Chaucer's text] suggests that however private or subtle a sin may be, the sins of Cresseid, Amiloun, and the Summoner erupt through their skins and allow anyone to read the states of their souls." On corporeal disfigurement and figurative associations of text, see also Cox (2004), where the Sotah ritual of ingesting text as a catalytic agent of disfigurement is evoked by Chaucer's Pardoner.

say, of course, that visible blemishes signify a person's moral substance or pattern of behavior any more than a person's having been named "Adam" upon birth exhibits any correlation to the biblical character of that name, itself a Hebrew metaphor. It is to say, however, that our consideration of the methods and strategies by which artists and writers incorporate symbolic correlations in their representations of human beings and human actions can lead to edifying and provocative insights on both the moral attributes and the codes both ecclesiastical and popular that frame them.

Dermal Reflexivity

Certainly the details germane to the physical characteristics of a person, foregrounded in the General Prologue portraiture's attention to clothing, accessories and other material trappings of social class and vocation, corporeal size and shape, somatic oddities (the Pardoner's goat-like squeak of a voice, for example, or his perpetual beardlessness), and facial features (the Prioress' "spanne"[19] of a forehead, the Host's bright eyes), are overtly symbolic attributes long used in visual and textual arts as indicators of symbolic values, be they conventional or idiosyncratic. As the copious notes in the *Riverside Chaucer* and elsewhere attest, the details set forth in the General Prologue portrait sequence create a composite effect, culled as they are from instructive biblical topoi, allusive imagery deriving from biblical commentaries and other learned traditions as well as from popular secular literature, correlations made familiar via "estates" and other categorical models of popular satire, recurring motifs informed by the iconographic conventions of the visual arts, and from Chaucer's own fertile imagination. Indeed, critics have long isolated and identified particular portrait details in relation to specific source texts and established literary and popular traditions, providing readers with a deeper understanding of the types, and stereotypes, on display without negating the pragmatic verisimilitude of the pilgrim fellowship as the dramatis personae of the pilgrimage narrative. The pilgrims are not, of course, limited to these familiar and conventional understandings, and, moreover, as composite portraits they additionally challenge the reader to consider their multivalent associations and correlations as participatory in overlapping, and sometimes seemingly conflicting, contexts. Malcolm Andrew (1989: 330) notes:

---

[19] A span of about seven to nine inches, according to Benson's (1987: 26 n. 155) gloss in *The Riverside Chaucer*.

I would argue that the decontextualization of the pilgrims from their physical and moral settings is essential to the meaning of the General Prologue, in that it facilitates Chaucer's freeing them from rigid and clearly definable contexts for judgment. To speak of the existence of such settings is itself, of course, a fallacy – though one which the poet could be claimed to have encouraged. The fictional mode of the General Prologue allows Chaucer, through his narrator, to refer, allusively and selectively, both to the pilgrims' physical settings and to potentially appropriate moral settings.[20]

In contrast to the more common correlations of theme and parchment – such as evocations of the biblical Passion narrative that self-reflexively delineate the process of the manuscript's production, or symbolic details of a character's wounding and scarring that parallel the parchment and markings[21] – Chaucer's portraiture emphasizes, figuratively and ambiguously, the cutaneous souvenirs of less lofty adventures: to provoke a sardonic humor, to challenge aesthetic sensibilities, and, as we shall see, to draw connections between the activities of textual production, both artistic and physical, and those of textual reception. What makes Chaucer's attention to skin in particular so intriguing is the contextual trope of the reworked parchment, the palimpsest, upon which these details have been written, indicative of the possibility of healing, renewal, and restoration (the "correcting" of the surface) accompanied by a visible, perceptibly tangible, history of the characters' errors, as it were. To illustrate, let us consider three examples set forth by General Prologue portraits, which, together, help establish and elucidate Chaucer's conflation: the Summoner, whose portrait is most overtly aligned with Adam's "scalle;" the Cook, bearer of the notorious "mormal" or ulcer that may or may not resemble the custardy creamed chicken upon which the Cook's culinary reputation implicitly rests; and the Wife/Woman of Bath, whose facial rosecea advertises her passion for self-presentation. Traces and residual echoes, much like the obscure and unexpected underpaintings that modern X-rays have discovered beneath the surface of well-known paintings by famous artists[22] hint at a secret history that requires exposure and revelation to be appreciated by anyone other than its artist/author.

---

20 See also Rigby (2014) on historically contextualizing the pilgrims as representatives of their occupations.

21 Reichardt (1984: 155) notes of *Sir Gawain and the Green Knight*, "The act of comprehending the mark on the flesh of the hero is not unlike the act of reading the marks of writing on the pages that convey the story about him."

22 Consider Picasso's *Blue Room* for example, with its recently revealed hidden portrait long suspected. On Picasso's *Blue Room* and the underpainting revealed, see "Hidden Painting" (2014) and "Multi-Institutional Collaboration" (2014).

A physical manifestation of Chaucer's threat to the hapless Adam, the Summoner's face exhibits the very visible characteristics of inflammation and infection, the compromised integrity of facial derma implicitly corresponding to inner corruption and contagion:

> A Somonour was ther with us in that place,
> That hadde a fyr-reed cherubynnes face,
> For saucefleem he was, with eyen narwe.
> As hoot he was and lecherous as a sparwe,
> With scalled browes blake and piled berd.
> Of his visage children were aferd. (ll. 623–628)[23]

His manifestation of Adam's "scalle" in his "fyr-red" and "saucefleem" face with "scalled browes" and the "whelkes white," said to defy all known medicinal remedies, results in disfigurement that frightens those who observe it, children in particular. As Sharon E. Rhodes (this volume), observes:

> While these skin conditions may not reveal the exact nature of the sinners' misdeeds, the unmistakability of the presence of skin disease legibly marks them as people to avoid – indeed, Chaucer tells us that "children were aferd" ('children were afraid,' l. 628) of the Summoner's face – and makes each character a cautionary tale: a negative and viscerally grotesque exemplum.

Via clever juxtapositions and assumptions, Chaucer crafts a portrait of someone both repulsive and oblivious, who exacerbates the former with the odoriferous breath of "garleek, onynons, and eek lekes" (ll. 634 and 635)[24] and "strong wyn, reed as blood," (l. 625)[25] and adds to the putrid imagery a hint of menace, that children fear his deformed and repellent visage, and, the narrator implies, with a euphemistic trope ("Ful prively a fynch eek koude he pulle," ll. 663–665),[26] lechery and improper sexual activity, according to Kittredge and others.[27] The latter, by extension in context, hints that the Summoner's vile behavior is at

---

23 'A Summoner was there with us in that place, / Who had a fire-red cherubim's face, / For pimpled and discolored it was, with swollen/narrow eyelids. / As hot he was and lecherous as a sparrow, / With *scalled* [having the skin inflammation scale] brows black, and balding beard, / Of his face children were afraid.'
24 'garlic, onions, and also leeks'
25 'strong wine, red as blood'
26 'Secretly/discreetly a finch also could he pluck'
27 Relevant critical studies of the Summoner include Braswell-Means (1991), Brody (1974), and Cox (1997: 113–133, esp. 116–117) on the indeterminacy of the Summoner's ailment. See also Boswell (1980: 29–31) on labels corresponding to youth.

least partly directed towards the young boys and girls to whom he has access, privately and hidden in his encounters, and for whom he provides incentive to sustain the secret: "In daunger hadde he at his owene gise / The yonge girles of the diocise, / And knew hir conseil, and was al hir reed" (ll. 663–665).[28]

The specific label of the Summoner's malady is neither indicated by name nor by conventionally identifiable details in the portrait. Critics have attempted to assign a speculative diagnosis, leprosy being the most common, following Walter Clyde Curry's (1960: 318) diagnosis: "The Summoner has been afflicted with a species of morphea known as *gutta rosacea*, which has already been allowed to develop into that kind of leprosy called alopecia." And the listed remedies that have failed are those described as curative agents in, for example, *Liber de Diversis Medicinis* (c. 1420s), a bit later than Chaucer's writing but indicative of a similarly accepted medical perspective. Others, including Saul Brody (1974), see the Summoner's affliction as more likely that of scabies, aptly described by Bryon Grigsby (2004: 85): "Scabies is a general term for a scaly skin disease caused by a parasite and is extremely itchy." But, as Grigsby notes, "[t]he essential problem with differentiating between scabies, leprosy, and any number of other skin ailments is that medieval doctors often grouped different types of skin ailments together" (2004: 85), though, he observes, "it seems likely that Chaucer expected the reader to conclude that the Summoner was leprous" (2004: 86). Thomas Garbáty (1963: 358), in his medically oriented analysis, observes in defending his case for a diagnosis of leprosy, specifically the type widely believed to be venereal in origin, "[t]he face of the corrupt Summoner, watchdog of morality, marks his own lechery." In his essay interrogating the tendency of such critics to establish interpretation based on their assuming a particular context, Malcolm Andrew (1989: 318) focuses on "the critical assessment of those moral judgments which Chaucer is taken by some to have intended as an effect of his portraits" and finds their results "unsatisfactory." He observes of Walter Clyde Curry et al.:

> [T]he question of how Chaucer's audience might have responded to the notion of a tight-knit group of pilgrims going cheerily on their way with a manifest leper in their midst is not addressed. Indeed, we may ponder not only how Chaucer's actual audience would have responded to the inclusion of so preposterous an idea in his fictional world, but also, within that fiction, how the fictive audience of pilgrims would have responded to so undesirable a fellow traveler and story-teller

---

28 'In [his] control he had after his own fashion (as he pleased) / The young people of the diocese, / And knew their secrets, and was of all their advisor.'

and notes of this "genuinely critical problem," that "it will hardly be solved by turning to the modern medical dictionary and proclaiming that the Summoner is in fact suffering from 'secondary syphilis (lues II) specifically a rosacea-like secondary syphiloderm with meningeal neurosyphilis'" (Andrew 1989: 323–324). Such overreaching attempts to diagnose fictional characters based on scant evidence can, however, help us gain an appreciation for the connotations of facial disfigurement and their associative if ultimately indeterminate origins. The ambiguities of the Summoner's portrait make a definitive diagnosis impossible, deliberately so, one might argue, as the narrator is impugning the Summoner's overall character rather than aligning him with any one particular foible or sin.

The surface layer of palimpsest, the scalle and whelkes, is correlated by narrator Chaucer with the character's vile indifference to ethics in his accepting of bribes, extorting favors, and, as is implied, abusing young people, boys and girls alike. Pustules, pimples, inflammation, and swelling aren't themselves indicative of evil, of course; ask any teenager combating adolescent acne, for instance. But textually, the juxtaposition of physical and moral attributes, in conjunction with Chaucer's wishful conflation in "Adam" and elsewhere, serves to underscore a figurative connection that readers are implicitly invited to consider further: that something untoward in the Summoner's abuse of office and ethics has occurred, and is evidenced by the physical corruption of the figurative parchment that tells this tale.

The Cook's famous leg ulcer likewise indicates the possibility of a back-story impugning its bearer:

> A Cook they [the guildsmen] hadde with hem for the nones
> To boille the chiknes with the marybones,
> And poudre-marchant tart and galyngale.
> Wel koude he knowe a draughte of Londoun ale [...]
> But greet harm ws it, as it thoughte me,
> That on his shyne a mormal hadde he.
> For blankmanger, that made he with the beste. (ll. 379–387)[29]

The Cook's "mormal" has been variously understood to be "a dry scabbed ulcer, gangrenous rather than cancerous" (Benson 1987: 814 n. 386) or "fetid" pustules (Curry 1960: 48), or "running," "not dry" (Braddy 1946: 267), theories derived

---

[29] 'A Cook they had with them for the occasion / To boil the chickens with the marrow-bones, / And poudre-marchant and galingale spices. / Well he knew how to assess a draft of London ale [...] / But it was a great harm, as it seemed to me, / That on his shin a *mormal* [type of sore] had he. / For white-pudding, that he made with the best [quality].'

from medieval medical writings by Guy de Chauliac, Bernardus de Gordon, and others (Benson 1987: 814 n. 386). The narrator Chaucer in the General Prologue portrait includes the detail so as to highlight an implicit correlation between the damaged and infected skin surface and the moral and ethical traits of the skin's owner/wearer.[30] Erin E. Sweany (this volume) observes:

> The Cook's skin continuously induces suspicion that there is something wrong with him. Both the Canterbury pilgrims and modern scholars combine this sense of wrongness with the Cook's behaviour and the accusations against him to speculate at diagnoses and to read deviance on the Cook's skin.[31]

The "mormal" is implicitly a kind of breach in the surface integrity of the skin that allows for the oozing of pus, if understood to be runny rather than dry, repugnant both physically, owing to the sight and presumed odor of infection, and socially, hinting at the likelihood of hygiene challenge pervasive in body and soul.

Recalled with an affected pity by the narrator Chaucer, the mormal is sardonically juxtaposed with the blancmange illustrative of the Cook's level of culinary skill. More than merely serving as a witty warning against consuming the culinary offerings of one so visibly neglectful of ordinary hygiene, even by late medieval standards, the juxtaposition heightens the reader's sense that the origin story of the Cook's ailment is likely as putrid as the gooey white substance oozing from the mormal, the flow of which unambiguously signals some kind of infection even if, as is the case with the Summoner, an exact diagnosis remains purposefully elusive. While the ethics of a hired cook might not seem to pose much of a threat beyond those in whose employment the Cook's efforts are put to work, the character is arguably a means for the narrator Chaucer to intensify his sequential correlations of skin and ethics without delving into ideological and ecclesiastical abuses for each portrait. Indeed, the Cook's all but irrelevant social presence ironically creates a more unsettling correlation, presented as so ordinary and banal, remarkable only because its visibility prompts the narrator to acknowledge it and remark upon the revulsion it provokes.

Similarly, the facial skin of the Wife of Bath broadcasts an ethical caveat in the implicit text constituted by the marred cutaneous surface of her face and the implications behind the signs of damage. The Woman/Wife is, in the General Prologue sequence, unexpectedly identified by body/sex/gender as a woman rather than the capable artisan and businesswoman in cloth making she is subsequently said to be, in keeping with the vocational identifications of the portrait

---

[30] See also Lynch (2007).
[31] See Sweany (this volume), who explores indeterminacy in greater detail.

sequence. The irregularity in categorical identity would appear to be connected to her being described and portrayed as obsessed with sexual matters, or, more accurately, with her ability to talk about them (the likelihood of their having occurred being suspect to an extent). Unsurprisingly, given the corporeal/gendered emphasis, the Wife is described with details corresponding to her interest in matters of sexual relationships:

> Boold was hir face, and fair, and reed of hewe.
> She was a worthy womman al hir lyve:
> Housboundes at chirche dore she hadde fyve,
> Withouten oother compaignye in youthe –
> But thereof nedeth nat to speke as nowthe. (ll. 457–462)[32]

The Chaucer narrator notes that the facial surface of the Wife of Bath is "boold [...] fair, and reed of hewe," that it is brazen, pleasing, and red in color, indicating that the overall hue (as opposed to the Summoner's localized pockets of inflammation) is one conventionally associated with lustful fixation.[33] Much has been made of the Wife's character in terms of gender, marriage, sexuality, and social hegemony, as noted above, though "she" is of course a literary creation who, like any other Canterbury pilgrim, exists via text; she is only as real as the words that create her portrait and that mimetically assign her the appearance of voice. Within the General Prologue portrait and later in the Canterbury sequence, and thus prior to the General Prologue's being voiced by the narrator in retrospect, the character's own prologue emphasizes her interest in sexual matters, particularly those ostensibly yet ambiguously claimed as autobiography. Hence the portrait's overt association of the bold, fair, red face with conventional symbolic values of lustful thoughts and desires.

In the Wife's case, however, her words of lustful fixation are displaced into the realm of text rather than lived experience. Hence her symbolic appearance additionally corresponds to her self-styled mendacious tendencies ("If that I speke after my fantasye," III.190),[34] as they are designed to titillate both herself and her audience via her act of speaking. The Wife is shown to derive great pleasure from entertaining audiences by speaking of sexual matters with no more authenticating evidence than her own claim of "fantasye." Prepared for

---

32 'Bold was her face, and fair, and red of hue. / She was a worthy woman all her life. / Husbands at the church door [place of marriage] she had five, / Outside of other company in youth – / But there isn't need of that to speak right now.'
33 On the WoB's ruddy hue and its conventional associations, see, for instance, Kennedy (2001: 17–19), Beidler (2000).
34 'If that I speak according to my fantasy/fancy'

her own prologue by the narrator's descriptive correlation of skin and text, readers are expecting the performance's lustful articulations of wishful thinking and purported recollections. As well, as Roberta Magnani (this volume) observes:

> The "Wife of Bath's Prologue" affords a cognate conceptualisation of skin as a site on which meaning is produced, inscribed and disseminated. As she describes her appearance, the Wife specifies: "I hadde the prente of seinte Venus seel" (III.604) [...] her – sensual, wanton and therefore fundamentally sinful – femininity is incontrovertibly signified on her body [...] Much like script on vellum, Alisoun's gender identity is textualised and stabilised corporeally through the "seel" and "prente" of Venus.

While the conventional marker of lust aptly corresponds to the character's subject matter, it is her eagerness for audience and her arrogant self-styled authority that warrants the pilgrims' caution. Isabel Davis (2013: 166) observes of the "incorrigibility of skin-bound humanity" in the "Wife of Bath's Prologue" and *Sir Gawain and the Green Knight*:

> Middle English poets continually wrote these eschatological dramas through the image of skin, making time cutaneous: susceptible, elastic, and plicated; skin, for all its apparent fixity and envelopment, was a way of conveying Christian omnitemporality, recursiveness, and the continued attachment of the past to the present.

Conclusion: *Pellem pro Pelle*

What this illustrative sequence suggests is that despite, or owing to, the tantalizing ultimate unknowability of the words in palimpsest, hidden and elusive and only partially recoverable at best, Chaucer sees a productive correlation between the material reality of a text's literary and social construction and the abstract, intangible potentialities thereby generated. Traces of error on a dermal surface – be their origins textual (as in the case of the hapless Adam's miscopied parchment) or behavioral (as is implied by the Summoner's facial eruptions, the Cook's oozing leg sore, and the Wife's chronic rosacea) – foreground the mimetic reality of tainted/corrupted skin as well as that of the medium by which their generative narratives are disseminated. Dermal blemishes, like scars though temporary, reveal a history, indirectly, signifying a back story that both accounts for the visible disfigurement and produces a context for its readers, as it were, those within the parameters of the fictive pilgrimage and those external to it receiving the *Canterbury Tales* narrative by way of text, the words inscribed on the surface of the manuscript parchment.

Symbolic associations of moral lapse and disease are rampant in medieval literature, as noted above and throughout this volume, and the General Prologue evinces Chaucer's (and, presumably, his readers') awareness of these commonplace images and the negative moral judgments they project, certainly. And yet, like Adam, the scribal doppelganger unaffected by Chaucer's imagined curse punishing hypothetical future instances of indifferent carelessness, these General Prologue pilgrims are described, at least indirectly, as being indifferent to the realities of dermal reflexivity: to whatever personal history is behind their blemished surfaces, and to however that implicit history might be read and understood by those in proximity. They show no concern with the associations that others might discern, and they make no attempt to hide their condition – nor, implicitly, to amend whatever behavior presumably aggravates it into an ongoing, perhaps chronic, manifestation of symptomatic displays. It is of course Chaucer himself who sees the figurative connections and who subtly coaxes his readers into considering the metaphoricity of skin in all its forms, vivifying it by way of dramatization, both in the pilgrimage narrative and its textual reality. "Pellem pro pelle," goes the cryptic and enigmatic biblical proverb (Liber Job 2.4), skin for skin. The skin tells its story.

Works Cited

Primary Sources:

"Archimedes Palimpsest." Issued by the Archimedes Palimpsest Program, April 2004. <http://archimedespalimpsest.org/about/> [accessed 13 September 2014].

Baum, Paull F. (trans.). 1967. *Anglo-Saxon Riddles of the Exeter Book*. Durham: Duke University Press.

Benson, Larry D. (ed.). 1987. *Geoffrey Chaucer: The Riverside Chaucer*. 3rd ed. Boston: Houghton Mifflin.

"Liber Job." In: *Patrologia Latina Database*. Volume 28. Columns 1079–1122. <http://pld.chadwyck.com/> [accessed 20 December 2016].

Ogden, Margaret S. 1938. *Liber de diversis medicinis*. EETS OS 207. London: Oxford University Press.

Winterson, Jeanette. 1992. *Written on the Body*. London: Jonathan Cape.

Secondary Sources:

Andrew, Malcolm. 1989. "Context and Judgment in the *General Prologue*." *The Chaucer Review* 23.4: 316–337.

Beidler, Peter G. 2000. "Chaucer's Wife of Bath's 'Foot-Mantel' and Her 'Hipes Large'." *The Chaucer Review* 34.4: 388–397.

Bitterli, Dieter. 2009. *Say What I Am Called: The Old English Riddles of the Exeter Book & the Anglo-Latin Riddle Tradition*. Toronto: University of Toronto Press.

Boswell, John. 1980. *Christianity, Social Tolerance, and Homosexuality: Gay People in Western Europe from Late Antiquity to the Renaissance*. Chicago: University of Chicago Press.

Braswell-Means, Mary. 1991. "A New Look at an Old Patient: Chaucer's Summoner and Medieval Physiognomia." *The Chaucer Review* 25.3: 266–275.

Brody, Saul. 1974. *Disease of the Soul: Leprosy in Medieval Literature*. Ithaca, NY: Cornell University Press.

Caplan, Jane (ed.). 2000. *Written on the Body: The Tattoo in European and American History*. Princeton: Princeton University Press.

Cox, Catherine S. 1997. *Gender and Language in Chaucer*. Gainesville: University Press of Florida.

Cox, Catherine S. 2004. "Water of Bitterness: The Pardoner and/as the Sotah." *Exemplaria* 16.1: 131–164.

Curry, Walter C. 1960. *Chaucer and the Mediaeval Sciences*. 2nd ed. New York: Barnes and Noble.

Davis, Isabel. 2013. "Cutaneous Time in the Late Medieval Literary Imagination." In: Katie L. Walter (ed.). *Reading Skin in Medieval Literature and Culture*. The New Middle Ages. New York: Palgrave Macmillan. 99–118.

DeMello, Margo. 2000. *Bodies of Inscription: A Cultural History of the Modern Tattoo Community*. Durham: Duke University Press.

Derrida, Jacques. 2002. "The Animal That Therefore I Am (More to Follow)." Trans. David Wills. *Critical Inquiry* 28.2: 369–418.

Desmond, Marilyn and Pamela Sheingorn. 2003. *Myth, Montage, and Visuality in Late Medieval Manuscript Culture*. Ann Arbor: University of Michigan Press.

Dinshaw, Carolyn. 1989. *Chaucer's Sexual Poetics*. Madison: University of Wisconsin Press.

Warwick Frese, Dolores and Katherine O'Brien O'Keeffe (eds.). 1997. *The Book and the Body*. Notre Dame: University of Notre Dame Press.

Garbáty, Thomas. 1963. "The Summoner's Occupational Disease." *Medical History* 7.4: 348–358.

Gellrich, Jesse M. 1985. *The Idea of the Book in the Middle Ages: Language, Theory, Mythology, and Fiction*. Ithaca, NY: Cornell University Press.

Gillespie, Alexandra and Daniel Wakelin (eds.). 2011. *The Production of Books in England, 1350–1500*. Cambridge: Cambridge University Press.

Gillespie, Alexandra. 2008. "Reading Chaucer's Words to Adam." *The Chaucer Review* 42.3: 269–283.

Grigsby, Bryon Lee. 2004. *Pestilence in Medieval and Early Modern English Literature*. New York and London: Routledge.

Hanna, Ralph. 2004. "Middle English Books and Middle English Literary History." *Modern Philology* 102.2: 157–178.

"Hidden Painting Found Under Picasso's *The Blue Room*." Issued by BBC, 17 June 2014. <http://www.bbc.com/news/entertainment-arts-27884323> [accessed 20 June 2014].

Holsinger, Bruce. 2009. "Of Pigs and Parchment: Medieval Studies and the Coming of the Animal." *PMLA* 124.2: 616–623.

Horobin, Simon. 2010. "Adam Pinkhurst, Geoffrey Chaucer, and the Hengwrt Manuscript of the *Canterbury Tales*." *The Chaucer Review* 44.4: 351–367.

Jablonski, Nina G. 2006. *Skin: A Natural History*. Berkeley: University of California Press.

Johnston, Michael. 2014. *Romance and the Gentry in Late Medieval England*. Oxford: Oxford University Press.

Kay, Sarah. 2006. "Original Skin: Flaying, Reading, and Thinking in the Legend of Saint Bartholomew and Other Works." *Journal of Medieval and Early Modern Studies* 36.1: 35–73.

Kennedy, Beverly. 2001. "'Withouten oother compaignye in youthe:' Verbal and Moral Ambiguity in the General Prologue Portrait of the Wife of Bath." In: Robert Myles and David A. Williams (eds.). *Chaucer and Language: Essays in Honour of Douglas Wurtele*. Montreal: McGill-Queen's University Press. 11–32.

Kwakkel, Erik. 2014. "The Skinny on Bad Parchment." In: *Medievalbooks*, 24 October 2014. <https://medievalbooks.nl/2014/10/24/feeling-good-about-bad-skin/> [accessed 5 December 2014].

Lynch, Kathryn L. 2007. "From Tavern to Pie Shop: The Raw, the Cooked, and the Rotten in Fragment 1 of Chaucer's Canterbury Tales." *Exemplaria* 19: 117–138.

MacKendrick, Karmen. 2004. *Word Made Skin: Figuring Language at the Surface of Flesh*. New York: Fordham University Press.

"Making of Medieval Book Exhibit May 20–September 28, 2003." Issued by the J. Paul Getty Museum Center. <http://www.getty.edu/art/exhibitions/making> [accessed 5 December 2014].

Manly, John M. and Edith Rickert (eds.). 1940. *Chaucer: The Text of the Canterbury Tales*. Chicago: University of Chicago Press. Digitized by the Internet Archives, 18 November 2011. <https://archive.org/details/textofcanterbury01manl> [accessed 5 December 2014]

Mann, Vivian B. 2014. "A Shared Tradition: Decorated Bible Pages of Medieval Bibles and Qu'rans." In: Stephen Prickett (ed.). *The Edinburgh Companion to the Bible and the Arts*. Edinburgh: Edinburgh University Press. 160–174.

Mooney, Linne R. and Estelle Stubbs. 2013. *Scribes and the City: London Guildhall Clerks and the Dissemination of Middle English Literature 1375–1425*. Woodbridge and Rochester: York Medieval Press and Boydell Press.

Mooney, Linne R. 2006. "Chaucer's Scribe." *Speculum* 81.1: 97–138.

"Multi-Institutional Collaboration Broadens Understanding of Pablo Picasso's Methods." Issued by The Phillips Collection, 2 September 2014. <http://www.phillipscollection.org/sites/default/files/press_material/press-release-blue-room-collaboration.pdf> [accessed 17 September 2014].

Nyffenegger, Nicole. 2013. "Saint Margaret's Tattoos: Empowering Marks on White Skin." *Exemplaria* 25.4: 267–283.

OED = *The Oxford English Dictionary*. 2000–. 3rd ed. online. Oxford: Oxford University Press. <http://www.oed.com/> [last accessed 20 December 2016].

Olson, Glending. 1979. "Making and Poetry in the Age of Chaucer." *Comparative Literature* 32: 272–290.

Partridge, Stephen. 2012. "'The Makere of this Booke:' Chaucer's *Retraction* and the Author as Scribe and Compiler." In: Stephen Partridge and Erik Kwakkel (eds.). *Author, Reader,*

Book: Medieval Authorship in Theory and Practice. Toronto: University of Toronto Press. 106–153.

Reichardt, Paul F. 1984. "Gawain and the Image of the Wound." *PMLA* 99.2: 154–161.

Reimer, Steven. 2015. "Scribal Error." *Manuscript Studies*, 30 May 2015. <https://sites.ualberta.ca/~sreimer/ms-course/course/scbl-err.htm> [accessed 20 September 2015].

Rigby, Stephen H. 2014. "Reading Chaucer: Literature, History, and Ideology." In: Stephen H. Rigby (ed.). *Historians on Chaucer: The 'General Prologue' to the Canterbury Tales*. Oxford: Oxford University Press. 1–23.

Rudy, Kathryn M. 2015. *Postcards on Parchment: The Social Lives of Medieval Books*. New Haven and London: Yale University Press.

Schmidt, A. V. C. 1987. *The Clerkly Maker*. Cambridge: D. S. Brewer.

Shoaf, Richard A. 2001. *Chaucer's Body: The Anxiety of Circulation in the Canterbury Tales*. Gainesville: University Press of Florida.

Williamson, Craig (ed.). 1977. *The Old English Riddles of the Exeter Book*. Chapel Hill: University of North Carolina Press.

Williamson, Craig. 1982. *A Feast of Creatures*. Philadelphia: University of Pennsylvania Press.

Wright, Thomas (ed.). 1872. *The Anglo-Latin Satirical Poets and Epigrammatists of the Twelfth Century*. London: Longman.

Erin E. Sweany
The Cook's "Mormal:"
Reading Disease, Doubt, and Deviance on the Body of Chaucer's Cook

Abstract: Diseased skin and moral deviance are key characteristics of the Cook in Chaucer's *Canterbury Tales*, but little consideration has been granted to the Cook's skin beyond the mere existence of the *mormal*. This essay reads the Cook's physical characteristics as potential symptoms of leprosy, not to definitively diagnose the Cook but rather to illustrate the pervasive ambiguity of the Cook's physical state. Reading the Cook's potential leprosy as an embodied uncertainty shows the power that such an undefined, afflicted body has over the pilgrims, even when it appears so briefly in the *Tales*, illustrating how damaged skin is the troubled point at which we negotiate the fraught relationship of self and community. Thus, this article also queries conflicting reports about the Cook (by the Cook versus those by his fellow pilgrims) to explore the relationship between the Cook's skin, disease, morality, and language in the *Tales*.

Chaucer's Canterbury pilgrim the Cook first appears in the General Prologue, where he is described in terms of his cookery skills and the infamous *mormal* on his leg, a vaguely described skin sore that has become one of many points of speculation about the Cook. Following the "Reeve's Tale," the Cook has a brief prologue (thirty-nine lines in which the Host accuses him of handling food unhygienically and of making his customers sick) followed by an only slightly longer fragmentary tale (fifty-two lines) of the irresponsible, thieving apprentice Perkyn Revelour. The fragment ends abruptly with Perkyn dismissed by his master and taking up with a companion who, like Perkyn, enjoys "dys, and revel, and disport" (l. 4420)[1] and has a wife who works as a prostitute. The Cook's final appearance is in the "Manciple's Prologue," where he is mocked and berated by the Host and the Manciple for his sleepiness and apparent drunkenness. The Cook's participation in the frame narrative of the *Canterbury Tales* is thin and his character and role are articulated mostly through his ambiguous dialogical links to the other characters and the abrupt termination of his tale.

---

1 'dice, and revel, and merry-making.' Translations are my own unless otherwise noted. All quotations from the *Canterbury Tales*, cited by line number, are from Benson (1987).

Chaucer's Cook has thus long been a figure of frustration and speculation for modern scholars.

Because there is no clear literary source for this tale, scholars have looked to history to develop strategies for reading the Cook and his tale. With this reliance on history comes a persistent interest in the historical authenticity of the Cook as a character – the possibility that Chaucer's inspiration for the Cook can be found in historical records (Lyon 1937); the naturalness of a cook's rivalry with a hosteller and a manciple (Tupper 1915: 261–265; Gray 1987: 852 ll. 4345–4352; Scattergood 1987: 953 ll. 46–47); the believability of the Cook's (un)professional activities (Carney Forkin 2007; Lynch 2007); or the insistence that the Cook's leg *mormal* can be precisely diagnosed (Skeat 1900; Curry 1921; Braddy 1946). Diagnosis in modern, medical terms tends to shut down interpretation, in that the diagnosis seems to solve the problem, answer the question, so that no further analysis is needed because the meaning of the symptom has been found. As an exercise, it suggests that if we can only know what is wrong with the Cook, perhaps then we will know what Chaucer meant by him. Skeat (1900: 37–38 l. 386) defines the *mormal* as "a cancer or gangrene" whereas Curry (1921: 274–276) describes the *mormal* as "a species of ulcerated, dry-scabbed apostema which is produced by the corruption in the blood of natural melancholia, or sometimes of melancholia combined with *salsum phlegma*." Curry also speculates that such a sore would have been extremely itchy. Braddy (1946: 267) agrees with Curry that *mormal* must refer to an ulcer or sore, but determines that the affliction was not a dry and scabby one but a wet and oozing one; and she further implies that the uncontained product of the sore could be contaminating the Cook's dishes.[2] Braddy's insinuation is made explicit by Jill Mann (1973: 168–170) who uses Braddy's characterization of the *mormal* as wet and oozing to transcend one-dimensional material readings of it. Mann sees special significance in the association of a physically revolting skin disease with the Cook's profession. She argues that the Cook is characterized by his work-life and he produces disgust in an audience because of the juxtaposition of his skin disease with his role as a food preparer. Mann reads the *mormal* as a site of not just physical deviance, but also of openness and legibility.

---

[2] The image of the *mormal* seeping fluid has evoked speculation about the contents of the Cook's *blancmanger* since Braddy implied it could be contaminated. Skeat (1900: 37–38 l. 387) lists a blancmanger as "a compound made of capon minced, with rice, milk, sugar, and almonds [...] named for its white color." For further information about this ubiquitous medieval dish, see the scholarship on medieval food and cooking by Scully (2005: 188–194) and Hieatt (1995).

This essay proposes that the physical openness of the Cook to the world is the key to the difficult legibility of both the Cook and his tale. Building on Mann's argument, it explores the possibilities inherent in the Cook's physical deviance and questions the perception of that deviance by modern scholars and Chaucer's other Canterbury pilgrims. Scholars have already spent a considerable amount of time considering the unfinished nature – the openness – of the tale. Higl (2012) reads the "Cook's Tale" as a riddle in the way it has provoked, since at least the fifteenth century, an impulse in its audiences to provide an ending – an "answer," in riddle parlance.³ Other recent scholars who have argued for the intentional, or at least satisfactory or formally sound, openness of the tale include Bahr (2016), Pigg (2012), Casey (2006), Burakov (2002), and Kang (1997). The paleographic and codicological openness of the manuscripts of this portion of the *Tales* is dealt with by Casey (2006) and Beadle (1992). The *mormal* can be read as a revolting door to the literary significance of the Cook and his tale, demanding that the reader focus on the Cook's body, though scholars have historically looked past or away from that body. The scholarly consensus is that the Cook's body is deviant due to the Cook's moral deviance – he is often referred to with some version of the phrase "Chaucer's drunken Cook," an offense of which both the Host and the Manciple accuse him. Certainly, body and morality are inseparable in the Middle Ages; for example, Virginia Langum (2013) traces the interrelation of the skin as revelatory of both sickness and sin back to Augustine and explains that the opacity of the skin and of language were understood as effects of the human fall from grace, a parallel that materially links diseased skin with a deviant soul.⁴ This reflective interrelationship of skin and soul, along with the metaphorical use of surgical terms in confessional texts to describe how confession is drawn out of the sinner, is further important, Langum argues, for understanding the medieval valuation of a careful and gentle extraction of sins from the penitent – harsh examination would be akin to physical violence.

Diseased skin and moral deviance are key characteristics of Chaucer's Cook, but little consideration has been granted to the Cook's skin and what might be read on it and through it beyond the mere existence of the *mormal*. Even less consideration has been given to the Cook's feeble insistence on his own physical state, although the aggressive assertions of the Host and the Manciple are gen-

---

3 Pinti (1996) reviews the alternate endings and tales that appear in medieval manuscripts following the "Cook's Prologue."
4 Furthermore, Cox, in her contribution to the present volume, discusses Chaucer's use of diseased skin as a signifier of suspect moral character in the case of the Summoner, the Cook, and the Wife of Bath to argue that Chaucer included a "sequential [correlation] of skin and ethics" in the *Canterbury Tales*.

erally accepted as accurate representations of the Cook's physical and moral status. Given Langum's (2013) firm linking of skin and spoken language in medieval confession and the further medical metaphors used in the practice of confession, we should be prompted to a closer examination of the Cook by the intersection of his skin disorder, his self-perception and the claims he makes, and other characters' perceptions of and claims about the Cook. This article proposes to dwell on the Cook's skin to find that, like his *mormal*, the Cook's body is a site of uncertainty. Medieval skin is the primary medieval human experience with liminality, marking bodies as simultaneously *apart from* and *a part of* – as forever physically individuated from all other bodies while also pointing toward the community of which the individual is a part of the composition. Damaged skin is the troubled point at which we negotiate the fraught relationship of self and community. Thus, this article also queries conflicting reports about the Cook (by the Cook versus those by his fellow pilgrims – his community) to explore the relationship between the Cook's skin, disease, morality, and language in the *Tales*.

The Cook is a disruptive figure for both the pilgrims and Chaucer's readers. We see from the description of the Cook in the General Prologue that his two defining characteristics are his cooking abilities and his leg sore. His physical form and his tale are punctuated with a gaping wound, the genesis and substance of both a mystery to the reader. Chaucer first calls attention to the Cook's skin, and the damage to it, in the General Prologue, where he very briefly states that "But greet harm was it, as it thought me, / That on his shyne a mormal hadde he" (ll. 385–386).[5] Certainly the twentieth-century arguments over the nature of the *mormal* – a dangerous cancer, a filthy, dry scab, or a runny sore, all possibly with a strong smell – are more stomach-turning than the narrator's original description (see above for the evolution of these readings). There are few certainties about the *mormal*; the terminology and the description are inadequate to make any diagnosis unquestionable. Furthermore, the Middle English description of the *mormal* as a "harm" (*MED harm* n.) immediately evokes ambiguity, as it refers to a range of states: physical damage done, an "injury," "a diseased part of the body," "moral evil," and "pain," among other similar concepts. Thus, we see that the Cook's *mormal* is something that the narrator highlights as a site that demands interpretation by the reader. With the implication of physical harm, illness, and moral deviance, the *mormal* might label the Cook as a victim or invalid of some sort (having been injured or having an illness), or he might be an unwholesome presence.

---

5 'But it seemed a great *harm* to me / that on his shin a *mormal* had he'

Reading uncertainty alongside of (instead of as a hindrance to the meaning of) the *mormal* is productive when one considers the further appearances of the Cook in the *Tales*. When the three appearances of the Cook are considered together, it is apparent that Chaucer calls our attention repeatedly, yet always with accompanying uncertainty, to the Cook's skin. The initial reference to the *mormal* in the General Prologue as something the narrator regards as a *greet harm* is echoed in both dermal focus and obscure style by an oblique reference to (questionably) itchy skin in the Cook's own prologue and to pale skin in the "Manciple's Prologue." It is this last appearance by the Cook, in the final fragment of the *Tales*, where the Cook's pallor is mentioned three times – once by the Manciple and twice by the narrator. The narrator describes the Cook as "ful pale and no thing reed" (l. 20);[6] after the Cook falls off his horse the narrator exclaims, "So unwieldy was this sory palled goost"[7] that he could remount only with "greet showvyng bothe to and fro" (l. 55)[8] and "muchel care and wo" (ll. 53–54).[9] The Manciple says he will rescue the Cook from having to tell a tale while in poor health: "I wol as now excuse thee of thy tale. / For, in good faith, thy visage is ful pale" (ll. 29–30).[10] The meaning of these references is fraught. Accusations of drunkenness by the Host and the Manciple in the Cook's final appearance have long coloured modern readings of the Cook, but these accusations do not reflect a thorough reading of the Cook's body nor a serious attention to the Cook's own words.

The representation of the Cook's alarming and readable skin at both the beginning and the end of the entire tale collection asks the reader to notice the unhealthy state of the Cook's body. The Cook has been variously labelled an unhygienic glutton, the proprietor of an unsanitary (and therefore dangerous) shop, a drunk, a lecher, a phlegmatic, and a spiritual leper. All of these labels suggest a man who is dangerous to society, a corrupting influence (Bertolet 2002). The Cook's skin continuously induces suspicion that there is something wrong with him. Both the Canterbury pilgrims and modern scholars combine this sense of wrongness with the Cook's behaviour and the accusations against him to speculate at diagnoses and to read deviance on the Cook's skin. Taken together, these alternate readings reveal the Cook to be a body onto which is collectively written the uncertain danger of a physical and spiritual sickness. Our

---

6 'entirely pale and not at all red'
7 'So unwieldy was this sorry, pallid ghost'
8 'great shoving to and fro'
9 'much care and woe'
10 'I will now excuse you from your [tale-telling responsibilities]. Because, [I say] in good faith, your visage is entirely pale'

very impulse to definitively diagnose him is a symptom of our discomfort with his indeterminacy.

I will show how the Cook's attributes, as given by the narrator and interpreted by the Host and the Manciple, combine to cast a shadow of both disease and doubt onto scholarly certainties about what is wrong with the Cook by analysing the details in the text as symptoms of leprosy, not to definitively diagnose the Cook but rather to illustrate the pervasive ambiguity of the Cook's physical state. Reading the Cook's leprosy as an embodied uncertainty shows the power that such an undefined, afflicted body has over the pilgrims, even when it appears so briefly in the *Tales*. In order to investigate the Cook as a figure of disease, I will first show how leprosy can be mapped onto the Cook's symptoms. But this diagnosis is not meant to fix the state of the Cook's physical body; rather, I show how the diverse symptoms of medieval leprosy in fact unmoor the Cook from a single diagnosis, either moral or physical. Understanding the Cook in light of his leprous symptoms offers insight into the overlay of medical and moral maladies of the Middle Ages and, more importantly, illustrates the multivalent nature of the Cook's symptoms and how they produce an indeterminate figure of disease.

"What eyleth thee?"

In the present volume, Michael Leahy and Sealy Gilles, in their respective essays, explore the broad range of medieval genres that put the leprous body to ideological use. Furthermore, they both engage with the leprous body as a site of societal dis-ease. Leahy's essay "Reading Leprous Skin in Late Medieval Culture" argues that the medieval leper as a textual figure is "protean" in form and appears in diverse medieval genres precisely because the leper was, to medieval audiences, a figure of "productive disgust." Gilles' contribution "Doctrinal Dermatologies" looks at the progression of textual leprosy, concluding that the representation of leprosy collapsed in complexity over the course of the Middle Ages, moving from a socially manageable (and well-managed) disease to a symbol of innate and inevitable corruption. Carole Rawcliffe explains some of the historical reasons behind the medieval leper's multiplicative identities in her comprehensive 2006 book *Leprosy in Medieval England*, in which she describes leprosy as a miasma of physical symptoms, with sometimes conflicting religious implications. Medieval humoral medicine regarded leprosy as a condition that could have a range of manifestations depending on the natural humoral state of the body that was afflicted.[11] Because the medieval version of humoral medicine attributed different natural balances to individuals based on sex and age, and because humoral balance could be easily shifted through "diet, environment, heredity and lifestyle," the presentation of leprosy was not uniform. Additionally, the symptoms could vary based on which humour had been thrown out of balance. To compound this complexity, a patient could experience a combination of unbalanced humours, resulting in many permutations of symptoms (Rawcliffe 2006: 71–75). In addition to physical causes and symptoms, leprosy was also inextricably bound up with spiritual health, being a state visited upon the body as punishment from God and paradoxically also a state associated with the body of Christ at his crucifixion (and therefore a state desirable to the penitent). Rawcliffe (2006: 47) points out that the positive quality of human suffering could "be regarded as an enviable opportunity for personal redemption, or even as a mark of divine grace. The moral stature, or spiritual health, of the individual was therefore crucial in determining his or her culpability, for saints as well as sinners might be leprous." Thus, medieval leprosy was a disease composed of a web of physical, spiritual, and social experiences and expectations.

Even with these myriad components, medieval leprosy was absolutely signalled visually, written on the skin in sores, cracks, pustules, and swellings. It is here we return to the Cook, because although he does not suffer from the full body disfigurements characteristic of the elephantiasis form of leprosy (the most severe form),[12] the *mormal* on his leg is, to the narrator, a *greet harm* (l. 385), a textually implied visual cue of leprous possibilities. Medieval leprosy is so enmeshed with spiritual health and therefore moral judgment that the combination of the *mormal* and the criticisms of the Cook by the pilgrims insistently raise the spectre of leprosy. In addition to the *mormal*, the Cook is associated with half a dozen other symptoms of leprosy. Combining

---

11 This model of bodily composition was based on Greek texts and filtered through Latin, Hebrew, and Islamic translations and scholarship (and then eventually into medieval Latin). It posits a body composed of the same four elements – earth, water, fire, and air – that made up the entirety of creation. The interactions of the qualities of these elements (coldness, moisture, heat, and dryness) were concretized in bodily fluids called the humours (melancholia, choler, phlegm, and blood). The ratio of humours in a body determined the governing humoral quality of a body: "The melancholic humour was cold, dry and earthy; the phlegmatic humour cold and wet, like water; the choleric humour hot and dry, like fire; and the sanguine hot, wet and airy" (Rawcliffe 2006: 65).
12 Elephantiasis was originally a condition accompanied by severe skin problems distinct from leprosy, but by Chaucer's age the distinction had been lost for centuries, and instead it was regarded as the most severe and invasive form of leprosy (Rawcliffe 2006: 74–78).

the narrator's, Host's, and Manciple's observations in each appearance of the Cook we have a man with pale skin, weakness, bad breath, immoderate sexual appetites, a violent temper, possibly itchy skin, a distorted voice (sounding hoarse and congested), and "dazed" (*MED daswen* v.) eyes.[13] These symptoms are general, but are all included or suggested in the thirteenth-century treatise by Gilbert the Englishman that compiled and summarized existing literature on leprosy.[14]

Additionally, if Chaucer means for his audience to understand the Cook as a leper, the destination of Canterbury is particularly apropos.[15] The shrine of Thomas à Becket was, by Chaucer's time, a well-established place for leprosy cures. Bathing leprous sores with healing waters was a common treatment for leprosy, and Becket's shrine was particularly known for healing waters that supposedly contained the blood of the saint. The shrine was a site of miraculous healing, and tales of healed lepers are one of the most pervasive types of miracles in the earliest recorded accounts of Thomas' miracles.[16] In William Fitz Stephen's account of these miracles, William makes a note of the number of lepers cured, asking: "Quid putas, agit inpraesentiarum Dominus curando tot leprosos?" (Robertson and Sheppard 1965 [1875]: I, 333).[17] The passage goes on to explain that, in fact, Thomas à Becket was chosen by God to be martyred for the purpose of making leprosy as curable as other physical ailments: "necessarium fuit hostiam vivam mactari, Deoque placentem, quae lepram, sicut et caeteras

---

[13] The narrator states that the Cook enjoyed the "Reeve's Tale" as much as a good back-scratching, suggesting that he might experience itchy skin: "The Cook of Londoun, whil the Reve spak, / For joye him thought he clawed him on the bak" ('The Cook of London, while the Reeve spoke, / thought that he scratched him on the back because of [his feeling of] joy [in the Reeve's tale],' ll. 4325–4326).

[14] Chaucer names Gilbert as a medical authority in his initial description of the physician (l. 434). Gilbert was a well-known, and indeed celebrated, medical authority both in England and on the continent (Rawcliffe 2006: 7; Wallis 2010: 339–341).

[15] Bertolet (2002: 229) states that the Cook is only present on the pilgrimage as a professional and not as a pilgrim. However, I would add that the presence of the Cook in a professional capacity does not immediately obviate a personal reason for his taking a job on a pilgrimage.

[16] The two earliest primary accounts of Thomas' miracles composed by William Fitz Stephen and Benedict of Peterbourgh privilege leprosy cures by clustering them together. Leprosy is, in general, one of the most oft-cured ailments by the saint. These accounts and others are available in Robertson and Sheppard (1965), a comprehensive edition of the medieval accounts of Thomas' life and miracles. See also Rawcliffe (2006: 170–171).

[17] 'Why, do you think, God is now curing so many lepers?' All Latin quotations of Thomas' miracles are from Robertson and Sheppard (1965). All translations are my own (as are any mistakes or inaccuracies). Thanks are due to my colleague Sean Tandy for reviewing my translation of this passage, and to the editors of this collection who made suggestions for improving them.

languores curare" (I, 333).¹⁸ The passage then goes on to celebrate Thomas' martyrdom and recount how many kinds of leprosy the saint cures. Finally, the answer emphasizes the superiority of the healing power of God over the healing powers of man (since God can heal spiritual leprosy as well as physical leprosy), a common message found in William's account of the miracles.¹⁹ The late twelfth-century Miracle Windows in Trinity Chapel in Canterbury Cathedral depict lepers who had been cured by Saint Thomas.²⁰ One of these windows is an image of Elias the leprous monk, whose account is present in both major miracle collections. Elias lies to his abbot so he can leave the monastery and travel to Canterbury for the healing waters. On the road, he encounters pilgrims returning from a pilgrimage to the site who give the monk a vial of the water, which cures him.²¹ Lepers could be represented pictorially with bespeckled skin, such as in the image of Elias in the stained glass of Trinity Chapel in Cambridge Cathedral. It is suggestive of medieval receptions of the Cook that the early fifteenth-century illustrator of the respective miniature in the Ellesmere manuscript depicted the Cook's entire leg as bare to reveal the mormal as a series of red dots occupying the space from the knee to the ankle and covered by an insufficient bandage. Mullaney (1999: 49) remarks that the bandage is "dirtied with a darker pigment and signs of infection are spreading out from beneath it in a rash of lurid, red spots of paint."²² Further miracle stories of Thomas include tales of leprosy that result from immoderate physical appetites, such as the tale of Odo de Beaumont, a penitent leper who had become leprous after consorting with a prostitute but is cured by a visit to the shrine (one of the earlier miracles attributed to Saint Thomas) (Rawcliffe 2006: 84–85).²³ Perhaps Chaucer

---

18 'it had become necessary that a living sacrifice be made, one that was pleasing to God, and that cured leprosy just as it cured other diseases'
19 Spiritual leprosy is described in this account as a disfigurement of the soul (*decor animarum sua lepra deturpatur*) (I, 333).
20 There is a third depiction of a leper in the same windows, but the identity of the leper is uncertain (Rawcliffe 2006: 171).
21 William of Canterbury has Elias meeting a group of pilgrims on the road, Benedict's account of Elias has the monk meeting only a single pilgrim, a knight. For William's recounting of Elias' pilgrimage see Robertson and Sheppard (1965: I, 417) and for Benedict's Robertson and Sheppard (1965: II, 242). Rawcliffe (2006: 175) remarks that Elias' case seems to be on the spectrum of leprosy at a more curable stage.
22 Mullaney (1999: 48–49) regards the Cook as artistically represented as a disgusting fool-like figure. She notes that the illuminator seems quite critical of the Cook and willing to take liberties to express his judgement, depicting him in shabby and insufficient clothing even though Chaucer does not describe the Cook's attire.
23 The tale of Odo can be found in Robertson and Sheppard (1965: I, 340).

had this story in mind when he gave the Cook part of a tale in which Perkyn Revelour goes to live with a prostitute.

For Chaucer's readers, the physical location of the fictional pilgrimage invokes a range of associations with leprosy: from Becket's well-circulated tales of miraculous healing, to the images of leprous suffering told in stained glass in the Trinity Windows, and finally, to the geographic proximity of the shrine to one of the earliest leper hospitals in England. Saint Nicholas' Hospital in Harbledown,[24] just outside of Canterbury and on the road from London, was well established by the fourteenth century.[25] Indeed, Henry II, on his pilgrimage to Canterbury in penance for Thomas' murder, stopped at St. Nicholas' to pray for forgiveness and make a substantial donation.[26] Chaucer invokes this location the last time we see the Cook, in the "Manciple's Prologue," giving prime place to the lines: "Woot ye nat where ther stant a litel toun / Which that ycleped is Bobbe-up-and-doun, / Under the Blee, in Caunterbury Weye?" (ll. 1–3).[27] These are the first three lines of the "Manciple's Prologue," and the narrator not only mentions the location where the Cook is so overcome with fatigue that he falls asleep on his horse but also engages the knowledge of the audience by asking, "Do you not know where a little town stands?" By asking a knowledgeable medieval audience to envision the town and the path to it (and thus

---

[24] This is the generally accepted location of the "litel toun / Which that ycleped is Bobbe-up-and-doun" (ll. 1–2), with "Bobbe-up-and-doun" speculated to be a corruption of Harbledown as noted by Scattergood (1987: 952 n. 2–3). Baker (1984: 79–80) reviews past debates about the location.

[25] Leper houses were not prison-like and the purpose was not the segregation of lepers. Rawcliffe (2006: ch.1) explains that strictly enforced segregation of medieval lepers was more of a nineteenth-century invention than a medieval reality. In the sixth and seventh chapter of Rawcliffe (2006), we see that the hospital rules shaped the spaces as monastic environments, promoting lives of chastity and prayer, while also providing care for sick bodies. While there was increasing fear of contagion, particularly following the plague in the mid-fourteenth century, the leper hospitals remained a refuge for the sick more often than not, rather than a prison. Rawcliffe (2006: 95) notes: "Even in the plague-ridden years of the later Middle Ages, well informed men and women recognized that the humoral balance or temperament of the individual would, in the final resort, determine his or her vulnerability to external influences."

[26] Rawcliffe (2006: 45–46, 149) also notes that Becket had invoked Uzziah in a warning to Henry II: "this warlike ruler had been smitten with leprosy 'in the forehead' for his presumption in defying the servers in the Temple and burning incense there." An exploration of the political tensions between Thomas and Henry II, the invocations of leprosy by Thomas in their feud, and Chaucer's possible references to leprosy would be fascinating, but beyond the scope of this study.

[27] 'Do you not know where a little town stands / that is called Bob-up-and-Down / alongside Blean Forest, on the road to Canterbury'

calling to mind the presence of Saint Nicholas' Hospital), Chaucer makes a sly suggestion about the significance of the location to the action.[28]

It is at Harbledown, near both a leper hospital and the shrine of Thomas à Becket, where the Cook's body and identity become openly contested. The "Manciple's Prologue" contains the most sustained participation of the Cook in the *Tales*, taking up one hundred and four lines, a shade over the ninety-seven lines of the "Cook's Prologue" and the "Cook's Tale" combined. In the Cook's portrait, the narrator says that the Cook's *mormal* is a *harm*, and now (l. 385), in the "Manciple's Prologue," the Cook insists: "As ther is falle on me swich hevynesse, / Noot I nat why, that me were levere slepe / Than the beste galon wyn in Chepe" (ll. 22–24).[29] Thus, in the characterization of the Cook, the narrator lists external hints of disease (see discussion of *MED harm* n. above), while the Cook simultaneously offers his own admission that he feels internally burdened. The other pilgrims, however, are committed to ignoring the Cook's declaration of bodily uncertainty and instead become enraged (the Manciple) and start mocking the Cook for sleeping on his horse (the Host). Harry Bailey, mocking the Cook for sleeping on his horse, asks:

> What eyleth thee to slepe by the morwe?
> Hastow had fleen al nyght, or artow dronke?
> Or hastow with some quene al nyght yswonke,
> So that thow mast nat holden up thyn heed? (ll. 16–19).[30]

In these lines, the Host suggests a variety of morally compromising attributes or behaviours that, in his mind, could explain the Cook's lethargy: that he is unhygienic (and thus flea-bitten), that he is a drunkard, and that he has immoderate sexual appetites. These accusations have helped to establish the Cook as Chauc-

---

28 Kensak (2001: 225) notes the nearness of Harbledown to Beckett's shrine and claims of the Cook's tumble into the dirt: "The Cook falls from his horse near Harbledown [...] which marks the beginning of the approach to the shrine of Thomas à Becket. The leaden Cook is transformed into dirt [...] just as the walls of Canterbury are coming into view over the trees of the Blee forest." Kensak is appealing to medieval alchemy to argue that the Cook is spiritually leaden and the events in the "Manciple's Prologue" are a mockery of the spiritual renewal that was a goal of medieval pilgrimage.
29 'Because such a heaviness has fallen on me, which I know not why, I would rather sleep than [drink] the best gallon of wine in Cheap[side]'
30 'What ails you that you sleep during the day? / Have you had fleas [biting you] all night or are you drunk? / Have you been laboring with a woman all night? / So that you might now not hold up your head?' *Yswonke* is from *MED swinken* v. which can, and very clearly does here, imply sexual activity. *MED queen* n.[1] b here refers to a woman in a pejorative sense: "a lowborn woman, quean; also, a harlot; also as a term of abuse."

er's ne'er-do-well pilgrim. In what follows, I will examine these possibilities in light of the suggestions of leprosy above and all three appearances of the Cook in the *Tales*.

"Hastow had fleen al nyght?"

The Host suggests that the Cook is sleepy because he has been awake all night scratching at vermin, implying that he is unclean. This is also evoked in the "Cook's Prologue" wherein the Host accuses the Cook of making his customers ill with unsanitary food. In the prologue to his tale, the Cook expresses his enjoyment of the preceding "Reeve's Tale," recites a moral to the story, and then says that he will tell a tale. The Host responds to the Cook by giving him leave to continue with a tale but warns him to tell a good one. Seemingly by way of rationalizing his suggestion that the products of the Cook's imagination require such a warning, he accuses the Cook of being an untrustworthy food vendor, doctoring the foodstuffs he sells in his shop and serving food that causes illness:

> Now telle on, Roger; looke that it be good,
> For many a pastee hastow laten blood,
> An many a Jakke of Dovere hastow soold
> That hath been twies hoot and twies coold.
> Of many a pilgrym hastow Cristes curs,
> For of they percely yet they fare the wors,
> That they han eten with thy stubble goos,
> For in thy shoppe is many a flye loos.
> Now tell on, gentil Roger by thy name.
> But yet I pray thee, be nat wroth for game;
> A man may seye ful sooth in game and pley. (ll. 4345–4355)[31]

These accusations by the Host, with the veneer of jest, name the Cook as someone who is willing to allow flies to remain loose in his shop and feed his customers substandard wares, from greens that will make them ill (and thus cause diners to curse the Cook) to pies that are several days old. The Cook's uncleanness is the most popular explanation for the presence of his *mormal*. We see this in Wal-

---

[31] 'Now continue your story, Roger; but see to it that it is good. You have let blood from many a pasty and sold many a Jack of Dover that has been twice hot and twice cold. You have had Christ's curse from many a pilgrim because they fared the worse for your parsley which they had eaten with your stubbly goose, for many a fly is loose in your shop. Now continue telling your tale, gentle Roger, by your name. But yet, I pray to you, do not be angry at the [tale-telling] game; a man might say the truth in both game and play.'

ter Clyde Curry's (1960: 50–51) work on the tale when he uses it to diagnose the Cook with *malum mortuum*, a skin condition "caused in the first place by uncleanly [sic] personal habits, such as lack of frequent bathing and the continuous wearing of soiled clothes, by the eating of melancholic foods and the drinking of strong wines, and by disgraceful association with diseased and filthy women." Curry's anachronistic moralizing is a positivist mode of scholarship that inadvertently models the medieval conflation of physical pathologies with moral pathologies.[32] Although Curry does not offer leprosy as a potential diagnosis, most of the behaviour listed above and included by Curry in his analysis could indicate leprosy, given a fuller consideration of the Cook's appearances in the *Tales*.

The Host's aspersions carry more weight than just the audience's disgust and suggest harm greater than food poisoning. There is potentially more at stake for the Cook than the purity of his *blancmanger*. Among the possible earthly causes of leprosy in the medieval period are "contaminated foodstuffs, most notably rancid oil and lard, infected pork, and rotten fish" (Rawcliffe 2006: 78–80). Furthermore, flyblown meat was thought to cause leprosy if eaten and if one *sells* food, as the Cook does, the danger of illness is spread from himself to his customers if authorities did not enforce food safety regulations: "Since the poor often had little choice to consume flyblown mean, the responsibility for removing 'pokky' or leprous wares from urban markets lay squarely at the door of local authorities" (Rawcliffe 2006: 78–80).[33] Thus, when the Host references old pies and fly infestations he may be alerting the pilgrims to a more significant danger than is initially obvious from encountering the Cook on pilgrimage. Additionally, the Host's accusations that the Cook is doctoring his old wares to sell as fresh includes medical imagery that has not been appreciated in the context of the Cook as a diseased character. The Host accuses the Cook of *laten blood* ('let blood') from his pies to make them seem fresh when they are not (l. 4346). This is certainly a reference to the widespread medieval (and beyond) practice of stra-

---

32 Rawcliffe (2006: ch. 1) discusses this movement in regards to leprosy. For information on the rise of the hygiene movement that was occurring during the birth of bacteriology and contributed significantly to anachronistic re-diagnosing of the past, see "Strong Microbes and Weak Hygienists" in Latour (1988). More recently, Whitney (2011: 369) has diplomatically moderated this moralizing to "[slothfulness] in his professional duties" in her diagnosis of the Cook as Chaucer's phlegmatic man.

33 An alternative interpretation is offered by Bertolet (2002: 234–235), who reads the parsley stuffing as the culprit of illness. He also argues that a problem with the Cook's food is that a legal statute made it illegal to use goose in pies (although the pies and the goose could be referring to two entirely different dishes).

tegically opening a patient's vein and allowing them to bleed to correct a humoral imbalance. The cook who *laten blood* from his pies is selling old pies, which are possibly beginning to go bad, but hiding it by draining off leaking liquids that might belie a claim of freshness. So, while the shadow of leprosy, specifically, is a peripheral one, disease in general is raised explicitly. Certainly, the Host's descriptions of old food and loose flies suggests more danger to the Cook's customers than to the Cook himself, but the descriptions cement the Cook as a figure of disease. Ambiguity is also an ever-present aspect of the Cook's identity, as we can see in the above passage where the Host concludes by asking the Cook to take his words in jest, but then warns him that "game and play" can nonetheless convey truth. Thus, Harry Bailey is asking the Cook to interpret this unsolicited review as simultaneously *game* and *sooth* (i.e., both a joke – implying falseness presented for enjoyment – and truth). Rhetorically, the Cook is, from his first interaction with the other pilgrims, being figured as uncertain – as belonging to both *sooth* and *game*.[34]

"Artow dronke?"

The Cook's drunkenness is by far the label most accepted in modern scholarship.[35] The case for it is not really made, so much as there is a history of taking Chaucer at his word (placed in the mouths of the Host and the Manciple). The Manciple and the Host turn the Cook into the butt of their jokes, and we have accepted this as the Cook's identity. Rather than letting the antagonistic Host and Manciple entirely determine the Cook's identity, we should instead regard indeterminacy as a state at least worth weighing against the claims of the Cook's apparent enemies. After all, scholars generally do not accept that Chaucer expects his readers to simply take the Reeve's word on the Miller's character. The Cook does not have much that is definite to say for himself; but he does object to the accusations of the Host and Manciple in terms that reinforce his own inde-

---

34 This slipperiness is perhaps carried even further with the word *pley* which is presented with *game* and thus seems immediately interpretable as MED *plei(e)* n., a reference to entertainment and merry making. However, the distinct word MED *plē* n. (sometimes spelled *plei*) refers to a conflict or complaint. Conflict, as we will see, characterizes the Cook's interactions with the other pilgrims that he is shown interacting with.
35 Gray (2003: 111) accepts this without doubt: "His skill in strong London ale leads to an unfortunate fall later, when his horse throws him, and he has to be lifted back, with considerable difficulty." Even Getz (1991: 89), who is considering the Cook in the context of medieval medicine, regards the Cook as only a drunkard, a character prone to excess.

terminacy. As will be presented below, the Cook feels unwell but has no conception of (or will not admit to) a reason.

After the Cook is discovered to have fallen asleep on his horse, the Host offers his accusatory list of possibilities as to why the Cook is so tired (as detailed above), while the Manciple initially speaks to the Cook courteously and even perhaps sympathetically, offering to tell a tale in place of the Cook and reiterating the narrator's observation that the Cook is pale while adding that his eyes look dazed:

> "Wel," quod the Maunciple, "if it may doon ese
> To thee, sire Cook, and to no wight displese
> Which that heere rideth in this compaignye,
> And that oure Hoost wole, of his curteisye,
> I wol as now excuse thee of thy tale.
> For, in good feith, thy visage is ful pale,
> Thyne eyen daswen eek, as that my thynketh [...]" (ll. 25–31)[36]

In the passage immediately above are traits that mark the Cook's body as ambiguous. The description by the Manciple of the Cook as "ful pale" echoes the description of the Miller in his prologue "for dronken was al pale" (l. 3120).[37] But, unlike the Miller who exhibits some self-awareness in his avowal that he knows he is drunk,[38] or the Pardoner who loudly insists on pausing for a drink and a cake before telling his tale, the Cook does not admit to being drunk or drinking anything at all. He claims he does not know why he would rather sleep. Paleness is an oft-mentioned trait of lepers; their skin was said to be light in colour and uncommonly smooth, hairless, and free of wrinkles. Additionally, their visages were said to be horrible to look at, partially due to their red-rimmed, runny, and protruding eyes.[39] This is perhaps a lot for Chaucer's description of the Cook's eyes as *daswen* to bear; but *MED daswen* v.[40] is a vague and thus flexible

---

[36] "'Well,' said the Manciple, 'if it may give relief to you, Sir Cook, and not displease anyone who rides here in this company, and if our Host wills it, out of his good will, then I will now excuse you from [telling] your tale. For, in good faith, your visage is very pale, your eyes are dazed, I think [...]'"
[37] 'because of drinking was very pale'
[38] "I make a protestacioun / That I am dronke; I know it by my soun" ('I declare / that I am drunk. I know it by my sound,' "Miller's Prologue," ll. 3136–3137).
[39] For example, Gilbert the Englishman as quoted in Wallis (2010: 341) describes lepers' eyes: "Their eyes become distorted, rimmed with red, striking horror into those who see them." Both Rhodes and Cox, in their contributions to this volume, discuss the repulsive skin of the Summoner's face and the suggestion of leprosy that scholars have historically read onto it.
[40] 'of eyes or vision: to grow dim, fail'

descriptor of failing or impeded vision and is used to describe both the experience of impeded vision and the appearance of the eyes as perceived by another person.[41] Indeed, the Cook is so open to interpretation before the Manciple diagnoses these details as drunkenness that a reader might not know what to think of the Cook before the Manciple and the Host forcefully insist on their interpretations.

Furthermore, the Manciple's accusation is surprising because his speech to the Cook is initially courteous but then suddenly, midway through, turns to vitriol:

> And, wel I woot, they breeth ful soure stynketh:
> That sheweth wel thou art nat wel disposed.
> Of me, certeyn, thou shalt nat been yglosed.
> See how he ganeth, lo, this dronken wight,
> As though he wolde swolwe us anonright.
> Hold cloos thy mouth, man, by thy fader kyn!
> The devel of helle sette his foot therin!
> Thy cursed breeth infecte wole us alle.
> Fy, stynkyng swyn! Fy, foule moote thee falle!
> A, taketh heede, sires, of this lusty man.
> Now, sweete sire, wol ye justen atte fan?
> Therto me thynketh ye been wel yshape!
> I trowe that ye dronken han wyn ape,
> And that is whan men pleyen with a straw. (ll. 25–45)[42]

The Manciple seems unnecessarily acrimonious considering the comparatively patient treatment the drunk Miller receives at the hands of the Host and even the Reeve, who narratively spars with the Miller.[43] The Cook's breath that "ful

---

[41] While Cox (this volume) focuses on the presence of both skin irregularities and the implications of their ambiguities from the perspective of the pilgrims' own (immoral) agency, the present essay calls our attention to the potential passiveness of the Cook's bodily deviance – thus asking the audience to consider an illness-etiology of the Cook's deviance, in addition to acknowledging the entanglement of disease and morality in the Middle Ages.

[42] 'And I know well that your breath stinks foully and this demonstrates that you are not well disposed. By me, certainly, you shall not be glossed; see how he gapes, lo, this drunken creature, it is as if he would swallow us right up. Hold your mouth closed, man, by your father's kin! The devil of Hell sets his foot therein! Your cursed breath will infect us all. Fie, stinking swine! Fie, foul might you fall! Take heed, sirs, of this lusty man. Now, sweet sir, will you joust at a fan? Thus, it seems to me that you are well-shaped! I suppose that you are wine-ape drunk and that is when men play at straws.'

[43] The Host courteously asks the Miller, in response to his drunken demand that he tell the next tale (at the close of the Knight's), to let another tell a tale ("Oure Hooste saugh that he was dronke of ale, / And seyde, 'Abyd, Robyn, my leeve brother; / Som better man shal telle us

soure stynketh" must certainly be powerful to have associations with the devil drawn to it and to cause the Cook to be the only pilgrim whose drunkenness is openly reviled in harsh and extensively detailed terms. Note that it is the Cook's breath that the Manciple claims alerts him that the Cook is "nat wel disposed" (IX, l. 33). While the Manciple is firm about the Cook's drunkenness, the Manciple's description of the Cook's disposition again suggests indeterminacy and multiplicity, *dispōsen* (*MED dispōsen* v.) being a term that describes behaviour, ethical disposition, and physical condition in regards to humoral health. Thus, this phrase might be the Manciple's judgment of the Cook's behaviour, moral composition, and/or physical state. The Manciple continues in the next stanza, saying that the Cook will "infecte" the rest of the pilgrims (IX, l. 39). The medieval idea of infection was not the same as the modern understanding, of course, but the verb *infecte* (*MED infecten* v.) did still convey an affliction by, as well as a spreading of, disease. This spreading was the result of clouds of corrupt air that might be breathed in.[44] Thus, the Manciple might be suggesting fear of more than just an unpleasant smell but of bad air that harboured disease. The medieval physician Gilbert the Englishman notes that a leper's breath, sweat, and skin all smell fetid.[45] So while the Manciple is explicitly attributing the Cook's bad breath to drunkenness, the language again raises the spectre of disease. Furthermore, just as the Manciple begins his tirade, he claims that the Cook will not be "yglosed" (IX, l. 34) by him (*MED glōsen* v.). This term implies both that the Manciple plans to speak frankly about the Cook and that he refuses to interpret the Cook. This playful wording simultaneously predicts the negative

---

furst another.'") (I, ll. 3128–3130). When the Miller responds that he will tell his tale or leave the company, the Host calls the Miller a fool, but also allows him to continue with his tale (I, ll. 3132–3135). The Reeve's objection to the Miller's statements that he will tell "[...] a legende and a lyf / Bothe of a carpenter and of his wyf" is abrupt and angry (beginning with "Stynt thy clappe!") but is comparatively short at six lines and does not go into great detail in his accusations ("Lat be thy lewed dronken harlotrye, / It is a synne and eek a greet folye / to apeyren any man, or hym defame, / And eek to bryngen wyves in swich fame.") ('[...] a legend and a life / about both a carpenter and his wife;' 'Hold your tongue;' 'Leave off of your lewd and drunken obscenities, / It is a sin and also great folly / to slander or defame any man, / and also to represent wives in such a report.' I, ll. 3141–3149).

44 This is a long-standing theory of how groups of people sharing physical space could become sick before the discovery of bacterial and viral pathogens. Isidore of Seville explains that *pestilential* "arises from corrupt air and maintains itself by penetrating the internal organs" and "as soon as it seizes on one person quickly spreads to many" (quoted from Barney, Beach, and Berghof 2006: 110). Additionally, Getz (1991: 82) cites a late thirteenth roll that states that putting animal dung in the streets is a public health hazard: "by it the air there is infected and corrupted to the serious damage and peril of loss of life [...]."

45 See Wallis (2010: 340).

accusations to come and casts the Cook as needing to be read and interpreted. It is yet another slippery expression used to describe the Cook; the Manciple is both claiming to tell a harsh truth about the Cook and rejecting any claims to interpretation. The rhetorical move echoes the Host's earlier wordplay that claims to be insulting the Cook in jest while reminding us that playful messages can still convey truth. The Manciple's claimed harsh truth is about the Cook's alcohol consumption, but the description asks for further consideration.

After the Manciple's tirade, the Cook, previously lethargic, becomes so angry that he falls from his horse and must be assisted to remount. The Manciple and Host continue to mock the Cook until the Manciple offers the Cook some wine, which wondrously restores him. The Manciple continues to diagnose the Cook as drunk after the Cook falls, saying that he does not know what the Cook has been drinking but that he is drunk because he is speaking in his nose, he is sneezing, and has a head cold (or sounds as though he does). For comparison, Gilbert remarks that lepers may be quick to anger and may have a hoarse voice and sound as though they have nasal congestion.[46] Finally, the way the Cook is revived from his stupor is suspicious. After being put back on his horse the Manciple appeases the Cook by offering him some good wine, which the Cook consumes in its entirety "And of that drynke the Cook was wonder fayn," which prompts the narrator to ask: "What neded hym? He drank ynough biforn" (ll. 87–93).[47] The narrator is calling attention here to not only the Cook's consumption of alcohol but his reaction to it. Isidore of Seville, in his seventh-century encyclopaedic *Etymologiae*, explains that the Greek word for antidote means "derived from the opposite."[48] This idea of using substances with the opposite qualities of those humours that are causing a problem is a governing idea in medieval medicine.[49] In the "Parson's Tale," which is separated from the final appearance of the Cook in the "Manciple's Prologue" just by the "Manciple's Tale," Chaucer includes Galen's cure for gluttony, which is MED *abstinence* n. *Abstinence* describes the avoidance of excessive consumption of food and drink and the consumption

---

[46] See Wallis (2010: 340–341).
[47] 'And the Cook was extremely happy for that drink [...] What need did he have? He drank enough before.' Whether the Cook was happy to have been given the wine, was desirous of the wine, or was made happy by the wine, what Chaucer presents is a change in the one aspect of the Cook's disposition from lethargic (which was, according to the Manciple and the Host, brought on by the Cook's drunkenness) to enthusiastic.
[48] See Barney, Beach, and Berghof (2006: 113).
[49] Isidore's text also lists the strategy of a like-for-like cure – that is, pharmaceuticals with the *same* properties as the humors causing the problem are used as treatment – this is an earlier strategy that seemingly did not survive into the Middle Ages.

of extravagant victuals.⁵⁰ It does not describe the refusal of all food, just a sparsity in amount and quality of those things that are consumed. The Parson explains that a component of *abstinence* is MED *sōbrenes(se)* n. that "restreyneth the outrage of drynke" (ll. 833).⁵¹ Thus, the Parson advises that the cure for gluttony would be to practice moderation in terms of both amount and quality of victuals consumed. It is important to note that the Parson's intent is not to offer cures for the physical body, but rather to instruct on the cultivation of the soul – which would be to practice qualities like *abstinence* with a good will, looking towards the reward of Heaven (and not just for the health of the body). But regardless of the quality of the Cook's will whilst consuming the Manciple's wine, the Cook's miraculous recovery from drunkenness via the consumption of "good" wine does not make sense in medieval medical or moralizing terms. It is moderation in neither sense of abstinence (nor does it align with humoral medicine) to consume more of that which is harming the body, and to consume that which is stated to be of high quality at that.⁵²

The Cook's consumption of wine prompts Chaucer to ask, "What neded hym?"⁵³ With the medieval philosophy of the curing power of opposites in mind, the remainder of the line, "He drank ynough biforn," enhances the mystery. Certainly, part of the function of the wine is to remedy the relationship between the Manciple and the Cook, but Chaucer notes that the Cook is *fayn*, that is, his mood is highly improved. Are we then to understand this to be a commentary on what kind of drunk the Cook is, or on his physical health? After all, paleness, the Cook's most remarked-on quality, can be caused by a body that is too cool, an indication of too much phlegm (Wallis 2010: 143). The heat from wine might then be restorative, and thus the wine would be medicinal.

We cannot entirely dismiss the popular diagnosis of drunkenness, but such a designation need not be an exclusive one. In the view of fourteenth-century medicine, being an unclean drunk is far more dangerous, far closer to illness,

---

50 The Parson warns against the "outrageous apparailynge of mete" ('elaborate preparation of food,' "Parson's Tale," ll. 833).
51 'restrain[s] the excess of drink'
52 The modern acceptance of the accusations of the Cook's drunkenness alongside his miraculous cure might have to do with the post-medieval idea that a person who became drunk and then experienced the negative physical side effects of drunkenness would then need more alcohol, the "hair of the dog," to recover. In contrast to this modern experience with a hangover, the medieval physician John of Gaddesden's cure for drunkenness (for men) is bathing the testicles in salt and vinegar and consuming cabbage juice and sugar, likely to cool the body from the heat-producing alcohol. Gaddesden is also listed as a medical authority by Chaucer in the description of the Physician (see l. 434).
53 Baker (1984: 2.10, 93) notes that most manuscripts read *it* rather than *hym*.

than it seems to modern readers. Such accusations could indicate a variety of dangerous physical states that either were caused by uncleanliness and moral vagaries or resulted in them. All the details offered about the Cook destabilize his identity, creating an amorphous, open, infinitely readable character rather than a stable image. Leprosy itself, as a diagnosis, also refuses to settle in the Middle Ages but rather colonizes the perceptions of any number of skin irregularities and is employed in texts ranging far afield from the medical.[54] Reading the Cook in light of leprosy thus draws attention to the fact that we cannot be sure precisely what ails him (spiritually, physically, and/or morally). It is this resistance to delineation that, rather than offering up equally possible options of disease and health, suggests only myriad and multiplying disease potentialities – an existence disturbing to the Cook's fellow pilgrims and perplexing to scholars.[55] Leahy's essay in the present volume also explores the convergence of instability and leprosy, specifically in regards to rhetorical uses that allow descriptions of leprosy to evoke, simultaneously, contradictory desires for both the engagement and effacement of leprous bodies for didactic purposes. Gilles (this volume), reading Henryson's *Testament of Cresseid* in conjunction with the ever-diminishing instances of leprosy starting from the late twelfth century and continuing through the Middle Ages, ultimately sees a figure who is the product of a society's inexperience with lepers as neighbours and thus fearful boundary-drawers. Both Leahy and Gilles look at the flexibility of leprosy, both seeing in this flexibility moralizing societal impulses. But in regards to the Cook, there are not enough established knowns to proscribe a definite purpose, leaving the Cook's body to stand as an unconfirmed case of leprosy – gesturing toward the terrifying multivalence of unwell bodies and the ways that these bodies can overlap with deviant morals.

---

[54] See Gilles (this volume) for an enlightening review of the various types of medieval genres leprosy appears in.

[55] Cox (this volume), reading Chaucer's pilgrims' skin alongside the medieval use of parchment as a writing surface, also argues that skin is a site of production and potential. Cox, engaging with the materiality of parchment through the idea of the palimpsest, argues that Chaucer's rhetoric of skin as ever generating meaning is his recognition that we read identities through the material marks that experiences can leave behind on skin while also reminding us of the incomplete access to and changeability of those skins and identities.

"Hastow with some quene al nyght yswonke?"

There has been relatively little discussion about the accusation that the Cook might be tired due to his sexual activity or sex partners. Certainly, extra-marital sex would mark the Cook as a morally deviant character in the Christian medieval west. His presence on a pilgrimage would seem to make this deviant sexual behaviour even more of a transgression,[56] although Chaucer's pilgrims do not make up the most ideally pious group of pilgrims, as has often been pointed out as part of the larger joke of the frame of the *Tales*. Perhaps the Cook's fragmentary tale that ends with a wife who makes a living for herself and her husband through prostitution makes the Cook's lechery a given, but as with the Host's other speculations about the reason(s) for the Cook's diminished state, Chaucer offers more than the Host's lewd suggestion to evoke speculation in a medieval audience.

The suggestion that the Cook is not just sexually active but also sexually active with a promiscuous woman again summons up the spectre of disease when faced with Chaucer's description of the Cook's body. Immoderate sexual appetites can cause changes to a man's body that are readable by others. In Constantine the African's translation of the *Isagoge*, sexual intercourse is said to cool the body because it dries the body out.[57] As we just saw above, an overly cool body could be restored with heat-producing foods or drinks (such as alcohol). Thus the medieval reader would have perhaps registered the Cook's recovery via wine as a signal that the Host has hit upon some truth in this final suggestion. Yet excessive sex was not just an opportunity for comedy but also potentially both cause and symptom of diseases.

Constantine also authored an eleventh-century treatise on sex which explains that weakness and paleness can be caused by too much semen loss – implying that a person is sexually overactive.[58] Constantine explains that having a lot of sex is not always bad for men; however, it is unquestionably bad for men who are already weak with illness. Sex was made further dangerous to men by women, who were thought to hold on to diseases like leprosy in their wombs (due to the cold and dampness that was the natural quality of women's repro-

---

[56] "Attitudes towards sexuality and pilgrims varied according to the viewpoints of those promoting pilgrimage or crusading [...] Sermons, papal letters and the law codes of some crusading armies exhorted pilgrims to avoid luxurious lifestyles, showy entourages, excessive eating and drinking, blasphemy, gambling, quarreling, and sex" (Bird 2012).
[57] See Wallis (2010: 146).
[58] Constantine is yet another well-known medical authority included by Chaucer in the portrait of the Physician in the General Prologue (l. 433).

ductive organs within a humoral medical system). Diseases could then pass from the womb to men through sexual intercourse (Rawcliffe 2006: 81–89). In his compilation of leprosy symptoms, Gilbert includes immoderate sexual appetites and enjoyment that leave a body weaker than they should.[59] Thus, while Chaucer could be implying that the Cook was simply lecherous, the Host's lewd suggestion, when paired with the Cook's physical traits, raises questions about the Cook's physical health while also reminding the reader that medieval disease and medieval morality were inextricably entangled phenomena.

Mis-reading the Cook's Body

While Chaucer winks at leprosy and its inextricability from the carnal appetites, he does not write a clear-cut leper in his presentation of the Cook. All the symptoms of the Cook correspond with leprosy to varying degrees, but not all the symptoms of leprosy are applied to the Cook by Chaucer. The Cook is a figure of uncertainty, as medieval leprosy could be. As noted earlier, medieval leprosy affected both sinners and saints for various reasons. Leprosy could be a sign of God's favour or indicate that one has no control over their carnal appetites. Indeed, Rawcliffe (2006: 47) even notes that indulgence in sex, food, and alcohol (all components of the Cook as we have seen in this essay) were considered a "lethal troika" that medieval authors regarded as practically calling leprosy down on oneself. Leprosy was *the* medieval moral disease. It was a bodily state that was wrapped up in implied moral transgressions and, more importantly, it pointed to morality more generally, asking the reader to question the afflicted person's moral state.

In the *Tales*, the pilgrims' accusations against the Cook, when considered together, raise more questions than they answer. The pilgrims that interact with the Cook do so on consistently antagonistic terms, and also in speculative terms – evoking doubt in nearly every characteristic of the Cook. In the "Cook's Prologue," the Host accuses the Cook of being unsanitary. In the "Manciple's Prologue," the Host questions the Cook's fatigue (has he been drinking or up all night with a woman?); and he and the Manciple are not satisfied with the Cook's protestations against their accusations as to the origins of his sudden lethargy. The Manciple insists on the Cook's drunkenness, but the narration of the Cook calls these labels into question. The Cook's skin, from the *mormal* in the General Prologue to his paleness in the "Manciple's Prologue," remains a

---

[59] See Wallis (2010: 341).

symptomatic site. The narrator repeatedly asks the readers to direct their attention to the Cook's skin – the surface on which leprosy is most often recognized in the Middle Ages, the organ that encloses the body, and the surface onto which identity and morality are most likely to be read, the skin being a physical mediator with characteristics that are visually perceived and interpreted as well as a surface onto which viewers inscribe their cultural beliefs and values. Interestingly, it is not the narrator who draws the conclusions about the Cook's paleness and his behaviour. It is only the Host and the Manciple who infer that the Cook is drunk. A medieval doctor might conclude instead that the Cook is a phlegmatic, as Elspeth Whitney does in her 2011 article.[60] The Cook's skin is an important site for the narrator to hint that there may be more to the Cook's problems than drunkenness. It is furthermore a site where the other pilgrims are forced to grapple with the ambiguously dangerous nature of an individual with whom they are sharing their fellowship. We are not given conclusive information about the Cook's bodily health to establish clearly that he is a leper, but reading the Cook through the lens of leprosy reveals the extent to which the unstable, indeterminate form of the Cook produces fear through even ambiguous references to sickness.[61]

Chaucer gives the reader only enough information about the Cook to speculate, and perhaps that is the crucial part of the Cook's identity. Efforts to diagnose the Cook with a single problem have revealed less about the Cook than they have about our understanding of diseased physical states as culturally and temporally static. That is, we have been missing Chaucer's clues that the pilgrims are mis-reading the Cook's body because we ourselves have mis-read the Cook through the very thick lens of modern medicine and modern medical myths about the Middle Ages. The modern attachment to disease as biologically discernible and absolute clouds the study of historical depictions of disease. We do better to attend to the multivalent phenomena of bodies compromised by physical and moral unwellness (self-inflicted and otherwise) that is illustrated in the uncertain figure of the Cook.

---

[60] Whitney (2011: 364–368) uses nearly all the characteristics discussed above, plus the implied largeness of the Cook, to categorize him as a model phlegmatic man.

[61] Rawcliffe's (2006) project is devoted to dispelling myths about medieval leprosy that started in the nineteenth century. One of those myths is that lepers were victims of extreme persecution and segregation. My suggestion that the Cook could be a body that evokes fear does not disregard Rawcliffe's important conclusions about the general inclusion of lepers in medieval English society. Rather, it evinces a less polarized, more nuanced, and thus more realistic place of leprosy. While there are clues about the Cook that give the pilgrims cause to question his nature, he is not entirely excluded from the fellowship.

The shadow of disease that Chaucer casts over the Cook serves to illuminate the difficulty of reading bodies, particularly in a medical age when diseases depended partially on individual humoral constitutions to determine their forms. The slippery and amorphous body of the Cook, difficult to get a firm grasp on (particularly if he has fallen off his horse), consistently unsettles, with ever-expanding possibilities, any delineation of his identity. This always forming, never completely concrete body nudges readers to question the accusations and labels cast on the Cook by the other pilgrims, illustrating that it is not just suggestions of moral or physical corruption that make the Cook a disruptive figure but also, and primarily, his indeterminacy. The Cook's *mormal* (and other damaged skin) breaks down the idea of skin as a marker of inside/outside, and thus troubles the notion of stable or entirely accessible identity.

Works Cited

Primary Sources

Baker, Donald C. (ed). 1984. *Geoffrey Chaucer: The Canterbury Tales*. Volume 2, part 10: The Manciple's Tale. A Variorum Edition of the Works of Geoffrey Chaucer. Norman: University of Oklahoma Press.

Barney, Stephen A., Jennifer A. Beach, and Oliver Berghof (eds. and trans.). 2006. *Isidore of Seville: The Etymologies of Isidore of Seville*. Cambridge: Cambridge University Press.

Benson, Larry D. (ed.) 1987. *Geoffrey Chaucer: The Riverside Chaucer*. 3rd ed. Boston: Houghton Mifflin.

Geoffrey Chaucer: *The Canterbury Tales*. MS EL 26 C 9f. 47r. Huntington Library, San Marino, CA. Digital Scriptorium. <http://dpg.lib.berkeley.edu/webdb/dsheh/heh_brf?CallNumber=EL+26+C+9> [accessed 30 September 2014].

Secondary Sources

Bahr, Arthur. 2016. *Fragments and Assemblages: Forming Compilations of Medieval London*. Chicago: The University of Chicago Press.

Beadle, Richard. 1992. "I Wol Not Tell Yit: John Seldon and a Lost Version of the Cook's Tale." *Chaucer to Shakespeare: Essays in Honour of Shinsuke Ando*. Cambridge: D. S. Brewer. 55–66.

Bertolet, Craig E. 2002. "'Wel Bet Is Roten Appul out of Hoord:' Chaucer's Cook, Commerce, and Civic Order." *Studies in Philology* 99.3: 229–246.

Bird, Jessalynn. 2012. "Sexuality and Pilgrimage." In: Larissa J. Taylor, Leigh A. Craig, John B. Friedman, Kathy Gower, Thomas Izbicki and Rita Tekippe (eds.). *Encyclopedia of Medieval Pilgrimage*. BrillOnline Reference Works. <http://referenceworks.brillonline.

com/entries/encyclopedia-of-medieval-pilgrimage/sexuality-and-pilgrimage-SIM_00011> [accessed 26 January 2017].

Braddy, Haldeen. 1946. "The Cook's Mormal and Its Cure." *Modern Language Quarterly:* 265–267.

Burakov, Olga. 2002. "Chaucer's The Cook's Tale." *Explicator* 61.1: 2–5.

Carney Forkin, Thomas. 2007. "'Oure Citee:' Illegality and Criminality in Fourteenth-Century London." *Essays in Medieval Studies:* 31–41.

Casey, Jim. 2006. "Unfinished Business: The Termination of Chaucer's 'Cook's Tale'." *The Chaucer Review* 41.2: 185–196.

Cholmeley, H.P. (ed.) 1912. *John of Gaddesden and the Rosa Medicinae.* Oxford: Clarendon Press.

Curry, Walter C. 1921. "Two Notes on Chaucer." *Modern Language Notes* 36.5: 272–276.

Curry, Walter C. 1960. *Chaucer and the Mediaeval Sciences.* 2nd ed. New York: Barnes and Noble.

Getz, Faye M. 1991. *Healing and Society in Medieval England: A Middle English Translation of the Pharmaceutical Writings of Gilbertus Anglicus.* Madison: University of Wisconsin Press.

Gray, Douglas. 1987. "Explanatory Notes: The Cook's Prologue" and "The Cook's Tale." In: Benson, Larry D. (ed.). *The Riverside Chaucer.* 3rd ed. Boston: Houghton Mifflin. 852–853.

Gray, Douglas (ed.). 2003. *The Oxford Companion to Chaucer.* New York: Oxford University Press.

Hieatt, Constance B. 1995. "Sorting through the Titles of Medieval Dishes: What Is, or Is Not, a 'Blanc manger'." In: Melitta Weis Adamson (ed.). *Food in the Middle Ages: A Book of Essays.* New York and London: Garland. 25–44.

Higl, Andrew. 2012. "Answering the Riddle of the Cook's Tale." *Playing the Canterbury Tales: The Continuations and Additions.* Farnham and Burlington: Ashgate. 141–171.

Kang, Ji-Soo. 1997. "The (In)Completeness of the Cook's Tale." *Medieval and Early Modern English Studies* 5: 145–170.

Kensak, Michael. 2001. "What Ails Chaucer's Cook: Spiritual Alchemy and the Ending of *The Canterbury Tales.*" *Philological Quarterly* 80: 213–231.

Langum, Virginia. 2013. "Discerning Skin: Complexion, Surgery, and Language in Medieval Confession." In: Katie L. Walter (ed.). *Reading Skin in Medieval Literature and Culture.* The New Middle Ages. New York: Palgrave Macmillan. 141–161.

Latour, Bruno. 1988. *The Pasteurization of France.* Cambridge, MA: Harvard University Press.

Lynch, Kathryn L. 2007. "From Tavern to Pie Shop: The Raw, the Cooked, and the Rotten in Fragment 1 of Chaucer's *Canterbury Tales.*" *Exemplaria* 19.1: 117–138.

Lyon, Earl D. 1937. "Roger De Ware, Cook." *Modern Language Notes* 52.7: 491–494.

Mann, Jill. 1973. *Chaucer and Medieval Estates Satire: The Literature of Social Classes and the "General Prologue" of the Canterbury Tales.* Cambridge: Cambridge University Press.

MED = *Middle English Dictionary.* 1952–2001. Ed. Hans Kurath, Sherman M. Kuhn, John Reidy and Robert E. Lewis. Ann Arbor: University of Michigan Press. <http://quod.lib.umich.edu/m/med/>.

Mullaney, Samantha. 1999. "The Language of Costume in the Ellesmere Portraits." *Trivium* 31: 33–57.

Pigg, Daniel F. 2012. "Imagining Urban Life and Its Discontents: Chaucer's *Cook's Tale* and Masculine Identity." In: Christopher R. Clason and Albrecht Classen (eds.). *Rural Space in the Middle Ages and Early Modern Age: The Spatial Turn in Premodern Studies.* Fundamentals of Medieval and Early Modern Culture 9. Berlin: De Gruyter. 395–408.

Pinti, Daniel J. 1996. "Governing the 'Cook's Tale' in Bodley 686." *The Chaucer Review* 30.4: 379–388.

Rawcliffe, Carole. 2006. *Leprosy in Medieval England.* New York: Boydell Press.

Robertson, James C. and Joseph B. Sheppard (eds.). 1965 [1875]. *Materials for the History of Thomas Becket: Archbishop of Canterbury (canonized by Pope Alexander III., A.D. 1173).* Volumes 1–2. Wiesbaden: Kraus Reprint.

Scattergood, V. J. 1987. "Explanatory Notes: 'The Manciple's Prologue'." In: Larry D. Benson (ed.). *The Riverside Chaucer.* 3rd ed. Boston: Houghton Mifflin. 952–953.

Scully, Terrence. 2005. *The Art of Cookery in the Middle Ages.* New York: Boydell Press.

Skeat, Walter W. 1894. *Notes to the Canterbury Tales.* Vol 5 of *The Complete Works of Geoffrey Chaucer.* 2nd ed., Volume 5. Oxford: Clarendon Press.

Tupper, Frederick. 1915. "The Quarrels of the Canterbury Pilgrims." *The Journal of English and Germanic Philology* 14.2: 256–270.

Wallis, Faith. 2010. *Medieval Medicine: A Reader.* Toronto: University of Toronto Press.

Whitney, Elspeth. 2011. "What's Wrong with the Pardoner?: Complexion Theory, the Phlegmatic Man, and Effeminacy." *The Chaucer Review* 45.4: 357–389.

Nicole Nyffenegger
Blushing, Paling, Turning Green:
Hue and Its Metapoetic Function in *Troilus and Criseyde*

Abstract: Hue is a mark on human skin that invites conceptualisations of skin as an inscribable and readable surface. I argue that Chaucer treats the faces of his characters in *Troilus and Criseyde* as *mise en abyme* pages that he inscribes by hue. Rather than just betraying the feelings of the characters at distinct points in the narrative, however, hue has overarching functions. First, the distribution of the diverse hue references across the narrative underlines the narrative's structure and traces the developing feelings of the protagonists throughout the narrative. Second, hue reinforces the intricate connections in *Troilus and Criseyde* between visual dynamics, emotions, and agency that have been at the centre of scholarly interest for some time. Third, the narrator introduces hue as a figure for the generic conventions of romance in his authorial apology in book II and thus gives it a metapoetic function that he explores further throughout the work. Whenever hue is used in *Troilus and Criseyde*, the narrator reflects on its suitability to adequately express feelings and consequently on his own poetic options when writing about love.

Human skin matters in the literature of the late Middle Ages. It is critical for our understanding of the bodies of humans and animals presented in the literary works of the period. At the same time however, human skin is not always easily visible because many texts do not refer to it explicitly by the relevant terms (*MED hīd(e)* n., *fel* n., *skin* n.).[1] This is probably due to the fact that skin was neither conceptualised as an entity of its own nor as a sensory organ (Connor 2004: 9–47). Instead, the Middle Ages had inherited the Aristotelian notions that skin is but the dried surface of flesh and that skin itself does not register touch but allows the flesh underneath to feel through it.[2] Consequently, before

---

[1] In Chaucer's works, these terms hardly ever appear and when they do, they usually refer to animal hides rather than to human skin – with the exception of the slack skin of January's neck in the "Merchant's Tale" (l. 1364). The invisibility of skin is reversed to grotesque exposure in accounts of flaying such as, most prominently, accounts of the life of Saint Bartholomew. See also Kay (2006), as well as the introduction to this volume.
[2] Aristotle, *Historia Animalium*, III:11 and Aristotle, *De Generatione Animalium*, V, II.6. See, e. g., Trevisa's (1975: 268) comment on the relative thickness of human skin: 'In men the skin is thin-

https://doi.org/10.1515/9783110578133-008

the rise of medieval skin studies in recent years, many scholars only implicitly included skin in their studies of the gendered, fragmented, and textualised bodies of medieval literature.³ In keeping with Katie Walter's (2013: 3) recent claim that skin is nevertheless "made to speak in wide-ranging ways to its aesthetic, philosophical, ethical, and political preoccupations," the task at hand is thus to discern the ways in which skin becomes visible in the texts despite the absence of explicit references.

Throughout this volume, we argue that skin that is in some way marked signifies differently from unmarked skin. One such mark is 'hue' (*MED heu* n.), denoting the skin tone of the face as, for example, rosy, red, or pale.⁴ Since hue cannot be imagined separately from the skin on which it appears, it makes skin visible in texts that do not explicitly mention it. What is more, the thus marked skin invites its conceptualisation as an inscribable surface that mirrors the processed and inscribable animal skin that is parchment. To be sure, the two writing surfaces are separate ones, each bearing marks of a distinctive kind and each forming a separate layer of signification, yet they are contiguous in that they are both skin (of human and animal respectively) that signifies differently once it has been inscribed. Since a character's marked skin however only exists by virtue of having been written into existence through words on the parchment page, the relationship between the two surfaces can be described in terms of a *mise en abyme*. Lucien Dällenbach (1989: 35) seminally defines the *mise en abyme* as a pluralistic concept that covers different types of duplication:

(a) *simple duplication* (a sequence which is connected by similarity to the work that encloses it);
(b) *infinite duplication* (a sequence which is connected by similarity to the work that encloses it and which itself includes a sequence that … etc.); and
(c) *aporetic duplication* (a sequence that is supposed to enclose the work that encloses it).

(emphasis and ellipsis in the original)

---

ner than in beasts, and that is to allow good touch and groping. For if it were hard and thick as is the shell of a shellfish, they should not feel by groping; and if it were rough and hairy as is the skin of an ass, then it would weaken and impede the sense of feeling and groping' (my translation). On the dialectic between outer and inner sensation see also Robertson (2013: 32).

3 E. g., Feher (1990), Grosz (1990), Lomperis and Stanbury (1993).

4 I employ the term hue in its limited sense as a reference to skin tone and I argue that so does Chaucer in *Troilus and Criseyde* (except for one single instance which I discuss in detail below).

While the generic term *mise en abyme*, according to Dällenbach, refers to not one but all of these three duplications, I propose to think of the relationship of marked human skin and parchment page in terms of a 'simple duplication' as defined above, i.e., a narrative sequence that describes marked human skin is connected, by similarity, to the parchment page on which it is inscribed. The human skin mirrors the parchment page and the marks on the skin mirror the letters or illuminations on the page. Thus, the skin of a character can be conceptualised as an additional surface of signification, an additional space for the poet to inscribe. The creative potential of such a layering of text, parchment, and human skin was arguably easier for medieval readers and writers to grasp than it is for us today.[5]

Hue was understood to signal a character's humoural disposition, his/her emotional state, or outward influences, as Bartholomaeus Anglicus' discussions of skin colour show.[6] Among the outward influences, Bartholomaeus identifies the heat of the sun and the dryness of the air, diverse illnesses and burning (Trevisa 1975: 1283). As for the humoural disposition, his description of the causes for changes of skin colour reads as follows in John of Trevisa's (1975: 1283)[7] translation:

> Also colour of skynne chaungeþ, and nameliche of mannes skynne, by many oþre causes: for sometyme yuel complexioun, as it fareþ in melancolik men; and for to grete passyng hete, as it fareþ in colerike men [...].[8]

---

[5] See especially Kay's (2004, 2006, 2011) and Holsinger's (2009, 2010) explorations of the relationship between human and animal skin, as well as Gutierrez-Neal's contribution to this volume. I am indebted to Roberta Magnani (especially for the term 'surface of signification'), Elizabeth Robertson, and Annette Kern-Stähler for their comments on how to describe the relationship between the two writing surfaces. See also Cox's discussion of Winterson's novel in this volume.

[6] For an overview of the medico-theoretical background as well as further references see Leahy's contribution in this volume. Colour is not discussed as a marker of race in these passages nor in this article. See, e.g., Jablonski (2006) for a more comprehensive theoretical discussion of skin colour.

[7] Due to uncertainty about Trevisa's base text, it is hard to pinpoint how close Trevisa's translation is, see e.g., Edwards (2003).

[8] 'Also, the colour of skin changes, and namely of man's skin, by many other causes: sometimes because of evil complexion, as it happens to melancholy men; and because of great passing heat, as it happens to choleric men' (my translation).

Finally, Bartholomaeus follows the tradition of Pseudo-Aristotle and identifies feelings (which he calls the "passions of the soul")[9] as another possible cause for changes of skin colour: "Also colour is tokne of accidentes and of passiouns of þe soule, for sodeyn palenes and discolour is tokne of drede [...] Sodeyn rednesse in þe face is tokne of schame or of wraþþe" (Trevisa 1975: 1283).[10] Afflictions or disturbances of the soul, such as dread, shame, and wrath, are inscribed on the face as sudden paleness or redness respectively, the word "sudden" indicating a quick and perhaps unexpected change from a different colour. In fact, Bartholomaeus' discussions of skin colour are, more precisely, discussions of the *changes* of skin colour: a character blushes, turns pale, red, or green, or "loses hue." A pale face, as well, is only recognisable against a previously rosy one. Thus, hue is an unstable and fluid inscription that invests skin with a palimpsestic quality. This is even more marked in cases in which feelings effect quick ("sudden") changes of skin colour. The immediacy with which skin inscribed by hue is able to register a character's feelings even suggests that the living and lively skin of a character may be the more suitable writing surface than parchment when it comes to the representation of feelings.

As to the question of what determines the attribution of the different causes to a certain character's changing or changed facial colour, John Block Friedman argues that genre plays a crucial role. Based on Walter Clyde Curry's studies of humoural physiognomy, Friedman (1981: 139–140) proposes the term 'affective physiognomy' for poetic descriptions of the face in which features such as eye movement and "colour of the cheeks" (i.e., hue) reveal emotions. He claims that affective physiognomy figures "particularly in courtly or aristocratic poems, such as the *Book of the Duchess* or *Troilus and Criseyde*," while humoural disposition as the cause for colour changes is more frequent in fabliau characters such as the Wife of Bath (1981: 139).[11] Friedman suggests that Chaucer follows Dante's notion of an 'aristocracy of feeling' when he chooses to use affective

---

9 McNamer (2007) argues for the use of the term 'feeling' rather than 'emotion' which only came to be used in the 16th century. For a precise differentiation of the relevant terminology and especially of 'affect' and 'emotion,' see Trigg (2014, "Introduction"), for an overview of the field see Downes and McNamara (2016). For the tradition of the passions of the soul starting from Pseudo-Aristotle see Friedman (1981).
10 'Also, the colour is a token of afflictions or of emotional disturbances of the soul, because sudden paleness or discolouring is a token of dread [...] Sudden redness in the face is a token of shame or of wrath' (my translation).
11 Compare also Sweany's discussion of the Cook's paleness and that of Bychowski on Virginia's paleness in this volume.

rather than humoural physiognomy for his "aristocratic figures with more complicated inner lives," such as Troilus and Criseyde (1981: 148–149).

Friedman's argument may appear precarious in view of the fact that Chaucer applies neither generic features nor social stereotypes slavishly but uses them creatively and in order to achieve certain effects.[12] However, in *Troilus and Criseyde*, Chaucer never uses hue to denote humoural disposition, but only to express feelings. With the exception of one instance (which I discuss below), all instances of hue in the work fit Friedman's definition of affective physiognomy. In what follows, I build on his argument to investigate how Chaucer uses hue in *Troilus and Criseyde* to make the characters' inner lives outwardly readable. I argue that the narrator treats the skins of his characters as *mise en abyme* pages, as additional writing space on which to explore his poetic options between verbal and non-verbal expressions of feelings. Both necessarily are expressed in the narrator's words, but in contrast to the reporting of a character's words and thoughts, the assignment of colour to a feeling evokes a powerful visual guide to a character's emotional state.[13] In addition, the narrator goes beyond inscribing a given feeling on the face at any discrete point in the narrative. Instead, he uses hue for a number of overarching purposes: first, the distribution of different hues across the narrative underlines the narrative's structure, second, the narrator's explorations of the characters' agency are supported by their non-verbal expressions of feelings, and finally, the narrator reflects on his role as a writer of romance. In his authorial apology at the beginning of book II, he introduces hue as a figure for the generic conventions of romance and thus gives it a metapoetic function that he explores further throughout the work.

Hue Underlining the Structure of the Narrative

Troilus, Criseyde, and Pandarus constantly blush, turn rosy and red, pale, green, or display a "dead hue." In *Troilus and Criseyde*, hue serves as an inscription on

---

[12] E.g., Strohm (1989: 49–51).
[13] Trigg (2016: 97) describes a similar problem in the case of Criseyde's 'speaking face:' "A text describes a visual appearance by seeming to translate it into a secondary text of direct, if unspoken speech. Criseyde's unspoken question functions like a caption, a *bandeau* or *banderole*, a scroll that floats next to a person illustrated in a manuscript, carrying words understood to be literally spoken by that figure." MacTaggart (2012: 317) claims that the scenes of Troilus' looking at Criseyde are "carefully drawn so that we do not merely read about Criseyde but, rather, gaze at her."

the face of feelings such as shame, shock, and grief, signalled by different colours or the loss thereof, to the point of looking dead in the extreme case.[14] The hue references fall into three distinct types, of which the first employs the term hue and specifies its colour, e. g., "red hue." One example is Troilus' changing hue from red to pale (and possibly back) when he addresses Criseyde in his bedroom: "now his hewes rede, now pale" (III: 94–95).[15] The second type omits a mention of colour and instead describes characters as changing or losing their hue or as displaying a "dead hue." Pandarus for instance reprimands Criseyde for her changing of hue because of her fear: "Ne chaungeth naught for fere so youre hewe" (II: 303).[16] Although no colour is mentioned explicitly, one can safely assume that "losing hue" and "dead hue" mean a loss of all colour leading to paleness, which is reminiscent of the paleness of a dead person's face in the case of "dead hue." Valerie Allen (2005: 196) suggests that both paleness and loss of hue are equivalent to "losing face" – against which a blush works defensively, "as an antidote to the gesture of recoiling, and restores the flow of vital spirits."[17] The third type, finally, omits the term hue and instead only refers to the colour on a character's face. An example is the rose simile used to describe Criseyde's blushing: "[Criseyde] wex as red as rose" (II: 1256).[18]

While they differ semantically, hue references of all three types are employed in the same way in *Troilus and Criseyde:* in all cases, hue is clearly used as an inscription of the characters' feelings on their faces. What is noteworthy, however, is the distribution of the different types of hue references across the narrative. It suggests that hue has the overarching function of underlining the structure of the narrative, from the two characters falling in love in books I and II to the consummation of their love in book III to, finally, their suffering from their separation in books IV and V.

In books I and II, Troilus' and Criseyde's feelings are mainly coyness and longing, inscribed on their faces as "changing hue" in six instances (one of which refers to the record number of sixty changes a day), and as red hue in four instances.[19] Two of the four instances of red hue employ the rose image

---

[14] See also Biggam (1993).
[15] 'his hue now red now pale.' All Middle English quotes for *Troilus and Criseyde* are from Benson (1987), all translations into modern English from *eChaucer* unless specified differently.
[16] 'Change not colour so for fear'
[17] Blushing with shame and embarrassment has been explored extensively, among others, by Flannery (2011, 2012). On the danger of losing face and face-saving strategies, see Bolens (2012). For a recent and comprehensive discussion of face and emotion, see Downes and Trigg (2017).
[18] 'grew ruddy like a rose'
[19] "Changing hue:" I: 441, 461, 487; II: 303, 1198, 1258. "Red hue:" I: 867; II: 645, 1198, 1256.

("rosy hewed," II: 1198; "red as rose," II: 1256). As a conventional image for freshly blossoming love, its exclusive presence in books I and II underlines the narrative's foregrounding of the beginning of a new love story in these two books. There is in these first two books only one single mention of pale hue caused by woe (II: 551). This stands in contrast to the many instances of paleness and "dead hue" later in the narrative. In Book III, when Troilus and Criseyde meet in person and intimately, hue is generally red (four instances)[20] but is also contrasted sharply with white and pale. The red faces of the lovers when standing in front of each other's respective beds (III: 94; III: 956) mark a stark contrast to Criseyde's "white sydes" ('white sides') and "snowissh throte" ('snowy throat') during the intimate encounter (III: 1248–1250). The physical fulfilment of the lovers' longing is thus not only presented as central through its placement in the third of five books, it also comes into sharper focus by the types of hue that are inscribed on the lovers' faces. In this context, Troilus' changing hue from red to pale at the beginning of book III (III: 94–95) foreshadows the colour contrasts during and after the bed scene. The morning after, when the lovers have to separate, their hue is described as changing (from red to pale, perhaps, in the sense of losing hue) and thus provides yet another colour contrast: "So wo was hem that chaungen gan hire hewe" (III: 1698).[21]

When in book IV the lovers learn of the prisoner-exchange and their imminent separation, their hue, "whilom bright" ('once bright') now turns pale (IV: 740). Criseyde, whose hue was once "fresh and fairest," now faints with a pale and green hue (IV: 1154–1155) and Pandarus reacts to the news by looking "ful ded and pale of hewe" (IV: 379).[22] There are four instances of pale hue in book IV,[23] in contrast to none in book I and only one each in books II and III (II: 551; III: 95). Again, hue thus clearly reinforces the structure of the narrative. After the climactic intimate encounter in book III, the story has changed to the worse and hue now attests to the characters' suffering. In book V, finally, Troilus' hue is described as pale, lost, dead or "deadly pale"[24] as he longs for Criseyde's promised return. Criseyde's once so bright face is likewise pale while she longingly looks towards her home (V: 708–711).

The one notable exception confirms the rule: there is one single instance of red hue in book V, elsewhere in the narrative suggestive of falling in love or of consummating love and consequently reserved for books I to III. In book V how-

---

20 III: 82, 94, 956, 1570; even the reference to the many ladies blushing fits the picture (III: 303).
21 'they changed color for woe'
22 'deadly pale'
23 IV: 235, 379, 740, 1154.
24 V: 1403; V: 559; V: 86, 536, 618, 1221 respectively.

ever, Diomede turns red after his wooing speech to Criseyde ("And with that word he gan to waxen red," V: 925).[25] Diomede's red hue here points to the beginning of a new love-story. This new one is obviously at odds with the main love story that is not yet quite over and thus underlines the tragedy of Troilus' ongoing idealism about this love. Before and after the passage in which Diomede turns red, Troilus' suffering is inscribed on his face as "dead hue" (V: 559) and "lost hue" (V: 1403). The stark contrast of red and white which brings the lovers' passionate encounter into focus in book III, has in book V become a stark contrast between the wooing Diomede envisaging a new beginning with Criseyde and the mourning Troilus reminiscing about his past love.

Thus, far from only showing the characters' feelings at distinct points in the narrative, hue functions in an overarching way: it supports the structure of the narrative in that the rosy colours in the first and second book, the stark red-white contrasts in the third, and the green, dead and pale hues in the fourth and fifth book underline the change in mood from one book to the next. This use of skin colour to structure a narrative is reminiscent of manuscript rubrics marking structural divisions. However, the use of hue goes further because ultimately, it traces the developing feelings of the characters across the narrative. In this context, Ardis Butterfield's (1995: 55) observation of the S1 scribe's rubrication would deserve further exploration. She shows that the scribe chose to rubricate the beginnings and endings of the songs and the lovers' letters, thus employing an otherwise purely structural device to emphasise specific passages in the text. These, like the passages marked by hue discussed above, are crucially linked to the characters' feelings. This specific connection between rubrication in the manuscript and description of hue in the text may perhaps be understood in a similar way as the connection between manuscript and text discussed by Martha Rust (2013: 404–405) who claims that the "weeping verses" and the "sorry face" from the very beginning of *Troilus and Criseyde* (I: 7; 14) "invite an image in a reader's mind of the very page before him as the face across which those lachrymose verses flow."

Explorations of Agency on Human Skin

In addition to underlining the structure of the narrative, hue also serves the narrator to explore questions of agency. He uses the *mise en abyme* pages of his

---

[25] 'with those words he began to grow red.' See also Hermann's (1985: 131–133) reading of this blush.

characters' faces as the surface on which to inscribe non-verbal expressions of feelings, and he uses hue as the inscription. Stephanie Trigg (2016: 95) argues in the case of Criseyde that "the narrator struggles to reconcile the unchanging beauty of the heroine's face with her changing affections" but that the work "offers a series of experiments in the expression of emotion on the human face." I suggest that the face inscribed by hue is just such an experiment. Once inscribed, it appears to be easily readable for everyone who sees it. The characters in the work do read each other's faces extensively, for example when Troilus suffers so much from his lovesickness that it shows in his hue for everyone to see: "ek his sorwe / Gan multiplie, that, whoso tok kep / It shewed in his hewe both eve and morwe" (I: 484–487).[26] The only one who does not understand Troilus' changed hue (or feigns not to, as the puzzled narrator comments) is Criseyde: "But how it was, certeyn, kan I nat seye / If that his lady understood nat this / Or feynede hire she nyste, oon of the tweye" (I: 492–494).[27] Criseyde's refusal to read Troilus' hue alongside everyone else points to the fact that the act of seeing and reading a character's face is counterbalanced by the act of refusing to look. There are of course many different acts of seeing at work in *Troilus and Criseyde* (e.g., seeing by chance, actively looking, refusing to see, refusing to be seen), each associated with a specific degree of agency.

The dynamics between these different acts of seeing, agency, and emotions in the work have been discussed extensively, among others by Sarah Stanbury (1991, 1992), Jill Mann (1989), Holly Crocker (2007), Stephanie Trigg (2016), and Elizabeth Robertson (forthcoming).[28] While the characters' blushes have in these discussions been tackled as one of the ways in which their faces invite or resist reading, the extent to which Chaucer's use of hue reinforces the "complex visual dynamics" (Stanbury 1992: 237) of his romance remains underexplored. There are many instances of hue that testify to the reaction of a character at seeing someone or at realising that he or she is being looked at. While the sense of sight (both seeing and being seen) causes the hue in this character's face to change, a second look at the facial skin then reveals the inscription of feelings that the first look has caused. Like a parchment page, the facial skin

---

[26] 'and his pains increased so much that, if one observed him well, they showed in his hue both evening and morning' (my translation, based on the *eChaucer* one).
[27] 'How it was I cannot say, whether his lady did not understand all this, or pretended she did not, one of the two'
[28] See also McTaggart (2012), Yager (1991), Allen 2005, and Mulvey (1975).

of the characters starts to signify and becomes potentially readable right after the mark on skin appears.[29]

In addition to the question of who reads the inscribed skin as in the passage above, one can hence also ask the question of who writes, i.e., who causes a certain hue to appear on a character's face and under which circumstances. Our readings of the different acts of seeing and their effects are complicated by the varying degrees of agency that the medieval theories of vision attributed to the seeing person. From Greek antiquity the Middle Ages had inherited various visual theories of intromission (in which the agent is the object, sending out its image to the passive seer) and extramission (in which the agent is the seer's eye, sending out a beam of light towards the object) (Lindberg 1981: 1–32). The late Middle Ages saw a synthesis of the two theories that resulted in the construction of reciprocity between viewer and object in which the viewer is both active and passive (Crocker 2007: 17–50). Among others, Stanbury (1992) has investigated the intricate interplay of sight and the different degrees of agency connected to seeing, being seen, and refusing to be seen in *Troilus and Criseyde* under these preconditions, claiming that the penetrating glances of both protagonists are simultaneously gendered and gendering and that activity and passivity consequently become reciprocal.

In her analysis of the first passage in book II in which Criseyde looks down from her window to watch Troilus passing in the street (II: 635–658), Stanbury investigates the connection of gaze and agency especially. In this passage, Troilus is looked at extensively by the crowd. His freshness and youth make him "heaven to see" for those who look at him (II: 635–637). He reacts to the shouts and supposedly to the looks by growing a little red with embarrassment: "For which he wex a litel reed for shame" (II: 645).[30] Then, he casts down his eyes. His refusal to return the gaze of the spectators heightens their pleasure of seeing him: "That to byholde it was a noble game / How sobrelich he caste down his yën" (II: 647).[31] This is the "chere" (the 'whole picture') that Criseyde sees. She is touched by the image that makes its way into her heart and her face reacts by turning red:

Criseÿda gan al his chere aspien,
And leet it so softe in hire herte synke,

---

[29] Similarly, Allen (2005: 198) describes that shame "circulates, like the rush of blood that it is; so do gazes. Each blush [...] occurs before the gaze of another."
[30] 'he grew a little red for shame'
[31] 'so that it was a noble sport to see how soberly he cast down his eyes'

> That to hireself she seyde, 'Who yaf me drynke?'
> For of hire owen thought she wex al reed (II: 649–652).³²

At the end of the passage, Criseyde, embarrassed, pulls her head back and thus simultaneously stops looking and removes herself from sight (II: 656–657).³³

The effects of Troilus' being looked at, of his refusal to return the gaze, of Criseyde's watching of Troilus, and of her embarrassment are all inscribed by hue on their respective faces. In addition to telling his audiences of the mutual embarrassment, the narrator also tells them about the surface on which this embarrassment can be seen, thus evoking a visual representation of feelings. What is more, no actual contact is established through the eyes of the characters. Instead, what connects the two lovers is their joint blushing. Stanbury points out how Troilus' and Criseyde's blushes here work as reciprocal gestures: "Troilus' blush reveals *her* sense of sudden exposure; his blush, we might say, is really her own" (1992: 237, emphasis in the original). Thus, skin here works as a legible surface of signification on which the intricate connections of emotions and agency are explored. This impression is substantiated by a second passage in book II (1247–1270) that parallels this first one and that suggests that these hue references are anything but accidental.

In an echo of the first procession in which the characters fail to make visual contact, Troilus rides by Criseyde's window a second time. This second procession is a setup by Pandarus who, as if in recognition of the askew glances of the first procession, now directs the lovers' gazes very consciously. He hereby achieves completely different 'visual dynamics,' to borrow Stanbury's term. In this scene as well, the effects of the lovers' gazes are inscribed on their faces. Pandarus commands Criseyde to come and see Troilus, blackmails her into not fleeing back into her room this time and exposes her and her blush to Troilus' gaze:

> 'Nece, ysee who comth here ride!
> O fle naught in (he seeth us, I suppose),
> Lest he may thynken that ye hym eschuwe.'
> 'Nay, nay,' quod she, and wex as red as rose (II: 1253–1256).³⁴

---

32 'Criseyde all the time took in his look, and let it softly sink into her heart, until she said, "Who has given me a potion?" At her own thought she grew all red'
33 Robertson explores this retraction, among others, as an instance of "snail-horn perception" in her forthcoming article of the same title.
34 '"Niece, see who comes riding this way. Ah, don't fly away! He sees us, no doubt, and he might think that you shun him!" "No, no!" she said, and grew ruddy like a rose'

This time, Troilus does not cast his eyes down but looks up. The final nod to Pandarus before riding away signals the complicity between the two men and reveals that this supposedly incidental encounter is a setup. However, Troilus is as moved by the ensuing feelings as Criseyde is. While Criseyde turns red as a rose, Troilus' hue is described as "moving," probably indicating a repeated change of one colour to another and back:

> With that he gan hire humbly to saluwe
> With dredful chere, and oft his hewes muwe;
> And up his look debonairly he caste,
> And bekked on Pandare, and forth he paste (II: 1257–1260).[35]

The concurrence of moving hue and being moved emotionally is not coincidental and suggests, again, that skin inscribed by hue may be especially suited for the expression of feelings.

Between this passage and the one discussed above, the visual dynamics differ greatly and the agency ascribed to each character, especially through their acts of seeing, has changed considerably. However, the inscriptions on their faces remain very similar. This shows that the non-verbal expression of feelings on skin, while it reinforces the visual dynamics of the work, is not a very refined one. Hue merely signals that emotional turmoil of a specific kind affects the character, but the emotions ultimately elude precise description. In what follows, I propose that the narrator comes to just that conclusion when he reflects on his poetic options of writing about love.

The Metapoetic Function of Hue

In my argument so far, I have suggested that hue in *Troilus and Criseyde* serves the overarching functions of underlining the narrative's structure and of further complicating the narrator's explorations of agency. While hue means 'colour of the face' throughout the work, it clearly does more than just to betray a character's feelings at any distinct moment of the narrative. However, there is one single instance of the term 'hue' in the work that does not seem to fit Friedman's category of affective physiognomy because it cannot unequivocally be identified as referring to skin tone. It occurs when the narrator offers an authorial apology at the beginning of book II (2–28) in which he presents himself as someone who

---

[35] 'With that Troilus humbly greeted her with a timid look, often changed color, and cast a look up courteously, nodded to Pandarus and passed on his way'

has great difficulties writing about love. In this apology, he portrays himself first as a historian of love when he invokes Clio as his muse (II: 8–11). Second, he presents himself as only a translator when he claims that he translates from Latin and thus wants neither to be thanked nor blamed for the work, and certainly refuses to be blamed for any "lame words" (II: 14–18). Chaucer scholars have argued that these self-reflexive comments are also in fact discussions of genre, in which the roles of the translator and of the historian are weighed against each other (e.g., Butterfield 2006).

The part of the apology that has however not been read in this context is the narrator's use of the proverb of the blind man that cannot judge well by the hue: "Ek though I speeke of love unfelyngly, / No wondre is, for it nothyng of newe is; / A blynd man kan nat juggen wel in hewis" (II: 19–21).[36] With this proverb, the narrator once more underlines that he cannot write about love with feeling because of his lack of experience. Most scholars have understood the term 'hue' here to mean colour, which places the proverb in a long European tradition (e.g., Kittredge 1910). Some have seen it as a pun by which Chaucer refers to the 'colours of rhetoric,' a term which he employs in the *Canterbury Tales* (e.g., Taylor 1983, 1989). Others, investigating colour in medieval literature, have claimed that it points to the significance of colour symbolism in the work (e.g., Huxtable 2006). However, these interpretations neglect the fact that Chaucer never employs the term 'hue' in *Troilus and Criseyde* to mean just colour. Apart from this one exception, every single reference to hue is a reference to the colour of the face, and more specifically the colour of the face as caused by feelings, i.e. corresponding to Friedman's concept of affective physiognomy. This at least opens the possibility of reading hue in this proverb as the colour on someone's face too. This interpretation does not alter the meaning of the proverb: Whether the blind man is unable to judge well by the colour or by the colour of someone's face results in the same protest of inability. However, I argue that this reading will help us see a new aspect of the authorial apology itself, namely a hint at a third role for the narrator, in addition to those of the translator and the historian.

In her seminal reading of this apology, Ardis Butterfield (2006: 11) interprets the hue-proverb as a further comment on Chaucer's self-presentation as historian and translator and his professed inability to write about love:

---

[36] 'And though I speak of love without due feeling, it is no wonder, for it is nothing new; a blind man cannot judge *well by the hue*' (the italics are my amendment of the *eChaucer* translation, in accordance with my proposed of reading the passage; *eChaucer* has 'cannot judge colors well')

> [Chaucer] presents himself as both [historian and translator], but each as an excuse to explain away the inadequacies of the forthcoming story. Narrative is not the answer to the problem of how to represent this history of love: it creates a false teleology and an account that distorts, ignores, or simply doesn't see ("a blynd man kan not juggen wel in hewis").

In the same way in which a blind man cannot see, she argues, the account that the narrator can provide, either in his role as a historian or in his role as a translator, is unable to grasp what is essential. But what if we read hue in the proverb as a reference to marked facial skin and bring the term here into conversation with the ways in which Chaucer employs it elsewhere in the work? Building on Butterfield's reading, I suggest that there is in fact a third role for the poet that is implicitly discussed in this apology, namely that of the romance writer. The third stanza supports this suggestion: when the narrator evokes the distant places and long bygone times to explain the utter dissimilarity of Troy to his own times ("Ek for to wynnen love in sondry ages, / In sondry londes, sondry ben usages," II: 27–28),[37] he points towards conventions of romance that neither fit the self-ascribed role of historian nor that of translator that Butterfield identifies for this passage. While the authorial protestations of inability are thus expanded by another role, the conclusion remains the same: the romance writer cannot provide a more valid account than the historian or the translator can, even with the specific poetic devices he has at his disposal, such as employing faces as additional surfaces of signification.

Hue, I have suggested with Friedman here, is clearly a feature of romance in *Troilus and Criseyde*. Friedman (1981: 146) claims that affective physiognomy, of which hue is one element, is a device for an *auctor* of romance to express emotion. However, on closer inspection one realises that the expression of the actual feeling is a crude one, with red hue signalling shame and pale hue signalling grief for example. If hue indeed is a device that the romance writer employs, then it is not in itself sufficient to express the complex inner workings of characters such as Troilus. Instead, hue only signals that there *are* feelings. It is a shortcut in the same way in which the many proverbs in *Troilus and Criseyde* are shortcuts.[38] The statement that a character blushes or pales triggers a contract between the narrator and his audience according to which this specific shortcut is a viable way of communication within the generic framework of romance. Both sides understand (or pretend to understand) what is meant without the narrator having to go into much detail. Thus, hue does not in fact help to describe what the protagonists are feeling; it only signals *that* they are feeling. As

---

37 'And in various ages and various lands, there have been various customs to win love'
38 See also Taylor (1989, ch. 4).

Stephanie Downes and Rebecca McNamara (2016: 453) claim: "Like the faint or swoon [...] descriptions of the effects of emotion on the body and the face often stand in for the emotions themselves, which are left unnamed and open to interpretation." John P. Hermann (1985: 134) consequently cautions against an "uncomplicated mapping of gestures to mental states." Thus, in the same way in which the specific instruments of historian and translator are not suitable to create an account that does not distort the love story, hue as the device of the romance writer is an insufficient instrument to write about love. Consequently, the narrator, a blind man in terms of love, does not even try to judge by the hue. Instead, he employs hue in his authorial apology as a figure for the generic conventions of romance and thus assigns it a metapoetic function. Consequently, whenever hue appears in the work, the narrator potentially reflects on its viability as an instrument of the romance writer. In what follows, I return to instances in the narrative where this is the case.

When Troilus sees Criseyde for the first time in the temple and falls in love at first sight (book I), he goes straight to his palace, into his bedroom, sits on the bed and there starts sighing and groaning due to his lovesickness. This clear inward movement from the temple to the palace to the bedroom to the bed does however not stop there.[39] It continues right into the character himself in what modern editors have called the *Canticus Troili*. In these twenty-one lines of interior monologue, Troilus' feelings are revealed, followed by a prayer to the god of love. Together, these passages result in five stanzas of direct thought in which Troilus expresses his feelings. Next, we learn that the fire of love burns so hot in Troilus that he loses his hue sixty times a day: "The fyr of love [...] brende hym so in soundry wise ay newe, / That sexti tyme a day he loste his hewe" (I: 435–441).[40] This sixtyfold losing of hue is an inscription on Troilus' face of his extreme inner turmoil. It is not much more than a signal, however, that something extreme is going on, because hue itself cannot express what, exactly, it is that tortures Troilus. Instead, the reader knows about Troilus' emotional state from the five preceding stanzas.

Clearly, the inscription of Troilus' feelings on his face is neither necessary nor particularly helpful here, but Chaucer nevertheless chose to present it. The remark about Troilus' losing hue is in fact his addition to his otherwise very close translation from Boccaccio. I suggest that Chaucer inserted the remark here exactly to provide the audience with another, second surface of significa-

---

39 On the spatial aspects of this passage see Kern-Stähler (2002: 192–195) and Strohm (2015: 52).
40 'The fire of love [...] burned him so ever anew in various ways that sixty times a day he grew pale' (i.e. 'lost his hue,' my translation)

tion. The description of hue is a romance writer's instrument to show rather than tell his audience about the feelings of the character. What happens in this passage, consequently, is that the narrator compares two of the roles he assumes: that of the romance writer and that of the translator. On the one hand, he presents himself as the translator of his fictional source Lollius (to whom he attributes the song, I: 394)[41] who seeks to represent Troilus' feelings in the song. On the other hand, he presents himself as the romance writer who seeks to represent the extremity of Troilus' emotional turmoil by describing the non-verbal expression of feelings on his face as wildly changing hues. Two possible approaches to the task of writing about love are thus compared and contrasted.

Another instance in which hue serves as a metapoetic comment is found in two almost identical passages from book III that are separated by 900 lines in the narrative. I present them side-by-side here for easier comparison:

This Troilus, that herde his lady preye	This Troilus ful soone on knees hym sette
Of lordshipe hym, wax neither quyk ne ded,	Ful sobrely, right be hyre beddes hed,
Ne myghte o word for shame to it seye,	And in his beste wyse his lady grette.
Although men sholde smyten of his hed.	But Lord, so she wex sodeynliche red!
But Lord, so he wex sodeynliche red,	Ne though men sholde smyten of hire hed,
And sire, his lessoun, that he wende konne	She kouthe nought a word aright out brynge
To preyen hire, is thorugh his wit ironne.	So sodeynly, for his sodeyn comynge.
(III: 78–84)[42]	(III: 953–959)[43]

In these two parallel passages, Troilus and Criseyde meet in person and speak in the privacy of their respective bedrooms. In the first passage, Criseyde addresses Troilus who is too embarrassed to speak and instead blushes. In the second, which echoes the first, the roles and the sequence are inverted: Criseyde, addressed by Troilus kneeling in front of her bed, first blushes and then fails to produce a word. Both male and female protagonist turn "sodenlyche red" (III: 82; 956) to the same extent and under the same circumstances. Against scholarly claims that blushes are gendered and gendering (e.g., Allen 2005: 192), the clear-

---

[41] Which is in fact a Petrarchan sonnet he added to his main source's account. On Lollius see, e.g., Minnis (1982: 24).

[42] 'When Troilus heard his lady ask him for lordship, he was between life and death for shame, nor could he have said a word in reply, even if someone had been about to smite off his head; and Lord, how red he grew so suddenly! And, sir, the lesson that he thought he knew by heart to beseech his lady with, had fully run out of his memory.'

[43] 'Soon Troilus was on his knees right at her bedside, and soberly in his best fashion greeted his lady. But, Lord, how red she grew suddenly! Even if men were to cut off her head, she could not have brought out a word, because of his sudden arrival.'

ly ungendered blushes here and throughout the work suggest that hue is purposefully presented as a literary device that lacks precision.

In both passages, the red hue also accompanies a sudden and violent halt of the speeches. The word "suddenly" is repeated insistently and the violence of the speechlessness is emphasised by the narrator's claim, in both passages, that the characters could not continue speaking even if they were threatened with beheading ("men sholde smyten of his [hire] hed," III: 81; 957). In both passages, words fail to express feelings. The characters' complete lack of words echoes the narrator's difficulties at finding the right words: the narrative flow is interrupted almost as violently as the characters' speeches. Again, the narrator adds hue to the words on his page, but he finds the device wanting: words fail, but so does hue. In both passages, an authoritative outside agent is required to bring the narrative back into motion:

Criseyde al this aspied wel ynough,	But Pandarus, that so wel koude feele
For she was wis, and loved hym nevere the lasse,	In every thyng, to pleye anon bigan,
Al nere he malapert, or made it tough,	And seyde, "Nece, se how this lord kan knele!
Or was to bold, to synge a fool a masse.	Now for youre trouthe, se this gentil man!"
But whan his shame gan somwhat to passe,	And with that word he for a quysshen ran,
His resons, as I may my rymes holde,	And seyde, "Kneleth now, while that yow leste;
I yow wol telle, as techen bokes olde.	There God youre hertes brynge soone at reste!"
(III: 85 – 91)⁴⁴	(III: 960 – 966)⁴⁵

In the first passage, the agent that brings the narrative back into motion is the "bokes olde" from which the narrator, in his role as a translator, claims to be translating. In the second passage, Pandarus steps in, he who knows so much about feelings ("that so wel koude feele") and who "sets the experience of emotion in motion" (Downes and McNamara 2016: 450).⁴⁶ In both passages, to quote

---

44 'Criseyde, because she was wise, noted all this well enough and loved him none the less, even though he was not presumptuous or self-assured or arrogant enough to sing a fool a mass. But what he said, when his shame had begun to pass, I will tell you as well as I can, as I find it in old books.'
45 'But Pandarus, whose feeling was so quick in every case, began then to make sport, and said, "Niece, see how this lord can kneel now to beg for your pledge! Only see this nobleman now!" And with that word he ran for a cushion and said, "Kneel now as long as you wish! And may God soon bring your hearts to rest!"'
46 Windeatt (1992: 214) likewise states that Pandarus "generates action from feeling" (as quoted in Downes and McNamara 2016: 450). Waswo (1983: 10) claims that this role makes Pandarus a "surrogate author."

Butterfield (2006: 11), "narrative is not the answer." Both of the roles that the narrator attributes to himself according to Butterfield's reading, that of the historian and that of the translator, are found to be wanting. Hue however is not the answer either. The role of the romance writer, too, is no more than an excuse to "explain away the inadequacies of the forthcoming story" (Butterfield 2006: 11). Thus, the audience is presented with a narrator who juggles with a complex set of roles and poetic options to write about love and who comes to the conclusion that, ultimately, he will fail in the task.

In conclusion, hue in *Troilus and Criseyde* invites conceptualisations of human skin as inscribable and potentially readable. As a mirror of the letters and illuminations on a parchment page, hue, the inscription on the *mise en abyme* page of the face, goes beyond betraying feelings and instead has the overarching functions of underlining the narrative, of reinforcing explorations of agency, and of functioning as a metapoetic comment on a romance writer's options when writing about love. In the authorial apology of book II, we hence encounter not just a translator and a historian, as Butterfield argues, but also a romance writer. In what can be read as a gesture of *dissimulatio*, the narrator tells his audiences, once more, that he is unable to write about love. But Chaucer shows them that the opposite is the case, in his nuanced explorations of the different poetic options of writing about love, one of which is to write on human skin.

Works Cited

Primary Sources

Benson, Larry D. (ed.). 1987. *Geoffrey Chaucer: The Riverside Chaucer*. 3rd ed. Boston: Houghton Mifflin.

"eChaucer: Chaucer in the Twenty-First Century." Issued by Gerard NeCastro. <http://machias.edu/faculty/necastro/chaucer/concordance/.> [accessed 10 August 2017].

Platt, Arthur (trans.) 1910–1952. "Aristotle: De Generatione Animalium." In: John A. Smith and William D. Ross (eds.). *The Works of Aristotle*. Volume 5, Book II.6. Oxford: Clarendon Press.

Seymour, M.C. (gen. ed). 1975. *John of Trevisa: On the Properties of Things*. Oxford: Oxford University Press.

Wentworth Thompson, D'Arcy (trans.). *Aristotle: Historia Animalium*. Book III. *Internet Classics Archive*. <classics.mit.edu/Aristotle/history_anim.3.iii.html> [accessed 26 April 2017].

Secondary Sources

Allen, Valerie. 2005. "Waxing Red: Shame and the Body, Shame and the Soul." In: Lisa Perfetti (ed.). *The Representation of Women's Emotions in Medieval and Early Modern Culture*. Gainsville: University of Florida Press. 191–210.
Biggam, Carole. P. 1993. "Aspects of Chaucer's Adjectives of Hue." *The Chaucer Review* 28.1: 41–53.
Bolens, Guillemette. 2012. *The Style of Gestures: Embodiment and Cognition in Literary Narrative*. Rethinking Theory. Baltimore: John Hopkins University Press.
Butterfield, Ardis. 1995. "*Mise-en-page* in the *Troilus* Manuscripts: Chaucer and French Manuscript Culture." *Huntingdon Library Quarterly* 58.1: 49–80.
Butterfield, Ardis. 2006. "Chaucer and the Detritus of the City." In: Ardis Butterfield (ed). *Chaucer and the City*. Woodbridge: Boydell and Brewer. 3–22.
Connor, Steven. 2004. *The Book of Skin*. London: Reaktion Books.
Crocker, Holly A. 2007. *Chaucer's Visions of Manhood*. New York and Basingstoke: Palgrave Macmillan.
Dällenbach, Lucien. 1989. *The Mirror in the Text*. Chicago: University of Chicago Press.
Downes, Stephanie and Rebecca F. McNamara. 2016. "The History of Emotions and Middle English Literature." *Literature Compass* 13.6: 444–456.
Downes, Stephanie and Stephanie Trigg. 2017. "Facing Up to the History of Emotions." *postmedieval: A Journal of Medieval Cultural Studies* 8.1: 3–11.
Edwards, A. S. G. 2003. "The Text of John Trevisa's Translation of Bartholomaeus Anglicus' *De Proprietatibus Rerum*." *Text* 15: 83–96.
Feher, Michel. 1989. *Fragments for a History of the Human Body*. 3 vols. New York: Urzone.
Flannery, Mary. 2011. "A Bloody Shame: Chaucer's Honourable Women." *The Review of English Studies* 62: 337–357.
Flannery, Mary. 2012. "The Concept of Shame in Late-medieval English Literature." *Literature Compass* 9.2: 166–182.
Friedman, John B. 1981. "Another Look at Chaucer and the Physiognomists." *Studies in Philology* 78.2: 138–152.
Grosz, Elizabeth. 1990. "Inscriptions and Body-Maps: Representations and the Corporeal." In: Anne Cranny-Francis and Terry Threadgold (eds.). *Feminine, Masculine and Representation*. Sidney: Allen and Unwin. 62–74.
Hermann, John P. 1985. "Gesture and Seduction in *Troilus and Criseyde*." *Studies in the Age of Chaucer* 7: 107–135.
Holsinger, Bruce. 2009. "Of Pigs and Parchment: Medieval Studies and the Coming of the Animal." *PMLA* 124.2: 616–623.
Holsinger, Bruce. 2010. "Parchment Ethics: A Statement of More than Modest Concern." *New Medieval Literatures* 12: 130–136.
Huxtable, Michael J. 2006. "The Medieval Gaze at Grips with a Medieval World." In: Carole P. Biggam, Christian J. Kay and Nicola J. Pitchford (eds.). *Progress in Colour Studies: Language and Culture*. Amsterdam and Philadelphia: John Benjamins. 199–218.
Jablonski, Nina G. 2006 *Skin: A Natural History*. Berkeley: University of California Press.
Kay, Sarah. 2004. "Flayed Skin as objet a." In: Jane E. Burns (ed.). *Medieval Fabrications*. New York: Palgrave Macmillan. 193–205.

Kay, Sarah. 2006. "Original Skin. Flaying, Reading, and Thinking in the Legend of Saint Bartholomew and Other Works." *Journal of Medieval and Early Modern Studies* 36.1: 35–73.

Kay, Sarah. 2011. "Legible Skins. Animals and the Ethics of Medieval Reading." *postmedieval: A Journal of Medieval Cultural Studies* 2.1: 13–32.

Kern-Stähler, Annette. 2002. *A Room of One's Own: Reale und Mentale Innenräume weiblicher Selbstbestimmung im spätmittelalterlichen England.* Tradition–Reform–Innovation 3. Frankfurt am Main: Peter Lang.

Kittredge, G. L. 1910. "Chauceriana." *Modern Philology* 7.4: 465–483.

Lindberg, David C. 1981. *Theories of Vision from al-Kindi to Kepler.* Chicago: University of Chicago Press.

Lomperis, Linda and Sarah Stanbury (eds.). 1993. *Feminist Approaches to the Body in Medieval Literature.* New Cultural Studies Series 14. Philadelphia: University of Pennsylvania Press.

Mann, Jill. 1989. "Shakespeare and Chaucer: 'what is Criseyde worth?'." *Cambridge Quarterly* 18.2: 109–128.

McNamer, Sarah. 2007. "Feeling." In: Paul Strohm (ed.). *Middle English.* Oxford Twenty-First Century Approaches to Literature. Oxford: Oxford University Press. 241–257.

McTaggart, Anne. 2012. "Shamed Guiltless: Criseyde, Dido, and Chaucerian Ethics." *Chaucer Review* 46.4: 371–402.

Mulvey, Laura. 1975. "Visual Pleasure and Narrative Cinema." *Screen* 16: 6–18.

MED = *Middle English Dictionary.* 1952–2001. Ed. Hans Kurath, Sherman M. Kuhn, John Reidy and Robert E. Lewis. Ann Arbor: University of Michigan Press. <http://quod.lib.umich.edu/m/med/>.

Minnis, Alastair J. 1982. *Chaucer and Pagan Antiquity.* Chaucer Studies. Cambridge: Boydell & Brewer.

Robertson, Elizabeth. 2013. "Noli me tangere: The Enigma of Touch in Middle English Religious Literature and Art for and about Women." In: Katie L. Walter (ed.). *Reading Skin in Medieval Literature and Culture.* The New Middle Ages. New York: Palgrave Macmillan. 29–55.

Robertson, Elizabeth. Forthcoming 2018. "First Encounter: 'Snail-Horn Perception' in Geoffrey Chaucer's *Troilus and Criseyde*." In: Helen Hickey et al. (eds.). *Contemporary Chaucer Across the Centuries.* Turnhout: Brepols.

Rust, Martha. 2013. "Blood and Tears as Ink: Writing the Pictorial Sense of the Text." *Chaucer Review* 47.4: 390–415.

Stanbury, Sarah. 1991. "The Voyeur and the Private Life in *Troilus and Criseyde.*" *Studies in the Age of Chaucer* 13: 141–158.

Stanbury, Sarah. 1992. "The Lover's Gaze in *Troilus and Criseyde.*" In: R. A. Shoaf and Catherine S. Cox (eds.). *Chaucer's Troilus and Criseyde: 'Subgit to Alle Poesye.'* Essays in Criticism. Binghamton: Medieval & Renaissance Texts & Studies. 224–238.

Strohm, Paul. 1989. *Social Chaucer.* Cambridge, Mass.: Harvard University Press.

Strohm, Paul. 2015. "The Space of Desire in Chaucer's and Shakespeare's Troy." In: Andrew J. Johnston, Russell West-Pavlov and Elisabeth Kempf (eds.). *Love, History and Emotion in Chaucer and Shakespeare: Troilus and Criseyde and Troilus and Cressida.* Manchester: Manchester University Press. 46–60.

Taylor, Karla. 1983. "A Text and Its Afterlife: Dante and Chaucer." *Comparative Literature* 35.1: 1–20.
Taylor, Karla. 1989. *Chaucer Reads* The Divine Comedy. Stanford: Stanford University Press.
Trigg, Stephanie. 2014. "Introduction: Emotional Histories–Beyond the Personalization of the Past and the Abstaction of Affect Theory." *Exemplaria* 26.1: 3–15.
Trigg, Stephanie. 2016. "'Language in her eye:' the Expressive Face of Criseyde/Cressida." In: Andrew J. Johnston, Russell West-Pavlov and Elisabeth Kempf (eds.). *Love, History and Emotion in Chaucer and Shakespeare: Troilus and Criseyde and Troilus and Cressida*. Manchester: Manchester University Press. 94–108.
Walter, Katie L. (ed.) 2013. *Reading Skin in Medieval Literature and Culture*. The New Middle Ages. New York: Palgrave Macmillan.
Waswo, Richard. 1983. "The Narrator of *Troilus and Criseyde*." *ELH* 50.1: 1–25.
Windeatt, Barry. 1992. *Troilus and Criseyde*. Oxford Guides to Chaucer. Oxford: Clarendon Press.
Yager, Susan. 1991. *Visual Perception in Chaucer*. Ann Arbor: University of Pennsylvania.

Part III: **Writing Dermal Identities**

Pax Gutierrez-Neal
Like a Second Skin:

Appropriation and (Mis)interpretation of Identities in *Sir Gawain and the Green Knight* and *William of Palerne*

Abstract: Skin functions as a transmutable, shaping force of identity in the fourteenth-century romances *Sir Gawain and the Green Knight* and *William of Palerne*. Animal hide or human flesh, the manifestations of skin formulate identity: the Green Knight's disguising flesh, Gawain's scarred neck, Alphouns' transformed skin, and William's and Meliors' animal hides. However, the appropriation of the skins for identity eventually becomes uncontrollable, vulnerable to multiple (mis)interpretations. Gawain's experiences at Hautdesert force him to reformulate himself, and Gawain is forced to echo his traumatic axe-stroke each time he ties the girdle around himself, but his peers cannot fathom his shamed reading of the green baldric. William's revelation of his unknown lineage leads to a crisis of identity, one that he attempts to alleviate as he wears various skins (bearskins, deerskin, the werewolf-shield) until his royal blood is revealed. William inevitably loses control of his appropriated signifiers. The lovers become more and more like their animal disguises until, finally, a queen cuts the hides away, effectively 'skinning' them from their animality. In these romances, the (inter)layering of skin is a powerful but ultimately uncontrollable signifier of identity, one that ultimately throws into question the human status of the signified.

Skin plays an important role in the fourteenth-century romances *Sir Gawain and the Green Knight* and *William of Palerne*, fulfilling the functions of armour and cloth in providing protection and identification. Animal hide or human flesh, armour or baldric, all perform much the same role in these romances. Ultimately, the (inter)layering of skin and armour culminates into a final amalgamation of identity that compromises the overladen bearer. The appropriation of such a composite symbol by the agent results in a loss of control over said symbol, rendering the agent's identity vulnerable to misinterpretation. The very skin of the agent becomes a slippery signifier of the self.

Skin is a site of transformation, permeable and potent. Sara Kay (2011) examines the role of skin both as a medium of writing (vellum) and as the subject of writing (werewolf tales, bestiaries, etc.); she utilises the idea of the "suture" as a mark of the vellum reassuming the significance of skin when flesh appears in a text, resulting in an "uncanny [...] sense that it [the suture] insinuates a disturbance in the field of symbolization, even if this disturbance is not itself symbolized" (Kay 2011: 15). Even the medieval Latin word *pellis* refers to both animal and human skin as well as parchment. One cannot forget, either, that "animal skins are bearers of meaning that can be assumed" by human speakers or human bodies (Kay 2011: 15). There is a possible conflation, then, of the animal skin held in hand and the human skin of that very hand. Skin is universal yet transmutable: animal skin, human skin, vellum, books – it remains skin even while it inhabits various forms, serves various functions. And yet the skin itself is "iconically [...] able to stand in for all skin:" the skin is the "symbolic language" of the body, of the self (Gonzales-Day 2002: 29). Taken a step further, a single patch of skin can imply not only the entirety of the physical body it encompasses, but also the very sense of identity held by said body.[1]

This function of skin is particularly potent to these questions of identity, as skin can act quite literally as a catalogue of the self: It is a signifier of trauma(s) not only through its potential metonymy for the body but also through the physical markers left behind. In their study of trauma narratives, M. J. Larrabee, S. Weine and P. Woollcott (2003: 353–354) define trauma as a shaping force that "undercuts the usual, slashes unspoken assumptions to shreds, and attacks the very meaning of one's life, even as the trauma experiencer [sic] sometimes continues the motions of everyday existence." It is a challenge to one's preconceived self-definition, a transfiguration of identity. And skin, as a transformative site, not only represents but also potentially transmutes those very signifiers of trauma and identity. Recall the use of skins in vellum: the animal's hide is shape-shifted from one form into another, metamorphosing signification from animal *pellis* to manuscript *pellis*.[2] The arguably traumatic process of cutting and (re)shaping skin from one *pellis* to another re-categorises the flesh from living animal to inanimate object, even as the texture, the scent, the known origins of the material insist on reflecting its old life, layering the skin-of-the-page onto the skin-of-the-holding-hand. Recall, too, how the line between animal skin and human skin erodes in this contact. Skin is not only transformative, but inherently ambiguous. Even as it displays traumas, reflects shaped identities, it also bears the echoes of its past alongside the marks of its present self, conflating mixed identities into an imperfectly translated whole; it is an unstable signifier. Even so, *Sir Gawain and the Green Knight* and *William of Palerne* focus on the flesh, depicting skin as invaluable in shaping and (mis)reading identities.

---

[1] This symbolic function is more literal for Rhodes' examination of skin and legible identity in *Amis and Amiloun* (this volume).

[2] Cox (this volume) discusses this process of manuscript production in greater detail.

Un/Lacing: Skinning and Arming

For *Sir Gawain and the Green Knight*, the most striking images of skin reside in the infamous hunting sequences. These scenes utilise sensually narrated descriptions of the skinning and processing of the animal. The flaying of the hart in the first hunt, for example, is rich in detail, providing over twenty lines of step-by-step procedures. Of particular interest in this lengthy passage are the lines "Lystily for laucyng þe lere of þe knot" (l. 1333),[3] "Alle þe rymez by þe rybbez radly þay lauce" (l. 1342),[4] and "Bi þe byȝt al of þe byȝes / Þe lapez þay lauce bihynde" (ll. 1349–1350).[5] Note the repetition of the specific terminology *lauce* and *laucyng*. These terms are forms of the verb *losen*, which can mean to 'detach' or 'loosen (skin),' while in gerund *laucing* signifies the '[u]ntying of knots, [or] bonds' (*MED losen* v.). The word appears three times in less than twenty lines, echoing throughout the skinning sequence. Why does the poet so emphasise this 'loosening of skin?'

While this terminology may not seem significant at first, one must note that skinning was a highly ritualised endeavor, moreso for hunted prey than for butchered chattel. As Anne Rooney (1993: 15) observes, medieval hunting practices were "taught and learnt as a system of precise language," and so the correct use of terminology was paramount. Satirically, Salisbury's (1994) *Policraticus* warns that incorrect skinning technique, or even the misuse of hunting terms, would result in severe beatings or brandings to display the culprit's ignorance; while these comments are parodic, their humour is rooted in truth. Hunting and skinning were so highly ritualised that breaches of procedure could be mockingly ascribed hyperbolic punishments that nonetheless reflect the importance placed upon those processes (Marvin 2006: 134). And, for hunters, skinning was the focal point of their endeavors: the power of the hunt rested in that "transformative moment of [...] the unmaking sequence" (Marvin 2006: 141). Skin, that useful and malleable surface, was integral to this ritualised activity, and itself held some inherent power. And *Sir Gawain and the Green Knight* self-consciously depicts this ritual, with only a few discrepancies – Rooney (1993: 181) observes that while a few stages of the hart's skinning and breaking

---

[3] 'Carefully loosening for the ligature of the knot.' Quotations for *Sir Gawain the Green Knight* are cited from Andrew and Waldron's (2010) revised *The Poems of the Pearl Manuscript*, while translations for *Sir Gawain the Green Knight* are adapted from Andrew and Waldron's (2002) earlier, bilingual edition of the same. Modernizations of *William of Palerne* are developed via reference to Bunt's (1985: 338–489) glossary notes.
[4] 'All the membranes on the ribs they quickly loosen'
[5] 'behind the fork of the thighs, they loosen the skin folds'

are slightly out of order, the *Gawain*-poet nonetheless remains precise in their terminology. The attention, then, that *Sir Gawain and the Green Knight* gives to this scene – the hart boasts the longest skinning sequence of the three hunts – fits with the importance of skinning itself, and its use of specific terminology is only appropriate.

However, if skinning is a "transformative moment of [...] unmaking," then arming itself could be an equally transformative moment of *making*. An armed knight is, after all, primarily identified by the markings and features of his arms. Both were procedural, with hunting rituals dominating skinning processes and arming requiring, for practical purposes, its own precise steps (Nickel 1995: 7, 10). In fact, skinning, with its specific terms of loosening and unbinding, creates a nearly perfect mirror for arming's own words of binding and lacing. The 'loosening of skin' becomes a 'fastening of armour,' in these mirrored transfigurations of shape.

One should note that arming is a common trope in medieval romance, appearing often as lengthy descriptions of both the arms and the arming process (Stock 1995: 56). And appropriately, *Sir Gawain and the Green Knight* provides us with a lengthy arming scene, wherein many such binding terms are employed:

> Þenne set þay þe sabatounz vpon þe segge fotez,
> His legez lapped in stel with luflych greuez,
> With polaynez piched þerto, policed ful clene,
> Aboute his knez knaged wyth knotez of golde;
> Queme quyssewes þen, þat coyntlych closed
> His thick þrawen þyȝes, with þwonges to tachched;
> [...]
> When he watz hasped in armes his harnays watz ryche:
> Þe lest lachet oþer loupe lemed of golde. (ll. 574–591)[6]

Gawain is *lapped* ('enclosed') and *hasped* ('latched') in his armour, *tachched* ('fastened') with *lachet* and *loupe* (loops of cloth or leather) and *þwonges* ('leather thongs'). The process of donning and doffing a knight's armour is parallel to the skinning and binding up process of gutting a game animal: Gawain is laced up in his equipment in a reversal of the prey animal being *vnlace[d]* ('unfas-

---

6 'Then they set the steel shoes upon the man's feet; his legs enclosed in steel by beautiful greaves to which were attached brightly polished knee pieces, fastened about his knees with gold knots. Fine cuisses then, that cleverly enclosed his thick muscular thighs, fastened with leather thongs; [...] When he was latched in armour, his accoutrement was rich: the least loop or loop-hole gleamed of gold.'

tened') from its hide, as the boar is later in the poem (l. 1606).⁷ While one is fastened tightly into his outer layer, rich in identifying markers, the other is unfastened and loosened from its own. The skin of the animal is a reflection of the armour of the knight, and vice versa.

As one can see from above, *Sir Gawain and the Green Knight* follows the arming trope as closely as it does its hunting ritual. When Gawain is armed, the text employs procedural terminology, noting in the first sequence that he is "Dubbed in a dublet of a dere tars, / *And syþen* a crafty capados" in his first arming scene (ll. 571–572, emphasis added).⁸ The second follows the pattern as well: "*Fyrst* he clad hym in his cloþez, þe colde for to were, / *And syþen* his oþer harnays" (ll. 2015–2016, emphasis added).⁹ The poem is almost self-conscious in its step-by-step portrayal of the arming and skinning sequences, loosely presenting both as procedural mirrors of each other.

This parallel of skin and armour is much clearer in *William of Palerne*. Despite its characteristics as a romance trope, *William of Palerne*'s arming scenes are neither lengthy nor detailed. While William does undergo several arming and disarming scenes, none are more than two lines: "Anon he was armed at alle maner poyntes" (l. 3278);¹⁰ "Þe quen him loveli ladde riȝt to h[er]e chaumber, / unarmed him anon, and afterward cloþed" (ll. 3475–3476);¹¹ and "and as blive þe burdes brouȝt him to hire chaumber / and unarmed him anon, and afterward him cloþed" (ll. 3669–3670).¹² Nor do these scenes provide any detail of William's arms or dis/arming. Their purpose is merely to inform the reader that dis/arming has occurred. In fact, the only arms-related scene given in great detail is William's choosing of a standard:

> a god schel of gold graiþed clene,
> and wel and faire wiþinne a werwolf depeynted,

---

7 Similar to the word *losen*, *vnlacen* is another hunting term for cutting or flaying game, meaning to 'loosen' or 'unfasten' (*MED unlāsen* v.). While etymologically unrelated, their usage and definition in hunting ritual renders them significant here. The term *vnlacen* is also specifically applied to moments of 'removing armour' (*MED unlāsen* v.), forging an analogue between skinning game animal and disarming a knight.
8 'Dressed in a jacket of splendid, rich fabric, *and then* a skillfully-made cape'
9 '*First* they dressed him in his clothes, to protect from the cold, *and then* his other armour'
10 'At once, he was armed in every respect to perfection.' Quotations for *William of Palerne* are taken from Bunt (1985).
11 'The queen gracefully led him right to her chamber, removed his armour immediately, and afterward dressed him'
12 'and at once the women brought him to her chamber and removed his armour immediately, and afterward dressed him'

> þat be hidous and huge, to have alle his riȝtes,
> of þe covenablest colour to knowe in þe feld. (ll. 3216–3219)[13]

Even here, however, Queen Felice's offer does not include armour: she asks, "'what signe is þe levest / to have schape in þi scheld to schene armes?'" (ll. 3213–3214).[14] The inquiry is what type of shield William wants for his arms, and not about the arms themselves. William himself claims that, beyond the shield, he "coveyte[s] nouȝt elles" ('covets naught else,' l. 3215). Armour, and the process itself of donning or doffing it, is not presented as relevant information in the poem.

However, this lack of detail surrounding William's arms is replaced by that given to their disguises. In order to escape an unwanted marriage, Meliors and her lover William don bearskins as a disguise. First, their helper Alisaundrine disguises Meliors, fastening her into the skin until none would believe she were anything but a bear:

> And sche melled hire Meliors ferst to greiþe,
> and festened hire in þat fel wiþ ful gode þonges
> above hire trie atir, to talke þe soþe,
> þat no man upon mold miȝt oþer parceyve
> but sche a bere were to baite at a stake,
> so justislich eche liþ joyned. (ll. 1719–1724)[15]

Meliors is *tiffed* in that *tyr*, or dressed in that attire, the skin presented as merely an additional, outer layer of clothing (l. 1725). And yet that seemingly simple depiction of lacing one's clothing transmutes Meliors into a convincing animal: Her disguise is so craftily laced that she is, to any who would see her, simply a bear. And, once Meliors is suitably dressed, Alisaundrine "in þat oþer bere-skyn bewrapped William þanne, / and laced wel eche leme wiþ lastend þonges" (ll. 1735–1736).[16] The donning of the skins is described quite like the donning of armour, with the imagery of fastening and tying on that evokes the arming trope that is otherwise absent in this romance. Moreover, the lovers are success-

---

[13] 'a good shield of gold finely arrayed, and a werewolf depicted well and fair within, that is hideous and huge, to claim all his rights, of the most suitable colour to know well in the field.'
[14] 'what device is most pleasing to have painted on your shield and bright armour?'
[15] 'And she busied herself to first array Meliors, and fastened her in that skin with thongs so exceedingly well above her excellent attire, to tell the truth, that no man on earth might otherwise perceive but that she were a bear to bait at the stake, so closely each joint fitted.'
[16] 'then in that other bear-skin wrapped William, and fastened well each limb with strong thongs'

fully transformed: in donning this skin-armour, they cannot be perceived as anything but bears. Even when the Roman emperor correctly connects the theft of two bearskins with the lovers' escape, he orders the hunt for "tvo white beres" ('two white bears,' l. 2175). The emperor, likely to save face, perpetuates their new identities, eliding their humanity and transmuting them into explicitly animal prey. The lovers' identities are not merely hidden, but transfigured through the flesh they have donned atop their own.

In addition, the text carefully observes in both dressing scenes that the hides are fastened with ties over the lovers' clothing: "above hire trie atir" and "above his cloþes, þat comly were and riche" (ll. 1721, 1737).[17] The inclusion of this detail for both dressing sequences may be significant. It was not taken for granted that the lovers would not go naked beneath the skins, but the text made a point to indicate both were clothed beneath. Why point this detail out? Perhaps this inclusion was to separate the romance from its possible folkloric predecessors, wherein the lovers were naked beneath the skins or even likely rendered as physically transformed (Walker Bynum 1998: 1012). Or perhaps it was to draw attention to the layering of clothes under the hides, not unlike how clothing was layered under armour.[18] If we accept the latter, then this insistent detail further fits the disguising scenes not only alongside the arming trope but also in place of that missing sequence.

But this scene is not the only time they dress themselves in skinned hides. Once their disguises are found out, the lovers must trade their bearskins for deerskins, must "lappe in þe ski[nn]es" (l. 2576)[19] of animals once more. But it is hardly treated as a burden: they are "greiþed gayli in þat gere" (l. 2597).[20] The skins are *gere* that they don, serving the same function of 'clothes' or 'armour' that the bearskins had previously served (*MED gere* n.). Furthermore, when the lovers skin and don the deerskins, the ritualistic process of removing the hide, as with donning armour, is glossed over entirely: "William hent hastili þe hert, and Meliors þe hinde, / and a[s] smartli as þei couþe, þe skinnes of turned. / Eiþer gamliche gan greþe oþer gailiche þerinne" (ll. 2589–2591).[21] The lovers grab the animals and, with no mention of skinning the hides, simply "change into" the skins as though they were simple cloaks, *gamliche* ('playfully') and *gai-*

---

17 'above her noble attire' and 'above his clothes, that were handsome and rich'
18 This layering of garments was so common that there was debate as to *what kind* of padded clothing was best to wear beneath a knight's armour (Linn 1936: 302–303, 309).
19 'wrap in the skins'
20 'dressed cheerfully in that apparel'
21 'William hastily seized the hart, and Meliors the hind, and as neatly as they could, changed into the skins. Either playfully began to dress the other cheerfully therein'

liche ('cheerfully') sewing each other up in their animal disguises. But the lovers' teasing play does not detract from the efficacy of their guises:

> þe skinnes sat saddeli sowed on hem boþe,
> as hit hade ben on þe beste þat hit growed.
> And better þei semed þan to siȝt semliche hertes,
> þan þei semed before, bere whan þei were,
> so justilion eþer of hem were joyned þe skinnes. (ll. 2592–2596)[22]

The skins are so tightly fitted to the lovers that these disguises are even better than their previous bearskins. Even the final line here echoes the text's previous assurances of the bearskins – the lovers' bodies are "so justisliche [...] joyned" ('so closely [...] fitted,' l. 1724) into the skins that that "no man upon mold miȝt oþer parceyve" (l. 1722)[23] but that they are those animals. The rituals of arming are marginalised in favor of these moments of literally dressing in skins, and yet the lovers' identities become that of the animal, recognised on sight as any knight is discerned by his arms. Both disguising sequences replace the arming scene, usurping the identity-forming function of the equipment described therein.

Identity Slippage: Losing the Self in the Skin

Skin is also used as a disguise in *Sir Gawain and the Green Knight* – the titular Green Knight relies on his transformed flesh to hide his identity. The ploy is effective, as Gawain does not recognise Bertilak as the Green Knight at Hautdesert nor at the Green Chapel; instead, the truth must be revealed to Gawain by the Green Knight himself.

However, the Green Knight's flesh is ambiguous and transmutable, it seems, with his attire. In his introduction, as Suzanne Craymer (1999: 50) argues, the Green Knight's body is mistaken *for* clothing: the initial description of the Green Knight's cape is contradicted by the later description of his hair and beard, enveloping his shoulders and hanging low over his chest (ll. 181–182); the two are conflated, body and cloth, hair and fabric rendered indistinguishable on this striking figure. This is not to say the Green Knight is not wearing a cloak. It is not a mutually exclusive dichotomy, but rather the cloth and the hair are interchangeable to the audience in the text. The Green Knight's disguise, Craymer

---

[22] 'the skins fit securely sewn on them both, just as they had been upon the beast that grew them. And they seemed better to sight than handsome harts, than they seemed before, when they were bears, so closely were either of them fitted in the skins.'
[23] 'no man on earth might otherwise perceive'

(1999: 50) further argues, hinges on the green hue of his flesh to keep him unrecognisable to Gawain, as the text uses similar terms in describing both the Green Knight and Bertilak (Craymer (1999: 58) highlights their corresponding descriptors of great height and strong legs). Even as his body and clothing are transmutable, his skin functions as the primary indicator of his identity, disguising or revealing it.

Furthermore, the text explicitly states that the Green Knight wears no armour but has left it and all his weapons "at home:" "'I haue a hauberghe at home and a helme boþ, / A schelde and a scharp spere, schinande bryȝt, / And oþer weppenes to welde, I wene wel, als'" (ll. 268–270).[24] Meanwhile, Gawain's own armour is redolent with markers of his identity. His red and gold armour "has a tradition behind it:" "When the poet garbs his hero in red and gold, he also clothes him in the glory of his past exploits, reminding all who know the stories how magnificent Gawain's career has been" (Day 1984: 55, 57). However, the Green Knight's lack of armour does not mark him as unidentifiable. His attire is described in great detail itself, reminiscent of the arming-scene-by-description:

> Ande al grayþed in grene þis gome and his wedes:
> A strayt cote ful streȝt þat stek on his sides,
> A meré mantil abof, mensked withinne
> With pelure pured apert, þe pane ful clene
> With blyþe blaunner ful bryȝt, and his hod boþe,
> Þat watz laȝt fro his lokkez and layde on his schulderes;
> Heme wel-haled hose of þat same grene,
> Þat spenet on his sparlyr, and clene spures vnder
> Of bryȝt golde, vpon silk bordes barred ful ryche,
> And scholes vnder schankes þere þe schalk rides. (ll. 151–160)[25]

Unlike the norm, this description begins with the knight's hood and moves down to his unshod feet, working in a sort of inverse arming scene. Even the detail of his being "scholes vnder schankes" ('shoeless under legs') serves to emphasise that the Green Knight is completely without even the smallest piece of armour: Instead of a knight's typical "steel shoes" (*sabatounz*), the Green Knight is wear-

---

24 'I have a hauberk and helm both at home, a shield and a sharp spear, shining bright, and other weapons to possess also, I know well'

25 'And all arrayed in green [was] this man and his clothes: a very smooth, close-fitting coat that clinged to his sides, a merry mantle above, adorned within with fur, openly trimmed, the edging very fair with lovely, bright ermine, and his hood both, that was drawn back from his hair and laid upon his shoulders; neat, well-pulled-up hose of that same green, that fastened on his calf, and bright spurs underneath of bright gold, upon silk bands barred very finely, and the man rides there shoeless under legs.'

ing stockings (Andrew and Waldron 2010: 213 n. 160). Additionally, the Green Knight is wearing "clene spures" ('bright spurs'); the sword and spurs are the "indispensable features of a knight's equipment" and are "themselves symbols of knighthood" (Linn 1936: 310).[26] The inclusion of the spurs is one of significance: Even without armour, the Green Knight's identity as a knight is unquestioned. While the Green Knight does not bear armour or its signifying power of identity, his identity is nonetheless to be understood by his clothes and flesh, by the green colour that marks him so utterly.

Similar to how the Green Knight uses skin to show (or obscure) his identity, the lovers rely on their animal disguises to hide their true identities. However, the lovers go further, nearly conflating their human identities into the animal skins they wear. When Queen Felice approaches them, she dons the skin of a hind, despite having seen "here comli cloþing þat kevered hem" under the sun-cracked hides (l. 3034).[27] This detail could very well be a leftover from the tale's aforementioned earlier tradition in which the lovers truly shapeshifted, suggesting that the queen's disguise was necessary for approaching actual deer (Walker Bynum 1998: 1012). Nonetheless, its lingering presence still serves to emphasise the lovers' animal identities: Even knowing they are human, Queen Felice still feels the need to dress herself as a hind to meet them.

Yet more, the lovers do not merely remove their deerskins here. We know that they are able to, as they remove both sets of disguises at various points. With the bearskins, after the ruse is discovered, the lovers venture forth "cloþed in here cloþes [...] / wiþ hem boþe bere-felles þei bere in here armes, / so loþe hem was þo to lese or leve hem bihinde" (ll. 2428–2431).[28] And yet, the lovers do not, or cannot, shed their deerskins. The text itself refers to them as þe hert and þe hinde as readily as it calls them by name and neglects their names in favor of their animal disguises entirely for passages at a time, such as the lovers' failed attempt to board a ship (ll. 2713–2785, 2805–2829). While the deerskins are fastened to the lovers like clothing, much as the bearskins were previously, they cannot so easily be removed. When Queen Felice takes the lovers into her chambers, the hides must be skinned from the lovers' bodies with a sharp knife: "Sone þe quen kauȝt a knif, and komli hireselve / William and his

---

[26] The climax of the ceremonial investing of a knight was the donning of sword and spurs, just as their removal acted as a symbolic degradation of the knight in the 1590 Booke of Honor and Armes (Linn 1936: 310).
[27] 'their handsome clothes that covered them'
[28] 'clothed in their clothes [...], with both their bear-skins they bore in their arms, so loath were they to lose or leave them behind'

worþi fere swiftli unlaced / out of þe hidous hidus" (ll. 3199–3201).²⁹ The queen's own removal of her hart's skin is not mentioned; it is her *unlac[ing]* of the lovers that the text emphasises, the unmaking moment that is so powerful in the ritual of the hunt. Despite their ability to remove the bear-hides as clothing, the lovers cannot remove this latest identity of the deer hides. Their identity has become inextricable from the animal skins they wear, and they cannot return to humanity of their own power: They must be flayed like hunted deer, peeling back their second skins to restore their original identities.

Skin is an important transformative site in *William of Palerne*. Not only the lovers, but the poem's werewolf, Alphouns, is a figure whose flesh is itself his identity. Alphouns' transfiguration from human to wolf is brought about by direct contact with his skin, which is "anoynted [...] wel al abowte" (l. 139)³⁰ by a charmed "noynement" ('ointment') created by his stepmother Braunde (l. 136). The Spanish prince retains his human intelligence, but is trapped in the ferocious form of the wolf. It is the change in his own skin that transforms him, rather than the more traditional mode of lycanthropy (the donning of a wolf's pelt, the skin of a separate creature).

Alphouns himself is not the typical werewolf: Wolves (and werewolves) were known in the Middle Ages as evil, murderous beasts (Salisbury 1994: 130). And yet Alphouns' lack of viciousness is almost parodic at moments. Alphouns puts on a show in three distinct instances: when hunters attack Alphouns while he is trying to protect William and Meliors, and when the wolfish prince twice mock-attacks travellers in order to steal their foodstuffs for the hapless lovers. In these instances, there is no reference to Alphouns' werewolf hide. The text's focus is on Alphouns performance, not his shape, even while the werewolf is acting "as a wod best" (l. 2371)³¹ or "bellyng as a bole" (l. 1891)³² or emitting a "rude roring" ('fierce howling,' l. 1851). The use of "as" to create a simile for Alphouns' behaviour only places its performativity into sharper focus: he is not *actually* "a wod best" ('a rabid beast') just as he is clearly not "a bole" ('a bull') but merely acting "as" one. Werewolf he may be, but Alphouns is no crazed, murdering beast. His antics are almost humourous, as he puts on a melodramatic show to startle his victims. He is less a werewolf in these moments and more an actor in costume. His wolfen shape and bristling fur are superficial, only skin-deep so to speak, and do not affect his human mind.

---

29 'Soon the queen seized a knife, and her beautiful self swiftly loosened William and his worthy companion out of the hideous hides'
30 'well anointed all about'
31 'as a rabid beast'
32 'bellowing as a bull'

That is not to say, however, that the text entirely ignores Alphouns' furred flesh or relegates it to mere disguise. Early in the poem, when he returns to his ward to find the young William missing, Alphouns "[f]or reuliche gan [...] rore and rente al his hide" (l. 86).[33] However, even this moment is distinctly human: he rends his hide as a human would tear at his hair in a traditionally human gesture of distress. In his acute *reuliche* ('sorrow'), Alphouns displays a "manlike 'dool'" and then, as Norman Hinton (1996: 136) observes, praises God upon finding William dwelling happily with the cowherd: "And hertily for þat hap to heveneward he loked, / and þroliche þonked God mani þousand siþes" (ll. 102–103).[34] Alphouns behaves with distinctly human mannerisms more than animal ones, even when he seems his most bestial.

There is only one other instance of a direct reference to the werewolf's flesh: When he later attacks Braunde in Queen Felice's court, the poem focuses onto the physical, animal signs of his anger and distress: "bremly his bristeles he gan þo areise, / and grisiliche gapande with a grym noyse" (ll. 4342–4343).[35] His "bristeles [...] areise," wolfish hackles rising with his anger and "grym" growls. In this moment, Alphouns seems to embody the vicious, murderous predator that the werewolf was known to be. However, his wrath is not immediate nor wholly unprovoked; first he "stared on his stepmoder stifli a hwile" (l. 4339).[36] It is only after "he saw [hire] with his sire sitte in murþe" (l. 4340)[37] that he falls into a rage: "Ful wroþ þan þat werwolf wax *of þat siȝt*" (l. 4341, emphasis added).[38] Even after long contemplation, it is only after he sees her happily reunited with his imprisoned father that his anger overcomes his rational intelligence. And in this case, his wrath is justified: Braunde is the cause of his forced transformation and subsequent loss of his royal inheritance: it is "[r]ightful vengeance" characterised by "rightful *human* fury" (Freeman 1985: 296, emphasis added).[39] Even when he is most like a werewolf, even when his wolfish skin is emphasised in the text, Alpohouns is still very human.

Nonetheless, Alphouns' identity is utterly wrapped in his skin. Even when Braunde restores his human shape through her charms and rituals, Alphouns'

---

[33] 'for sorrow [...] began to howl and tore all his hide'
[34] 'And for that good fortune he devoutly looked heavenward, and profusely thanked God many thousand times'
[35] 'he fiercely began to raise his bristles, and horribly gaping with a terrifying noise'
[36] 'stared unwaveringly at his stepmother a while'
[37] 'he saw [her] sit in joy with his father'
[38] 'Then the werewolf grew exceedingly angry *at that sight*'
[39] While Freeman is here discussing the twelfth-century lay *Bisclavret*, the attack scenes are similarly motivated by a wrong inflicted upon the rational werewolf.

reaction (immediately after being "gretli glad" ('greatly happy,' l. 4441) to be human again) is that of shame: "Soþli þat he was so naked sore he was aschamed" (l. 4443).[40] And it is this shame that marks Alphouns as once more human. As Jacques Derrida (2008: 5) postulates, one separation of man from animal is this very *knowledge* of nakedness:

> He would be a man only to the extent that he was able to be naked, that is to say, to be ashamed, to know himself to be ashamed because he is no longer naked [...] On the other hand, because the animal is naked without consciousness of being naked, it is thought that modesty remains as foreign to it as does immodesty. As does the knowledge of self that is involved in that.

Alphouns' sudden shame upon his reversion to humanity is the clearest indication that he has, indeed, left his animality behind; his new clothes, as "one of the 'properties' of man," define his new identity as human (Derrida 2008: 5). Accordingly, when Braunde informs William that Alphouns has requested clothing, William's response is both joy and suspicion of the veracity of her claims: "'Is þat soþ,' saide William, 'mi swete lady hende? / Cleymeþ he after cloþes, for Cristes love in heven? / Deceyve me nouȝt with þe dedes, but seie me þe soþe'" (ll. 4480–4482).[41] Braunde must defend herself, twice invoking God – swearing "'bi Crist'" ("'by Christ'") (l. 4483) and exclaiming "'heriȝed be God'" ("'praised be God,'" l. 4484) – to convince William that she is telling the truth. She must reiterate that Alphouns is once more human, is as "'hol [...] in alle maneres as to man falles'" (ll. 4484–4485).[42] Alphouns' request for clothes, then, is no minor detail: It is the mark of his human status. To wear clothing is the same as to wear his animal flesh: It signifies his identity.

And much like William and Meliors' return to humanity after being skinned from the deer hides,[43] Alphouns is bathed and clothed: "And Alphouns anon þanne [...] / buskes into þe baþ boute more noyse, / and fond it treuli atired

---

40 'Truly he was greatly ashamed that he was so naked'
41 "'Is that so,'" said William, "my dear, noble lady? He asks for clothes, for Christ's love in heaven? Deceive me not with the affair, but tell me the truth'"
42 "'whole [...] in all manners as fall to man'"
43 After taking them in and removing the skins, Queen Felice clothes the lovers, embraces them, *and then* ensures they bathe: "Þe quen hire clipt and kest and gret comfort made, / and seþþen blive dede hem baþe boþe tvo wel faire, / and greiþed hem gaili in garnemens riche" ('The queen embraced and kissed them and made great comfort, and then quickly made both of the two bathe very graciously, and dressed them splendidly in rich garments,' ll. 3205–3207).

and tidili warme" (ll. 4452–4454).⁴⁴ It is only after this private bath under Braunde's care that the matter of clothing arises; yet despite his shame he does not ask for clothing – Braunde must broach the subject, just as she offered him his bath when she saw his shame. If the clothes are indeed a signifier of Alphouns' full return to humanity, then this mediation of them through his original assailant befits his previous curse: Even restored to a bipedal shape, Alphouns is not yet fully human again until Braunde has also guided him through this symbolic restoration of his humanity.

Additionally, this recurring need to cleanse the skin highlights the root of transformation as one of that very skin. Underneath the ointment, underneath his clothing of wolfish fur, Alphouns had always possessed human flesh. His shame at his nakedness, then, can be read not only as a mark of restored humanity, but also as a mark of his obscured humanity underneath the skin he had *worn as clothing*. Caroline Walker Bynum (1998: 1012) interprets this restoration as fully appropriate for the werewolf, "as if the human body were under the wolf skin all along." His changed skin had marked him as werewolf, dominating his identity such that when William first sees him as a man, there is no recognition: "of þat companie, be Crist, þer ne knew him none" (l. 4505).⁴⁵ After Alphouns chastises William for his generic welcome, William must admit to Alphouns that he does not recognise him: "'I ne wot in þis world what þat ȝe are'" (l. 4517).⁴⁶ Despite knowing that Braunde had undone her curse and that Alphouns was desirous of clothing, William is still confused by Alphouns' human shape. It is not until Alphouns directly states, "'I am he, þe werwolf'" (l. 4520)⁴⁷ that William finally makes the connection. Alphouns utilises the present tense, "'I *am* he,'" instead of the past, indicating that his identity is still intertwined with his animal form. Further, this scene is not the only moment when Alphouns claims his werewolf identity in the present tense: When telling of how he snatched William as a child, he says once more, "'I *am* þe werwolf, wite ȝe for soþe'" (l. 4627, emphasis added).⁴⁸ Even obviously human once more, he still identifies himself as his old wolfish skin. It is a signifier he cannot escape, one that has consumed his human identity.

---

44 'And then at once Alphouns [...] hastens into the bath without more noise, and found it faithfully prepared and suitably warm'
45 'of that company, by Christ, none knew him there'
46 "'I don't know what in this world you are'"
47 "'I am he, the werewolf'"
48 "'I *am* the werewolf, you may know for certain'"

Overcome Identities: The Wolfen Shield and Gawain's Girdle

As mentioned previously, William takes the werewolf as his standard to defend Palerne, intentionally identifying himself with the multi-skinned identity of Alphouns. Such a move was not unusual in the mid-fourteenth century, as it was a popular custom in England "to adopt freely chosen personal badges" (Nickel 1995: 14). Heraldry was also of great importance in the fourteenth century, boasting animal symbols resplendent in meaning, and for a particular creature to appear on one's shield or crest was "sign and warrant to the world" that that knight and/or his family was known for possessing or displaying the same corresponding traits of said creature, whether in fame or infamy (Savage 1928: 8). Therefore, William's choosing of the werewolf, "hidous and huge" ('hideous and huge,' l. 3218), is a direct alignment of his own identity with that of the creature, in this case to the wolfish Alphouns.

And indeed, in battle, William is frequently identified by his standard: he "'bereth in his blasoun of a brit hewe / a wel huge werwolf wonderli depeinted'" (ll. 3572–3573);[49] "'he it is þat þe werwolf weldes in his scheld'" (l. 3752);[50] "'War be he þat þe wolf weldes in his scheld'" (l. 3832).[51] And it is not the humanly rational Alphouns to whom William is equated, but the ravenous, beastly werewolf itself; as the King of Spain laments his losses, he calls William a murderer of men and a devil wreaking destruction: "'[he] haþ murþered mi men and swiche harm wrouȝt!'" (l. 3883)[52] he exclaims, "'[he] is sum devel degised þat doþ al þis harm!'" (l. 3888).[53] The King of Spain goes on to say that he wishes to hunt William down and has, already, unleashed a multitude of hounds upon him: "'I wold him hunte as hard as ever hounde in erthe / honted eny werwolf! But wel he is ware / þat I so many hondes have on him uncoupled'" (ll. 3835–3837).[54] William is explicitly depicted as a werewolf and, once more, an animal to be hunted. The shield he bears formulates his identity as animal as clearly as Alphouns' werewolf flesh did his own, and William is transmuted from rational human to ravenous beast. Despite his appropriation of the wolfish symbol, William loses control of its meaning: The signifier is misconstrued to indicate tradi-

---

49 "'bears on his brightly-coloured blazon a very big werewolf, wonderfully depicted'"
50 "'it is he who has the werewolf on his shield'"
51 "'Where is he who has the wolf on his shield'"
52 "'he has murdered my men and wrought such harm!'"
53 "'he is some devil disguised that does all this harm!'"
54 "'I would hunt him as hard as any hound on earth hunted any werewolf! But he is well aware that I have uncoupled on him so many hounds'"

tional werewolf traits instead of the unique intelligence and *hende*-ness of one particular werewolf – Alphouns.

With William's use of the werewolf on his shield, the significance of Gawain's use of the love-lace as his insignia – covering his armour as a baldric and creating a 'bend' atop his heraldic colours – becomes more potent. Gawain initially wears the girdle as a type of armour, one that will protect him from death: "'For quat gome so is gorde with þis grene lace, / While he hit hade hemely halched aboute / [...] / he myȝt not be slayn'" (ll. 1851–1854).[55] After the confrontation at the Green Chapel, however, it becomes a "token of vntrawþe" ('token of dishonor') to Gawain (l. 2509), a signifier that he "perceives himself to be defined by" (Gross 1994: 166). The baldric is an inextricable part of his new identity as a shamed knight. And the girdle does seem to signify Gawain's shame, or at least it cohabitates that signification: He wears it laced "þeraboute" ('thereabout,' l. 2485) the scar on his neck and diagonal across his torso. Moreover, when Gawain is telling his peers about his adventure, he "þe lace hondeled" ('the lace handled,' l. 2505) before saying,

> Þis is þe brende of þis blame I bere in my nek.
> Þis is þe laþe and þe losse þat I laȝt haue
> Of couardise and couetyse, þat I haf caȝt þare;
> Þis is þe token of vntrawþe þat I am tan inne. (ll. 2506–2509)[56]

It is unclear to what Gawain is referring in this passage – what precisely is the "Þis" that is token and brand of his shame? His immediate fiddling with the girdle seems to indicate that it may be the subject, the symbol of his shame and cowardice. Andrew and Waldron (2010: 299 n. 2506–2509) interpret the line in this manner: "this (the belt) is the ribbon of this reproof (the scar)." However, it may be that it refers to the scar that the baldric covers – thus his need to "hondel" ('handle') it, to move it aside and reveal the mark it obscures. If one reads the girdle as knotted *over* the scar, hiding it from view, then the symbol of the scar is appropriated into that of the girdle, which is itself bound up in the symbolism of the Green Knight. Its use here as a marker, and possibly cover, of Gawain's *lauced* flesh serves to double the signifier of his ruptured identity. Nonetheless, the hiding of the scar, as the primary and direct effect of Gawain's

---

[55] "'For what man is so girt by this green lace, while he had it closely fastened about [...] he may not be slain'"

[56] 'This is the brand of this blame I bear on my neck. This is the injury and the loss that I have received from cowardice and covetise, that I have obtained there; this is the token of dishonor that I am discovered in.'

unchivalrous behaviour, seems to diminish the impact of that lesson; it is subordinated to the girdle and its multiple significations. The lesson itself, however, may not be of such dramatic import as Gawain's reaction indicates. As Michael Foley (1974: 76) asserts, Gawain's guilt rests not in committing the "mortal sin of forswearing an oath," but instead in merely "cheating in a *layk* or game." Foley (1974: 77) reads Gawain's reaction as "exaggerate[d]," and cites the knight's youth and idealism for his "excessive remorse." Gawain does not seem to grasp that his fault is minor or forgivable, treating his slight in a game as a mortal sin against his chivalric nature and obscuring the direct mark of that infraction with the amalgamate meanings of the girdle. The scar's symbolism, then, becomes inextricable from that of the belt, and so is inseparable from its connection to the supernatural Green Knight. The lesson is not enough; the connection to Bertilak must also be present in the symbolism. The girdle absorbs multiple significations, including the scar that it covers, obscuring and representing the ruptured flesh beneath.

Gawain ultimately wears the girdle over his armour, crossing his iconic red and gold heraldry. Gregory Gross (1994: 161) notes that "[b]ecause it is the last article of dress that Gawain puts on, and because he wears it so prominently, it is clear that it overrides the pentangle as the symbol of his identity." His chivalric reputation, as identified through his infamous red surcoat, is slashed across by this mark of his failure – a bright, contrasting scar across his torso, "like a bar sinister" (Day 1984: 57).[57] This detail is made more potent when one again considers Gawain's initial arming scene, wherein the final items are his spurs and sword, as befits a good knight:

> Wyth ryche cote-armur,
> His gold sporez spend with pryde,
> Gurde with a bront ful sure
> With silk sayn vmbe his syde. (ll. 586–589)[58]

Recall that the sword and spurs are symbolic of knighthood itself. Nickel (1995: 11, emphasis added) reads the lines as meaning the spurs are "buckled on *over*" his surcoat. If read in this way, the text presents Gawain's most characteristic fea-

---

[57] Day is, of course, punning on heraldic terminology, referencing Gawain's fall from courtly ideal; it is a humourous but inaccurate play on words. As heraldry operates from the viewpoint of the bearer, and not the observer, Gawain's tying it atop his right and under his left shoulder creates a *bend dexter* – or simply *bend*, as devices are assumed to be *dexter* unless otherwise noted as *sinister* (MacKinnon 1966: 21, 44–45, 55, 58).

[58] 'With fine surcoat, his gold spurs fastened with pride, girt with a reliable sword with a silk girdle around his side.'

ture, the symbol that covers his token red armour, as the symbol of his very knighthood. But this place of ultimate identification is replaced by the girdle, which itself is riddled with significations: It is marked by Lady Bertilak, who wore it before giving it to Gawain; it is evocative of the love token and, so, the sexual suggestiveness of the bedroom scenes during which it was given; it is tied to secrecy both in Gawain's withholding it from Bertilak and the lady's urging for him to be discreet;[59] it is tied to the supernatural as an object that prevents death; the girdle is also signified by Bertilak, who explicitly claims it as his own ("my wede [...] þat ilke wouen girdle," l. 2358).[60] Furthermore, it is associated with the Green Knight himself, who gives it to Gawain "For hit is grene as my goune" (l. 2396).[61] Bertilak wishes Gawain to remember and speak of the girdle as a "token / Of [...] þe Grene Chapel" (ll. 2398–2399)[62] to his peers, yet Bertilak prefaces this claim with an initial reason: the girdle is green like the clothing of the Green Knight himself. It is not enough that Gawain tells of Bertilak and his role in the tale (including the wealth and power of his holdings), but he must also visually intertwine his identity with that of the Green Knight. Gawain's wearing the girdle as a baldric immediately associates him with the Green Knight, almost as if it were acting as a piece of heraldry declaring Gawain's connection to Bertilak. This connection clouds Gawain's identity as strictly human. Gawain's affiliation with the Green Knight also invests his identity with said knight's fantastical nature, investing his knightly status with Bertilak's magical, nigh inhuman, status. As Barbara Goodman (2011: 50) observes: the text "never actually states that the Green Knight returns to his form of Bertilak," an ambiguity of shape that she parallels to Gawain's own "obscured" values. She also considers Gawain's self-questioned values as the reason Bertilak, as the transformed creature in the tale, is not "absorbed by the hero-knight's own society" as is typical of the trope (Goodman 2011: 50). However, I would argue that it is not merely that Gawain fails to absorb and normalise the supernatural Bertilak, but also that the Green Knight has transferred his supernatural signifiers onto Gawain via the girdle.

---

[59] An urging that Gawain ignores: when dressing to go to the Green Chapel, Gawain dons the girdle last: "Þe gordel of þe grene silke þat gay wel bisemed, / Vpon þat ryol red cloþe, þat ryche watz to schewe" ('The girdle of green silk well suited that fine [knight], upon that splendid red cloth, that was fine to display,' ll. 2035–2036). The girdle is a slash of green over his "red cloþe," wrapped as it is around his "haunchez [...] double hym aboute" ('waist [...] twice about him,' ll. 2032–2033).
[60] 'my garment [...] that same woven girdle'
[61] 'For it is green as my robe'
[62] 'token of [...] the Green Chapel'

The girdle acts as the conduit for this transference of the Green Knight's otherworldly signification onto Gawain: he now bears the *grene* of Bertilak's supernatural form. But Gawain refuses to embrace this signification. Norman Simms (2002: 286–287) notes that Gawain is "marked in two new ways, only one of which he can share with the rest of the court:" the girdle, which is imitated by the other knights, and the scar on his neck which he "cannot share [...] even though it is the stigma which assigns its meaning to the green girdle." Gawain's skin is the root of his identity, and the rupture in his flesh acts as a signification in that identity, but one that cannot be expressed. Yet the expressible girdle is itself an unreliable signifier, misconstrued as it is by Arthur's court: they wear the girdle as a mark of distinction to be respected forever, a symbol of the "renoun of þe Rounde Table / And he honoured þat hit hade, euermore after" (ll. 2519–2520).[63] Gawain's self-imposed mark of shame is misconstrued and twisted into one of "honour" by the court. This misinterpretation is not groundless, either, as Gross (1994: 167) observes:

> In their eyes, his status as a worthy knight is greater than ever, for only the worthiest could survive against such impossible odds. Gawain's profession of 'Vntrawþe' must sound to them, therefore, as if it were an ironic courtly expression of humility, similar to the speech Gawain had made to Arthur when he sought to accept the Green Knight's challenge.

The court reads Gawain's baldric in light of his previous self; they cannot conceive of his new identity. Instead, they interpret the girdle as an inclusive signifier, one that consolidates and unites the "broþerhede" ('brotherhood') of the Round Table (l. 2516). For Gawain, however, it is a mark of "isolation," replacing the pentangle and its community-based values and defining Gawain "in relation only to himself" (Gross 1994: 161). Yet, as previously asserted, the girdle is a multilayered symbol, laden with various significations. The girdle's nexus of meanings, then, makes it a slippery signifier of identity, one that defies Gawain's agency over it. The knight loses control of the very symbol he appropriated, and as such, his identity is left vulnerable to various misinterpretations.

Additionally, as stated above, the girdle absorbs the signification of the scar it covers, taking on the identity-shaping meaning of Gawain's very flesh. In this way, the girdle itself becomes something inexpressible, signifying the damaged skin that cannot be shared. And yet Gawain refuses to wear the girdle beneath his armour, next to the very flesh to which it is so intimately tied. In fact, during his climactic confrontation with the Green Knight, he throws the girdle away from himself: "Þenne he kaȝt to þe knot and þe kest lawsez, / Brayde broþely

---

63 'renown of the Round Table and he that had it [was] honored evermore after'

þe belt to þe burne seluen" (ll. 2376–2377).⁶⁴ Gawain's initial reaction is to remove the girdle from his person, a response that has not been mitigated by his guilt: He wears the lace outside of himself, above his armour, as far from his skin as it can be while still being worn. He externalises this mark, what to him is "þe token of vntrawþe" (l. 2509),⁶⁵ refusing to accept it as a formulation of his new identity. It remains outside, moulding his identity even while he denies and rejects its signification. Even so, it remains in contact with his neck, the only item he must "hondel" ('handle') to expose his scar. His rejection is, ultimately, ineffective.

Tracing Trauma through the Skin

Sir Gawain and the Green Knight and *William of Palerne* use skin to question identity, whether one is wearing armour or hide, human skin or wolfish fur. However, their identities become obfuscated, blurred between human and non-human. Recall Derrida's aforementioned embrace of difference: rather than a single, hard line separating the non-human animal from the human animal, there are small, variegated distinctions across the spectrum of animal life. In the blurring identities – skin or armour, beast or knight, prey or person – these two romances do not settle on a clear distinction. Skin is removed like clothing, armour donned like a reversed skinning, flesh is shaped and altered and cleansed. The boundaries between what makes one shape, one flesh, one identity a human one and another an animal is left open and vulnerable. Let us look briefly at John Simons' (2002: 120) "strong anthropomorphism," a category that represents animals as humans so as to either highlight the differences between human/non-human experiences or call into question the true "extent to which humans and non-humans are really different." When a text presents this strong anthropomorphism, when it questions whether humans are not, in fact, so different from non-humans, then it also begs the question of what, precisely, *is* the human? For these texts, the response appears to be a mirrored, indistinct definition that reflects itself in the conflated and obscured identities of their main characters. The misinterpreted identities of the skin, then, are not merely an anxiety of permeable selfhood, but a question of what even separates that "self" from the "other."

---

64 'Then he seized the knot and burst the fastening, flung the belt violently to the same man'
65 'the token of dishonesty'

As has been shown, definition of selfhood and identity (and, in fact, humanity) is of much concern in both texts, in particular as regards to the traumas suffered within the texts. As previously discussed, trauma can act as a transformative catalyst on identity, challenging those boundaries – and anxieties – of self and identity on which these texts focus. However, trauma is, by its very nature, not a single instance but a continuous echo: "its very unassimilated nature – the way it was precisely *not known* in the first instance – returns to haunt the survivor later on" (Caruth 1996: 4, emphasis in original). Cathy Caruth (1996: 101, 107) expounds on the phenomenon of "traumatic repetition," as the unknowable, inexpressible nature of trauma requires repetition, recurring echoes of the original trauma – echoes that are not precisely the same as the initial event.

To apply this theory to the texts examined here, it is in this manner that William's transitions from cowherd to knight to bear to hart to werewolf-knight and finally to King of Palerne can be seen as traumatic echoes, each conflated and false identity is both a match to and distinct departure from his identity of unknown lineage. William was devastated to discover that his foster father was not his biological sire, and his subsequent slippage in identities can be seen as the effects of that trauma as he tries on various identities, seeking the one that "fits." Recall that even as a fugitive in the animal skins, falling further and further into animality, William is constantly wishing for the arms of a knight. He cannot commit to a single identity, but must confuse and conflate the various signifiers he has appropriated. Later, when he is faced with Queen Felice, his mother, professing how very much he reminds her of her lost husband and son,[66] William dismisses her theory as maternal wishful thinking for loved ones long dead:

> "Madame, of þat mater no more now þinkes.
> What be ȝe now þe beter so bitterli to wepe,
> seþþe boþe þe sire and þi sone arn boþe dede?
> Þeiȝh ȝe driȝen swiche duel al ȝour lif-dawes,
> ȝe gete hem never agayn!" (ll. 3701–3705)[67]

---

[66] William scolds Queen Felice for being sorrowful when she should be celebratory, and when she tells him the reasons for her sadness, she notes "how hire þouȝt he was liche hire lord þe king þanne, / and hou þe sorwe of hire sone dede hire so to wepe" ('how she thought he was like her lord the king then, and how the sorrow of her son made her weep,' ll. 3698–3699).

[67] "'Madam, think no more of that matter. How are you now the better for weeping so bitterly, since both the father and the son are both dead? Although you suffered such sorrow all your lifedays, you never win them again!'"

William rejects the queen's comparison, telling her to never think of the two (or their similarities to him) again. He cannot accept that identity either. It is not until Alphouns relates the truth of William's parentage that William ceases to shift from identity to identity, that he accepts his own skin instead of relying on that of others, like his werewolf standard.

Alphouns' own trauma is that of his initial transformation. His stepmother Braunde rubs him over with ointment, changing his human form into that of a wolf's, but retaining his human intelligence; his realisation and reaction are a violent episode in which he attacks Braunde and nearly strangles her to death:

> And whanne þis witty werwolf wiste him so schaped,
> he knew it was bi þe craft of his kursed stepmoder,
> and þou3t, or he went away, he wold, 3if he mi3t,
> wayte hire sum wicked torn, what bitidde after.
> And as blive boute bod he braydes to þe quene,
> and hente hire so hetterly to have hir astrangeled,
> þat hire deth was nei3 di3t, to deme þe soþe. (ll. 141–151)[68]

Alphouns immediately displays a bloodthirstiness that, as stated above, aligns him with the murderous reputation of the werewolf. He nearly kills Braunde, but her shouting, "so kenely and lowde" (l. 152),[69] bring many to help her and Alphouns flees the scene. His pseudo-attacks on the passing men, from whom he takes food and wine for the lovers, are a parodic mimicry of this violence, a lingering phantom of his murderous rage. However, at the reunion with his stepmother, Alphouns' wrath is no parody but an animal rage of bristling fur and gaping jaws:

> Ful wroþ þan þat werwolf wax of þat si3t,
> and bremly his bristeles he gan þo areise,
> and grisiliche gapande with a grym noyse
> he queite toward þe quene to quelle hire as blive. (ll. 4341–4344)[70]

---

[68] 'And when this shrewd werewolf knew himself to be so shaped, he knew it was by the magic of his cursed step-mother, and thought, before he went away, he would, if he might, inflict on her some wicked turn, whatever may happen after. And quickly without delay he rushes to the queen and seized her so violently as to have strangled her, that her death was nearly brought about, to tell the truth.'

[69] 'so urgently and loud'

[70] 'Then the werewolf grew exceedingly angry at that sight, and he fiercely began to raise his bristles, and horribly gaping with a terrifying noise he rushed toward the queen to kill her quickly.'

Alphouns tries to attack her again, and William must bodily restrain him: he "ful wiȝtli þe werewolf þan hent / anon in his armes aboute þe necke" (ll. 4357–4358)[71] and carefully talks him out of his rage. Alphouns' violent episode can be read as a traumatic repetition of his original trauma. The sight of Braunde triggers the same mindless outburst as his previous, traumatic encounter with her. It is only after he has been changed back, after the trauma has been reversed in a reflection of its application (anointed versus bathed skin), that he is able to escape these violent repetitions. In both cases, the trauma is centered on identity and the skin as its signifier.

Thus, while Gawain's trauma can be examined in many ways (the first encounter with the Green Knight in Arthur's court; his three swings of the axe; his betrayal by the "wyles of wymmen" ('wiles of women,' l. 2415); or his long, tumultuous journey to Hautdesert), it is his scar that is the center of his own trauma of identity. Scars are "an unchosen mark of suffering" and "a record of difference" from one's previous self, and act "as a figure for the relationship between inside and outside, between self and world" (Hartman 2004: 164, 175).[72] Gawain's scar, signifier of his identity, is also the mark of his trauma, a record of the new difference in his self that goes unrecognised and misinterpreted by his peers. And so, as William is skinned from his various identities only for his new signifier to be misconstrued, so is Gawain skinned by the Green Knight's axe. The *lace* of the girdle and the *lauced* hide of his neck, the signifiers of his trauma and identity, are ultimately misconstrued by the court around him. However, the texts go even further: the incorrect readings of the signifiers are never amended. The opposite, in fact, takes place: the false interpretations become the truth. For William, his reputation in battle is known to be as ferocious as the werewolf on his banner; for Alphouns, he is to himself still the beast that others cannot quite extricate him from; and for Gawain, Arthur's court forever wears his baldric as a mark of honor. And, as mentioned above, Gawain's echoing trauma is doubled through the layering of that very green lace and the mark on his neck. If his scar is a symbol of the relationship between his inner and outer identity, then his own confusion and conflation of that mark with and in the girdle is mirrored in the relationship of his identity and its vulnerability to misinterpretation by the outside world. His trauma is unspeakable, inexpressible, yet he repeats it each time he once more laces on the girdle over the scar etched into his very flesh,

---

[71] 'very quickly then seized the werewolf in his arms about the neck at once'
[72] Hartman is writing specifically about scars from mastectomies. However, her analysis of breast cancer poetry can be applied to Gawain's own scarring.

each re-tying of the baldric an echo of his original, shameful donning of the lace and subsequent slice of the axe.

Conclusion

Skin is central to identity in these texts. The flesh is the site of rupture and transformation; skin and that which covers it reflects the mutability of identity as it shifts between shapes, ideals, and traumas. The ambiguous line between clothing and skin, hide and armour, garments and fur correspondingly blur the distinction between one conception of self and another. Covered or exposed, the flesh forms the identities that are defined and (mis)read in these two romances. To wit, Gawain's struggle for the chivalric ideal leaves his flesh and surcoat scored, a scar across his neck and arms that cannot be expressed or understood by his peers but aligns Gawain with the supernatural Green Knight. William requests his witty werewolf for a standard and receives the monstrous, animal identity that follows it until he, too, is seen as an animal to be hunted down. Alphouns' bodily shape is transfigured through his skin, and even once his human flesh is restored, his identity irrevocably altered, he cannot escape his animal monikers. William and Meliors don animal hides and cannot remove their identifying significance until even the text refers to them interchangeably as human and beast. Skin and arms echo each other, shaping identity and its perception beyond the bearer's control.

The implications take us further, however, as the (mis)read signifiers reveal a slippage not only in personal identity but also in species identity. The definition and perception of the human is thrown into question, left vulnerable to transformation with and through external perception. While the specific manifestations of this identity formulation are different between the two texts, both ultimately expose an anxiety of identity – its permeability, malleability, and vulnerability to different misinterpretations. Agency cannot be maintained over the appropriated symbol, and control over the definition of one's self is essentially lost in the ensuing conflations.

Works Cited

Primary Sources

Andrew, Malcolm and Ronald Waldron (eds.). 2010 [2007]. *The Poems of the Pearl Manuscript*. Exeter: Exeter University Press.

Bunt, G. H. V. (ed.). 1985. *William of Palerne: An Alliterative Romance*. Groningen: Bouma's Boekhuis.

Secondary Sources

Caruth, Cathy. 1996. *Unclaimed Experience: Trauma, Narrative, and History*. Baltimore: Johns Hopkins University Press.

Craymer, Suzanne. 1999. "Signifying Chivalric Identities: Armor and Clothing in *Sir Gawain and the Green Knight*." *Medieval Perspectives* 14.1: 50–60.

Day, Mildred L. 1984. "Scarlet Surcoat and Gilded Armor: Literary Tradition and Costume in 'De Ortu Waluuanii' and 'Sir Gawain and the Green Knight'." *Interpretations* 15.2: 53–58.

Derrida, Jacques. 2008. *The Animal That Therefore I Am*. Ed. Marie-Louise Mallet. Trans. David Wills. New York: Fordham University Press.

Foley, Michael. 1974. "Gawain's Two Confessions Reconsidered." *The Chaucer Review* 9.1: 73–79.

Freeman, Michelle. 1985. "Dual Natures and Subverted Glosses: Marie de France's 'Bisclavret'." *Romance Notes* 25.3: 288–301.

Gonzales-Day, Ken. 2002. "Analytical Photography: Portraiture, from the Index to the Epidermis." *Leonardo* 35.1: 23–30.

Goodman, Barbara. 2011. "The Female Spell-Caster in Middle English Romances: Heretical Outsider or Political Insider." *Essays in Medieval Studies* 15: 45–56.

Gross, Gregory. 1994. "Secret Rules: Sex, Confession, and Truth in 'Sir Gawain and the Green Knight'." *Arthuriana* 4.2: 146–174.

Hartman, Stephanie. 2004. "Reading the Scar in Breast Cancer Poetry." *Feminist Studies* 30.1: 155–177.

Hinton, Norman. 1996. "The Werewolf as *Eiron*: Freedom and Comedy in *William of Palerne*." In: Nona Flores (ed.). *Animals in the Middle Ages: A Book of Essays*. New York: Garland. 133–146.

Kay, Sara. 2011. "Legible Skins: Animals and the Ethics of Medieval Reading." *postmedieval: A Journal of Medieval Cultural Studies* 2.1: 13–32.

Larrabee, M. J., S. Weine and P. Woollcott. 2003. "'The Wordless Nothing:' Narratives of Trauma and Extremity." *Human Studies* 26.3: 353–382.

Linn, Irving. 1936. "The Arming of Sir Thopas." *Modern Language Notes* 51.5: 300–311.

MacKinnon of Dunakin, Charles. 1966. *The Observer's Book of Heraldry*. London: Frederick Warne & Co.

Marvin, William. 2006. *Hunting Law and Ritual in Medieval English Literature*. Rochester: D. S. Brewer.

MED = *Middle English Dictionary*. 1952–2001. Ed. Hans Kurath, Sherman M. Kuhn, John Reidy and Robert E. Lewis. Ann Arbor: University of Michigan Press. <http://quod.lib.umich.edu/m/med/>.

Nickel, Helmut. 1995. "Arthurian Armings for War and for Love." *Arthuriana* 5.4: 3–21.

Rooney, Anne. 1993. *Hunting in Middle English Literature*. New York: Boydell & Brewer.

Salisbury, Joyce. 1994. *The Beast Within: Animals in the Middle Ages*. New York: Routledge.

Savage, Henry L. 1928. "The Significance of the Hunting Scenes in *Sir Gawain and the Green Knight*." *The Journal of English and Germanic Philology* 27.1: 1–15.

Simms, Norman. 2002. *Sir Gawain and the Knight of the Green Chapel*. New York: University Press of America.

Simons, John. 2002. *Animal Rights and the Politics of Literary Representation*. New York: Palgrave.

Stock, Lorraine. 1995. "'Arms and the (Wo)man' in Medieval Romance: The Gendered Arming of Female Warriors in the 'Roman d'Eneas' and Heldris's 'Roman de Silence'." *Arthuriana* 5.4: 56–83.

Walker Bynum, Caroline. 1998. "Metamorphosis, or Gerald and the Werewolf." *Speculum* 73.4: 987–1013.

Roberta Magnani
Queer Skin in the "Wife of Bath's Prologue" and Its Manuscript Glosses

Abstract: Writing on skin amounts, on one side, to a fantasy of perfect legibility and, on the other, to a violent act of surveillance. This is made apparent in the "Wife of Bath's Prologue" and its manuscript glosses, as they inscribe dominant gender constructs on Alisoun's skin and on parchment. Harnessing queer theory, especially Karen Barad's queer ontology and Sara Ahmed's queer phenomenology, this essay, however, demonstrates that skin, as a porous surface, rejects paradigms of monolithic readability and, instead, signifies queerly. As her skin is marked by both the seal of Mars and that of Venus, the Wife dis-orients the "straight" hermeneutics of clerical exegesis to which she juxtaposes her own carnal interpretative paradigm. Simultaneously, the manuscript glosses, intended as cautionary narratives against the emasculating power of a masculine woman, use circumcision as a cutaneous mark which signifies maleness in unequivocal ways. However, in so doing, they also reveal themselves as sites of queer disjuncture, since circumcision, much like the Wife's skin, is far from an unproblematically legible surface. As they bleed, the manuscript parchment, the foreskin, and the Wife's body, subjected to her husband's violence, become uncontainable surfaces of resistance. As excoriated membranes, they bleed meaning rather than containing it.

Introduction: The Queer Textuality of Skin

Skin is a textual surface on which meaning is inscribed. Both medieval and contemporary theories engaging with the cultural valence of skin maintain that these inscriptions make it a hermeneutic surface which signifies monolithically and whose legibility is unequivocal. Pushing forward recent criticism which has aligned ontologically human skin with the animal skin on which medieval texts were copied and transmitted, in this essay, I will demonstrate how binary conceptualisations of gender are violently written on the Wife of Bath's body and in the glosses to her prologue, scraped onto the organic surface of its manuscripts. Queer theory, especially Karen Barad's queer ontology and Sara Ahmed's queer phenomenology, affords a portable and effective paradigm through which to unseat the premises of unproblematic legibility which are underpinned by violent surveillance. Instead of offering an inert surface on which a "straight,"

https://doi.org/10.1515/9783110578133-010

monolithic hermeneutics can be deployed, skin signifies queerly, that is, in multiple and divergent ways. By re-assessing the function of a number of largely neglected manuscript glosses, I will depart from a critical tradition which has cast glossing as a locus of orthodoxy and surveillance aimed at containing Alisoun's erratic exegesis. In particular, a source gloss warning against the emasculating agency of powerful women uses the Pauline theology of circumcision to redirect the Wife's non-conforming subject position towards desirable constructs of binary relations predicated on women's subordination and men's dominance. Circumcision, the incontrovertible cutaneous signifier of masculinity, functions as a strategy of containment of the queer by inscribing these binary relations on the surface of the penis and of the parchment. However, much like Alisoun's skin, the cut of circumcision refuses to signify monolithically; as it bleeds, it disperses meaning on both skin and manuscript page. In other words, instead of guarding boundaries and assuaging cultural anxieties about unstable signification, skin disorients hegemonic power dynamics.

"Rubbe and scrape:" The Violence of Cutaneous Legibility

The paradigm of perfect readability of cutaneous marks comes at a cost. Inscription is a violent act perpetrated on the organic surface of human skin and manuscript parchment. As Nicole Nyffenegger and Katrin Rupp explain in detail in the introduction to this volume, the conceptualisation of skin as locus of signification is an epistemological paradigm which, founded on Augustinian theology, still informs contemporary theory. In St Augustine's work as in Didier Anzieu's (2016 [1995]) theory of the 'Skin Ego,' skin is configured as a stable signifier on which meaning is sealed and the destabilising possibility of multiple significations is averted.[1]

This configuration of skin as readable surface has received much scholarly attention especially in the works of Catherine Innes-Parker (1995, 1999), Elizabeth Robertson (1991, 2013), Caroline Walker Bynum (1982, 1991, 2011), and Adrienne Williams Boyarin (2009), among others, who have engaged extensively with the corporeality of medieval female martyrs. Despite its markedly secular and carnal context, the "Wife of Bath's Prologue" affords a cognate conceptualisation of skin as a site on which meaning is produced, inscribed and disseminated. As she describes her appearance, the Wife specifies: "I hadde the prente of seinte

---

[1] For a comprehensive overview of contemporary and medieval theorisations of skin, see also Kay (2011).

Venus seel" (III.604).[2] Following Walter Clyde Curry's (1960) study of scientific discourse in Chaucer's works, editors and critics such as Larry D. Benson have glossed Alisoun's cutaneous mark as a "violet or purplish birthmark located upon the 'loins, testicles, thighs, or perhaps upon the neck'" (Benson 1987: 870). The genital location of the mark gestures towards its sexual connotation and Alisoun has no qualms in identifying the "seel" as a signifier of her wantonness and profligacy: "Venus me yaf my lust, my likerousnesse" (III.611).[3] In her analysis of the significance of the image of the seal in this passage, Karma Lochrie (2005) draws from medieval medical and theological traditions, and points out that the female body and genitals in particular are a passive and malleable surface ready to be moulded by male creative activity – sexual or otherwise. She specifies that "female genitals are not typically seen as themselves capable of activity" and are "the passive anvils, wax [...] compared to male sexual activity during intercourse" (Lochrie 2005: 94). A mere receptacle, a woman's body is conceptualised as an inert site whose identity is written or sealed upon its skin by a male agent. A textual surface or a wax tablet, female skin is inscribed with the markers of innate passivity and sinfulness which, according to Isidore de Seville's *Etymologiae*, as quoted in Blamires (1992: 43), are inextricably linked to one another:

> Man [*vir*] is so named, because there is greater force [*vis*] in him than in women [*feminis*] – hence also the word 'strength' [*virtus*] – or, he is so named because he controls woman [*feminam*] forcefully [*vi*]. Woman [*mulier*] gets her name from 'softness' [*mollitie*], or as it were 'softer,' *mollier*, with a letter taken away or changed.

To a man's virtue Isidore juxtaposes a woman's physical and, by extension, moral weakness. His pseudo-etymologies construct and fix this unresolvable binary in language. In Alisoun's case this essentialism becomes legible on her skin, as her – sensual, wanton and therefore fundamentally sinful – femininity is incontrovertibly signified on her body. The accompanying gloss, found in the Ellesmere manuscript (MS EL 26 C 9) and a number of related codices, consolidates a reading of femininity as inherently corrupt and weak by cementing it in a discourse of astrological determinism:

---

2 'I had the mark of saint Venus' seal.' All translations are mine unless otherwise stated. All references to Chaucer's works are taken from *The Riverside Chaucer* (Benson 1987) and will be given in parentheses in the body of the essay. Henceforth references to the *Canterbury Tales* will indicate the manuscript fragment and the line number(s); references to other works by Chaucer will indicate page number(s).
3 'Venus gave me my lust and my lasciviousness.'

> Cumque in ascendente fuerint infortune
> turpem notam in facie pacientur In nati
> uitatibus mulierum cum fuerit ascendens
> aliqua de domibus Veneris Marte exis
> tente in eis vel e contrario erit mulier impudica (f. 69v).[4]

In the Latin translation of the astronomical treatise *Almansor's Propositions* (twelfth century), the seal is read as a *nota* ("turpem notam"). Letter and tattoo mark at once, as the *DMLBS* explains, the *nota* or "Venus seel" inks the Wife's moral corruption and its physical manifestation on the surface of her skin. Her turpitude thus becomes permanently legible on her body. Much like script on vellum, Alisoun's gender identity is textualised and stabilised corporeally through the "seel" and "prente" of Venus. Despite Lochrie's generative reading of the seal and wax analogy, the rhetoric of inscription and its technologies deployed in this passage merit further analysis.

I contend that editors' glossing of the seal of Venus as a birthmark perpetuates the essentialist binaries put forward in much medieval medical and religious discourse on gender and sexuality, as it configures Alisoun's skin as a hermeneutic site of unequivocal signification which makes legible what is natural and innate. This ideology of perfect readability is predicated on a dual strategy of authorisation which is at once documentary and theological. The technology of inscription used to write Alisoun's identity on her skin can be aligned to the cutaneous marks found on the bodies of female saints. For instance, Adrienne Williams Boyarin's (2009) work on Christ's seal on St Margaret's body offers helpful insights in these processes of authorisation made legible on skin. Boyarin (2009: 92) argues that the seal "is the public charter of a powerful lord who has repeatedly authorised the document by affixing his seal on the parchment." As well as legally sanctioned, the meanings written on the female body also have a Christic valence. Building on the important work on the generative intersections between the carnal secularity of the Wife's narrative and medieval hagiography (Cox 1993; Wogan-Brown 1994; Boenig 1995; Winstead 1997), what interests me here is that the indelible and perfectly readable mark of Alisoun's wanton

---

[4] 'Whenever they are in ascendance unfortunately one will bear an unseemly mark upon the face. At the nativities of women when a sign is ascending from one of the houses of Venus while Mars is in it, or vice versa, the woman will be unchaste' (Benson 1987: 870). Transcriptions of all glosses cited in this essay are mine and taken from the Ellesmere manuscript whose digital facsimile I have accessed online. Abbreviations have been expanded silently. For further information about the distribution of the glosses and manuscript variants, see Manly and Rickert (1940: III.496–502). Unless otherwise stated, all translations are taken from *The Riverside Chaucer* (Benson 1987).

femininity is cognate to a charter, that is, a legal as well as a spiritual document. In other words, the "seel" amounts to an unbreakable contract which aligns the Wife's body to the late medieval "Charter of Christ" poems whose "elaborate conceit is that Christ's body stretched on the cross is like animal skin stretched on a frame to create the parchment that bears his contract with humanity" (Williams Boyarin 2009: 98).[5] Similarly, according to the *MED prente* n. is simultaneously a synonym for seal and a term indicating the impression left by Jesus' face on St Veronica's veil. This consolidates the legal-theological sanctioning of Alisoun's configuration of skin as malleable and legible surface, or a passive recipient of – largely damning – signification.

These cutaneous narratives of femininity as fundamentally weak and wanton are at the centre of the "book of wikked wyves" (III.685), a digest of misogynistic material owned by Jankin, a cleric and Alisoun's fifth husband. Not an isolated instance, but a widespread textual tradition, this book comprises a number of anti-feminist *exempla* with which Jankin taunts his wife much to her annoyance. One such *exemplum*, from Proverbs 11.22, harnesses the Aristotelian paradigm of a woman's skin as pliable surface of inscription and perfect readability: "'A fair womman, but she be chaast also, / Is lyk a gold ryng in a sowes nose'" (III.784–785).[6] A woman's moral and physical "softness" or "mollitie," to use Isidore's pseudo-etymology, is incised on her skin. Rhetorically, this quotation from Proverbs is founded on a bestialising simile which berates femininity, since it casts beauty as fundamentally corrupt and necessitating moral containment. Because of women's innate profligacy, the beautiful but morally incontinent female body is presented as non-sensical and grotesquely misplaced as is a golden ring pierced through a sow's nose. The accompanying source gloss, found in the Ellesmere manuscript and a small number of related codices, radicalises the anti-feminist tone of the passage by making women's moral corruption far more overt: "Circulus aureus in naribus Suis / Mulier formosa et fatua .i. impudica" (f. 71r).[7] The annotation glosses the adjective *fatua* ('foolish') as *impudica* ('unchaste'), implying that a beautiful wife is not only inherently unwise, but also incapable of remaining pure. The pierced skin of the sow, grotesquely adorned with a golden ring, functions as a permanent reminder that a woman's –

---

5 Kay (2011: 20) also discusses the "Charter of Christ" poems as a primary paradigm for the alignment of textual and cutaneous surfaces.
6 'A beautiful woman, unless she is also chaste, is like a golden ring in a sow's nose.'
7 'A beautiful and foolish, that is unchaste, woman [is like] a golden ring in the nose of a pig' (my translation). Manuscripts related to British Library, MS Egerton 2864 follow the Latin Vulgate version of the Bible and therefore omit the accretion "impudica" and offer "pulcra" [sic] instead of "formosa."

beautiful – body is a marker of her innate licentiousness. Misogyny is made apparent through a ridiculing penetrative wound on the skin of the bestialised woman and through the incision made by the scribe's quill when penning the anti-feminist gloss on the organic surface of the Ellesmere manuscript. Cutaneous and textual surfaces are, therefore, sites on which anxieties about the incontinence of women are overtly and violently written in order to be exorcised and contained through a penetrative cut.

The pierced nose of the sow signifies the violence on which writing, whether on parchment or human skin, is founded. In particular, Alisoun defines the biblical laws on polygamy as "sharp word" (III.14). The Wife construes the policing of sexual agency through the practice of monogamy as a wounding gesture. The "sharp" instruments of scriptural containment of her polygamous appetites resonate with the poem "Chaucers Wordes unto Adam, His Owne Scriveyn," also scrutinised in the introduction and in Catherine S. Cox's essay for this volume. In this brief text, the poet addresses Adam, his scribe, and chastises him for his propensity for error; Chaucer denounces the consequent corrections on parchment as a vicious violation: "So ofte adaye I mot thy werk renewe, / It to correcte and eke to rubbe and scrape, / And al is thorugh thy negligence and rape" (650 ll. 6–7).[8] The fundamental violence of the quill wounding, scratching and cutting the organic surface of a codex is discussed in the influential work undertaken by Bruce Holsinger (2009, 2010) and Sarah Kay (2006, 2011), alongside the scholarly reflections on parchment that they inspired, partly in response to the 'animal turn' in literary studies.[9] The ethical implications of this argument extend to the horrors of wounding inscriptions scraped on the organic surface of the manuscript page. As Holsinger (2009: 620) observes, medieval textuality is profoundly imbricated with discourses of violence and death: touching a manuscript reveals "the palpable signs of the death of a fellow creature for our use." Similarly, Mary Carruthers defines the act of excoriating the skin as a mnemonic strategy that is performed on both the book and the flesh by the overt use of brute force (Carruthers 2008: 166–168). On a narrative level, the animal suffering which foregrounds any act of writing resonates with the violence which is woven in the fabric of the "Wife of Bath's Prologue" and "Tale." The "sharp word" of medieval anti-feminist writing is accompanied by overt scenes of domestic violence, from Jankin's beatings to the rape of the virginal *mayde* perpetrated by

---

8 'So often each day I have to revise your work, correct it, and also rub and erase it [by scraping it off the parchment]; and all because of your negligence and haste/plundering.'
9 For recent responses see Walter (2013).

one of King Arthur's knights who, at the beginning of the "Wife of Bath's Tale," "by verray force [...] rapte hire maydenhed" (III.888).[10]

Despite being broadly sanctioned in legal and religious practice as well as in conduct literature, Jankin's marital brutality towards his wife is so extreme that it results in impairment (Vandeventer Pearman 2010: 46–48): "By God, he smoot me ones on the lyst, / For that I rente out of his book a leef, / That of the strook myn ere wax al deef" (III.634–636).[11] The semantic choices made by Alisoun in her description of her fifth husband's attack, namely the two verbal forms "smoot" (*smiten*) and "strook" (*striken*), echo the penetrative wounding of the pen on parchment. As well as meaning 'to strike' and 'to deal a blow,' *smiten* can also signify 'to pierce,' 'to penetrate,' and 'to wound,' much like Adam Scriveyn's careless quill. Similarly, a "strook" is indeed 'a blow,' but it is also a 'slash' or a 'cut' and, specifically, 'the stripes suffered by Christ in his Passion,' or, a reminder of Christ's wounds (*MED strōk(e)* n.). As discussed at length by Edna Edith Sayers (2010: 90), the rhyming couplet "leef"/"deef" aligns cutaneous and textual membranes by setting up an association between the violated parchment and the violated body of the Wife. As Tory Vandeventer Pearman (2010) and Sayers (2010) have eloquently pointed out, Jankin's punitive and normative blow results in disability; Alisoun's deafness is, in Augustinian terms, a diagnostic tool or a legible physical marker, a "battle scar" which manifests the Wife's inherent wantonness and, at the same time, chastises her for it (Vandeventer Pearman 2010: 63). Following Vandeventer Pearman's lead, I concur that the alignment of femininity with disability precedes the disabling punishment inflicted by the husband, as, according to classical and medieval medicine, women were seen as naturally monstrous and "defective in both mind and body" (Vandeventer Pearman 2010: 61). As she explains, "medical and scriptural discourse implicitly link the overtly sexualized woman and the disabled person" (Vandeventer Pearman 2010: 63). Alisoun's deafness and the marks on her skin, therefore, simply reveal her inherent monstrosity. Marked by the seal of Venus and therefore prone to "ryot and dispence" (III.700),[12] the female body is configured as incontinent, bestial and grotesque. In Isabel Davis' (2013: 110–111) words, "Alison is [...] a digest of anti-feminist material 'bounden in a volume' (681). [...] Alison is book-like: she is made out of skin that has been pre-inscribed by others." As Davis herself suggests, Alisoun is more than "book-like;"

---

[10] 'By sheer force [he] took her virginity.'
[11] 'By God, he hit me once on the ear because I had torn a leaf [page] from his book; as a consequence of the blow I became completely deaf in that ear.' On domestic violence and marriage see also Desmond (2006).
[12] 'debauchery and profligacy'

the ontological association is complete: much like the virgin martyrs, she *is* a book, a text whose perfect legibility signifies culturally-constructed narratives of feminine moral and physical corruption couched as natural disposition. Anxieties about women's perilous incontinence are clearly and violently inscribed on their skin and function as the corporeal signifiers of their disruptive otherness.

Heteronormative Glossing: The Teleology of the Pauline Theology of Circumcision

The violence with which clerical misogyny inscribes the female body affects both skin and parchment. The act of wounding the surface to create meaning has a hermeneutic function which closes femininity to the possibility of multiple signification, and therefore confines it to a received construct of moral and physical incontinence. The piercing of the skin and the "sharp" scratching of the quill on parchment are forceful acts of containment which serve a normative agenda or "straight" hermeneutics. In this section of my article, I wish to attend to glossing as a technology of cutaneous inscription. As the glosses I have discussed so far testify, a manuscript annotation functions as a strategy of clerical policing which is aimed at reproducing dominant – in this case anti-feminist – ideologies and re-orienting non-conforming subject positions. These modes of surveillance operate spatially, as they re-direct queer bodies towards culturally-sanctioned identities. Therefore, a paradigm of spatial positioning and re-positioning, which builds on Sara Ahmed's (2006) work on queer phenomenology, proves to be a very useful framework through which to read the strategies on which policing is founded. These strategies become apparent on the material surface of the wounded skin. As a material space of inscription, its valence is phenomenological as well as hermeneutic. As Ahmed puts it, "[p]henomenology helps us to consider how sexuality involves ways of inhabiting and being inhabited by space" (Ahmed 2006: 67). Identity, sexual and otherwise, is, in other words, a matter of spatiality, that is, of how bodies occupy space and are oriented in it. She identifies heterosexuality as "straight" or "compulsory orientation" (Ahmed 2006: 84), while queer, non-normative bodies are "twisted" (Ahmed 2006: 67) and a form of "derailment" (Ahmed 2006: 76). Their deviance, here conceptualised as spatial as well as moral, requires "straightening devices that follow the straight line or even 'can only see straight,' given how they conflate this line with what is right, good, or normal" (Ahmed 2006: 72). Anxieties about the ever deviant, derailed and deformed female body, as articulated in Jankin's book, result in the deployment of such 'straightening devices.' By signifying "slantwise" (Ahmed 2006: 107), queer objects allow unsanctioned identities to be imagined or even performed. The manuscript gloss, as a 'straightening device,' re-orients the text towards desirable significations.

This function becomes apparent in a manuscript annotation appended to a much-studied passage in the "Wife of Bath's Prologue" in which Alisoun co-opts the theological and judicial principle of the conjugal debt. By dis-orienting the "straight" heteronormative structure of marriage, she claims access to sexual pleasure and financial emancipation in marriage:

> Myn housbonde shal it have bothe eve and morwe,
> Whan that hym list come forth and paye his dette.
> An housbonde I wol have—I wol nat lette—
> Which shal be bothe my dettour and my thral. (III.152–155)[13]

Alisoun's considered appropriation of the Pauline doctrine of marriage bolsters her desire for "power" over her husband's body and material possessions. Her act of re-orientation of traditional paradigms of female submission and male dominance causes a rupture in the "straight" hermeneutics of medieval anti-feminist discourse; now oriented "slantwise," her figuration of marriage makes non-conforming femininity not only visible, but also possible. In response to Alisoun's queering of heteronormative power structures, the annotative apparatus to the "Wife of Bath's Prologue" polices and straightens her dislocations of marital relations. Taken from St Jerome's anti-marital and anti-feminist treatise *Against Jovinianus* (fourth-century), the gloss articulates and addresses anxieties about Alisoun's scrambling of the natural binary divides between masculinity and femininity which are sealed on her skin in the shape of a natural (birth) mark. Masculinity and the challenging of its superiority through the spectre of feminisation is what is really at stake here, as it is made apparent in the accompanying manuscript annotation: "Qui vxorem habet et / debitor dicitur et esse in prepucio et seruus vxoris / et quod malorum seruorum est alligatus" (f. 64v).[14]

In line with the conceptual cognancy of textual and corporeal skin, which underpins my essay and this volume more broadly, it is important to note that this source gloss operates as a dual strategy of policing, as it operates simultaneously on the space of the manuscript page, by enclosing the Wife's queer text within a framework of Latinate orthodoxy, and on the cutaneous surface of the

---

13 'My husband will have it both in the morning and in the evening, whenever he wishes to come forth and pay his debt. I will have a husband – and I will not forsake this – who will be both my debtor and my slave.'
14 'He who has a wife is regarded as debtor, and is said to be uncircumcised, to be the servant to his wife, and like bad servants to be bound.' (Benson 1987: 866–867).

penis, on which the mark of masculinity is incised through the rite of circumcision. It is an instance of the triple layering of text-parchment-skin which Nyffenegger and Rupp discuss in the introduction to this volume. The undesirability of being "in prepucio" – or 'uncircumcised' – stems from the cultural significance of foreskin as a marker of masculinity. As multiple samples of Christ's foreskin circulated as a relic in the Middle Ages, they were identified, in Carolyn Dinshaw's (1989: 165) words, as "an index of virility." The uncircumcised body is, however, primarily a queer and undefined entity. The presence of the foreskin marks the impossibility to discriminate between masculinity and femininity as the physiological boundaries between the two sexes become indistinct. According to Lochrie's (2005: 95) account of medieval medical knowledge, the foreskin of the uncircumcised penis is morphologically and lexically analogous to the clitoris, especially those anomalous forms like the hypertrophic clitoris. This hybridity invalidates essentialist models of sexuality and the gloss advocates a reinstatement of the Augustinian paradigm of the perfect legibility of skin. It is no accident that in St Paul's new theology of circumcision (Romans 2.28–29) the ritual is associated with naming and "straight" hermeneutics. As Bernard de Clairvaux (1090–1153) explains in his twelfth-century sermon "On the Circumcision," the excising of the foreskin is a signifier of incarnation and revelation:

> Before his birth the angels, who possessed the secrets of God, were allowed to know and utter the sacred name of salvation, but till this day of the Circumcision we knew it not. On this day it was first given me to pronounce confidently the blessed name of Jesus. (Bernard de Clairvaux, "On the Circumcision," 148)[15]

On the surface of the foreskin, therefore, the divinity of God becomes manifest and audible, as it is only at the moment of the Circumcision that Christians can partake in the knowledge of Christ the saviour, previously only accessible to the angels, and are able to speak His name. As Elisheva Baumgarten (2005: 315) explains, in the Middle Ages Christian baptism and Jewish circumcision had a shared cultural function: they were "rites in which children became members of their communities and received names." Circumcision, especially, being marked on the male skin, acts as the legible marker of (homo)sociality and identity. Through this ceremonial incision on the surface of his genitals, a boy is, using a critical term borrowed from Louis Althusser, 'interpellated,' that is, his masculinity and social subject position are publicly established (Althusser 1971: 121–176).

---

[15] Quotations and translations for the Sermons of St. Bernard are from Hedley (1909) and referenced by page number in the main text.

Karen Barad's (2012a) conceptualisation of epistemology and ontology as a 'cut,' or as a process of differentiation between phenomena, offers a framework for my reflection on circumcision and other modes of inscription of meaning on skin. Borrowing Barad's terminology, I contend that the penile incision is meant to function as a 'Cartesian cut,' as it operates according to the "given-ness of a distinction," or "an inherent distinction – between subject and object" (Barad 2012b: 77). This "metaphysics of individualism" (Barad 2012b: 77) separates absolutely and necessarily masculinity from femininity and, as I shall discuss shortly, in reference to Bernard de Clairvaux' theology of circumcision, Christianity – as fulfilled prophecy – from Judaism – a faith marked by the imperfections of infancy. As "seinte Venus seel" writes an incontrovertible narrative of femininity on Alisoun's skin, similarly, circumcision has an overt masculine valence which arguably counteracts the Wife's disorientation of the conjugal debt and heteronormativity. It is precisely a husband's condition as "seruus uxoris" ('a servant to his wife') that the gloss warns against and strives to rectify by recasting the gender binary within a heteronormative orthodoxy. Both cutaneous and textual, the cut of circumcision becomes the documentary and dermal seal of "God's covenant with the Jewish people" (Baumgarten 2005: 318).[16] The adjacency of the gloss to the text in the material space of the codex affords, therefore, an ontological and hermeneutic re-orientation of the Wife's text: the annotation "straightens" Alisoun.

However, as Ahmed points out, 'straightening devices' operate on a temporal level as well as on a spatial one. Echoing Judith Halberstam's (1998: 2) work on the temporality of the "life experience" and the family in particular, Ahmed (2006: 21) posits that "our 'life courses' follow a certain sequence, which is also a matter of following a direction or of 'being directed' in a certain way (birth, childhood, adolescence, marriage, reproduction, death)." The temporality of the 'Cartesian cut' of circumcision is also markedly teleological, as it is founded on St Paul's new theology of the Jewish ritual. According to Kathleen Biddick (2003), this *telos* is paradigmatic of Christian models of temporality especially in their relation to Judaism; practices of Christian "supersession [...] cut off a Jewish 'that was then' from a Christian 'that is now'" (Biddick 2003: 1):

---

[16] The valence of circumcision as a marker of the covenant between God and humanity is dominant in both Jewish and Christian theology, and discussed extensively in scholarship. Studies of medieval Christian and Jewish theological-cultural attitudes towards circumcision include Walker Bynum (1988, 1991); Kuefler (1996); Steinberg (1996); Biddick (2001); Mazo Karras (2005); Bale (2010).

> For he is not a Jew, which is one outwardly; neither is that circumcision which is out in the flesh: But he is a Jew, which is one inwardly; and circumcision is that of the heart, in the spirit, and not in the letter; whose praise is not of men but of God. (Romans 2.28–29)

Structured on a series of dichotomies, the Pauline theology of circumcision implies an Augustinian binary between an imperfect body and a godly soul, and a teleology of linear perfectibility from Judaism to Christianity. Paradoxically, St Paul usurps the term *Jew* to validate the spiritual superiority of baptism and Christianity more widely. Following the Pauline theology and Christianisation of the rite, Bernard's sermon on the circumcision also articulates its linearity and proto-Cartesian epistemology:

> While the human race was yet, as it were, in infancy as to faith and love, man received a commandment suited to his imperfect condition. When he had grown to the age of the more perfect man, he received the command of baptism, by which the entire man is circumcised. (138)

A teleology of perfectibility, therefore, underpins Christian readings of the cut of circumcision as a harbinger of difference predicated upon the spiritual-political superiority of a fully-realised Christianity over an infantilised Judaism, and masculinity over femininity. Christian temporality is overtly positioned as male-coded or patrilineal – with its use of the masculine pronoun "he" to signify metonymically humanity as a whole – and underpinned by a "straight" directionality.

A legible 'Cartesian cut,' circumcision incises homosocial hierarchies on the skin of the young male Jew while consolidating the cultural hegemony of male authority and sanctioning teleological paradigms of time. Much like "seinte Venus seel," the manuscript gloss engages with circumcision as a 'straightening device' which marks the skin with the readable signifiers of an essentialist binary. However, the urgency of this process of re-orientation of deviance brings into focus the presence of the queer in culture. Once opened, the disjunctures caused by the "slantwise" signification of queer subjectivities hinder the paradigms of perfect readability and teleological directionality of the normative. In the remainder of this essay I will return to and problematise the supposedly "straight" hermeneutics of circumcision, as I will contend that wounded skin reveals its porosity and bleeds meaning instead of signifying monolithically.

Skin Signifying Queerly

Notwithstanding the cultural hegemony of Augustine's theory of skin as perfectly legible surface and of anti-feminist "straight" hermeneutics, Alisoun's body refuses to function as an unproblematic space of inscription on which male agents "rubbe and scrape" meaning. It acts, instead, as site of resistance. The Wife's dissent is made apparent in her exegetical practices and responses to male-coded modes of glossing and interpreting texts, including the female body conceptualised as legible surface. Dinshaw's (1989) nuanced reading of the Wife's appropriation of glossatorial practices echoes this line of investigation, as she argues that "[t]he Wife is a source of delight for this male author precisely because through her he is able to reform and still to participate in patriarchal discourse; he recuperates the feminine *within* the solid structures of patriarchy" (Dinshaw 1989: 116). Instead of positioning Alisoun firmly within the discourse of heteronormativity, my reading is indebted to an alternative scholarly tradition which casts Alisoun as an agent of dissent. Mary Carruthers (1994: 40) famously responded to the criticism with which her essay "The Wife of Bath and the Painting of Lions" was received by distancing her work from that of critics who berated Alisoun for not seeing "beyond the misogynist discourse." However, rather than reading Alisoun's resistance to clerical strategies of violent inscription on skin simply within a binary framework of heteronormativity, I argue that she advocates and articulates a queer hermeneutics founded on acts of 'derailment,' to borrow again from Ahmed (2006), which demonstrates that signification transcends binary constructs.

Recent scholarship has recognised the hermeneutic porosity of skin and has refuted fixed paradigms of unproblematic readability. For instance, according to Elizabeth Robertson (2013: 30), in religious discourse, skin is figured as a "semipermeable membrane," and Virginia Langum (2013) reflects on the opacity of cutaneous surfaces, which is predicated upon a dialectic between obfuscation and readability. As Langum (2013: 141) concludes in her study of medieval confessional literature, the function of skin is at once "to reveal and to obscure" the original sin. Because of its polysemous quality, skin does not make meaning plainly legible but complicates it instead. Its semantic multivalence in medieval and early modern medical discourse underpins the verbal cloaking operated by its polyvocality. According to Mariacarla Gadebusch Bondio's (2005: 540) detailed examination of medical taxonomy, the sixteenth-century Venetian doctor Giovanni Marinello could avail himself of a variety of terms, ranging from *cutis, derma, cuticula, epidermis*, and the vernacular *pelle*, when providing dermatological advice in his treatise *Gli ornamenti delle donne* (1563). In other words, the unstable taxonomy of skin manifests its semantic opacity and its resistance to monolithic signification. The polysemy of skin chimes with Karen Barad's (2012a) queer ontology to which I referred earlier. She builds a persuasive case for the scientific untenability of classical ontology "based on a belief in a world populated by independently existing things with determinate boundaries and properties that move around in a container called 'space'" which informs a "straight" hermeneutics of singular readability (Barad 2012a: 43). Barad proposes, instead, a queer or quantum ontology predicated on the "irreducible heterogeneity" (2012a: 46) and "radical openness" (2012: 29) of all naturally occurring phenomena.

This queer "irreducible heterogeneity" manifests itself on the Wife's skin. Lochrie (2005: 90) sees her as a "masculine woman whose frequent allusion to her genital makeup constitutes a *lingua queynte*, or vernacular of female desire, that is perilously independent not only of reproduction but of heterosexual erotics as well." The Wife's use of the seal is, in Lochrie's account, one of a number of instances of "lexical colonization" (2005: 97), that is, an act of appropriation of the plural taxonomy designating female genital organs (e.g. "chose," "thynges," "pith," "bren," "quoniam," "queynte," etc.) which the Wife uses to articulate overtly and unapologetically her sexual agency. Through the playful appropriation of the lexicon of female sexuality, especially the clitoris, she claims control over the language of female desire and indulges in its repeated assertion. I concur with Lochrie (2005: 97) that "[t]he seal image thus reverses the common medieval idea of the female genitals as passive wax to the active penis signet." Despite being inscribed with the traditional marks of femininity, the Wife's skin signifies queerly; as a hermeneutic surface, it is porous and capacious in its ability to open up its apparent perfect legibility to more complex readings of femininity and sexuality. The Wife's skin becomes a site of resistance to anti-feminist heteronormative narratives.

Much like a manuscript leaf, her skin is a palimpsest on which she overwrites an essentialist narrative of gender binary with one which re-casts the seal as a manifestation of sexual desires and the queer possibilities towards which it gestures.[17] Specifically, she queers the gender binary which systematises identity in two unmovable categories: Venus and Mars, femininity and masculinity. A few lines after describing her female-coded seal, Alisoun points at another mark inscribed twice on her skin: "Yet have I Martes mark upon my face, / And also in another privee place" (III.619–620).[18] Alisoun reveals herself as a phallic

---

[17] For a detailed discussion of palimpsests, from Anglo-Saxon riddles to Winterson's novel *Written on the Body* (1992), see Cox's essay in this volume.
[18] 'Yet I have the mark of Mars on my face and also in another secret/private place.'

woman: while she is certainly of Venus, she also undeniably belongs to Mars. As the adversative adverb ("yet") signals, the Wife's skin is a permeable and expansive space on which apparently contradictory significations can be inscribed. Her queer skin rejects the Augustinian paradigm of cutaneous legibility and exposes the epidermis as an oblique site which accommodates queer configurations of gender and sexuality. The Wife articulates the queerness of her skin at a narrative and structural level, as she positions a terse statement about her alterity between her two references to the gender-coded marks: "For certes, I am al Venerien / In feelynge, *and* myn herte is Marcien" (III.610–611; emphasis added).[19] Notwithstanding her – and Chaucer's – unwillingness to abandon the Aristotelian dichotomy founded on the alignment between femininity and emotions, and masculinity and the soul, her skin becomes a queer surface of negotiation on which identity can be imagined and performed as both feminine *"and"* (III.611, emphasis added) masculine beyond heteronormative signification.[20]

Alisoun's critique of glossing is co-extensive with the figuration of her skin as queer and multivalent, and, by extension, with her resistance to the violent operations of perfect legibility. In the famous opening lines of her prologue, she firmly sets the epistemological foundations of her narrative against the dominant male-coded written authorities epitomised by Jankin's anti-feminist book: "Experience, though noon auctoritee / Were in this world, is right ynogh for me / To speke of wo that is marriage (III.1–3).[21] She replaces "straight" "auctoritee" with the affective, bodily, feminine epistemology of "experience." Dinshaw (1989), and Ruth Evans and Leslie Johnson (1994), among others, have commented on the overt gendering of this binary: male-coded glossing or exegesis and female-coded carnal experience. An irrelevant interpretative tool, "auctoritee" is deemed redundant when attempting to account for the Wife's traumatic experience of marital suffering. However, in an even more radical act of resistance, she extends the inadequacy of traditional scholarship from the affective realm to hermeneutics. Much of the critical debate on the Wife's exegetical practice has focused on the inaccuracies and short-comings of her appropriation of interpreta-

---

19 'Certainly, in feeling I am under the influence of Venus, and my heart [soul] under that of Mars.' According to the *MED, herte* n.² a can also signify "the Christian soul, the center of spiritual life and moral virtues."
20 Pugh (2004) reads the correlation between Mars and Venus on Alisoun's skin as a strategy used to queer genre and its conventions; their "fabliau spirit," in particular, queers the "pretensions of romance" (2004: 66).
21 'Even if there were no written authorities in this world, experience would be good enough for me to express the suffering of marriage.'

tive discourses.²² Her experiential or literal hermeneutics is read as evidence of her unreliability and self-serving manipulations. These readings cast the manuscript page as a hierarchical and divided space in which the sustained errors of the queer Wife are juxtaposed to the orthodoxy of the glosses. In response to this enduring scholarship, Theresa Tinkle (2010) has put forward a very persuasive counterargument which has led her to conclude that "a significant number of medieval scribes represent Alison of Bath as dependable (and sometimes) amusing authority" (2010: 114) as "glosses lend intellectual authority to Alison's anti-matrimonial argument" (2010: 110). Tinkle therefore imagines parchment less as a polarised surface and more as dialectical one. However, while she argues for both Alisoun's exegetical proficiency and "feminine resistance" (Tinkle 2010: 39) to clerical exegesis, she specifies that her dissent is couched – and dismissed – as "domestic comedy" (Tinkle 2010: 43). Although I find her discussion of the relations between annotations and text helpful and convincing, I would like to push her argument forward and figure the material space of the codex as a queer site of radical resistance and of perpetual dislocations in which signification is constantly redirected beyond binary constructs.

An example of Alisoun's queer hermeneutics can be found in her disruption of the heteronormative gender binary constructed in clerical discourse and inscribed on her body in the guise of "seinte Venus seel." In an act of further dislocation, she articulates her disruption *before* she asserts the immovable femininity written on the seal and, in so doing, pre-empts its fallacies:

> Glose whoso wole, and saye bothe up and doun
> That they were maked for purgacioun
> Of uryne, and oure bothe thynges smale
> Were eek to knowe a femele from a male,
> And for noon oother cause – say ye no?
> The experience woot wel it is nought so. (III.119–124)²³

Once again, the Wife's queer voice disorientates the "straight" determinism of clerical writing which reduces sexuality and, by extension, gender to genitality, as she calls into question the unequivocal legibility of female and male genitals.

---

22 Such assessments of Alisoun's exegesis include D. Robertson (1962); Disbrow (1986); Alford (1986); Schibanoff (1988); Knapp (1989); Martin (1990); Cox (1993, 1997); Heinrichs (1995); Caie (1976).

23 'Go ahead and gloss [genital organs], and argue back and forth, that they were made for the purpose of urination, and that both our small things [genitals] were also made to distinguish between a female and a male, and for no other purpose – would you say no? Experience knows well that it is not so.'

According to St Jerome, the "auctoritee" which glosses sexuality as binary (Lochrie 2005: 95), the "thynges smale," have an exclusively functional purpose, either as organs in the urinary system or as signifiers of sexual identity. "Experience," however, suggests otherwise and gestures towards a more expansive hermeneutics of sexuality beyond genital functionality. By implicating the reader ("say ye no?" III.123), the Wife alludes to a shared erotic response of genitals as instruments of sexual pleasure.[24] Also, as I briefly pointed out earlier, semantically and morphologically, female and male sexual organs are analogous. Lochrie (2005: 95) explains that often the morphological similarities between the penis and the vulva are signified by using the same lexicon such as the term "thynges smale" found in this passage; the noun "chose" narrows these similarities down to the alignment of the foreskin of the penis with the clitoris, an association to which I shall return. Despite clerical attempts at glossing or fixing the meaning of female sexuality on their skin, the Wife convincingly demonstrates its fluidity. By denouncing glossing as fallacious, the Wife explodes the ideological containment violently written on her skin and reconfigures it as queer. Instead of the unmovable orthodoxy of male clerical discourse, she puts forward a queer epistemology which discloses the incontrovertible readability of phenomena purported, for instance, by St Augustine's figuration of skin, as an unfounded myth.

While enacting her dissent, the Wife defines the operations of glossing as adirectional and dislocated:

> Men may devyne and glosen, up and doun,
> But wel I woot, expres, withoute lye,
> God bad us for to wexe and multiplye;
> That gentil text kan I wel understonde. (III.26–33)[25]

In her prologue, Alisoun uses the adverbial locution "up and doun" twice to substantiate her refutation of clerical interpretative practices: here in the context of biblical laws forbidding polygamy and, in an instance I introduced earlier, when rejecting the legibility of genital organs. Having both phenomenological and hermeneutic valence, this locution pertains to "verbs of pondering" (*MED up*

---

24 Cox's essay in this volume follows arguments already articulated in some of her existing scholarship as she puts forward a more skeptical reading of Alisoun's carnal hermeneutics and the extent to which it remains a textual rather than a lived experience. In my essay I hope, instead, to demonstrate how far-reaching her queer hermeneutics is.

25 'Men may speculate and interpret from every angle, but I know well, and clearly, without lying, that God commanded us to grow and multiply; I can understand that noble text well.'

adv. 10) as it does to "verbs of locomotion" (*MED up* adv. 5). The Wife unsettles dominant modes of pondering and glossing by disorienting them spatially as well as intellectually. She claims that their supposed teleology is in fact haphazardly multidirectional ("back and forth, here and there, up and down" *MED up* adv.⁵). Although it signifies thoroughness in cognitive processes ("considering [...] from every angle" *MED up* adv.¹⁰), "up and doun" also indicates a refracted orientation whose movements are horizontal and vertical at once. As the marks on her skin unseat the "straight" hermeneutics of binary determinism, so does her spatial configuration of glossing. No longer the harbinger of monolithic signification, glossing is now recast as a "slantwise" figure of 'derailment.' The Wife's queering of heteronormative power dynamics becomes apparent in the only other instance of usage of the locution "up and doun" in the prologue: "And for her squiereth me both up and doun" (III.309).[26] Here she reverses the patriarchal paradigms of female subjugation and male dominance by harnessing chivalric discourse: Jankin, the squire, attends assiduously to his wife imagined as a knight and, therefore, as an embodiment of female masculinity. Also, Jankin's 'service' opens itself up to sexual connotations which afford the Wife a further opportunity to articulate her access to pleasure despite the clerical surveillance of female bodies. By refusing to serve as a pliable surface of unequivocal signification, Alisoun's queer skin disorients all forms of inscription violently inflicted on the female corporality as text. As I will demonstrate in the final section of this essay, such acts of disorientation are also performed on the surface of the male body: circumcision, too, rejects paradigms of perfect legibility.

The Queer Time and Space of the Foreskin

As Alisoun's epistemology of "experience" proves, on the queer surface of the skin signification is invariably dislocated and plural. These "slantwise" modes of production and dissemination of meaning are not confined to the non-conforming queer body of the Wife of Bath, but, and most importantly, they inhabit the spaces traditionally occupied by hegemonic constructs of gender and sexuality. Even glosses, policing technologies of inscription by excellence and sites of "straight" hermeneutics, are in fact sites of slippage. A paradoxical and, almost certainly, unwitting, instance of such slippage is the source gloss articulating anxieties about female agency and its emasculating effect. Specifically, this gloss centred on circumcision configures both the parchment on which it is writ-

---

26 'And because he attends to me so assiduously.'

ten and the (fore)skin of circumcision as palimpsested porous surfaces on which multiple meanings can be scripted and layered. Much like Alisoun's skin, the foreskin does not signify unproblematically and thus does not lend itself to "straight" legibility. As the manuscript page of Chaucer's "Wife of Bath's Prologue" suggests, (fore)skin is a gendered permeable surface as it creates a queer space in which acts of resistance can be imagined in response to signifiers of cultural hegemony. Similarly, parchment is a space of negotiation between clerical power and the counter-culture advocated by the Wife. In other words, skin is a pervious textual and gendered membrane on which and through which perpetual processes of negotiation take place. Once the (fore)skin is cut with a knife or quill, it wounds the surface which, because of its porosity, bleeds meaning beyond the rigid confines of clerical exegesis and creates apertures which, instead of closing down signification, open it up to feminine and queer hermeneutics.

Circumcision is messy. Unlike the desired linear differentiations operated by the 'Cartesian cut' and the *telos* of Pauline theology, the excised skin of circumcision is a site of cultural diaspora and paradox. Scholarly examinations of the ritual in medieval Christian culture appear to concur in assessing the foreskin as a space of conflict particularly in terms of Jewish/Christian theological disputation (Kuefler 1996; Biddick 2001, 2003). Leo Steinberg (1996: 165), for instance, explains that Renaissance artists refused to represent the "visual effect" of the ritual cut because of the underlying "unresolved conflict of attitudes," while Sylvia Tomasch (2000: 77) describes the "intolerable primariness" of the Jews who "first possessed the (Christian) book – from which they needed to be displaced." The Christian theology of circumcision is, therefore, founded on a fundamental oxymoron which Tomasch (2000: 69) cogently articulates as the "absent presence" of the Jews in medieval culture. As Larissa Tracy (2013: 11) tersely posits, "[c]ircumcision, like castration, was a paradox for Christian theologians because Christ was circumcised" and the contentious quality of this issue is apparent in Bernard's sermon in which he describes the ritual as a "humiliating ceremony" (136). His questioning mode ("To what end could circumcision serve Him, Who had neither contracted sin nor committed it?" 135) and quasi-anaphoric use of adversative adverbs speak of the Christian unresolved ambivalence towards the ritual:

> Notwithstanding all this, the Child, the Lamb without spot, is circumcised. Though He stood in no need of circumcision, He willed to submit to that humiliating ceremony. Though He was without wounds, He shrank not from binding up our wounds. (136)

In other words, cultural anxieties about unstable boundaries between categories are articulated on the skin of circumcision: Judaism and its unacceptable imbrication with Christian history and the Wife's female masculinity disorient the linearity of Cartesian signification by configuring skin as a surface on which complex dialectical relations are possible. The source gloss aimed at policing Alisoun's queering of male authority, instead of containing her resistance, foregrounds a configuration of skin – both parchment and prepuce – as a capacious membrane capable of accommodating apparent paradoxes and conflicting meanings.

In Biddick's (2001: 199) words, the foreskin becomes, therefore, a text on which "queer possibilities" and cultural "crisscrossing" can be inscribed and performed. Steinberg (1996: 53) echoes this assessment as he describes the "manifold" functions of circumcision by the end of the seventh century: "initiatory, exemplary, sacrificial, eschatological." The fantasy of pure legibility of the cutaneous cut of circumcision is thus an impossible proposition. As Biddick (2003: 67) points out, in the Pauline doctrine of the ritual, expounded in Romans 2, the cut becomes "an illegible inscription" founded on a series of supposedly irreconcilable dichotomies: outwardly/inwardly; flesh/heart; spirit/letter; men/God. Rather than signifying linearly and unequivocally, the foreskin, much like the Wife's skin, signifies obliquely, opaquely and therefore queerly. Her epidermis is a queer palimpsested membrane on which the boundaries between gender categories are disturbed and rendered fluid.

Blood signifies such fluidity and porosity. In his annotations to the *Canterbury Tales*, Walter W. Skeat, quoted in Benson (1987: 870), identifies the source of the reference to the "Martes mark" (III.619) as Ptolemy's *Centum Dicta* and notes that "mark" translates the Latin *cicatricem*, also a scar or wound. As a *cicatricem*, this blemish on her genitalia is cognate to the blood-stained cut of circumcision. As I pointed out earlier, the Wife's extensive taxonomy of female genitals, especially the term "chose," and her reversal of the image of the seal to signify a woman's access to sexual desire rather than passivity, draw on the morphological and lexical proximity of the penis and the vulva. In its associations with female genitals, and the clitoris in particular, the foreskin, the ultimate marker of virility, is dislocated and queered. Unlike the clean 'Cartesian cut,' which is founded on "an inherent distinction – between object and subject" (Barad 2012b: 77), the cut of circumcision bleeds meaning across category boundaries. To borrow from Barad's (2012a) queer ontology, circumcision can be more accurately defined as an 'agential cut' because of its manifest potential for constant slippage in signification. Differentiation is indeed not obliterated, but the cultural-ontological mechanisms which produce it are at once interrogated and perpetually displaced:

> Agential realism does not start with a set of given or fixed difference, but rather makes inquiries into how differences are made and remade, stabilized and destabilized, as well as their materializing effects and constitutive exclusions. (Barad 2012b: 77)

The Wife's mark, in other words, prompts an interrogation of the imperatives of heteronormativity — i.e. a paradigm of male hegemony and female subjugation — advocated by clerical anti-feminist voices. Rather than cutting legible meaning onto her skin, her streak, reminiscent of the fluidity of blood, indicates "the liveliness of indeterminacies that bleed through the cuts" (Barad 2012b: 80). In sum, the Wife's skin confuses the categories of male and female as circumcision confuses the categories of Jew and Christian. The membrane of the manuscript folio, on which the source gloss is inscribed, and the cutaneous surface of Alisoun's genitalia are cognate with Barad's agential realism and definition of matter as "becoming – not a thing, but a doing, a congealing of agency […] morphologically active, responsive, generative, and articulate" (Barad 2012b: 80). Cutaneous sites of inscription cannot serve the clerical fantasy of "straight" signification; as organic surfaces, they are porous and pervious. Signification is written, but once scripted, it is in a state of "becoming," as it is immediately susceptible to slippage and palimpsesting.

Conclusion

In this essay, I have argued that writing on skin amounts, on one side, to a fantasy of perfect legibility which serves an essentialist agenda and, on the other, a violent act of surveillance. However, because of its ontological "irreducible heterogeneity," skin signifies queerly. This is made apparent on the porous surface of Alisoun's skin and in her re-orientations of the "straight" hermeneutics of glossing. As her skin is marked by both the seal of Mars and that of Venus, the Wife claims her sexual agency and queer subject position. Simultaneously, the manuscript glosses, intended as cautionary narratives against the emasculating power of a masculine woman, use circumcision as a cutaneous mark which signifies maleness in unequivocal ways. However, in so doing, they reveal themselves as sites of queer disjuncture, since circumcision, much like the Wife's skin, is far from an unproblematically legible surface. As they bleed, the foreskin and the Wife's body, subjected to her husband's violence, become open, fluid, uncontainable surfaces. As excoriated surfaces, they bleed meaning rather than containing it. The Wife counter-glosses cutaneous inscription as a site of resistance rather than as one of violent subjugation; in other words, she is able to control the instruments of signification and write on her violated skin as a surface of empowerment. The narrative of her subjectivity is now, queerly, her own.

Works Cited

Primary Texts

Benson, Larry D. (ed.). 1987. *Geoffrey Chaucer: The Riverside Chaucer.* 3rd ed. Boston: Houghton Mifflin.

Geoffrey Chaucer: The Canterbury Tales. MS EL 26 C 9. Huntington Library, San Marino, CA. Huntington Digital Library. <http://hdl.huntington.org/cdm/ref/collection/p15150coll7/id/2838> [accessed 16 January 2018].

Hedley, J. C. (ed. and trans.). 1909. *Sermons of St. Bernard on Advent and Christmas: Including the Famous Treatise on the Incarnation called "Missus Est."* London: R. & T. Washbourne.

Manly, John M. and Edith Rickert. (eds.). 1940. *The Text of the Canterbury Tales: Studied on the Basis of all Known Manuscripts.* 8 vols. Chicago: Chicago University Press.

Winterson, Jeanette. 1992. *Written on the Body.* London: Jonathan Cape.

Secondary Texts

Ahmed, Sara. 2006. *Queer Phenomenology: Orientations, Objects, Others.* Durham and London: Duke University Press.

Alford, John A. 1986. "The Wife of Bath versus the Clerk of Oxford: What Their Rivalry Means." *The Chaucer Review* 21: 108–132.

Althusser, Louis. 1971. *Lenin and Philosophy and Other Essays.* London: NLB.

Anzieu, Didier. 2016 [1995]. *The Skin-Ego.* Trans. Naomi Segal. London: Karnak Books.

Bale, Anthony. 2010. *Feeling Persecuted: Christians, Jews and Images of Violence in the Middle Ages.* London: Reaktion Books.

Barad, Karen. 2012a. "Nature's Queer Performativity." *Kvinder, Køn & Forskning* 1.2: 25–53.

Barad, Karen. 2012b. "Intra-actions." Interview by Adam Kleinman. *Mousse* 34: 76–81.

Baumgarten, Elisheva. 2005. "Marking the Flesh: Circumcision, Blood, and Inscribing Identity on the Body in Medieval Jewish Culture." In: Thalia Brero (ed.). *Micrologus XIII. La pelle umana/The Human Skin.* Florence: Edizioni del Galluzzo. 113–330.

Biddick, Kathleen. 2001. "Translating the Foreskin." In: Glenn Burger and Steven F. Kruger (eds.). *Queering the Middle Ages.* London and Minneapolis: University of Minnesota Press. 193–212.

Biddick, Kathleen. 2003. *The Typological Imaginary: Circumcision, Technology, History.* Philadelphia: University of Pennsylvania Press.

Blamires, Alcuin. (ed.). 1992. *Woman Defamed and Woman Defended: An Anthology of Medieval Texts.* Oxford: Clarendon Press.

Boenig, Robert. 1995. *Chaucer and the Mystics: The Canterbury Tales and the Genre of Devotional Prose.* Lewisburg: Bucknell University Press.

Caie, Graham D. 1976. "The Significance of Early Chaucer MS Glosses (With Special Reference to the *Wife of Bath's Prologue*)." *The Chaucer Review* 10: 350–360.

Carruthers, Mary. 1994. "The Wife of Bath and the Painting of Lions: Afterword." In: Ruth Evans and Lesley Johnson (eds.). *Feminist Readings in Medieval English Literature: The Wife of Bath and All Her Sect*. London and New York: Routledge. 39–53.

Carruthers, Mary. 2008. *The Book of Memory: A Study of Memory in Medieval Culture*. 2nd ed. Cambridge: Cambridge University Press.

Cox, Catherine S. 1993. "Holy Erotica and the Virgin Word: Promiscuous Glossing in the Wife of Bath's Prologue." *Exemplaria* 5: 207–237.

Cox, Catherine S. 1997. *Gender and Language in Chaucer*. Gainesville: University Press of Florida.

Curry, Walter C. 1960. *Chaucer and the Mediaeval Sciences*. 2nd ed. New York: Barnes and Noble.

Davis, Isabel. 2013. "Cutaneous Time and the Late Medieval Literary Imagination." In: Katie L. Walter (ed.). *Reading Skin in Medieval Literature and Culture*. The New Middle Ages. New York: Palgrave Macmillan. 99–118.

Desmond, Marilynn. 2006. *Ovid's Art and the Wife of Bath: The Ethics of Erotic Violence*. Ithaca, NY and London: Cornell University Press.

Dinshaw, Carolyn. 1989. *Chaucer's Sexual Poetics*. Madison: The University of Wisconsin Press.

Disbrow, Sarah. 1986. "The Wife of Bath's Old Wives' Tale." *Studies in the Age of Chaucer* 8: 59–71.

DMLBS = *Dictionary of Medieval Latin from British Sources*. 2012–. Ed. Richard Ashdowne, David Howlett and R. E. Latham. Oxford: Oxford University Press. <http://www.dmlbs.ox.ac.uk/> [last accessed 28 July 2017]

Evans, Ruth and Leslie Johnson (eds.). 1994. *Feminist Readings in Middle English Literature: The Wife of Bath and All Her Sect*. London: Routledge.

Gadebusch Bondio, Mariacarla. 2005. "La Carne di fuori: Discorsi medici sulla natura e l'estetica della pelle nel '500." In: Thalia Brero (ed.). *Micrologus XIII. La pelle umana/The Human Skin*. Florence: Edizioni del Galluzzo. 537–570.

Halbertsam, Judith. 1998. *Female Masculinity*. Durham and London: Duke University Press.

Heinrichs, Katherine. 1995. "Tropological Woman in Chaucer: Literary Elaborations of an Exegetical Tradition." *English Studies* 3: 212–214.

Holsinger, Bruce. 2009. "Of Pigs and Parchment: Medieval Studies and the Coming of the Animal." *PMLA*. 124.2: 616–623.

Holsinger, Bruce. 2010. "Parchment Ethics: A Statement of More than Modest Concern." *New Medieval Literatures* 12: 131–136.

Innes-Parker, Katherine. 1995. "Sexual violence and the Female Reader: Symbolic 'Rape' in the Saints' Lives of the Katherine Group." *Women's Studies* 24: 205–217.

Innes-Parker, Katherine. 1999. "'Mi bodi henge wix zi bodi neiled o rode:' The Gendering of the Pauline Concept of Crucifixion with Christ in Medieval Devotional Prose for Women." *Studies in Religion/Sciences Religieuses* 28: 49–62.

Kay, Sarah. 2006. "Original Skin: Flaying, Reading and Thinking in the Legend of Saint Bartholomew and Other Works." *Journal of Medieval and Early Modern Studies* 36.1: 35–73.

Kay, Sarah. 2011. "Legible Skins: Animals and the Ethics of Medieval Reading." *postmedieval: A Journal of Medieval Cultural Studies* 2.1: 13–32.

Knapp, Peggy A. 1989. "Alisoun of Bathe and the Reappropriation of Tradition." *The Chaucer Review* 24: 45–52.

Kuefler, Mathew. 1996. "Castration and Eunuchism in the Middle Ages." In: Vern L. Bullough and James A. Brundage (eds). *Handbook of Medieval Sexuality*. New York and London: Garland. 279–306.

Lochrie Karma. 2005. *Heterosyncrasies: Female Sexuality when Normal Wasn't*. Minneapolis: University of Minnesota Press.

Langum, Virginia. 2013. "Discerning Skin: Complexion, Surgery, and Language in Medieval Confession." In: Katie L. Walter (ed.). *Reading Skin in Medieval Literature and Culture*. The New Middle Ages. New York: Palgrave Macmillan. 141–160.

Martin, Priscilla. 1990. *Chaucer's Women: Nuns, Wives, and Amazons*. Iowa City: University of Iowa Press.

Mazo Karras, Ruth. 2005. *Sexuality in Medieval Europe: Undoing unto Others*. New York and London: Routledge.

MED = *Middle English Dictionary*. 1952–2001. Ed. Hans Kurath, Sherman M. Kuhn, John Reidy and Robert E. Lewis. Ann Arbor: University of Michigan Press. <http://quod.lib.umich.edu/m/med/>.

Pugh, Tison. 2004. *Queering Medieval Genres*. New York and Basingstoke: Palgrave Macmillan.

Robertson, D. W., Jr. 1962. *A Preface to Chaucer: Studies in Medieval Perspectives*. Princeton: Princeton University Press.

Robertson, Elizabeth. 1991. "The Corporeality of Female Sanctity in *The Life of St. Margaret*." In: Renate Blumenfeld-Kosinki and Timea Szell (eds.). *Images of Sainthood in Medieval Europe*. Ithaca: Cornell University Press. 268–287.

Robertson, Elizabeth. 2013. "Noli me tangere: The Enigma of Touch in Middle English Religious Literature and Art for and about Women." In: Katie L. Walter (ed.). *Reading Skin in Medieval Literature and Culture*. The New Middle Ages. New York: Palgrave Macmillan. 29–55.

Sayers, Edna E. 2010. "Experience, Authority, and the Mediation of Deafness: Chaucer's Wife of Bath." In: Joshua R. Eyler (ed.). *A World of Difference: Essays on Disability in the Middle Ages*. Burlington: Ashgate. 81–92.

Schibanoff, Susan. 1988. "The New Reader and Female Textuality in Two Early Commentaries on Chaucer." *Studies in the Age of Chaucer* 10: 71–108.

Steinberg, Leo. 1996. *The Sexuality of Christ in Renaissance Art and in Modern Oblivion*. 2nd ed. Chicago and London: Chicago University Press.

Tinkle, Theresa. 2010. *Gender and Power in Medieval Exegesis*. New York: Palgrave Macmillan.

Tomasch, Sylvia. 2000. "Postcolonial Chaucer and the Virtual Jew." In: Jeffrey J. Cohen (ed.). *The Postcolonial Middle Ages*. New York and Basingstoke: Palgrave. 243–260.

Tracy, Larissa. 2013. *Castration and Culture in the Middle Ages*. Cambridge: D. S. Brewer.

Vandeventer Pearman, Tory. 2010. *Women and Disability in Medieval Literature*. The New Middle Ages. New York: Palgrave Macmillan.

Walker Bynum, Caroline. 1982. *Jesus as Mother: Studies in the Spirituality of the High Middle Ages*. Berkeley and Los Angeles: University of California Press.

Walker Bynum, Caroline. 1991. *Fragmentation and Redemption: Essays on Gender and the Human Body in Medieval Religion*. New York: Urzone Publishers.

Walker Bynum, Caroline. 2011. *Christian Materiality: An Essay on Religion in Late Medieval Europe*. New York: Zone Books.

Walter, Katie L. (ed.). 2013. *Reading Skin in Medieval Literature and Culture*. The New Middle Ages. New York: Palgrave Macmillan.

Williams Boyarin, Adrienne. 2009. "Sealed Flesh, Book-Skin: How to Read the Female Body in the Early Middle English *Seinte Margarete*." In: Kathryn Kerby-Fulton (ed.). *Women and the Divine in Literature before 1700: Essays in Memory of Margot Louis*. Victoria: ELS Editions. 87–106.

Winstead, Karen A. 1997. *Virgin Martyrs: Legends of Sainthood in Late Medieval England*. Ithaca, NY: Cornell University Press.

Wogan-Brown, Jocelyn. 1994. "The Virgin's Tale." In: Ruth Evans and Leslie Johnson (eds.). *Feminist Readings in Middle English Literature: The Wife of Bath and All Her Sect*. London: Routledge. 165–194.

M. W. Bychowski
Reconstructing the Pardoner:
Transgender Skin Operations in Fragment VI

Abstract: This chapter reclaims the Pardoner as a critically trans figure in the Middle Ages through an analysis of the discursive and historical reconstructions of skin. Given how narratives of transition and the politics of surgery become written on the skin of countless transgender lives across time, a trans literary approach to Fragment VI of the *Canterbury Tales* cannot ignore that the Pardoner's presence and story arises in response to the Physician's tale of medical authority and the nature of gender. Putting the medieval praxis of castration in dialog with Judith Butler's theorizing of the 'sharp-machines' that construct culturally intelligible trans bodies, this study looks at how the narratives of Fragment VI fashion skin as a natural signifier of gender in the "Physician's Tale" and as a mark of unnatural reconstruction in the "Pardoner's Prologue." Indeed, the deployment of the Pardoner's body, relics, and voice speak back with tenants of what might be called medieval trans feminism against the subjugation of noncisgender men and the devaluation of surgically altered bodies throughout Fragment VI. A critical outcome of such a reconsideration of Geoffrey Chaucer's sexually complex figure is that while we may never know definitively what is between the pilgrim's legs – as with many transgender persons – nonetheless, based on the physical and social operation of gender he embodies, the Pardoner evidently stands at the crossroads of medieval trans discourse.

> Malleability, as it were, is violently imposed.
> And naturalness is artificially induced.
> — (Butler 2004: 66)

This article concerns itself with how gender is not only constructed but reconstructed in Fragment VI of Geoffrey Chaucer's *Canterbury Tales*, using critical transgender theory of 'sharp-machines,' as articulated by Judith Butler, to revisit how the text presents surgery on the bodies, particularly on the skin, of Virginia and the Pardoner. Such surgery provides a sense of the naturalness of sex or conversely the unnatural artifice of social gendering.[1] While predominantly concerning 'trans' bodies, Butler avoids offering a fixed definition of transgender when

---

[1] Citations of Chaucer's texts in this chapter are taken from Benson (1987). All translations are mine.

discussing sharp-machines, engines of discourse that enact physical and social reconstruction. Rather, sharp-machines may be understood as the network of physical and social operations at work in transitioning bodies (i.e. trans bodies) from one gender designation to another. I argue that in Fragment VI, the work of transgender skin operations is key to reading the Pardoner as speaking in response to the "Physician's Tale." As will be explored, neither modern nor medieval sharp-machines fully reposition a body from one gender to another. Instead, a body remains in tension between definitions. This between/across position also exists in the person's relation to the machines that neither fully subdue the body according to natural or social authorities nor become fully mastered by the body undergoing reconstruction. Bodies physically defined by their skin as a point of entrance as well as resistance come to function socially as mediators, co-operating with the sharp-machines that exert power on them while bringing these bodies into contact with other bodies that are often divided from them by sharp distinctions of discourse.

To accomplish this argument, the chapter is divided into four sections. First, the trans theory of Butler is examined to explicate the meaning of sharp-machines in transgender skin operations. Second, the Pardoner is located within pre-modern discourses of trans embodiment, specifically within the cultural context of medieval castrates. Previous scholarship has interrogated the Pardoner as a figure of debatable gender, yet there is a persistent tendency to read his gender as either inherited from birth, given by others, or vacated, voluntarily, by the Pardoner for the benefit of social ideals such as the authority of the church, the temperate control of the body, or the dangers of greed. This chapter responds to these traditions by locating the Pardoner's body within trans theories of co-operative agency, wherein subjects submit to degrees of physical and social construction in order to exert degrees of control that lead to a reconstruction of their identity that is not exactly as nature, God, or society assigns. Third, I argue that the Pardoner follows the "Physician's Tale" in Fragment VI to serve as a response to how the story naturalizes the use of surgical violence as a reparative to threats against a body's assigned gender; i.e. the cutting off of Virginia's head to assure that she will never cease being a virgin. Finally, a close reading of the language related to skin and the cutting of skin demonstrates how the Pardoner appears to reflect similar virginal qualities as Virginia, while also suggesting a very different cultural genealogy and social context, which link him with the associations and embodiment of castrates, geldings, and eunuchs. Nonetheless, as will be shown, virgins and castrates share overlapping social positions and associations. Indeed, as this study will show, the gender of both Virginia and the Pardoner are denaturalized through a critical trans approach, so that the identities of virgin, gelding, woman, and man are no longer read as fully assigned by either nature or society but as arising out of the co-operation of a person's agency with associations written within and on their skin.

A general understanding of how the Pardoner's gender has been reduced to a construct of nature or society by medieval studies can be summarized with a collation of how the figure has been read in association to the different eunuchs from Matthew 19.12. Providing such a useful overview, in "The Pardoner's (Over-) Sexed Body," Robert S. Sturges (2000) knits together an expansive literary review of scholarship on Chaucer's Pardoner through the relation of different readings of his polemic sex with an exegesis of eunuchs from Matthew 19.12: "sunt enim eunuchi qui de matris utero sic nati sunt et sunt eunuchi qui facti sunt ab hominibus et sunt eunuchi qui se ipsos castraverunt propter regnum caelorum qui potest capere capiat."[2] Various scholars argue for the Pardoner to be considered as *eunuchus ex nativitate* ('eunuch from birth'), a sterile, hermaphroditic, or female bodied person by nature (Rayner Myers 2000).[3] Others, based on the suggestion that he is a "gelding," comment on him being a *eunuchus qui castratus est*[4] whether physically constructed as a castrate, or socially constructed as a queer outcast (Taylor 2000: 154; Kuefler 2000: 186; Tracy 2013: 5–9). Readings of the Pardoner as *eunuchus Dei* ('eunuch of God') focus on the Pardoner's real or feigned surrender of his body and meaning to God; or alternatively as a queer person who has failed to surrender his body and meaning to God, identified as *eunuchus non Dei* ('eunuch not of God') (Miller 1955).

While drawing readers closer to a critical trans understanding of the Pardoner, queer medieval studies have also fallen victim to reducing the figure to a *eunuchus Dei* who sacrifices his body and significance to wider social meanings or a *eunuchus non Dei* who fails to sacrifice himself. The Pardoner in this situation is either a successful tool of the Church or a else failed tool. In "Eunuch Hermeneutics," Carolyn Dinshaw (1989: 156–184), like other queer theorists, uses psychoanalysis to read castrated skin as signifying a lack, absence, or partial object

---

[2] 'For there are eunuchs who have been so from birth, and there are eunuchs who have been made eunuchs by others, and there are eunuchs who have made themselves eunuchs for the sake of the kingdom of heaven. Let anyone accept this who can.' Latin quotations from the *Vulgate Bible* are from Swift (2011). Translations are taken from the *New Revised Standard Version, Catholic Edition*.

[3] Others describe the Pardoner as naturally feminine based on the description of his skin. "Effeminacy might be suggested by both anatomical disabilities, including missing or defective testicles and blocked pores in the penis or facial skin, or physiological problems, including impotence, nocturnal emissions, the generation of female children, and the inability to grow a beard, or more generalized markers, such as soft, abundant flesh and pale skin and hair" (Whitney 2011: 284).

[4] 'eunuch who has been castrated'

that deconstructs gender but also moves away from material operations of the body.[5] Eunuchs here become a signifier of a lack of essential embodiment. In *Getting Medieval*, Dinshaw (1999: 100–142) develops her reading of the Pardoner as signifying a partial body but continues to stress the negative motion of the castrate to represent absence, a hermeneutic of unknowing. Nonetheless, Dinshaw's work on the Pardoner helps to disrupt how the figure had been framed by conventional forms of knowledge and desire, opening up the text's uncertainty about gender and sexuality. From this uncertainty arise queer alternative readings. In particular, Dinshaw's scholarship opens up space for transgender studies to make critical interventions.

While previous gender and sexuality studies of the Pardoner have not addressed the reconstructive capacity of skin and identities in Fragment VI, many of the conclusions drawn by Sturges (2000) and Dinshaw (1989, 1999) suggest the need for a critical trans study. Sturges (2000) acknowledges how each form of writing has its place in making and remaking gender. Indeed, through a critical approach to skin, we discover that castrates are not created by any single act. Birth alone does not make someone a castrate. Nor does castration alone make someone a castrate. Nor does one make oneself a castrate in isolation. Each of these events participates in a wider cultural system of socially constructed and reconstructed gender identities. Likewise, in what Dinshaw (1999: 1–2) calls a "contingent" reading based on touch and enfolding intimacies, there remains room for a biopolitical extension of this work towards material skin operations, from unknowing to a partial re-knowing.

In this tradition, a critical trans study of the narratives of Fragment VI through the focal point of skin may seem counter-intuitive. Yet familiarity with how trans studies reexamine the reconstruction of gender reveals the role that skin plays not only as the organ where the world meets the body physically but also as the plane on which society and the self struggle over the significance of one's flesh.[6] White blemish-free skin becomes encoded in the Middle Ages with naturalness. Virgins are marked as exemplary products of nature by their fair skin. Likewise, castrates (such as eunuchs) are either naturalized by praise of their skin or else denaturalized by condemnation of their scars. Such a conflict plays out in the naturalized virginity of Virginia and the ambiguous gender of the Pardoner. Yet, I argue, however nature and social norms may be invoked, Fragment VI is full of persons using their skin rhetorically to assert agency over en-

---

5 See also Stockton (2011: 97–118) and Sturges (2000: 69–80).
6 An excellent study of transgender skin is available in Prosser's (1998) *Second Skins: the Body Narratives of Transsexuality*.

tangling systems of control and to reconstruct the gendered meaning of their bodies. As such, supposedly pre-sexual (virginal) and post-sexual (castrate) bodies are revealed as intimately tied to the making and unmaking of "natural" gender as they co-operate with violent systems that exercise power (and potential resistance) through the mode and site of such operations: the knife and skin. While the fairness and smoothness of skin may suggest purity, as products of piercing and cutting skin, scars remain to narrate the costs of making and securing sex.

Although consistently paired together in the manuscripts, and understood as making up two halves of Fragment VI, too often the Pardoner is not considered in relation to the narrative that introduces his prologue and tale: the "Physician's Tale." Yet when the "Physician's Tale" is read through skin operations, which affect a range of different bodies from virgins to castrates to relics, "by nayles and by blood" (l. 288),[7] it can be seen as mapping the medieval debate occurring in Fragment VI between the Physician and the Pardoner on the subject of surgical violence and what forces can claim control over a body's gender (ll. 288–289). The Physician's exemplum on chastity presents Virginia's body as a white "lilie," ('lily,' l. 32) painted by Nature, as being (se)cured from violent sexuality by a knife put to her throat. Facing the potential of one kind of forced penetration altering a virgin's naturalized body, the tale argues that it is better to carve out a part of Nature's wholeness than to let it transition. As scholars have attempted to fix the Pardoner's sex by reducing it to a product of nature or else primarily the work of social operations, likewise Virginia from the "Physician's Tale" can be too easily reduced to a natural embodiment of virginity or else an agency-free victim of violent systems of gender and sexuality.

A contributing factor to why Virginia may not often be considered in relation to the Pardoner in medieval gender studies is that the one gender seems so natural and the other so unnatural or performative. Yet critical trans studies insist that no body is wholly made by nature nor wholly made by society. Understanding how Virginia's gender is constructed and prohibited from being reconstructed (moving from virgin to wife and mother) is integral to an understanding of how the Pardoner reflects and refracts this narrative in the narration of his body and relics. In Fragment VI, the silent dismemberment of Virginia is answered by the Pardoner's body, which is at one point threatened with dismemberment by the Host, concluding a series of associations drawn between the Pardoner and the knife. These associations begin with the portrait of the Pardoner, where the narrator describes his skin, stating: "[n]o berd hadde he, ne nevere

---

7 'by nails and by blood'

sholde have; / as smothe it was as it were late shave" (General Prologue ll. 689 – 690).[8] From this the narrator draws a conclusion about the Pardoner's gender identity, stating that he is either "a geldyng or a mare" (General Prologue, l. 693).[9] While the exact meaning of this passage has been long debated, this chapter will consider how the relation between skin and gender identity situates the Pardoner as a post-sexual castrate reflection of Virginia's pre-sexual virginity. A critical trans reading of the Pardoner's portrait and prologue reveals how the Pardoner reanimates butchered bodies through the openly artificial power of relics and words. As part of this process, the Pardoner demonstrates the way in which skin matter is reconstructed through cultural and physical operations that cluster in and around the skin. In doing so, the Pardoner practises transgender skin operations as a form of rhetoric that reconstructs supposedly unnatural, broken, absent fragments of bodies and society into new – if scarred – wholes through life-giving narratives. By showing how a sheep's bone may become a relic, the Pardoner provides hope for his and Virginia's butchered flesh.

Yet is the Pardoner's own skin butchered, cut, or castrated? Whether or not the Pardoner has had the medieval sex change operation associated with geldings and eunuchs, i.e. castration, transgender studies insists that a body may function within such a trans identity without necessarily having or revealing such a surgery. Without declaring unequivocally one way or another, Chaucer provides reasons to associate the Pardoner with castrates. Scholarship on skin demonstrates that medieval surgeons may have had "pre-sexual" virgin bodies in mind when surgically manufacturing and valuing "post-sexual" castrates.[10] Kathryn Reusch (2013: 36) notes that castration manufactures soft tissue "includ[ing] soft smooth skin [...] lack of body hair [...] following a female shape." Medieval humoralists would have been aware of the production of

---

8 'No beard had he, nor never should have; as smooth it was as it were late shaven'
9 'a gelding or a mare'
10 Eunuchs were constructed and valued for more than what was between their legs. Castrates, like women, and other feminine phlemic bodies were bonded by physiological traits formed in the skin due to a lack of heat from the testes: "Every individual had a characteristic physiology or an innate temperament that persisted through secondary modifications caused by natural processes, such as aging, changes in environment, or habit (although these too affected humoral balance in the shorter term). This characteristic physiology could be identified through external signs such as body type, hair and skin color and texture, and degrees of hairiness" (Whitney 2011: 366). Freitas (2003: 247) argues that the purity and security of sexuality suggested by fair smooth skin reinforce the social value of eunuchs and may have helped motivate their production: "The literature, art, and historical accounts of the period confirm that, whereas now masculine eroticism is epitomized perhaps by firm muscles, a 'healthy' tan, and maybe even an unshaven face, the earlier period prized a soft body, pale skin, and smooth cheeks."

soft smooth skin as a result of castration, which we would now attest to hormone changes.[11] "The root cause of the beardlessness of the eunuch," argues Elspeth Whitney (2011: 378), "is not the loss of the testicles per se, but primarily the cold constitution produced by that loss, which prevented the transformation of residues into hair and closed the pores of the face." Virginal women and castrates were supposed to share such hormonal/humoral registers and skin qualities.

Yet just as trans persons insist that their gender goes beyond their embodiment, that they do not need to reveal information on their genitals or surgery to function as trans, so too the Pardoner and his skin can socially and narratively operate as a non-specified trans identity in general or as a castrate in particular without conclusively revealing physical reconstruction. Beyond virginal and castrate skin's metaphorical or spiritual signification of lack, the Physician and the Pardoner exist within a medieval understanding of *Christus Medicus* ('Christ as physician') or "oure soules leche" ('our soul's doctor') as the Pardoner names him (l. 916). While one is a medical and the other a religious professional, both Physician and Pardoner operate in a culture influenced by medico-religious discourse developed in part via St. Augustine's sermons and letters (Arbesmann 1954), texts inspired by passages describing Christ's cures and teachings, such as Matthew 18, "if your hand or your foot causes you to stumble, cut it off and throw it from you; it is better for you to enter life crippled or lame, than to have two hands or two feet and be cast into the eternal fire." This doctrine could excuse laying hands on another if the violence is justified as promoting personal or social health (Taylor 2000: 72; Tracy 2013: 9–10; Kuefler 2000: 282–283; Tougher 2008: 68–82; Scholz 199: 159–164). Despite prohibitions against deforming the body, castration becomes "permissible mutilation if used to save the whole person" (Kuefler 2000: 286). Testicles and more are cut off in what begins as a cure for illness but also as a way of curtailing sexuality (Tracy 2013: 5–18; Kuefler 2000: 286). Castrates, like virgins (and chaste women) are deemed sexually secured (pre-/post-sexual), because of a supposed lack in the body and of agency.

---

11 Freitas (2003: 226) notes many of these secondary sexual characteristics, reflecting those of a virginal woman, including and in addition to the skin as a product of the manufacturing of the eunuch's body: "The destruction of the testes before puberty creates the condition of eunuchoidism, in which the male secondary sexual characteristics are not expressed: The penis remains small; beard growth does not occur; axillary and pubic hair follow a female rather than male pattern, as does the distribution of body fat; and of course the larynx does not grow. In addition, as mentioned above, the proportions of the body are sometimes upset by the lack of the hormone that arrests bone growth."

To understand how virgins and castrates operate under the *Christus Medicus* concept, it is critical to consider how Christ's words on eunuchs in Matthew stress the importance of reclaiming one's own body, even from nature, and follow directly after his teaching on cutting apart one's body to save the whole in chapter 18. Indeed, the meaning of 19.12 is not complete until eunuchs choose to engage in operations enacted on their body (Matthew 18–19). Matthew 18 is followed by a meditation on forgiving those who have done violence and Christ's words on eunuchs in 19 follow the apostles' whining that if they cannot cast off their wives (like they might other parts of their body) it is best not to marry. In 19.12, Christ invokes eunuchs as a hermeneutic not of missing or discarded parts of the self but of recollecting the corporate self with all its scars. In Matthew 18 and 19, Christ instructs Christians to not only be operated on by nature or society but to become operatives in the reconstruction of their body and life. For pilgrims such as the Physician and the Pardoner, the reconstructed body would be understood as existing in tension between the body as given by nature and the body remade for Christ. As such, medieval conceptualisations of gender cannot be read as merely natural or social but, as critical trans studies suggests, as co-operative with mechanisms of gender that intermittently reconstruct the flesh and its social signification.

In order to establish a common theoretical methodology, and before a medieval trans reading of Fragment VI can move forward, it is useful to consider how contemporary critical trans studies has framed the skin of those undergoing some form of surgical reconstruction as part of undergoing a wider social reconstruction. While using different terms and language, trans theorists like Judith Butler and medieval theologians like Peter of Abelard offer compatible ways of reading transgender skin operations in literature through mechanisms of physical reconstruction and social control, revealing the co-operative power of skin (Kuefler 2000: 280). While medieval eunuchs and modern transsexuals exist in different centuries, they share a relation and response to sharp-machines that work to fix gendered bodies and control the transition of identities.

As Nature Made Him: Transgender Skin Operations

While existing as a modern way of understanding identity, in recent decades, transgender has also grown in an archive of critical theory and literature that offer methodologies by which to understand diverse texts and histories. Laying the foundations for trans theory, Butler's (1990) *Gender Trouble* (which the author later commented should have been named *Doing Gender*),[12] denaturalized the meaning of sex and gender, although the scholar did not directly address transgender or transsexuality in depth until 2004, when she published *Undoing Gender*. In the third chapter of this latter book, "Doing Justice to Someone: Sex Reassignment and Allegories of Transsexuality," Butler considers David Reimer, as described in *As Nature Made Him* by John Colapinto (2000), a person who does not necessarily identify as transgender, but finds himself placed in a trans position within a wider system of gender reconstruction which she calls "technologies of the knife" (Butler 2004: 64) or "sharp-machines" (Butler 2004: 66). According to these theories, transsexuality exists as an allegory, or what I call a 'genre of embodiment,' that connects a wide range of bodies existing in different cultural times and places. As will be shown in the following sections, examining such systems of gender reconstruction that occur time and again offers a critical trans way of composing and reading bodies, connecting narratives from the Middle Ages until today. In particular, the ability to identify the operations of sharp-machines is integral to analyzing how transgender skin operations not only reconstruct the bodies of figures such as Reimer or the Pardoner but critique the wider social mechanisms that direct and limit such changes as well as define the social significance of transsexual and castrate, intersexual and virgin, man and woman, modern and medieval.

Within a critical trans lens, skin does not have a neutral relationship to the knife, nor is it passive when tools cut across, burn, or penetrate it. The archeology of castrates demonstrates how the social construction of eunuchs, castrati, and geldings were not merely written on the body but transformed skin through "the technology of the knife." To show the power and resistances within sharp-machines, Butler discusses Reimer's life as an exemplum of/for operations, where "malleability [...] is violently imposed. And naturalness is artificially induced" (Butler 2006: 187).[13] By applying Butler's theory of the reconstruction of transgender and the intersex body, we can better understand the long genealogical relationship between the various operators of sharp-machines and the pre- and post-operative bodies which they work to construct.

Butler presents Reimer's life as an exemplum of the physical and social operations employed to preserve and construct skin that appears as natural. Identified male at birth, Reimer underwent surgery on his penis to alter his foreskin, which was burned off when the doctor "elected to use not a scalpel to cut away [the] foreskin, but a Bovie cautery machine. This device employs a generator to

---

[12] See *Judith Butler: Philosophin der Gender* (2006, dir. Zadjermann).
[13] See also Angier (1997).

deliver an electric current to a sharp, needlelike cutting instrument, which burns the edges of an incision as it is made" (Colapinto 2000: 12). After the accident marked Reimer's skin as not normatively male, doctors encouraged surgery to re-naturalize the body as a girl, making "a rudimentary exterior vagina using the remaining scrotal skin" (Colapinto 2000: 54). The parents agreed and David became Brenda. The use of the Bovie machine and transsexual/intersex protocols is represented as unusual, but reflects an impulse implicit in technologies of the knife, where operations cut away parts not conforming to gender norms while cauterizing the skin to assert a naturalized wholeness.

The division of bodies and the erasure of the past have become signatures of such trans narratives. In the 1950s, doctors developed the language of pre- and post-operative in what Sandy Stone (2006: 226) describes as part of a clinical "strategy of building barriers within a single subject." As genitals underwent operations to bring the body in line with the prescribed gender, the clinic's 'charm school' taught transsexual and intersex persons to continue to expunge parts of their history that did not fit into models of natural gender (Stone 2006: 227). The doctors brought in transsexual women to teach Brenda to be feminine. Here the transsexual state is replicated as *eunuchus ex nativitate*, a naturalized genus. Considered transsexual, however, Brenda was used to substantiate the naturalness of feminine characteristics. She was made to train her brother for supposedly natural sexual relations through "mock coital activities" (Butler 2004: 60). Made to present herself naked for study, doctors examined her body, "with its small stumplike protrusion under the skin and its apparent scarring" (Colapinto 2000: 92). This was published as proof of effective operations to naturalize female gender. While praised as a post-op transsexual, the marks of artifice were most praised when invisible, counterfeiting pre-op virginity.

After years as a transsexual and a girl, later in life Reimer decided to seek operations to remake himself physically and socially male. "David," writes Colapinto (2000: 184), using Reimer's reclaimed masculine name, "underwent surgery to create a rudimentary penis. Constructed of muscles and skin from the inside of his thighs, the penis was attached to the small stump of remaining penile corpora under the skin." In this logic, the title of Colapinto's book on Reimer's life, *As Nature Made Him*, suggests the primacy of Nature determining the form of a body's gender.[14] Yet again, the post-post-op Reimer is supposed to reflect natural pre-op forms of gender.

---

14 Other authors followed the model of declaring Reimer's gender as proof of the failure of transformation, such as Angier's (1997) "Sexual Identity Not Pliable After All, Report Says."

As an exemplum of skin operations, Butler's reading of Reimer's life draws readers to look at castration as signifying more than naturalized or absent knowledge, to consider the physical as well as the biopolitical reconstructions of the operative body. Butler (2006: 187) asks, "is the surgery performed in order to create a 'normal-looking' body after all? [...] mutilations and scars that remain hardly offer compelling evidence that this is what the surgeries actually accomplish." The physical and social operations of being "mutilated" and "scarred" function to justify becoming artificially "normal" looking – as Nature made him (or would have made him). It is a paradox and a double bind, revealing that the operations of sharp-machines are the unmaking and making of naturalness itself.

For castrates, medieval eunuchs or modern transsexuals, "[m]alleability [...] is violently imposed," writes Butler (2004: 66), critiquing assumptions that becoming post-op is ever an essential telos, "[a]nd naturalness is artificially induced." Castrates cannot be made to unproblematically signify a fundamentally unfixed form of embodiment or time. Nor can cisgender masculinity and femininity be taken as fixed natural forms that are retained across time, whether in a personal or collective history. All bodies become produced as a result of operations where skin touches, folds, and cuts across genres of embodiment.[15] Moving beyond mere contact, the contingency that trans studies consider involves a greater attention to scars and the work of sharp-machines, the way in which skin is transformed by its encounters with the world. In *Word Made Skin*, Karmen MacKendrick (2004: 11) describes how discourse and skin continually construct and reconstruct one another, "[t]ouching, folding, and cutting form the modes of surface contact. Across these senses, with these modes, we can mark the scar that makes the skin, the path traced by the sense of words." The skin is not a blank background on which gender is inscribed but it is remade by language and even resists the inscription of certain genders. The way in which transsexuality has been constructed and used to control the bodies of others, much like how eunuchs and castrates were used in the Middle Ages, causes scars that can alienate some from claiming such identity even as their histories are caused to touch and enfold into one another.

Indeed, transgender studies arose in no small part in response to how gender reconstruction was being defined, limited, and coerced. To be critically trans is to not passively submit either to the gender assigned by nature or society but to reclaim agency and liberty over systems of transformation. Thus, while rejecting a transsexual identity, Reimer exemplifies a critical trans mode of resistance.

---

15 See also MacKendrick (2004) and Nyffenegger and Rupp's introduction to this volume.

It is the call for those operative within the apparatus of sharp-machines, "to begin to articulate their lives not as a series of erasures [...] but as a political action begun by reappropriating difference and reclaiming the power of the reconfigured and reinscribed body" (Stone 2006: 232). Critical trans histories include the difficult workings of skin operations. Whether a pre-op boy, naturalized girl, transsexual, or post-op man, scars made Reimer testify to the operations of sharp-machines, pulling flesh into systems of power and resistance, using his skin to make and redefine his body.

A Genealogy of Medieval Sharp-Machines

While the word *transgender* arose at a specific twentieth-century moment, the forms of physical embodiment and systems of social gender transition it describes can be traced back for centuries. A critical trans approach to medieval literature and history draws readers to identify a wider mechanism of gender reconstruction that may otherwise go unnoticed but which nonetheless is embodied within specific cultural contexts. The reasons that such a system may require critical interventions are that such social structures and narratives assert the naturalness of certain forms and changes in gender while marking others as unnatural. Far from eschewing historicism, critical trans theory demands that scholars pay attention to historical contexts and associations that might otherwise go unnoticed because they are so "natural" as to be assumed as true from the offset or so "unnatural" as to be considered an exception not necessary to include. Thus, to understand the sharp-machines that construct and reconstruct the meaning of Virginia and the Pardoner, a critical study of transgender skin operations in the Middle Ages insists that readers should consider the wider social machines at work informing fourteenth-century approaches to the body.

Such a medieval genealogy of castrate operations can be traced through the scar tissue on the skin, showing that the violence of laying hands on another body is systematic to the cultural work of sharp-machines.[16] Since the development of classical medicine, surgery operated by coding certain bodies as "parts" (that which is discarded), while coding others as "wholes" (that which is preserved) (Taylor 2000: 56; Kuefler 2000: 286). By the fourteenth century, the post-op castrate body had collected a range of cultural practices and meanings

---

[16] "Emasculated men, usually described incorrectly as eunuchs, can now be found among transvestites, transsexuals, and other members [...] Some who consider themselves transsexuals in the West, although they have actually become castrati, extol this operation as a liberation" (Scholz 1999: 234).

that owe much to Peter Abelard's *Historia Calamitatum*.[17] In the *Historia*, Abelard considers his castration by political opponents who laid hands on him as a means of punishment.[18] In the Roman and Byzantine empires, eunuchs were constructed mostly of a slave class.[19] While castrate slaves did not form an evident part of medieval English culture, records show castration as a punishment for a host of crimes.[20] This punitive act sustained associations with those whose liberties and bodies are curtailed by the law.[21]

In regards to sexual and reproductive freedoms, the enslaved or criminal eunuch was regarded as a post-op, post-sexual body. In his *Historia*, Abelard considers his castration as just such an end to a certain kind of sexual and social agency. "What path lay open to me thereafter?" asks Abelard, "[h]ow could I ever again hold up my head among men, when every finger should be pointed at me in scorn, every tongue speak my blistering shame, and when I should be a monstrous spectacle to all eyes?" (ch. 8).[22] Abelard struggles to see how he will productively operate in society at all after his castration. The shift into becoming post-sexual is in a very real sense an end to his life as a normative male. Physically and socially made *eunuchus castratus*, Abelard is exempted from key masculine activities, marked by the scars on his skin as an exemplary body. [23]

The physical and social effect of reconstructed gender as readable on the skin cannot be underestimated. Abelard's new life establishes associations for

---

17 See McLaughlin and Muckle (1956) for the text in Latin and Bellows (1999) for the text in English.
18 Because older laws dictated that sexual transgressions could be punished by death, the move to castration was seen as a merciful shift. See Kuefler (2000: 287–289); Tracy (2013: 19–28); Irvine (1999: 96–99); Bremmer (2013); Taylor (2000: 52–55).
19 As various Muslim states claimed the region, the practice of utilizing eunuch servants was adopted and spread through conquests in Asia and Eastern Europe. See Scholz (1999: 198); Tougher (2008: 119).
20 See Irvine (1999); Wheeler (1999); Ferroul (1999); Tracy (2013: 9–19); Tougher (2008: 11); Scholz (1999: 246–255); Kuefler (2000: 289–290).
21 The job of enslaving and surgically producing eunuch servants largely fell to Christians, particularly in monasteries (Scholz 1999: 198–199; Kuefler 2000: 284–290).
22 "Qua mihi ulterius via pateret! qua fronte in publicum prodirem, omnium digitis demonstrandus, omnium linguis corrodendus, omnibus monstruosum spectaculum futurus." All Latin quotes are from McLaughlin and Muckle (1956). Translations are from Bellows (1999).
23 The work of these operations on and through these slaves moved around the Mediterranean, encouraging the spread of physical surgery as well as social practices aimed to erase old sexual, national, and religious identities. See Scholz (1999: 203–214, 232); Kuefler (2000: 280); Tougher (2008: 60–67, 119).

a post-sexual life.[24] To be a post-sexual castrate is in a sense to no longer exist within the commerce of community life. He becomes a non-entity. Abelard considers the implications of Leviticus and Deuteronomy for eunuchs, "He that is wounded in the stones, or hath his privy member cut off, shall not enter into the congregation of the Lord."[25] The life of a castrate is supposed to be sexually, socially, and spiritually over, even while he still lives.

Beginning as a site of lack, Abelard uses the operations of his body to reclaim his post-op life as distinctly productive. "Scarcely had I recovered from my wound," recollects Abelard, "when clerics sought me [...] They bade me care diligently for the talent which God had committed to my keeping, since surely He would demand it back from me with interest" (ch. 8).[26] The proposition at hand became that castration was not an end to life in the church, making him a *eunuchus non Dei*, but partial entrance into *eunuchus Dei*, providing unique "talents" and social value to castrates co-operating with the mechanisms that formed them. Rather than surrender his body as a passive object of social discourse, Abelard claims power over tools that touch him. "Therein above all," writes Abelard, "should I perceive how it was the hand of God that had touched me, when I should devote my life to the study of letters in freedom from the snares of the flesh" (ch. 8).[27] Identifying with the liminal operations of skin, Abelard turns the exit from a life supposedly fixed in nature into an entrance to an exemplary spirituality.[28] He pushes back against the snares of knife and flesh that made him operate in a trans position between genders, flesh, and spirit. The machine that lays hands on him is no longer the violent arm of justice but the empowering touch of *Christus Medicus*, "whose work on earth had been depicted by the synoptic gospels as that of a physician of soul and body" (Arbesmann 1954: 3). Since the early Christian period, the healing (making whole) of the flesh was understood as the redemption of the person back into community.

---

24 See Scholz (1999: 160–164); Kuefler (2000: 282–286); Tracy (2013: 12–13).
25 "Non intrabit eunuchus, atritis vel amputatis testiculis, et absciso veretro ecclesiam Dei." Deuteronomy 23.1 as quoted in McLaughlin and Muckle (1956) and translated in Bellows (1999).
26 "Vix autem de vulnere adhuc convalue, cum ad me eonfluentes clerici tam ab abbate nostro quam a me [...] attendens quod mihi fuerat a Domino talentum commissum, ab ipso esse cum usuris exigendum."
27 "ob hoc maxime dominica manu me nunc tactum esse cognoscerem, quo liberius a carnalibus illecebris."
28 See Irvine (1999: 87–106); Wheeler (1999: 107–128); Ferroul (1999: 129–150); Tracy (2013: 9–19); Tougher (2008: 11); Scholz (1999: 246–255); Kuefler (2000: 289–290).

The double-bind of social expectations may be considered the double-edged blade that at once carves out lives and demands that they grab the blade in order to replicate those divides as a tool of the system. Upon further reflection on the power and position afforded to him by his castration, Abelard begins to assert himself as a medium for controlling the sexual formation of others. Abelard writes, "[i]n truth, that which had happened to me so completely removes all suspicion of this iniquity [lust] among all men that those who wish to have their women kept under close guard employ eunuchs for that purpose" (ch. 14).[29] Abelard plays upon an etymological as well as social genealogy of "the eunuch" as a guardian of women and the marriage bed. "[E]unuch derives from the ancient Greek," writes Gary Taylor (2000: 33), from the roots meaning 'to guard' as well as 'marriage bed.'[30] While eunuchs developed other meanings and associations, especially as they gained responsibilities, being a guardian of the marriage bed remains inscribed in their identity.

In medieval as well as modern contexts, the decision to co-operate with sharp-machines is not made with unfettered free will, but represents a form of contingent personal resistance to a system from which a body cannot extricate itself. Voiced in the description of Reimer's and Abelard's lives, the post-sexual castrate and pre-sexual young women and men often find themselves sharing the same spaces physically and socially. Abelard writes, "[s]uch men, in truth, are enabled to have far more importance and intimacy among modest and upright women by the fact that they are free from any suspicion of lust" (ch. 14).[31] This opens up a point of empathy and co-operation between sexually managed lives. Embracing the power of operations that are nonetheless forced on participants represents a point of resistance for these supposedly secured bodies, allowing them to potentially reclaim socially erased pleasures and agency over bodies repeatedly stolen from them by sharp-machines of diverse forms, including laws, knives, and shame.

A critical trans study of medieval castration has the ability to reframe premodern eunuchs and castrati from isolated historical phenomena to fellow constructs in the surgical and social operation of sharp-machines that seize hold

---

29 "Adeo namque res ista omnem huius turpitudinis suspitionem apud omnes removet, ut quicunque mulieres observare diligentius student, eis eunuchos adhibeant." Eunuchs became, as Abelard writes, supposed safe-keepers that bordered off women of the lord's possession, managing servants, the estate, armies, and the Church. See Tougher (2008: 54–82); Taylor (2000: 32–39); Kuefler (2000: 282–292); Tracy (2013: 4–9); Scholz (1999: 200–209).
30 See also Tracy (2013: 6); Scholz (1999: 232).
31 "Tales quippe semper apud verecundas et honestas feminas tanto amplius dignitatis et familiaritatis adepti sunt quanto longius ab hac absistebant suspitione."

of monks and nuns, virgins and castrates, transsexuals and geldings. While sharing struggles and tactics within a centuries-old system of controlling the gendered body, each individual and genre of embodiment may nonetheless experience the sharp-machines in historically distinct ways. As Piotr Scholz (1999: 234) writes in *Eunuchs and Castrati: A Cultural History*, while castration and being made a eunuch was a source of violent slavery or punishment for some, this transformation of body and identity may be a path to grace and reclamation for others, "[s]ome who consider themselves transsexuals in the West, although they have actually become castrati [rather than eunuchs], extol this operation as a liberation." Just as modern trans persons must reckon the historically distinct contexts in which eunuchs arise, a comparison of the social oppression between male castrates and female virgins must be done with care. While sharp-machines affect both Virginia from the "Physician's Tale" and the Pardoner, placing them in a shared social position, it is necessary to nonetheless consider how they touch each person in very distinct ways.

Nature's Paintbrush: The "Physician's Tale"

Fragment VI presents Virginia and the Pardoner as bodies subject to transgender skin operations, the one struggling at the edge of virgin and sexually active woman and the other at the edge of sexually active man and castrate, yet each with stories that produce very different results. While the Pardoner is described in association with artifice, unnatural and de-painted with skin "smothe [...] as it were late shave" (General Prologue, l. 690)[32] Virginia is described as having smooth fair skin made for her by nature. Yet despite naturalization of her body, the central figure of the "Physician's Tale" retains her virgin skin by becoming subject to an operation that cuts her skin and fragments her body, thus revealing the role of sharp-machines in continually constructing and enforcing virginity as a genre of embodiment.

The "Physician's Tale" begins with a challenge: "Lo! I, Nature / Thus kan I forme and peynte a creature, / Whan that me list; who kan me countrefete?" (ll. 11–13).[33] The claim that nature is a master artisan is not unusual in medieval literature, but it is provocative coming out of the mouth of a medical doctor. While physicians are students of nature, compiling and passing down knowledge about bodies, this knowledge is employed in the fight to battle the natural

---

32 'smooth it was as if it were lately shaved'
33 'Lo! I, Nature, thus can I form and paint a creature when I wish; who can counterfeit me?'

forces of mutability (Whitney 2011). Fixed around a defense of virginal skin, the Physician presents the co-operation of natural and surgical authorities that construct and reconstruct Virginia's gender and sexuality. "In hire," the Physician diagnoses, "ne lakked no condicioun" (l. 41).[34] An exemplum of pre-sexual states, the "Physician's Tale" presents the preservation of Nature's unblemished and pre-penetrated skin as justifying the operations that cut her flesh and end her life.[35]

A key signifier of Nature's artistry is the virginal whiteness of pre-sexual skin. Virginia, the tale's exemplary body, is marked as a

> mayde of age twelve yeer [...] and tweye
> In which that Nature hadde swich delit.
> For right as she kan peynte a lilie whit,
> And reed a rose, right with swich peynture
> She peynted hath this noble creature (ll. 30–34).[36]

The repetition of the Middle English words for paint, painting, and pigments draws readers to pay careful attention to the construction and colors of Virginia's skin. Compared to a painted white "lilie" ('lily') and a red "rose," Virginia's skin is associated with the hue of virginity, white, as well as the color of sexual activity and violence, red.[37] It is significant that her skin is not compared to works of art but rather to other products of Nature. Virginia's skin is untouched, forever pre-sexual, secured from intercourse and violence that may de-paint or re-paint her fair body. The maiden's gender is readable through the artifice of her skin as a painting on a canvas. Nature claims that no one can counterfeit or best her painting skills: "Pigmalion noght, though he ay forge and bete, / Or grave, or peynte" (ll. 14–15).[38] Not even the Gods' craftsman can beat Nature's power of painting skin, nor "Apelles" or "Zanzis" who she dares "to grave, or peynte, or forge, or bete, / If they presumed me to countrefete" (ll. 16–18).[39]

---

[34] 'In her [...] she lacked in no condition'
[35] The Physician mixes medical and religious sterility, framing Virginia as one managed by *Christus Medicus*, whole in body and spirit, "As wel in goost as body chast was she, / For which she floured in virginitee / With alle humylitee and abstinence" ('As well in soul as in body she was chaste, for which she flowered in virginity with all humility and abstinence,' l. 45).
[36] 'Maid of an age of twelve years [...] and two in which Nature had such delight. For well as she can paint a lily white, and a rose red, so with such pains she painted this noble creature'
[37] Like eunuchs, women's cooler phlemic humors were thought to invest them with more "pale, hairless skin; limp, light-colored hair" (Whitney 2011: 368).
[38] 'Not Pygmalion, though he always forge and beat, or grave, or paint'
[39] 'To carve, or paint, or forge, or beat, if they presumed to counterfeit me'

These examples represent exaggerated versions of human artists, whose skills at manipulating bodies are set in opposition to the authoritative work of Nature. "For He that is the formere principal," says Nature, citing God as the supreme shaper of forms, "[h]ath maked me his vicaire general, / To forme and peynten erthely creaturis / Right as me list, and ech thyng in my cure is" (ll. 19–22).[40] Each created thing is subordinate to Nature's painting and "cure" (i.e. control) as the second highest authority after the author and savior of all things, *Christus Medicus*. This slippage between terms for the natural and artificial, however, suggests the simultaneous making and unmaking of Nature's "cure."

What happens when the control over the body is wrestled away from Nature? What if other systems paint over or "cure" the virgin skin, reconstructing her body and gender identity through violent hands, sharp blades, and sexual intercourse? "Youre is the charge of al hir surveiaunce," (l. 95) warns the Physician, "by youre necligence in chastisynge, / That they ne perisse" (ll. 98–99).[41] The consequence of mutability is death. The premise that one can "kill death" in the "Pardoner's Tale" responds to the cut-throat solutions of the "Physician's Tale" by begging the question: Isn't the work of a surgeon another attempt to conquer mortality by knife work? If operations save the futurity of the whole by sacrificing the part, who gets to determine what is the whole and what is the part? In the "Pardoner's Tale," each reveler is effectively equal in social value, but each determines that he is most deserving of futurity and stabs another in the back.

The drama of the "Physician's Tale" begins with a team of assailants competing over who has the right to lay hands on Virginia's body and determine the humoral state of her skin through the operations of sex and/or violence. The men convince the courts that Virginia is an escaped slave. This forces her father, Virginius, to hand her over to them. Fearing the loss of control over his daughter and wanting to protect her pre-sexual state, Virginius opts to cut off her head rather than hand her over to enslavement and rape. Virginius' decision follows the surgical principles of the *Christus Medicus* that physicians enact through technology of the knife: sacrifice the part to save the whole.

Once the dispossession of his daughter (and her virginity) is immanent, Virginius follows Abelard and secures her spiritual purity by dividing it from her flesh. Confessing that such surgery should only be performed in dire circumstances, Virginius coerces Virginia to accept his decision to cut apart her body. "O

---

[40] 'For He this is the first actor;' 'Has made me his vice general, to form and paint earthly creatures right as I will, and each thing is under my control'
[41] 'You are in charge of her surveillance [...] or by your negligence in chastising, that they will perish'

gemme of chastitee, in pacience / Take thou thy deeth," (ll. 223–224) he entreats her, "[t]o dyen with a swerd or with a knyf" (l. 217).⁴² Laying hands on Virginius' neck, the site where he will soon put a blade to, Virginia appeals to him as she would to a doctor: "Is ther no grace, is ther no remedye?" (l. 236).⁴³ Calling for alternatives, Virginia invokes grace and remedy, represented by *Christus Medicus*, co-operating with other mechanisms of her formation to circumvent Nature's determination of her body as naturally devoid of sexual power and resistance.

It is perhaps not surprising that spiritual grace fails in the "Physician's Tale," leaving Virginia to turn towards physical and social resistance over the sharp-machines of paint-brush and knife blade that secure her as a perpetual virgin. Virginia asks "to compleyne a litel space; / For, pardee, Jepte yaf his doghter grace / For to compleyne, er he hir slow, allas!" (l. 239–241).⁴⁴ Space and grace are rhymed and constitute the small amount of agency that Virginia might be able to exert over the cure (control) of her body. Without waiting for a response, Virginia swoons, challenging her father to operate on her without her will. The gambit is effective and Virginia is able to assert and protect control over her body. This resistance continues so long as she has the power to remain vulnerable.

When alternatives and resistance prove insufficient, Virginia turns to co-operation with the sharp-machines that will at once control and compel her mutability. When Virginia rises and prays, "Blissed be God that I shal dye a mayde" (l. 248)⁴⁵ she claims power over the impending operation and re-inscription of virginity in her body. Although Virginia is denied ownership over her embodied gender, painted on her skin by Nature and repainted by her father's blade, by thanking God for dying a maid, Virginia claims a degree of authority. She co-operates with the technologies of the knife pressed against her skin and enacts agency through them. "Dooth with youre child youre wyl" (l. 249) she tells her father and surgeon.⁴⁶ Blessing her death, Virginia takes a liminal position of power between a passive pre-op body awaiting operation and a post-op body receiving it, at once the subject and object of the surgery, exerting power and resistance on both sides. Presenting herself to her father, "she preyed hym ful ofte / That with his swerd he wolde smyte softe" (ll. 251–252).⁴⁷ Here, not only

---

42 'Oh gem of chastity, in patience take thou thy death […] to die with a sword or with a knife'
43 'Is there no grace, is there no remedy?'
44 'To complain in a little space; For, indeed, Jeptha gave his daughter grace in which to complain before he slew her, alas!'
45 'Blessed be God that I shall die a maid'
46 'Do with your child what you will'
47 'She prayed to him repeatedly that with his sword we would smite softly'

does she take ownership over the event of the surgery that will end her life, but she controls the manner in which it will cut her skin and part her head from her neck. Although Virginia does not have a choice of the cure, as she has "no grace or remedy" to alter that course, she claims some "space" and "grace" where agency can be enacted. She cannot exist without the brush or the blade that "forme and peynten" ('form and paint') her body, but like Reimer and Abelard, she exerts agency on these sharp-machines through co-operation. By its end, the "Physician's Tale" gives a model of the struggles and tactics of some who are caught in the mechanisms that enforce as well as limit the construction and reconstruction of the gendered body. Limitations exist for this medieval virgin that are not shared by others such as the male Pardoner. Yet they offer points where strategies may be given for others who are caught in extensions of similar systems. They also offer points where the agency and artifice are erased which call for further critique.

Nature De-Painted: The Pardoner's Portrait and Prologue

Not all transgender skin operations need to come to the same conclusion. Readers may find room for critiques and alternative narratives. Such readings may allow for a greater degree of liberty and pride for physically and socially reconstructed bodies. Indeed, by pairing the "Physician's Tale" and the "Pardoner's Tale" together in one compact fragment, Chaucer offers a sort of call and response on the subject of knives being used to violently impose a gender identity on a transitioning body; be it one moving from virgin to sexually active woman or from sexually reproductive man to castrate. The "Physician's Tale" ends with a mess of blood and scarred broken bodies, presenting a thesis the Pardoner will counter, namely that the sharp-machines operated by Nature and in the defense of natural forms overwhelm all agencies into parts and wholes. Represented by Chaucer as a body associated with shaved skin and potentially surgically removed genitals, the Pardoner may be identified with Virginia on conflicts over skin and gender, while also posing a counter-thesis through physical and social reconstructive operations of his relics: that those bodies discarded as parts may be recollected and reconstitute new forms of life.

While critical insights have been given to the speculation on the Pardoner's gender ("I trowe he were a geldyng or a mare," General Prologue, l. 961),[48] few scholars have considered the transgender skin operations that lead directly to

---

[48] 'I thought he was a gelding or a mare'

this conclusion. "No berd hadde he, ne nevere sholde have," narrates Chaucer, "[a]s smothe it was as it were late shave" (ll. 689–691).⁴⁹ This rhymed couplet draws readers to seriously consider the Pardoner's skin as a signifier and physical product of being either a gelding or a mare. Why compare his smooth skin to a "late shave?" There are other possible references for smooth skin, but the invocation of a shave underlines the operation of a blade on the body as producing virginal skin either from a shave to the face or a shave in the form of castration. Although it is possible that the Pardoner keeps clean-shaven, Chaucer clarifies that not only does he have no beard but that also he shall never have one. While allowing for different readings, including a natural lack of pronounced hair, the mention of shaving invokes associations with other unnatural/artificial bodies that also boast a smooth chin, from shavers to castrates. Indeed, Chaucer's words play on an awareness of how skin and hair, soft-tissues, are not merely the artistry of Nature but products of surgical interventions.⁵⁰ By the fourteenth century, medieval people were aware of the effects castration had on the soft-tissue.⁵¹ Castrates develop less body and facial hair than non-castrates, making their skin smoother (Reusch 2013: 36; Freitas 2003). Castration also produces a high voice, smooth hair, and thin frame.⁵² Anticipating insights from transgender studies, Chaucer's portrait of the Pardoner as a body suggesting reconstruction and gender transition while not confirming details of his body or life affirms many aspects of a trans identity. Thus, while the medieval author would not have used the term *transgender*, the Pardoner may be considered critically trans because of his agentive co-operation with systems of reconstruction that may at once violently force bodies to conform to gender ideals while also allowing for the dangerous power to alter and resist Nature's paintbrush.

While the attention of readers regularly returns to the trans state of the Pardoner's own body, which seems to exist between or across forms of gender, as a speaker he continually points away from himself towards other reconstructed

---

49 'No beard had he, nor never should have […] as smooth as it was lately shaved'
50 The Pardoner's skin reflects Virginia's skin due to a shared humoral register caused by a lack of testes and/or sexual heat which gives them both "pale, hairless skin; limp, light-colored hair" (Whitney 2011: 368).
51 Numerous debates on circumcision continued throughout the Middle Ages and after, as noted by Kuefler (2000: 184). Intersex surgery on hermaphrodite/intersex children were in regular use, they were conceptually folded in as "eunuchs from birth" and continue today; see Tougher (2008: 31–32); Kuefler (2000: 286); Scholz (1999: 5–13); Chase (2013); Winkerson (2012).
52 Whitney (2011: 379) notes that other features, besides skin, can also arise from the lack of heat and dryness produced by testes and associated with sexual agency, including, "Light-colored hair and pale skin were commonly seen as indicative in classical medical literature of a phlegmatic temperament," as well as "a high, languid voice."

bodies. In what constitutes a critical trans argument, the Pardoner directs readers to his relics that – through the artifice of narratives that enfold – physically reconstruct bodies through the smooth words of his well polished tongue (l. 712), a metonymic extension of his smooth skin. These words wrap around and redefine relations to butchered or otherwise cut body parts so that "Relikes been they, as wenen they echoon" (l. 349).[53] Regardless of what former wholes and parts they have been, the discarded have become remade and reclaimed, treated now as if they were relics. Scholars have noted how the Pardoner's relics suggest fragmentation (Sturges 2000: 107–109; Stockton 2011: 97–118) but what remains to be emphasized is how the narration of these relics co-operates with systems that define the relation between reconstructed bodies to produce a smooth sense of wholeness. How is it that a person who is candid that his relics come from questionable origins convinces others to buy into him and his works? How does he reveal fragmentation yet produce a sense of wholeness? How does candid artifice counterfeit Nature's virgin smoothness? What if "pigges bones" ('pig's bones,' General Prologue, l. 700) can be made indistinguishable from those of a saint when they are reframed as a relic? An early move within transgender activism and theory was the insistence that there is value in identifying a body and life as trans. This trans meaning arises as form embodiment and identity marked in part through transitional processes that co-operate with nature and society in order to reconstruct meaning. The Pardoner does not allow his relics to pass as relics by nature but affirms them as trans bodies arising from the reconstruction of bodies and meaning.

Empowered as relics by the "Pardoner's Prologue," these fragmented bodies boast the power claimed by technologies of the knife: to reconstruct bodies and reclaim their meaning. Whatever the actual super-natural capacities of these relics, power flows through the Pardoner's words as he shows how to re-narrate fragmented, scarred, and discarded bodies into holy bodies that promise to physically and socially produce a sense of re-claimed, artificial wholeness.[54] When speaking of his many relics, the Pardoner spends the most time on emphasizing the efficacy of a part of a slaughtered lamb, "a sholder-boon" from "an hooly Jewes sheep" (ll. 350–351).[55] Such shoulder-bones, following the surgical logic of discarding parts as refuse, would have been thrown away after butchery. The relic points to rejected parts of the body as mechanisms by which the

---

[53] 'relics they were, or so they seemed'
[54] For an excellent historical examination of relics see Walker Bynum (2011).
[55] 'a shoulder-bone from a holy Jew's sheep'

smooth appearance of wholeness is formed.⁵⁶ While certain effects supposedly given by the relics directly involve the skin, the Pardoner promises other changes that nonetheless fulfill the goals of transgender skin operations: to transition a body from a state of rejected fragmentation into a state of wholeness and co-operation with society.

The first form of reconstruction promised by the Pardoner goes to those who "taak of [his] wordes keep" ('heed his words') and physically place the shoulder-bone in a well, live-stock pierced by "any worm [...] or worm ystonge" (l. 355) and washed in the water will be made "hool anon" (l. 357).⁵⁷ Whether "worm" refers to a snake, reptile, parasite, or dragon, it certainly suggests the unwanted entrance of a body by a invader. The idea of a wormy invader of the body might echo the threat an invading penis presents to Virginia. Likewise, a castrate would fear the knife, another phallic invader that penetrates the body. Chaucer nearly turns this latter association into a reality when the Host threatens to cut off the Pardoner's genitals, as will be explored shortly. Whatever the kind of invader, however, the physical power of the shoulder-bone and the Pardoner's words wash over the marks of these breaches in the skin's supposed natural impenetrability, to make it smooth and "hool anon." Thus the first transmutation occurs as unchanged material facts take on new doctrinal meaning.

The second form of reconstruction is promised to bodies penetrated or punctured by disease, "[o]f pokkes and of scabbe, and every soore" (l. 358), claiming that if they drink of the well in which the relic is placed the fragmented body shall be whole.⁵⁸ Here the Pardoner draws an association between the scars caused by technologies of the knife and the wounds caused by disease. Such physical wounds would be present on the skin of those touched by the plague in London. Such outbreaks also caused social and emotional breakdowns, fragmenting a community's sense of the wholeness and health of the body politic. In producing these wounds on the skin, the disease reveals the porousness of the body and society that allowed the plague to pass through it. Making the skin "hool" from these "pokkes" and curing the "scabbe" of unwanted penetration, the relic smoothes over the history of dangerous ecological co-operation and contingency. Such a reconstruction would provide similar outcomes as transgender skin operations have given to the Pardoner. Not only does he have smooth skin but he is associated with forms of gender that are characterized by smooth skin, geldings, and women. By thus tying together the reconstruction of his relics

---

56 For more information on readings of this relic, see Sturges (2000: 102–139); Dinshaw (1999: 121–136); Burger (2003: 140–156); and Stockton (2011: 97–118).
57 'Any worm [...] or worm stung;' 'whole again'
58 'Of pocks, and of scabs, and every sore'

and his body, the Pardoner implicitly suggests that he may have used the relics himself.

The third form of reconstruction arises if listeners "keep eek what [the Pardoner] tell[s]," and the bone will multiply the number of whole bodies in society. "If that the good-man that the beestes oweth [...] drynken of this welle a draughte / [...] / His beestes and his stoor shal multiplie" (ll. 361).[59] This movement inverts the drive from wholes existing at the expense of fragments to insist that wholeness exists *because* of the presence and power of fragmented bodies. If one drinks in the words of the Pardoner's artificial wholeness and reclaims butchered bodies from the refuse of society, then the number of recognized wholes will multiply. If fewer fragmented and reconstructed bodies are discounted as lacking positive value or signification, not only will more lives be positively counted but more lives will be livable. One is less likely to refuse wounded, sick, or otherwise fragmented bodies if one is aware that they can be reconstructed and serve society. While animals are named most among those who are ill and among those whose possessions are multiplied by relics (indeed the Pardoner's relic itself comes from an animal), the way we relate to body fragments and relics reflects how we view trans, transitional and reconstructed bodies in general. Furthermore, we might accept that all these reconstructed trans bodies might have special "treasures" to give to society. Like Abelard, the relics demonstrate that trans bodies are critical and instrumental in wider social operations. That which itself has been reconstructed and transitioned in meaning can assist others in transforming their lives as well. In this way, whether or not the Pardoner is transgender in identity, he is critically trans in activity. If we accept that a pig's or sheep's bone can be a relic and that wounded and sick cattle can be made whole, we may be more willing to accept that a gelding or a mare might be reconstructed as a man with something to give to the society.

Conclusions

In the end, the "Pardoner's Prologue" offers a more positive alternative to trans skin operations than the "Physician's Tale," but his revivifying co-opting of sharp-machines cannot redeem all the violence that they have done and may do. Trans narratives can assert the mutability of bodies and gender systems but diversifying the use of such mechanisms does not mean the changes will

---

[59] 'Hold close what [the Pardoner] tells;' 'If that good man that owns the beasts [...] drinks of this well a drink [...] his beasts and his possessions shall multiply'

not be rejected and the old violence continued. Dangerously, the power of reconstruction operates both for the making and unmaking of lives. When systems begin to be reclaimed by those they oppress, there will be those on the oppressor's side that will react. Fragment VI follows the Pardoner's discourse with the reactivity of one who would defend Nature's primacy and the naturalized distinctions between man and woman, sexual and pre-/post-sexual, part and whole. A patriarch representing those who reject the reorientation of power, the Host refuses the reconstructions of the Pardoner's body, relics and words as counterfeit (ll. 925–926). This prompts the Host to assault him with the threat of turning or returning each and all of the refused parts into refuse. "Nay, nay!" cries the Host, "[t]hou woldest make me kisse thyn olde breech, / And swere it were a relyk of a seint, / Though it were with thy fundement depeint!" (ll. 948).[60] Remade bodies are not fundamentals painted by Nature, he claims, but de-painted "fundements," refused as shit. The Host confirms that any whole may become a refused part. Wholeness is not itself a naturally fixed state but requires constant rhetorical operations of sharp-machines whether it is by a father who would rather cut off his daughter's head than lose her virgin wholeness or an angry Host who would rather make threats of violence than accept transitioning and reconstructed embodiment as valuable.

The complaint against the artifice of the Pardoner's operations echoes Nature's challenge for anyone to attempt to counterfeit her work. The revaluation of discarded parts as constituting wholes in their own right is rejected. Parts remain parts. Refuse is refused. Painting becomes depainting. "I wolde I hadde thy coillons in myn hond," says the Host, "[i]n stide of relikes [...] / Lat kutte hem of, I wol thee helpe hem carie; / They shul be shryned in an hogges toord!" (ll. 952–955).[61] Such is the irony of those who defend the constancy of naturalized gender through threats of violent mutability. This contradiction is ultimately allowed because deciding who gets to claim authority over the transformed body may be considered more important than denying that such systems of transformation exist. Nature as the author of a person's gender is most useful to those who can claim that their form of gender and power is natural. Yet when other authorities, such the Pardoner's super-natural relics, claim to trump Nature and society, presumptions fall away, and the scarring struggle for power is laid bare. The Host would rather cut off the Pardoner's testicles (perhaps for the second time) than acknowledge the power of a reconstructed body to be redefined

---

60 'Thou would have made me kiss thy old breeches, and swear it was a relic of a saint, though it were with thy fundaments stained.'
61 'I wish I had thy testicles in my hand [...] instead of relics [...] cut them off, I would help you carry them; they shall be shrined in a hog's turd.'

and valued as equal to those who claim their body and identity as natural. Like a transphobic man who will not accept a trans woman as a woman and insists that the person be treated as a broken man, the Host would rather enact violence than accept change. Just as the Pardoner's skin resembles Virginia's, here again the Host plays upon the reflection between the two by threatening to ensure that the stories of the virgin and castrate share similar ends. The "Physician's Tale" ends with the transitioning body cut to pieces and if the Host has his way, the "Pardoner's Tale" may likewise end with a trans figure butchered.

Is there hope in the critical trans operations of the Pardoner or will scars remain a sign of a refused body? The Pardoner's silence after the threat is a sign of passive absence, yet this silence may function like the relics, acknowledging mutability in order to pressure others to exert sway in defense of trans bodies. Submitting to the Host's sharp words and knife, the Pardoner compels the Knight's help. "Namoore of this, for it is right ynough!" cries the Knight, "Sire Pardoner, be glad and myrie of cheere; / And ye, sire Hoost, that been to me so deere, / I prey yow that ye kisse the Pardoner" (ll. 960–968).[62] The Knight has the social authority but also the physical power gained from co-operation with sharp-machines in "mortal batailles" ('mortal battles,' General Prologue l. 61) to defend the Pardoner. In an act of non-violent resistance, the Pardoner, like Virginia, bears his vulnerable flesh to compel others to see that any body may soon be under the knife and to call out, "Namoore of this, for it is right ynough."

Perhaps the threat against the Pardoner reminds the Knight, and the readers, of the countless bodies caught on either side of the bloody operations of sharp-machines. Unlike the authority of nature which erases the marks of transition and change in order to secure its primacy, the open making and unmaking of the skin reveals the dangerous instability of all lives enfolding transsexuals, castrates, virgins, geldings, and mares in a shared position of vulnerability and resistance. Whether it is Reimer's body under the knife of doctors, Abelard's under the knife of his enemies, Virginia's under the knife of her father, or the Pardoner's under the knife of the Host, by testifying to the trauma and the power of sharp-machines, the skin offers unique forms of resistance. By revealing some level of vulnerability, these trans bodies connect to the agency of those around them in ways that put pressure on the system that makes and unmakes all bodies.

We may wonder if the power of skin operations must always be so violent. This concern brings the kiss of peace concluding the "Pardoner's Tale" into

---

[62] 'No more of this, for this is enough;' 'Sir Pardoner, be glad and merry with cheer; and you, sir Host, that is so dear to me, I pray that you kiss the Pardoner'

sharp relief. The moment "they kiste" (l. 968), the relationship between the aggressor and victim may begin to shift. No longer is one body active and the other passive, but both exert power and resistance against each other. The contact of lips emphasizes that the skin of either body is not purely smooth but full of porous openings through which the inside and outside enfold. It is at such openings that eunuchs and virgins, geldings and mares, medieval and modern may meet. It is at this point of intercourse that the Host's body touches and receives the Pardoner's body and vice versa. While the tension that led to the violence may remain, their "neer" ('near') co-operative relationship will guard them, as Christ taught husbands about their wives in Matthew 19.12, because neither can easily part with the other and retain unscarred wholeness. What comes of this may not cure the victim of the scars the assault has given but critical trans histories are often full of such abuses that must be reckoned as they are critiqued.

Full of still stinging cuts and telling scars, narratives of transgender skin operations testify to the countless lives physically and socially made through the artifice of sharp-machines which continually make and unmake supposedly natural states. Working at the level of skin, readers come into contact with the enfolding of spheres too easily held separate: medieval and transgender studies, transsexuals and eunuchs, virgins and castrates. Engaging in these operations allows for critical applications of power and resistance in systems that govern gender. Perhaps most importantly, this engagement would insist that we not perpetuate dismissive surgical assumptions where problematic bodies are marked as parts and expunged as always already absent in order to sustain those privileged lives marked as pure, smooth and whole. We recollect departed, discarded, de-painted fragments of personal and collective histories by reclaiming the operations that may yet carve out alternatives for the skin and the lives enfolded within.

Works Cited

Primary Sources

McLaughlin, Mary and J. T. Muckle (eds.). 1956. "Peter Abelard: Historia Calamitatum and Letters 1–7." *Medieval Studies*. Volume 18. Toronto: Pontifical Institute of Mediaeval Studies.

Bellows, Henry (trans.). 1999. "Peter Abelard: Historia Calamitatum." *Medieval Sourcebook*. New York: Fordham University Press.

Benson, Larry D. (ed.). 1987. *Geoffrey Chaucer: The Riverside Chaucer*. 3rd ed. Boston: Houghton Mifflin.

Swift, Edgar (ed.). 2011. *The Vulgate Bible: Douay-Rheims Translation*. Cambridge, MA: Harvard University Press.

Secondary Sources

Angier, Natalie. 14 March 1997. "Sexual Identity Not Pliable After All, Report Says." *The New York Times*. <www.nytimes.com/1997/03/14/us/sexual-identity-not-pliable-after-all-report-says.html> [accessed 1 April 2017].

Arbesmann, Rudolph. 1954. "The Concept of Christus Medicus in St. Augustine." *Traditio* 10: 1–28.

Bremmer, Rolf H., Jr. 2013. "The Children He Never Had; the Husband She Never Served: Castration and Genital Mutilation in Medieval Frisian Law." In: Larissa Tracy (ed.). *Castration and Culture in the Middle Ages*. Cambridge: D. S. Brewer. 108–130.

Burger, Glenn. 2003. *Chaucer's Queer Nation*. Medieval Cultures 34. Minneapolis: University of Minnesota Press.

Butler, Judith. 1990. *Gender Trouble: Feminism and the Subversion of Identity*. Thinking Gender. New York: Routledge.

Butler, Judith. 2004. *Undoing Gender*. New York: Routledge.

Butler, Judith. 2006. "Doing Justice to Someone: A Transsexual Allegory." In: Susan Stryker (ed.). *The Transgender Studies Reader*. New York: Routledge. 183–193.

Chase, Cheryl. 2013. "Hermaphrodites with Attitude: Mapping the Emergence of Intersex Political Activism." *The Transgender Studies Reader*. London: Routledge. 300–314.

Colapinto, John. 2000. *As Nature Made Him: The Boy Who Was Raised as a Girl*. New York: HarperCollins.

Dinshaw, Carolyn. 1989. *Chaucer's Sexual Poetics*. Madison: University of Wisconsin Press.

Dinshaw, Carolyn. 1999. *Getting Medieval: Sexualities and Communities, Pre- and Postmodern*. Durham: Duke University Press.

Ferroul, Yves. 1999. "Abelard's Blissful Castration." In: Jeffrey J. Cohen and Bonnie Wheeler (eds.). *Becoming Male in the Middle Ages*. The New Middle Ages 4. New York: Garland. 129–150.

Freitas, Roger. 2003. "The Eroticism of Emasculation: Confronting the Baroque Body of the Castrato." *Journal of Musicology* 20.2: 196–249.

Irvine, Martin. 1999. "Abelard and (Re)Writing the Male Body." In: Jeffrey J. Cohen and Bonnie Wheeler (eds.). *Becoming Male in the Middle Ages*. The New Middle Ages 4. New York: Garland. 87–106.

Judith Butler: Philosophin der Gender. 2006. Dir. Paule Zadjermann. ARTE France & Associés.

Kuefler, Mathew S. 2000. "Castration and Eunuchism in the Middle Ages." In: Vern L. Bullough and James A. Brundage (eds.). *Handbook of Medieval Sexuality*. New York: Routledge. 184–292.

MacKendrick, Karmen. 2004. *Word Made Skin: Figuring Language at the Surface of Flesh*. New York: Fordham University Press.

Miller, Robert P. 1955. "Chaucer's Pardoner, the Scriptural Eunuch, and the Pardoner's Tale." *Speculum* 30.2: 180–199.

Prosser, Jay. 1998. *Second Skins: The Body Narratives of Transsexuality*. New York: Columbia University Press.

Rayner Myers, Jeffrey. 2000. "Chaucer's Pardoner as Female Eunuch." *Studia Neophilologica* 72.1: 54–62.

Reusch, Kathryn. 2013. "Raised Voices: The Archeology of Castration." In: Larissa Tracy (ed.). *Castration and Culture in the Middle Ages*. Cambridge: D. S. Brewer. 29–47.

Scholz, Piotr. 1999. *Eunuchs and Castrati: A Cultural History*. Trans. John Broadwin and Shelley Frisch. Princeton: Markus Wiener.

Stockton, Will. 2011. *Playing Dirty: Sexuality and Waste in Early Modern Comedy*. Minneapolis: University of Minnesota.

Stone, Sandy. 2006. "The Empire Strikes Back: A Post-Transsexual Manifesto." In: Susan Stryker (ed.). *The Transgender Studies Reader*. New York: Routledge. 221–235.

Sturges, Robert S. 2000. *Chaucer's Pardoner and Gender Theory*. New York: St. Martin's Press.

Taylor, Gary. 2000. *Castration: An Abbreviated History of Western Manhood*. New York: Routledge.

Tougher, Shaun. 2008. *The Eunuch in Byzantine History and Society*. New York: Routledge.

Tracy, Larissa. 2013. "Introduction: A History of Calamities: The Culture of Castration." In: Larissa Tracy (ed.). *Castration and Culture in the Middle Ages*. Woodbridge: Boydell & Brewer. 1–28.

Walker Bynum, Caroline. 2011. *Christian Materiality: An Essay on Religion in Late Medieval Europe*. New York: Zone Books.

Wheeler, Bonnie. 1999. "Origenary Fantasies: Abelard's Castration and Confession." In: Jeffrey J. Cohen and Bonnie Wheeler (eds.). *Becoming Male in the Middle Ages*. The New Middle Ages 4. New York: Garland. 107–128.

Whitney, Elspeth. 2011. "What's Wrong with the Pardoner?: Complexion Theory, the Phlegmatic Man, and Effeminacy." *The Chaucer Review* 45.4: 357–389.

Winkerson, Abby L. 2012. "Normate Sex and Its Discontents." In: Robert McRuer and Anna Mollow (eds.). *Sex and Disability*. London: Duke. 183–207.

Elizabeth Robertson
Afterword: Skin Matters

The earliest uses of the word *skin*, a word borrowed from Scandinavian, in Old English texts refer not to a covering on human beings but rather to a skin removed from an animal and used as protection. It occurs often either interchangeably with, or along with, the word *hide* – *skin* referring to the covering of larger animals such as an ox and *hide* to that of smaller ones such as a calf. It does not come to denote a human covering until later in the Middle English period. Skin, then, was first understood as an object taken from an animal for human use. As the word develops to embrace more various and specific kinds of coverings it is still characterized in terms of its relationship to the animal. The *Oxford English Dictionary* (*OED skin* n.) divides the word into two major categories: skin that is removed from an animal used for a variety of purposes (including parchment) or skin that remains on an animal. When the fourteenth-century poet William Langland refers to a human covering he uses a word other than skin, namely *fel*. Holy Church explains to Will the dreamer that the "fader of faith," Truth (or God) "fourmed yow alle / Bothe with fel and face" (Passus I, l. 15).[1] In this formulation a covering, *fel*, and that attribute of the human that facilitates communication with the social world, the face, constitute the basic elements of the human. Even though Langland does not here use the word *skin* – perhaps simply for metrical reasons – he makes clear what is suggested by many of the essays in this collection: skin is fundamental to the identity of living beings.

The *OED* continues to define that protective entity that both animals and humans share as the "layer of tissue forming the external covering of the body in vertebrates." That substance, the dictionary explains further,

> is composed of two layers, the epidermis and dermis, and may contain specialized structures such as hairs, feathers, or scales, and various types of gland. It serves a general protective function and plays an active role in many important physiological processes such as thermoregulation, gas exchange, waste elimination, and sensation.

The medical writers Lanfranc of Milan (d. 1315) and Guy de Chauliac (c. 1300 – 1368), according to Michael Leahy, describe skin "as composed of little threads of veins arteries, and nerves;" they understand its function as both a boundary and a medium, and grant it significant status in the body as "governoure of alle

---

[1] 'father of faith,' Truth (or God) 'formed you all / Both with skin and with face.' My translation. Quotation taken from Robertson and Shepherd (2006).

þe body" (quoted in Leahy, in this volume).² Skin furthermore, as Guy de Chauliac goes on to explain, provides the body with "knowledge of the qualities, temperature, and texture of the objects in the world" (quoted in Leahy, in this volume). These medieval and modern definitions point to skin's density as well as to some of its multiple functions.

An important aspect of skin, then, is its thickness: often conceived of as only two-dimensional, made up of an inside and outside, skin actually has three dimensions, and it is that three-dimensionality that in part grants skin its complexity and asks of us a 'thick description,' that is one that penetrates beyond the surface layer and probes skin's opaque depths. This collection explores skin's opacity by considering the various ways skin surfaces, whether animal or human, interact with inscriptions on animal skins and in turn reveal skin's hermeneutic depth. Today, human skin is understood to be an organ, the largest organ of the human body, but in the Middle Ages, according to Aristotelian understandings of the human body, skin was not an organ, but rather a medium. Aristotle's definition helps us focus attention not on the skin's essence or its parts but rather on its mediating functions. As a thick semi-permeable substance, skin is a site in which complex transactions take place between inside and outside, self and other. Skin mediates not only between inner and outer and self and other, but also between many other states – between the animal and the human, for example, or between life and death. One major feature of skin that this collection brings to the fore though rarely discusses in detail is its abjection. As an entity whose fundamental function is to mediate, skin is abject: neither inside or outside, subject or object, the skin occupies a place in the middle, between subject and object, the abject position. As an abject entity, skin both attracts and repels and repeatedly destabilizes binary categories and identities. Its destabilizing features allow it the potential not only to challenge, but also to articulate new identities including queer and transgendered ones. This wide-ranging collection explores skin's mediating functions as a thick, three-dimensional entity as well as its capacity, emerging from its abjection, to critique and dismantle binary divisions and identities of all kinds.

Skin is Abject

The first third of this collection focuses on diseased skin and particularly on the marks left on the skin by leprosy, a condition of the skin that may or may not in

---

2 'governor of all the body'

the Middle Ages have been produced by Hansen's disease. Although one might think that it is only diseased skin that is abject, leprosy is such a wide-ranging term that it comes to signify skin that is marked in any way. Medieval discourses of leprosy such as those discussed here thus provide a backdrop for many of the discussions of inscribed skin to follow. As the essays make clear, leprosy was a capacious term that might have referred to Hansen's disease or a range of other viral diseases and skin conditions from measles to smallpox to syphilis to scabies to eczema. Ultimately, we can all be described as lepers since, like lepers, we all bear on our skin the marks of our past whose origins are often opaque and indiscernible. When you get close to any skin, whether leprous or not, and probe its depth, its abject state comes to the foreground.

For centuries, whatever its condition, marks on the skin were understood to be an external manifestation of the inner moral condition of the individual. We learn from Sealy Gilles that leprous skin has been the focus of moral commentary from the earliest writings of the Bible. In the Old Testament, leprosy was understood either as a disease requiring careful diagnosis and treatment (Leviticus 13.4–6), a punishment for moral failing (as for Miriam, sister of Moses in Numbers 12.9–10) or a test of faith (e.g. Job). In the New Testament, leprosy, while often allegorized as a word for heresy, also offered opportunity for the sufferer, one who is already *quasi mortuus* to become *quasi Christus*. The leper could imitate Christ by patiently enduring his or her suffering and by welcoming vilification and isolation. Healthy humans sought to contract leprosy in order to imitate Christ's suffering and his compassion for the sufferings of others. Of Christ's healing of a leper, Matthew tells us that he "took on our infirmities and endured our diseases" (quoted in Gilles, in this volume). For Christ, leprosy, then, is part of what it means to become human. Gregory uses leprosy as a metaphor for the extreme humility Christ exhibits in taking on humanity:

> Who indeed in human flesh is more sublime than Christ who is exalted above angels? And who in human flesh is more abject that the leprous, who is deformed with swelling wounds and filled with fetid exhalations? But behold in the form of a leper he appears; and he who is revered above all is not ashamed to be seen as despised below all men. (quoted in Gilles, in this volume)

For the leprous, sin manifests itself on the skin, but that same skin, just like the sinful human body itself, is redeemable and renewable.

Leprosy, sexual transgression and doctrinal deviancy became linked although, as Gilles argues, over time leprosy's meanings became narrower and darker and the leper was seen increasingly as corrupt, dangerously contagious and therefore to be isolated from the community. Leahy (this volume) summarizes leprosy's conceptual capaciousness:

it is linked to blasphemy, gluttony, erotic excess, political misrule, and the exemplary sufferings of Christ. Its protean qualities allow it to assume moral and devotional potency across medical writings, romance literature, didactic prose, and devotional works; its projection of the internal body and soul upon the sufferer's skin enables articulations of disgust, fear, devotion, and desire.

What Leahy calls the "multiple and unstable meanings" of leprosy, makes it difficult for us to interpret the status of characters who appear in literary texts as lepers such as Tristan, who disguises himself as a leper in order to help Isolde outwit her accusers concerning her sexual fidelity. Literary lepers can inspire moral approbation, moral condemnation, or both.

As a quintessentially abject condition, leprosy in the Middle Ages inspired two primary but conflicting responses: repulsion, whereby lepers were exiled from the community, and attraction, where they were embraced either by Christ or by the devotional penitent in imitation of Christ. Gilles (this volume) pinpoints leprosy's isolating function by defining it as "a condition of radical dissolution and exclusion from self and community." Like the corpse, the hideously deformed skin of the leper simultaneously repels and attracts, fascinates and disgusts – and ultimately destabilizes the identity of the observer.

The essays in the first cluster of this collection describe many of the repellent aspects of leprosy. Leviticus points to the following attributes characteristic of leprosy: "boils, swellings, white patches, burn-like spots, itching and loss of hair" (Gilles, this volume); Guy de Chauliac's list of the symptoms of leprosy makes clear its abjection:

> Rowndenesse of þe eyʒen and of þe eres, spredynge of þe browes, and writhinge or crokynge of þe nose þirles, [...] fowlenesse of þe lippes, an hose voyce as þoghe he spak with his nose þirles, stynkynge of brethe and of al þe persone, stable lokynge and horrible in þe maner of a beste þat highte satoun. (quoted in Gilles, in this volume)[3]

One or more of these features appear in the various skin conditions described in literary texts of the period. In the *Canterbury Tales*, Chaucer's Cook, for example, not only displays a mormal oozing with pus similar to leprous lesions, but also manifests other features closely associated with leprosy; in Erin E. Sweany's summary, he has "pale skin, weakness, bad breath, immoderate sexual appe-

---

[3] 'rounding of the eyes and ears, swelling of the eyebrows, and twisting or deviation of the nostrils [...] coarseness of lips, a hoarse voice as though he spoke through his nostrils, fetor of breath and of the body, a fixed stare as of the beast they call an ape.'

tites, a violent temper, possibly itching skin, a distorted voice (sounding hoarse and congested), and 'dazed' (*MED daswen* v.) eyes" (Sweany, this volume).

However disgusting and repellent the leper's suppurated flesh, the viewer is drawn to it, compelled to make moral judgments about it and yet unable finally to categorize what he or she has seen. The skin's legibility is further complicated by the fact that it is temporally dense: marks on the skin in the present record marks acquired in the past that can predict the future. As Catherine S. Cox puts it in this volume,

> damaged skin communicates not its owner's ideas, opinions, ideological affiliations, aesthetics, desire for self-expression, or attention-seeking, but rather its owner's material history, the chronological, linear timeline punctuated by events leaving traces, the extent of their significance not necessarily correlating with the prominence of the physical marks that incite curiosity, revulsion, or both.

Recording past, present, and future events as well as reflecting inner conditions and outer experiences, skin is also highly changeable. A mark can appear suddenly or slowly over time and then can fade or disappear entirely. Skin's changeability is especially notable in the various hues on the skin discussed by Nicole Nyffenegger. In her discussion of *Troilus and Criseyde*, Nyffenegger shows how changing hues throughout the poem structure the development of the love story. The meaning of the character's hues changing rapidly from blushing red to deadly pale is not immediately transparent. That a hue both invites and resists interpretation is indicated by the ways in which the poem repeatedly foregrounds complex ocular dynamics where characters observe and yet fail to comprehend the meaning of a blush or a pale face. The words on the skin of the parchment page themselves are like the hues on faces and both are difficult to interpret. Finally, Chaucer probes the significance of hue for his own poetic process when he describes himself as like a blind man who cannot judge hues.

The temporally fluid abject records of internal conditions and external experiences, whether marks of disease or changing hues, invite and often defy interpretation. Chaucer's narrator cannot take his eyes off the Cook's oozing pus-filled wound, but fails to provide the reader with a moral interpretation of that wound. The Cook's wound destabilizes categories: the blancmange he creates in the kitchen while his inflamed mormal oozes shares the mormal's creamy white wobbly characteristics. The boundaries between what is inside the body, on the surface of the body, or intended to be ingested by the body become blurred. The mormal, along with the other signs of his ill health such as his pale skin and bad breath, raises questions about his physical health and his possible leprosy as well as about his internal moral condition and ultimately destabilizes his identity. Along with his other leprous symptoms, the mormal ultimately makes the Cook's identity illegible. Furthermore, the fact that the cook's job is to serve a community with food, his mormal troubles his relationship to the other pilgrims. As Sweany (this volume) writes recalling Claudia Benthien, "[d]amaged skin is the troubled point at which we negotiate the fraught relationship between the self and the community." The various ways abject damaged skin can destabilize not only the identity of the sufferer but also of those who observe that suffering is captured in the narrator's comment: "But greet harm was it, as it thought me / That on his shyne a mormal hadde he" (ll. 385–386).[4] The formulation of the comment asks us to question who experiences the "harm:" the cook or the narrator – or both? The strange skin of the Summoner and the Pardoner – one full of pockmarks, the other unusually smooth – similarly call for, but resist, moral assessment.

That leprosy is at least metaphorically shared by all the Canterbury pilgrims is suggested by the fact that they are all going to Canterbury to seek help from the relics of Beckett, "that hem hath holpen whan that they were seke" (l. 18).[5] As Sweany points out, Canterbury was particularly known as a site where one could be cured of leprosy. Numerous miracle stories found in the lives of Beckett as well as in images in the windows of Canterbury Cathedral's Trinity chapel recount Thomas' miraculous cure of lepers.

The figure that most pitiably demonstrates the abject effects of leprosy is the one discussed in several of the essays in this volume, Crisseid in Robert Henryson's *Testament of Cresseid*. Although technically punished with leprosy because of her blasphemy, Cresseid is understood to have been condemned because of her sexual immorality. The abject condition her skin will manifest is foretold by Cynthia: "Thy cristall ene mingit with blude I mak / Thy voice sa cleir vnplesand hoir and hace / Thy lustie lyre ouirspred with spottis blak / and lumpis haw appeirand in thy face" (quoted in Gilles, in this volume).[6] The effect on her eyes and voice are, as Sharon E. Rhodes points out, in keeping with medical descriptions of leprosy. The description of her once beautiful face as "sa deformait / With bylis blak ovirspred her visage" (quoted in Rhodes, in this volume) crystallizes the abjection produced by her leprosy. As the embodiment of the abject – she is called in the poem the "abiect odious" ('contemptible outcast,' see Gilles, this volume) – Cresseid repels but also fascinates those who see her. Those look-

---

4 'But it was a great pity, as it seemed to me, that he had an ulcer on his shin.' Citations of Chaucer's texts are taken from Benson (1987), translations are my own.
5 'that helped them when they were ill'
6 'I mix with blood your crystal clear eyes. / Your voice, so clear, [I make] unpleasing, rough, and hoarse, / Your lovely complexion covered in black spots, / and leaden lumps appearing on your face.'

ing at her recoil – "Now is deformit the figour of my face / To luik on it, na leid now lyking hes" – and she is warned that all shall flee from her: "Quhair [Cresseid] cummis, ilk man sall fle the place" (both quoted in Rhodes, in this volume).[7] She is forced to leave her community to live as an exile in a leper house outside the city. Her leprous skin furthermore becomes the site for moral lessons, many of which she herself draws. Cresseid condemns herself for being "fickill and frivolous" ('fickle and frivolous') and for having been "inclynit to lustis lecherous" (quoted in Rhodes, in this volume).[8]

Although the primary focus of Henryson's poem seems to be to illustrate the punishments that await those who are sexually immoral, especially women, we might push the analysis of this paradigmatic text a bit further by considering to what degree Cresseid's abject state destabilizes the very moral conclusions the text asks us to draw and thereby opens up more redeeming aspects of her condition. Cresseid, first of all, teaches the reader that all beauty fades; she warns the reader: "[n]ocht is your fairness bot ane faiding flour" (quoted in Gilles, in this volume).[9] She becomes, therefore, an emblem of the vanity of all human wishes. Second, it is significant that it is Cresseid herself who voices her own self-condemnation. The sympathy her self-denigration elicits not only from the aging narrator but also from the reader inspires the reader to recognize his or her own moral failings and to strive to reach the depth of Cresseid's self-knowledge. Finally, given that medieval lepers were denied all legal identity, it is particularly significant that Cresseid makes her own will and testament. It is only when leprosy has stripped away her outer beauty that Cresseid discovers that she has something of value within – that which allows her to express her will, her soul.

Wanted Dead or Alive: Human and Animal Skins

A variety of medieval literary works, as several of the essays in the collection show, explore the dependence of the human on other skins, either animal or cloth, for protection or as a disguise. That numerous romance protagonists adopt animal skins for such purposes raises the question of what constitutes the dividing line between the human and the animal. In *Amis and Amiloun*, as Sharon E. Rhodes shows, the skin of the werewolf marks the ways in which

---

[7] 'Now the figure of my face is deformed; no one has pleasure in looking on it now;' 'where Cresseid comes, each man shall flee that place'
[8] 'was inclined toward lusty lecherousness'
[9] 'your beauty is nothing but a fading flower'

sin complicates even the seemingly compassionate gestures of the human. Pax Gutierrez-Neal shows us how skins of various kinds, bearskins, deerskins, armour, nicked skin, green skin, and a green girdle problematize the identity of its wearer. Gawain's identity in *Sir Gawain and the Green Knight* is destabilized through the poem's focus on skin or skin-like coverings from Gawain's nicked skin, to his armour, to the green girdle he wears to save his skin. By pointing simultaneously to Gawain's cowardice in trying to protect himself from death at the hands of the Green Knight and his courage at having endured the Green Knight's blows, both the girdle and the nick in the neck reveal the precarious legibility of skin. It becomes impossible to separate the cultural artefact that Gawain always wears, the girdle, from the human skin as a sign which is always with him. The Green Knight's skin is also hermeneutically complex – his green physical skin blends seamlessly with his green hair, his green cape and his green armour.

The skins the protagonists of the romance *William of Palerne* adopt – from bearskins to deerskins to wolfskins – also make it difficult for the reader to interpret their bearers' identities. The characters use dead animal skins to protect and disguise their human skin, but these disguises blur the distinction between the human and the animal. The fact that Felice has to flay the deer-skinned lovers Meliors and William from their deerskins suggests their close affinity with the animal. Yet they become closely allied with the deer only through a fundamentally human activity, sewing, when they are closely sewn into their skins. Animal skins are supplemental or accidental for the human – but what is the substance of human skin without some form of covering? In *William of Palerne*, when Alphonse is transformed back from werewolf to human, he is ashamed of his nakedness. Is it nakedness that distinguishes the human from the animal? Is it shame that marks the human? Is the skin naked only because of original sin? What is the human skin like before the fall? Animal skins not only protect and shape human identities, but they also make fundamentally ambiguous the identity of that animal that has only human skin as covering.

The abjection of these hybrid characters whose skin is part animal and part human is further intensified by the fact that their new hybrid skin is half alive and half dead. Even on a non-hybrid living being, skin is partially dead: from one moment to the next, parts of the skin change from live skin to dead skin. As we shed parts of our skin daily, do we also shed parts of our identity? When do we acquire a completely new skin? Within a medieval ideology, skin is renewable, that is, capable of resurrection. After resurrection, the body will be fully restored but we will be encased in new skins – ones that no longer show the marks of our history.[10] Is that resurrected skin, relieved of history, our true skin? As these essays show, all skins are marked in one way or another – indeed, the status of each person as a bearer of original sin implies that the individual will always exhibit marked skin. Does the fact that such marks disappear in heaven suggest, then, that human experiences – those that cleanse the individual of sin – are ultimately irrelevant in the afterlife? We might wish to explore further the meanings of marked skin on earth when understood as a surface destined to be wiped clean in heaven or forever marked as sinful in hell.

Skin is Queer and Skin is Transgendered

Several essays in this collection pay special attention to the fact that as medievalists we encounter dead skins in almost all of our primary reading in our encounters with the dead skins of parchment. Drawing on Sarah Kay's analysis of parchment, the essays explain how these dead skins carry on them the history of the living animals from where they came – in the animal bites piercing the parchment skin, in the hair follicles that can be stroked on the hair side of a manuscript page, in the worm holes chewed through some of the pages. Parchment leaves with their various marks on them, like skin bearing the marks of leprosy, carry a history and tell stories of past violence. The poem addressed to Adam Scriveyn attributed to Chaucer as well as the poignant Exeter Riddle 24, as several of the essays point out, highlight the ways in which texts written on parchment not only trouble the dividing line between the human and the animal but further problematize what it means to be human.

Marks on parchment bear a complex relationship to marks on human skin. As Cox shows, just as parchment is a palimpsest bearing a history of holes, stretching, scraping, so, too, the skin of Chaucer's pilgrims, especially the skin of the Wife of Bath, the Summoner, and the Pardoner, are palimpsests manifesting signs of secret histories that we as readers are invited to parse. Those ambiguous marks make it impossible to articulate a definitive identity for anyone. Explaining the ambiguities of the Wife of Bath's manifestation of both "the prente of seinte Venus seel"[11] and the "Martes mark" ('mark of Mars') upon her face, Roberta Magnani (this volume) explains the ways in which the Wife of Bath's skin destabilizes the legible "straight" sexuality clerical anti-feminist texts assign her. As she writes of the Wife, "her queer skin rejects the Augustinian para-

---

10 For a discussion of the resurrected body see Walker Bynum (1995).
11 'the mark of saint Venus' seal'

digm of cutaneous legibility and exposes the epidermis as an oblique site which accommodates queer configurations of gender and sexuality." She concludes that "the material space of the codex [is] [...] a queer site of radical resistance and perpetual dislocations in which signification is constantly redirected beyond binary constructs."

The queer effects Magnani describes here are not unlike those aimed for in the transgendered readings M.W. Bychowski urges us to adopt. Bychowski shows how two gendered identities – the virgin and the eunuch – are produced by the violent intervention of 'sharp-machines.' In a moving analysis of the cuts that maintain Virginia's virginity in the "Physician's Tale" and that produce the Pardoner's eunuchry, Bychowski (this volume) shows how

> [f]ull of still stinging cuts and telling scars, narratives of transgender skin operations testify to the countless lives physically and artificially made through the artifice of sharp-machines which continually make and unmake supposedly natural states.

Bychowski's analysis allows us to recognize the horrific violence involved in the creation of certain specific forms of gendered identity (virgin and eunuch), as well as the physical and cultural violence involved in the production of all gendered identity. Ultimately, skin's abject nature is always already both queer and transgendered and its meanings are always culturally rather than naturally determined.

The Word Made Flesh/Skin

The text that most clearly demonstrates the relationship between the skin of parchment and that of the human is the *Charter of Christ*, mentioned in several essays in the collection, a poem that appears in various versions including the fifteenth-century manuscript, Additional 37049. That version presents an image of the suffering Christ unfolding a document that almost entirely covers his body and indeed looks like the skin of his own body. The upper half of Christ's body is represented pierced with wounds that are marked in red ink. Those red marks drip onto the document and announce in words, also written in red ink, the salvation Christ's suffering guarantees to the reader. This particular version of the poem is on paper but other versions appear on parchment. This version recalls those poems which bring together the pierced and marked animal skin of the parchment, the pierced and tortured skin of the suffering Christ, and the skin of the reader marked by sin but capable of being redeemed and resurrected through Christ. The readers come to understand that promise by taking in the Charter not only through their eyes, but also through their own skin as they touch the parchment or paper page.

To carry the work of this volume's essays on parchment further, one might consider the abject nature of the primary marks on a manuscript page: words. The *Charter of Christ* presents the marks recorded on the parchment as the Living Word of Christ. But all words on a parchment page are in some sense alive or at least bear a relationship to the living. The words differ from the once alive but now dead animal skin upon which they are transcribed, yet, like the skins, they bear the history of the living person or persons (author and scribe) who once produced them. Of course, that transmission from the living author to the living scribe to the once alive parchment skin is fraught with difficulty, as the poem, "Adam Scriveyn," with which the editors begin this collection, makes clear.

The two poems by Tatwine and Eusebius discussed by Catherine S. Cox highlight the uncertain space between the living and the dead occupied by the marks on parchment skin that become words. In Tatwine's "De Membranis" the parchment speaks of its "blooming meadows:"

> A fierce robber ripped off my hide,
> Plundered the breath-pores of my skin.
> I was shaped by an artist and author
> Into a flat field. Furrowed and wet,
> I yield strange fruit. My meadows bloom
> Food for the healthy, health for the sick.
> (quoted in Cox, in this volume)

Similarly, Eusebius' parchments describe themselves as dumb in their previous animal life and as "answering back" now that the animals are dead and have been made into parchment:

> Once silent, voiceless, wordless, dumb—
> Now voiceless, silent, bearing words we come,
> White fields crossed by myriad black tracks:
> Alive we are dumb—dead, answer back.
> (quoted in Cox, in this volume)[12]

These haunting poems tell of the transformation of the three-dimensional animal that becomes a two-dimensional surface, but, then, when unfolded, be-

---

[12] For the Latin original as well as for the references to the Latin and the modern English translations of both poems, see Cox in this volume.

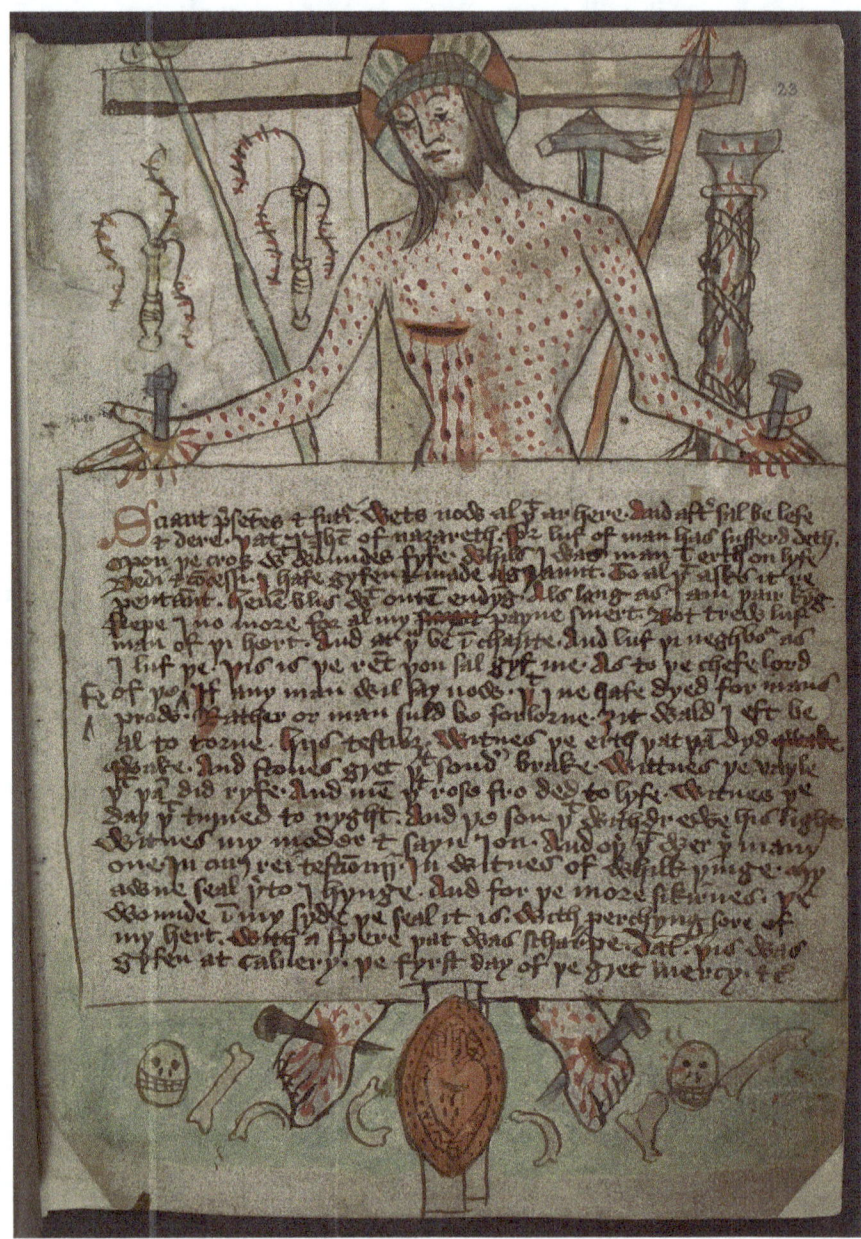

Figure 2: "Charter of Christ," BL Add MS 37049, fol. 23r, reproduced with permission of the British Library.

comes three-dimensional again – a fertile meadow – marked by the furrows made by the scribe's pen. The two authors draw on a common metaphor of verse as a plough's furrow: just as a farmer turns his plough to make furrows in the field, so the lines of poems themselves, the black tracks, create turns at the end of the lines, that is, verse. These two poems open up yet another perspective on the skin of parchment that might also be pursued further, an ecocritical one: the poems celebrate the interdependence of the animal (the sheep from which parchment is made), the human (the scribe and author who produce poetry) and the natural and the agricultural (the meadow and the ploughed field) – all of which share the crucial feature of being animate. The second poem ends with the paradoxical affirmation of the animal's ability, although dead, to answer back or respond to the human violation of nature ("responsum mortua famur"). The words themselves also have a life of their own when they are brought into being through the reader's engagement with the text. In the last line of this poem, the speaker (the animal skin) commands the reader to respond. In addition to inviting the reader to respond actively to the suggested command of the last line of the poem ("answer back"), the poem like all poems also asks the reader to animate the words through the reading process: the reader reanimates the once living words of the author/scribe when he or she infuses those words with his or her own breath.

The essays in this collection make clear the tremendous range of theoretical perspectives that can be brought to bear on the topic of skin including those of medical humanities, queer and transgendered studies, animal studies, eco-criticism and textual studies that focus on the materiality of the text. The essays illuminate the many and various ways skin functions as an abject entity. The hideous marks of leprosy that both attract and repel are not dissimilar ultimately from any marks on a person's skin and indeed those found on the animal skins used for a writing surface. Given that these marks are difficult to diagnose and their histories difficult to recover, abject marked skin fundamentally destabilizes identities. The nature of human skin becomes further problematized by human dependence on and use of animal skins either as protection or as a writing surface. Engaging poems written on the once living skin of parchment asks us to consider not only the fine line between the human and the animal but also the precise nature of living skin. Finally, texts on parchment also invite us to contemplate the abject nature of the words on the page, themselves at once both dead and alive. These essays show how the ambiguous abject liminality of skin as well as its opaque thickness elicit a wealth of responses and generate numerous questions still to be answered.

Works Cited

Primary Sources

Benson, Larry D. (ed.) 1987. *Geoffrey Chaucer: The Riverside Chaucer*. 3rd ed. Boston: Houghton Mifflin.

Robertson, Elizabeth and Stephen H. A. Shepherd (eds.). 2006. *William Langland: Piers Plowman. A Norton Critical Edition*. New York: Norton.

Secondary Sources

OED = *The Oxford English Dictionary*. 2000–. 3rd ed. online. Oxford: Oxford University Press. <http://www.oed.com/> [last accessed 09 January 2018].

Walker Bynum, Caroline. 1995. *The Resurrection of the Body in Western Christianity, 200–1336*. New York: Columbia University Press.

Contributors

M. W. Bychowski is an Anisfield-Wolf SAGES Fellow teaching courses on transgender and intersex history, disability culture, queer Christianity, racism, and medieval literature. She completed her Ph.D. in English Literature at the George Washington University. In addition to her academic writing on transgender, disability, and the Middle Ages, she engages actively in the Digital Humanities, maintaining a website on trans and crip culture, www.ThingsTransform.com, through which she offers "Transform Talks," workshops and training for businesses, schools, and faith communities. Such work has brought her to work with the White House twice in 2016 as part of the "LGBTQ Champions of Change" and "the Forum on LGBT and Disability Issues."

Catherine S. Cox is Professor of English at the University of Pittsburgh's Johnstown campus, where she teaches biblical and medieval literature and culture and contemporary critical theory. She is the author of numerous articles on Chaucer, Dante, the Gawain Poet, in relation to topics in religion, gender, and language, in the journals *Chaucer Review*, *Exemplaria*, *Intertexts*, and elsewhere, and has published two books, *Gender and Language in Chaucer* and *The Judaic Other in Dante, the Gawain Poet, and Chaucer*. She is currently working on a book project on ethics and subjectivity in medieval literature, considering the relationship of ethical dilemmas and contiguous religious traditions.

Sealy Gilles recently retired from the English Department at Long Island University, Brooklyn, New York. She has published on early medieval geography, Anglo-Irish colonialism, and John Manly and Edith Rickert's edition of the *Canterbury Tales*. Her article, "Love and Disease in Chaucer's Troilus and Criseyde" (*Studies in the Age of Chaucer* 2003) examines the impact of the bubonic plague pandemic on Chaucer's rewriting of Boccaccio's *Il Filostrato*. The current article, "Doctrinal Dermatologies," continues work on the cultural response to disease.

Pax Gutierrez-Neal is a Ph.D. Candidate in medieval literature at the University of Texas at Austin, where she works as an Assistant Program Coordinator at the University Writing Center. Her research interests are the human/animal divide as well as sex-, gender- and species-identities. In addition to receiving the 2014 Outstanding Master's Report Award in the UT English Graduate Department, she has also presented research at the 2013 Modern Language Association Congress in Boston, the 2014 Vagantes Medieval Graduate Student Conference in Austin, the 2015 International Congress on Medieval Studies in Kalamazoo, and the 2016 International Medieval Congress in Leeds.

Michael Leahy is an honorary visiting fellow at the University of Nottingham. His research focuses primarily on the incorporation of medical knowledge and language in English culture in the later Middle Ages. He is currently completing his first monograph entitled *Circulating Medicine: Medical Discourse and its Cultural Dissemination in Late Medieval England*.

Roberta Magnani is a Lecturer in English Literature at Swansea University. She has research interests in late medieval literature with a specific focus on Geoffrey Chaucer's works, manuscript studies and gender theories (especially queer theory). Her monograph, *Chaucer's*

Queer Textualities: The Challenging of Authority, is due to be published by Palgrave Macmillan in the 'New Middle Ages' series in 2018. She has also published on the intersections between medicine, spirituality and gender, as well as on the trope of the *hortus conclusus* in the works of Chaucer.

Nicole Nyffenegger is a Senior Lecturer in Medieval and Early Modern Literature and Culture at the University of Bern, Switzerland. Her main research interests are in discourses of the (gendered, wounded, violated) human body, gender and performance, and the senses. Her current projects bring together modern tattoo and body modification theories with questions of the textuality of human skin in medieval and early modern literature. She has published on bodies, margins and marginality, cultural conflict, and on questions of authorship, especially in medieval historiography.

Sharon E. Rhodes completed her PhD in English Language and Literature at the University of Rochester in 2016. Her dissertation, *Turning the Tide: Fathoming the Great Flood in Old English Literature*, looks at poetic and prose translations of the Flood Story in Old English in order to explore how Old English translators and the Old English language itself transform the story of the Flood so that it resonates in both the physical and cultural context of Christian, Anglo-Saxon England. In addition to Old English literature and Translation Theory, Dr. Rhodes' research deals with women and gender studies, Medieval spirituality, Chaucer, and Virginity Literature. She teaches Queer Theory at the University of Rochester. Her recent publications include an article entitled "Orm's Pre-Reformation Vernacular Bible Translation" in *The Medieval Translator* (2017) and an article on *Sir Gawain and the Green Knight* in the *Oxford Research Encyclopedia of Literature* (2017, co-authored with Thomas Hahn).

Elizabeth Robertson is Professor and Chair of English Language at the University of Glasgow. Co-founder of the Society for Medieval Feminist Studies in 1986, she publishes books, editions, essays and collections of essays on Middle English literature and especially on gender and religion in Middle English literature from 1190–1450, with a primary focus on the *Ancrene Wisse*, the Katherine Group, Chaucer, Langland and Julian of Norwich. She is currently co-directing an international interdisciplinary project funded by the Royal Society of Edinburgh, "Understanding the Senses: Past and Present." She is also in the process of completing a book, *Chaucerian Consent: Women, Religion and Subjection in Late Medieval England*.

Katrin Rupp is a Senior Lecturer in Medieval Literature at the University of Neuchâtel, Switzerland. Her research interests are in medieval representations of the body. She has co-edited a collection of essays in *Fleshly Things and Spiritual Matters* (2011). Her recent publications include an article on the obscene body in Geoffrey Chaucer's "Miller's Tale" and its telefilm adaptations by the BBC (*Neophilologus* 2014), on Osbern Bokenham's St. Margaret in *Fashioning England and the English. Literature, Nation, Gender* (forthcoming with Palgrave Macmillan) and on the Wife of Bath and Anne Elliott as author figures (co-authored with Anne-Claire Michoux, forthcoming with Narr Francke Attempto).

Erin E. Sweany received her Ph.D. from Indiana University, where she currently serves as a Visiting Lecturer in English. Her current book project, *The Anglo-Saxon Medical Imagination: Bodily Integrity, Conglomeration, and Autonomy*, based on her dissertation, combines literary and philological studies with medical humanity and scientific studies to examine representations of bodies, health, and illness in the Old English medical, poetic, and religious corpora. Her other research includes a forthcoming article that combines her interests in the medical humanities and philology with feminist scholarship to examine the representations of women in the Old English medical corpus.

Index

abstinence 69, 91, 136f., 237
Agrate, Marco d'
– Saint Bartholomew 7, 145
Ahmed, Sara 195, 202, 205, 207
Alighieri, Dante 148
Almansor's Propositions 198
Althusser, Louis 204
Ami et Amile 9, 21, 35
Amis and Amiloun 4, 78f., 86f., 89, 92f., 170, 257
amorphous 138, 142
antifeminism 5, 199–203, 206, 208f., 215, 259
antiheroine 77, 85
Anzieu, Didier 7, 196
Arbesmann, Rudolph 227, 234
Archimedes Palimpsest 104f.
Avicenna 60

baptism 204, 206
Barad, Karen 195, 204f., 207, 214f.
Baumgarten, Elisheva 204f.
Benthien, Claudia 20, 50, 256
Bériou, Nicole 31f., 37
Bernard de Clairvaux 204, 206
– "On the Circumcision" 204, 206
Béroul 9, 21, 36f., 39
– *Tristran and Iseut* 9, 21, 36f., 39
Bible 7, 9, 22f., 25, 79, 81, 102–104, 199, 223, 253
– Book of Job 9, 26f., 29f.
– Chronicles 26, 29, 80
– Deuteronomy 234
– Isaiah 27f., 30, 32f.
– 4 Kings 79, 81
– Leviticus 9, 22–25, 28, 31, 34, 41, 50, 234, 253f.
– Luke 27, 29, 31, 67
– Matthew 27, 30, 223, 227f., 247
– New Testament 9f., 27, 70, 253
– Numbers 26, 79f., 253
– Old Testament 9, 22f., 25, 28, 78f., 253
– Proverbs 199
– Romans 204f., 214
Biddick, Kathleen 205, 213f.
black bile 56, 62
blasphemy 9, 19, 34, 45, 63, 73, 77, 80, 83f., 92, 139, 254, 256
blemish 24, 29, 49, 63, 89, 101, 107, 114f., 214
blush 12, 148–155, 158, 160, 255
Boccaccio 63, 159
Bodel, Jean 33
Bourgeois, Albert 21, 36, 40f., 43
Boyarin, Williams Adrienne 4, 196, 198f.
Braddy, Haldeen 111, 120
Brody, Saul N. 63, 79, 81, 84, 86, 91, 109f.
Butler, Judith 3, 49, 221f., 228–231
Butterfield, Ardis 152, 157f., 162
Bynum Walker, Caroline 175, 178, 182, 196, 205, 242, 259

Canticus Troili 159
Carlin, Martha 42
Caruth, Cathy 189
castrate 9, 222–229, 231f., 234–236, 240f., 243, 246f.
castration 213, 221, 224, 226f., 231, 233–235, 241
Charter of Christ 4, 31, 198f., 260f.
chastity 128, 225, 238
Chaucer, Geoffrey 1–5, 10–13, 19, 47–49, 55, 61–66, 77–79, 81f., 84, 89–93, 97–101, 105–115, 119–123, 125–129, 131f., 136–142, 145, 148f., 153, 157–159, 162, 197f., 200, 209, 212, 221, 223, 226, 240f., 243, 255f., 259
– *Book of the Duchess* 148
– *Canterbury Tales* 11f., 55, 77–79, 89, 91f., 105, 114, 119, 121, 197, 214, 221, 254
– "Chaucer's Wordes Unto Adam, His Own Scriveyn" 1, 5, 200, 259, 261
– "The Cook's Tale" 121, 129
– "The General Prologue" 55, 139

– "The General Prologue"   78, 107 f., 112 f., 115, 119, 122 f., 140
– "The Knight's Tale"   12
– "The Manciple's Tale"   136
– "The Merchant's Tale"   11, 145
– "The Pardoner's Tale"   238, 240, 246
– "The Parson's Tale"   136 f.
– "The Physician's Tale"   9, 221 f., 225, 236–240, 244, 246
– "The Prioress' Tale"   107
– "The Shipman's Tale"   12
– "The Summoner's Tale"   4 f., 78, 89–92, 109, 133
– "The Wife of Bath"   5, 12, 97, 112–114, 121, 148, 195 f., 200, 203, 207, 212, 259
– *Troilus and Criseyde*   12, 19, 61, 63–65, 77, 82, 84, 145, 148–150, 152–154, 156–158, 162, 255
Chauliac, Guy de   10, 19, 39–41, 46, 49 f., 55–63, 67, 70–73, 82 f., 90 f., 112, 251 f., 254
– *Chirurgia Magna*   10, 56
– *The Cyrurgie*   19, 58, 83, 90
Christ   11, 21, 27, 29–31, 34, 50, 59, 67 f., 70–73, 89, 125, 130, 181 f., 198 f., 201, 204, 213, 227 f., 247, 253 f., 260 f.
circumcision   195 f., 202–206, 212–215, 241
cisgender   221, 231
clitoris   204, 208, 211, 214
Colapinto, John   230
– *As Nature Made Him*   228–230
complexion   5, 47, 58, 60, 62, 64, 66, 82, 147, 256
Connor, Steven   10 f., 57, 145
Constantine the African   64, 139
– *Isagoge*   139
contagion   9, 22, 25, 28, 34, 39, 44, 59, 72, 81, 91, 109, 128
Craun, Edwin D.   83
Craymer, Suzanne   176 f.
Crocker, Holly   154
Curry, Walter Clyde   90, 110 f., 120, 130 f., 148, 197
curse   27, 81, 83 f., 92, 97, 99, 106, 115, 130, 134, 182, 190

Davis, Isabel   3, 114, 201
Day, Mildred L.   185
deformity   23, 63, 68
Demaitre, Luke   22, 36, 40, 42, 46, 59, 61, 79
Derrida, Jacques   102, 181, 188
– "The Animal That Therefore I Am"   102
deviance   9, 35, 45, 119–123, 134, 202, 206
Dinshaw, Carolyn   2, 97, 204, 207, 209, 223 f., 242
disguise   29, 169, 174–176, 178, 180, 183, 254, 257 f.
dismemberment   225
drunkenness   119, 123, 132, 134 f., 137, 140 f.

Eckbert of Schönau   34
eczema   22, 79, 99
Edward III   43
elephantiasis   30, 79, 125
Ellesmere Manuscript   5, 127, 197–200
Eusebius   102 f.
Exeter Book Manuscript   102
Exeter Riddle #24   5, 102, 104, 259

Farina, Lara   6
Fastoul, Baude   33 f.
Fitz Stephen, William   126
flaying   101, 145, 171, 173, 179, 258
Foley, Michael   185
folklore   175
foreskin   5, 195, 204, 211–215, 229
Freeman, Michelle   180
Friedman, John Block   55, 148 f., 156–158

Gadebusch Bondio, Mariacarla   207
Garbáty, Thomas J.   90 f., 110
gender   9, 12, 112 f., 195, 198, 205, 208, 210, 212, 214, 221–225, 227–233, 237–241, 243–245, 247, 260
Gerard of Berry   64
Gilbert the Englishman   126, 133, 135
gluttony   43, 68 f., 73, 136 f., 254
Gonzales-Day, Ken   170
Goodman, Barbara   186
Gordon, Bernard de   39, 46, 49 f., 112

Gregory the Great (Pope Gregory I)   9, 28–30
– *Homiliarum in Evangelia*   30
– *Magna Moralia*   29 f.
Grigsby, Bryon   58, 110
Gross, Gregory   184 f., 187
Grosz, Elizabeth   3, 146

Halberstam, Judith   205
Hansen's disease   19, 21, 26 f., 29, 31, 40, 42–44, 57, 79, 253
Hartman, Stephanie   191
Hawthorne, Nathaniel   77
– *The Scarlet Letter*   77
Henry II   128
Henryson, Robert   4, 9 f., 19–21, 34 f., 37, 39, 42–50, 55 f., 61–63, 65 f., 69, 73, 77, 81–86, 90, 138
– *Testament of Cresseid*   4, 9 f., 19, 34, 37, 42, 44 f., 49, 55, 57, 61, 77, 79, 82–84, 92 f., 138, 256 f.
heteronormativity   202 f., 205, 207–210, 212, 214
Higl, Andrew   84, 121
Hinton, Norman   180
Holsinger, Bruce   6, 100, 104, 200
Hsy, Jonathan   72
hue   12, 113, 145–162, 177, 237, 255
Hume, Kathryn   44, 87
humours   55 f., 125, 136

infection   9, 22–25, 34, 43, 45, 78–80, 90, 106, 109, 112, 127, 135
Isidore of Seville   9, 28 f., 34, 135 f.
– *Etymologiae*   136, 197

John of Salisbury   68
– *Policraticus*   68, 171

Kay, Sara   4, 6 f., 24, 101, 103, 145, 147, 169 f., 196, 199 f., 259
Kempe, Margery   10, 55, 57, 71–73
Kern-Stähler, Annette   159
King Arthur   37, 200
King James I of Scotland   43
Kratins, Ojars   87

Kuefler, Mathews   205, 213, 223, 227 f., 232–235, 241
Kwakkel, Eric   98, 100, 105

Landfester, Ulrike   10
Lanfranc of Milan   57 f., 251
– *Science of Cirurgie*   57
Langum, Virginia   10, 121 f., 207
Lazarus   19, 21, 27 f., 32, 59, 70
lechery   4, 72, 90–92, 109 f.
Legat, Hugo   42 f., 55, 67–70, 73
leprosy   2, 4, 9–11, 19–21, 26, 28–48, 55–63, 65–73, 77–84, 86–90, 92 f., 110, 119, 124–128, 130 f., 133, 138–141, 252–257, 259, 263
Leurens, Waultier of Aire   41
Liber de Diversis Medicinis   110
Lieber, Elinor   22 f., 25 f.
Lindberg, David   154
Lochrie, Karma   197 f., 204, 208, 210 f.
lovesickness   61, 63–67, 84, 159
lust   9, 36, 87, 91, 114, 197, 235, 257

MacKendrick, Karmen   3, 101, 231
maleness   195, 215
Mann, Jill   120
Mannyng, Robert   81, 93
– *Handlyng Synne*   81, 93
Marinello, Giovanni   207
– *Gli ornamenti delle donne*   207
martyr   7, 32, 92, 127, 196, 201
Marvin, William   171
Mathews, Jana   43
measles   22, 253
melancholy   46, 62, 65
metamorphosis   47
metapoetics   145, 149, 156, 159 f., 162
Miracle Windows (Trinity Chapel, Canterbury Cathedral)   127 f., 256
miraculous healing   30, 126, 128, 256
mise-en-abyme   12, 145–147, 149, 152, 162
Moore, Robert   34
mormal   5, 11, 108, 111 f., 119–123, 125, 129 f., 140, 142, 254–256
mutilation   227, 231

nakedness   181 f., 258

New Testament
– Luke 59, 70
– Matthew 70, 253
Nickel, Helmut 172, 183, 185

Odo de Beaumont 127
Old Testament
– Book of Job 28f., 33, 115, 253
Orlemanski, Julie 27, 65, 83
outcast 47, 93, 223, 256
Ovide moralisé 4

pagan 45, 104
paleness 133, 137, 139–141, 148, 150f.
pariah 21, 92
patriarchal 5, 207, 212
penis 196, 203, 208, 211, 214, 223, 227, 229f., 243
Peter of Abelard 228
– *Historia Calamitatum* 233
phlegm 56, 120, 123, 125, 137, 141
piercing 101, 202, 225, 259
plague 22, 44, 128, 243
porosity 206f., 213f.
pox 22
promiscuous 19f., 38, 45, 49, 84, 139
psoriasis 22, 26, 79, 99
Ptolemy 214
– *Centum Dicta* 214
pus 5, 25, 112, 254f.

quarantine 22f., 25, 49
queer 10, 195, 202f., 206–212, 214f., 223f., 252, 259f., 263

rape 1, 36f., 99, 200, 238
Rawcliffe, Carole 21, 30, 32, 43f., 59, 62, 78, 81, 93, 124–128, 131, 140f.
Raymond of Toulouse 34, 50
Rayner Myers, Jeffrey 223
relic 38, 204, 221, 225f., 240–246, 256
Richards, Peter 42, 59
Riddy, Felicity 46, 49
Riley, H. T. 43
Robertson, Elizabeth 126f., 146, 153, 155, 196, 207, 251

Rooney, Anne 171
Rubin, Stanley 79, 92f.

Saint Augustine 121, 196, 206, 211, 227
Saint Jerome 203, 210
– *Against Jovinianus* 203
Saint Margaret 4, 198
Saint Nicholas' Hospital 128f.
Saint Paul 204–206
Salisbury, Joyce 171, 179
salvation 19, 28, 70, 204, 260
Satchell, Max 42
Savage, Henry L. 183
Sayers, Edna Edith 201
scabbe 58, 67f., 89, 111, 120, 243
scalle 1, 89, 97, 99, 106, 108f., 111
scars 100, 106, 114, 191, 224, 228, 231–233, 243, 246f., 260
Scholz, Piotr 227, 232–236, 241
semen 25, 139
Simms, Norman 187
Simons, John 188
Sir Gawain and the Green Knight 6, 108, 114, 169–173, 176, 188, 258
Skeat, Walter W. 120, 214
Stanbury, Sarah 146, 153–155
Steel, Karl 3, 7
Steinberg, Leo 205, 213f.
Stock, Lorraine 172
Stockton, Will 224, 242
Stone, Sandy 230, 232
Sturges, Robert S. 223f., 242
swelling 30, 60, 111, 125, 253f.

tattoo 3, 11, 106, 198
Tatwine 102, 261
Taylor, Gary 223, 227, 232f., 235
Teochimus 4
Thomas à Becket (Saint Thomas) 126f., 129
Tinkle, Theresa 209f.
Tomasch, Sylvia 44, 213
torture 4, 103, 159, 260
Tracy, Larissa 213, 223, 227, 233–235
transformation 3f., 32, 62f., 66, 101f., 169, 180, 182, 190, 192, 227, 230f., 236, 245, 261

transgender   221f., 224, 226, 228f., 231f., 236, 240, 242–244, 247, 252, 259f., 263
transgression   19f., 22, 25, 35, 139f., 233, 253
transphobia   245

ulcer   60, 108, 111, 120
unhygienic   119, 123, 129

Vandeventer Pearman, Tory   73, 201
vellum   100, 105, 169f., 198
virgin   72, 201, 222, 224–229, 236, 238–240, 242, 245–247, 260

virus   79
Vitry, Jacques de   31f., 43, 50
– *Sermo*   32, 34

Walter, Katie L.   7, 11f., 58, 146, 200
Whitney, Elspeth   131, 141, 223, 226f., 237, 241
William of Palerne   6, 169–171, 173, 179, 188, 258
William the Monk   34
Winterson, Jeanette   5, 105f., 208
– *Written on the Body*   5, 105, 208

Zovic, Neda Chernack   38

www.ingramcontent.com/pod-product-compliance
Lightning Source LLC
Chambersburg PA
CBHW061935220426
43662CB00012B/1916